BPP College
Library & Information Service

346.017 P
(n)

Contact: The New Deal

D0317736

Contact: The New Deal

Piers Pressdee

John Vater

Frances Judd QC

Jonathan Baker QC

Family Law

Published by
Jordan Publishing Limited
21 St Thomas Street
Bristol BS1 6JS

Whilst the publishers and the author have taken every care in preparing the material included in this work, any statements made as to the legal or other implications of particular transactions are made in good faith purely for general guidance and cannot be regarded as a substitute for professional advice. Consequently, no liability can be accepted for loss or expense incurred as a result of relying in particular circumstances on statements made in this work.

©Jordan Publishing Limited 2006

Crown copyright material is reproduced under Class Licence Number C01W0000451 with the permission of the Controller of HMSO and the Queen's Printer for Scotland.

All rights reserved. No part of this publication may be reproduced, stored in a retrieval system, or transmitted in any way or by any means, including photocopying or recording, without the written permission of the copyright holder, application for which should be addressed to the publisher.

British Library Cataloguing-in-Publication Data

A catalogue record for this book is available from the British Library.

ISBN 0 85308 973 6

Typeset by Columns Design Ltd, Reading, Berkshire
Printed and bound in Great Britain by Antony Rowe Ltd, Chippenham, Wilts

FOREWORD

The publication of a book entitled *Contact: The New Deal* to coincide with the passing of the Children and Adoption Act 2006 might lead readers to conclude that the book is simply a short commentary on this modest but important new statute. Such a conclusion, whilst understandable, would seriously undervalue this work, which is much, much more than a book about a new Act.

The topic of contact between separated parents and their children is one about which headlines are generated and passions run high. Whilst much of the public debate is ill-informed and sensationalised, it is widely recognised that there is justification in the main thrust of the criticisms that are made of the present approach. The arrival of a book which seeks to provide a detailed exposition of the historical, social, psychological and legal context within which this topic sits is extremely welcome. It has been thoroughly researched and written by four highly respected family law barristers, who are to be commended for mastering the wealth of background material and presenting it in such a clear and digestible style.

For the first time, this book draws together in one place each of the disparate developments and themes, both legal and non-legal, that impact upon the system's ability to resolve contact issues in individual cases. Even those who feel that they know this topic well will find much within these pages that is either 'new', or at least makes better sense of what has gone before. Had *Contact: The New Deal* been available, it would have been an extremely useful resource for those involved in the development of the Children and Adoption Act 2006. Its arrival now, at the stage when a new approach to contact is becoming established, makes this truly excellent book required reading for all in the Family Justice System.

The Hon Mr Justice McFarlane
August 2006

PREFACE

The division of parenting time represents the single biggest challenge to the family justice system today.

But what the law knows as questions of contact and residence are far from being purely legal issues. Topical, newsworthy, complex and emotive, these are matters of genuine social debate and firm fixtures on the political agenda.

The last two years particularly have been marked by a vast amount of time and energy devoted to how best to meet this challenge; and, correspondingly, that period has seen an array of reforms, initiatives and developments in this field, including and culminating in the Children and Adoption Act 2006. Significant in their own right, they cumulatively represent the State's wide-ranging response to that considerable challenge.

Through this book, we seek to draw together within one cover the key components of that response, which we have collectively termed 'the new deal' for contact. Our aim thereby is to provide a user-friendly guide to, and analysis of, the various means, statutory and non-statutory, by which the State is seeking to improve the situation for the children of separated parents.

In so doing, we in part draw on our own experiences as children law barristers who have acted for mothers, fathers, relatives and the children themselves, who have represented the intransigent, the flexible, the dogmatic, the indifferent and the wronged, and who have particular experience of the ways of the family court.

Before looking in more detail at the reforms and initiatives themselves, we have sought in this book's first three chapters to establish the context in which they arise. We start by considering the impact and importance of contact and by examining how the current system of law in this regard has evolved, considering within the ambit of Chapters 1 and 2 the need and pressure for change. In Chapter 3 we then outline the guiding principles of the present law, which remain fundamentally unaltered by the changes that we later discuss, although we seek through that survey to identify the trends in the case-law which may in more subtle fashion be reshaping the legal landscape.

In the next four chapters, we look in some detail at the ways in which the State has acted. Appropriately, given the increasing emphasis on non court-based resolution, we begin by considering in Chapter 4 the options and developments in that realm, with particular focus on the promotion of mediation, the advent of collaborative law and the provision of information through parenting plans and otherwise. In Chapter 5 we look at the improvements to and affecting the court system, aimed at bettering practice and procedure for the cases that do reach the court door – principally the Private Law Programme and its promotion of in-court conciliation and the new, changed role for CAFCASS.

In Chapter 6 our focus is exclusively on how courts deal with private law children's cases in which the issue of domestic violence arises, and there we analyse the recent statutory and non-statutory developments in that important sphere. In Chapter 7, we then outline and discuss the changes to the Children Act 1989 geared to improve the facilitation and enforcement of contact orders, brought in by the Children and Adoption Act 2006.

It is essential, however, not to focus too narrowly and, in Chapter 8, we look at three broad areas where change will inevitably impact on how private law children's cases are handled in the future – opening up the family courts, creating a single family court and the means by which the voice of the child is to be heard.

We conclude in Chapter 9 by providing our own views on what we have described as 'the new deal' for contact. We seek to understand its underlying philosophy, to examine the extent to which it does constitute a new and better deal for the children concerned and to analyse its prospects for success. The core relevant legal provisions and a compendium of useful organisations, websites and addresses are to be found within the appendices.

We write at a time of considerable debate about opening up the family courts. It is a debate that we welcome and one that has shaped the way in which we have written this book. This is not just a book for lawyers, but one for all those involved in the family justice system. We hope that all professionals working in that system will find it helpful, but also, and notwithstanding the inevitable drier aspects that we have had to cover, that the non-professional reader will find it sufficiently accessible to be of assistance too.

We cannot confidently predict whether the system, as modified, will significantly improve matters for the children who are its concern; only time will tell in that regard. But it seems plain to us that in some measure its success must depend on the knowledge, expertise and outlook of all those who look to guide and assist families through difficult and stressful times, and also on how those very families perceive and respond to the system that seeks to help them.

That in turn highlights the value of access to information – for the families themselves and for those who seek to shape their futures. Whoever the reader – be they legal or non-legal, part of the system or one affected by it – our primary aim is to help to increase awareness and understanding of what the State is trying to do to improve the lives of the children of separated parents and thereby to contribute to an ongoing debate of very real and widespread importance.

The law is stated as at 1 August 2006.

Piers Pressdee
John Vater
Frances Judd QC
Jonathan Baker QC

Harcourt Chambers
(London & Oxford)

ACKNOWLEDGEMENTS

Particular thanks are due to the Jordans team (Greg Woodgate, Jennifer Cowan and Helen Pettet) for their support, to our clerking team (especially Tim Wheeler and Judith Partington) for their understanding, to Mavis Maclean for her advice, and to Mr Justice McFarlane for his foreword and for providing (together with David Hershman QC) the inspiration for us all.

Additional thanks are due to the following who have provided us with access to documentation used in the preparation of this book: Chelsey Bonehill, Kate Chapman, District Judge Nick Crichton, Edward Devereux, Mark Higgins, Suzette Waterhouse and Alison Williams.

This book is dedicated to our respective families: Sally, Charlotte, Georgina, Ellie, Alex, Caroline, Hilda, Bill, Mira, Lila, Chloe, Monty, Gordon, Joan, Gordon, David, Thomas, Henry, Helen, James and Clare.

CONTENTS

TABLE OF STATUTES

*References are to paragraph numbers. Paragraph numbers printed in **bold** type indicate where the Act is set out in part or in full.*

TABLE OF
STATUTORY INSTRUMENTS

References are to paragraph numbers.

TABLE OF EUROPEAN/UN MATERIAL

References are to paragraph numbers. Paragraph numbers printed in **bold** *type indicate where the material is set out in part or in full.*

TABLE OF CASES

Chapter One

THE IMPORTANCE OF CONTACT AND THE NEED FOR CHANGE

1.1   What parent would wish their child to end up offending? To abscond from home? To become a teenage parent? To enter adulthood unqualified? To be unemployed? To engage in substance abuse? To develop mental health problems? To suffer emotional and behavioural difficulties, with implications not only for the child himself or herself, but for any relationship that they have and any children that they produce?

1.2   For most parents, the birth of a child is a source of great joy and happiness; for many, the desire to give that child a better upbringing (or at least no worse) than they had themselves is a significant impulse. Yet, each year, between 150,000 and 200,000 parental couples separate and, of the 12 million children in the country, in the region of a quarter now have had to endure the separation of their mother and father.[1] Predictably, the consequences for the child will vary from family to family (and it should not be thought that by necessity separation has to lead to adverse effects), but the message from research is clear and sobering – that the child of separated parents stands a greater chance of each and every one of the negative outcomes outlined above than the child who has not had that experience.[2]

1.3   The question for the families concerned and for the State as a whole is how best to avoid or at least ameliorate those outcomes and enable those children to reach their emotional, physical and educational potential. Inevitably, in what will be a complex situation, there are a number of factors potentially influencing the outcome – the extent of financial hardship, the amount of subsequent changes in family structure, parental ability to recover from the distress of separation, and the degree of any family conflict all have

---

1   HMG July 2004 Green Paper *Parental Separation: Children's Needs and Parents' Responsibilities* – Cm 6273 – available at www.dfes.gov.uk/childrensneeds/.

2   See J Pryor & B Rodgers *Children in Changing Families: Life After Parental Separation* (Oxford, Blackwell Publishers, 2001), *The Cost of Family Breakdown* (Family Matters Institute, 2000), *Young Runaways Report* (Social Exclusion Unit, 2002), *Teenage Pregnancy Report* (Social Exclusion Unit, 1999), K Kiernan *The Legacy of Parental Divorce: Social economic and demographic experiences in adulthood,* CASE Paper No 1 (STICERD, 1997), A Buchanan, J Hunt, H Bretherton & V Bream *Families in Conflict: Perspectives of children and parents on the Family Court Welfare Service* (Bristol Policy Press, 2001).

significant bearings.[3] But there is now increasing recognition of the importance of contact – and to be more accurate, contact that is safe – in achieving those very ends.

1.4   In this chapter, and from a research perspective, we seek to set the scene for the reforms, developments and initiatives that we later discuss. There is unsurprisingly a large amount of research in this area. We cannot and do not cover it all. Our purpose here simply is to highlight those aspects which have had some influence on how the State has responded to date and which could have an influence on how the State responds in the future. It is inevitably, therefore, a selective guide which does not purport to provide the level of in-depth analysis that might be seen in a book solely about research into contact.

1.5   This chapter begins by looking at the impact (positive and negative) that contact can have on the child. It then goes on to consider the merits and demerits of the system by and within which contact issues were being addressed. In light of the State's recognition that change was necessary, it focuses thereafter on the context for change and what is known about contact that does work. It ends by setting out the State's response in outline.

1.6   However, we make clear from the start that, whilst this is a book about contact and this is a chapter specifically about its importance, we use that word simply because the law does. The observation that contact is a 'cold word', suggesting 'a brief, casual, perhaps unwanted, connection with another'[4] does not seem misplaced. It is indeed an odd word to describe something that should be anything but cold and it is easy to understand why so many 'contact parents' feel devalued by the term.

THE IMPACT OF CONTINUING CONTACT

1.7   As will be examined further in Chapter 3 (in which the existing legal principles in this area are reviewed), the law proceeds on the assumption that a child will benefit from continued contact with his or her parent, which assumption can always be displaced if the child's interests indicate otherwise. At the outset, and before we look at the extent to which it is in fact observed, we consider the validity and importance that ought to be accorded to that principle.

The children's perspective

1.8   In looking at the significance of contact, the starting-point has to be what the children themselves say. One of the more striking and positive features of

---

3   See B Rodgers & J Pryor *Divorce and separation: The outcomes for children* (Joseph Rowntree Foundation, 1998).

4   J Herring *Connecting Contact: Contact in a Private Law Context* in A Bainham, B Lindley, M Richards & L Trinder (eds) *Children and Their Families: Contact, Rights and Welfare* (Hart Publishing, 2003).

recent years has been the increasing recognition of children's rights. The incorporation into domestic law of the European Convention for the Protection of Human Rights and Fundamental Freedoms 1950 (ECHR)[5] and the greater awareness of the UK's obligations under the United Nations Convention on the Rights of the Child 1989 (UNCRC)[6] have begun to sound in a more rights-based and less paternalistic approach when considering the voice of the child.[7]

1.9 Research similarly stresses the overriding importance of 'the centrality of the child',[8] the need to listen to and take seriously what the child says (factoring in appropriately their age, understanding and circumstances) and the damage that can be done to a child (especially an older child) if its views are ignored.[9]

1.10 Too much of the focus in earlier research was on parental accounts of their children's behaviours as opposed to children's accounts of their own experiences. What is really important is to hear and respect what the children themselves say about the contact issues that inevitably affect them so closely. An appraisal of the various research findings (necessarily limited and conditioned by the numbers and circumstances of the children involved) would suggest the following:[10]

- most children want contact;
- most children value contact;
- most children view the non-resident parent as an important figure who is still part of their family – the loss of contact is painful;
- most children miss the non-resident parent and many would like to see more of them;
- it is not so much the arrangements in themselves that matter most to children but how their relationships are managed;
- children value the effort and commitment of their non-resident parent in making a family life for them;
- children may vary in their responses to the same arrangements, even within the same family – for the older child, flexibility and the ability to accommodate other parts of his or her life may particularly matter, whilst, for the younger child, frequency and regularity may be more important;

---

5   Now set out in Schedule 1 to the Human Rights Act 1998. Reproduced at Appendix 3.
6   Reproduced at Appendix 4.
7   The issue of how the voice of the child should be heard is examined at para 8.44 et seq.
8   Per Dame Elizabeth Butler-Sloss in *Re L (Contact: Domestic Violence); Re V (Contact: Domestic Violence); Re M (Contact: Domestic Violence); Re H (Contact: Domestic Violence)* [2000] 2 FLR 334, at p 337, summarising the views of Drs Sturge & Glaser (see footnote 9).
9   See J Sturge & D Glaser *Contact and Domestic Violence – the Experts Court Report* [2000] Fam Law 615, at p 624.
10 See A O'Quigley *Listening to Children's Views and representing their best interest: A summary of current research* (York: Joseph Rowntree Foundation, 1999), J Pryor & B Rodgers *Children in Changing Families: Life After Parental Separation* (Oxford, Blackwell Publishers, 2001), J Hunt *Researching Contact* (London: National Council for One-Parent Families, 2003), J Dunn *Contact and Children's Perspectives on Parental Relationships* in A Bainham, B Lindley, M Richards & L Trinder (eds) *Children and Their Families: Contact, Rights and Welfare* (Hart Publishing, 2003), J Fortin, C Ritchie & A Buchanan *Young adults' perceptions of court-ordered contact* (Child and Family Law Quarterly, Vol 18, No 2, p 211, 2006).

- children who are consulted about decisions and are able to talk to a parent about problems are more likely to feel positive about the contact arrangements that concern them;
- children given an active role in decisions about contact arrangements are more likely to have positive feelings about their divided lives;
- whilst children usually enjoy contact, it can cause distress and problems – the cancellation by the non-resident parent of plans to see the child is a source of particular distress to children;
- among other less frequent complaints of children are: having torn loyalties; being exposed to conflict, harassment or abuse; being used as a go-between; managing relationships with a parent's new partner; missing their resident parent; being bored; and simply having the stress of moving between two homes;
- some children, for a whole range of reasons, resist contact – a phase that may be temporary but can be more sustained;
- many children are aware that their parents did not like them talking about the absent parent;
- children do not always feel that their views about contact are taken into account.

The positive power of contact

1.11   So, is contact in itself a good thing? The first point to make is that the clock ought not to start at the point of separation. These were not always children of separated parents. Given that still the vast majority of residential parents are mothers,[11] there has to be force in the assertion that:

> '... in considering the issue of contact ... the growing body of research showing the benefits of "father involvement", albeit mainly carried out in intact families, is highly relevant.'[12]

1.12   Of particular importance in this context is the research demonstrating that, regardless of the quality of the mother–child relationship, the closer children were to their father, the happier, more satisfied and less distressed they were.[13] Significant too is the research carried out by Flouri and Buchanan[14] to explore the relationship between father involvement and outcomes for UK children, which produced the following strong findings:

- father involvement established before the age of 7 is associated with good parent–child relationships in adolescence and also later satisfactory partnerships in adult life;
- children with involved fathers are less likely to be in trouble with the police;

---

11   See para 1.81.
12   A Buchanan & J Hunt *Disputed Contact Cases in the Court* in A Bainham, B Lindley, M Richards & L Trinder (eds) *Children and Their Families: Contact, Rights and Welfare* (Hart Publishing, 2003).
13   See P Amato *Father–Child Relations, Mother–Child Relations, and Offspring Psychological Well-Being in Early Adulthood* (Journal of Marriage and the Family, 1994).
14   Various papers published by E Flouri & A Buchanan 2002–2004, with the use of data from the British National Child Development Study.

- father involvement is strongly related to children's later educational attainment.

1.13 As to the research into contact post-separation (of which in the UK there is not enough), there is fairly widespread recognition of the *potential* benefits of contact. As Drs Sturge and Glaser observe,[15] contact can serve a variety of purposes and can deliver a number of benefits, including the meeting of the child's needs:

- for warmth, approval, feeling unique and special to a parent – 'experiences that can be the foundation for healthy emotional growth and development';
- for extending experiences and developing (or maintaining) meaningful relationships;
- for information and knowledge; and
- for reparation of distorted relationships or perceptions.

1.14 The word 'potential' is highlighted for a reason. Taken as a whole, research has tended to show that it is the nature and quality of parenting provided by the contact parent that is crucial, not contact in itself.[16] The 2001 study by Smith et al provides a good example. In reporting that it is the nature of the relationship rather than the frequency of contact that is important to children's outcomes, it supports the argument for a focus on the quality of child–father relationships rather than just on contact frequency.[17]

1.15 More recent research, however, sends out a somewhat different message. Children's relationships with their non-resident fathers, and associations between these relationships, children's relationships with mothers and stepfathers, and the children's adjustment were the subject of a two-year study of 162 children of separated parents (involving both single-parent and step-parent families), selected from a representative community sample in the UK.

1.16 This research was carried out by a team of four, including leading academic Professor Judy Dunn.[18] It involved all the children (who were in each case older than 7) being interviewed about their relationships with their mothers, fathers and stepfathers, and sought to address 'the unresolved issue of the links between relationship quality, child–father contact and children's outcome'. In so doing, the authors first examined two rival proposals – that children's accounts of the closeness or conflict in their relationships with their non-resident fathers were unrelated to the frequency of contact *or* that a positive relationship between child and non-resident parent was associated with the frequency of contact.

---

15   J Sturge & D Glaser *Contact and Domestic Violence – the Experts Court Report* [2000] Fam Law 615, at p 617.

16   See J Hunt & C Roberts *Child Contact with Non-resident Parents* (University of Oxford, 2004).

17   See M Smith, J Robertson, J Dixon, M Quigley & Z Whitehead *A Study of Stepchildren and Step-Parenting* (London, Thomas Coram Research Unit, 2001).

18   J Dunn, H Cheng, T O'Connor & L Bridges *Children's Perspectives on their Relationships with their Non-resident Fathers: Influences, Outcomes and Implications* (Journal of Child Psychology and Psychiatry, Volume 45:3, 2004, pp 553–566).

1.17   Having weighed up the alternatives, Dunn et al come to a clear conclusion:

> 'Earlier studies have reported some inconsistent findings on the significance of contact. Our findings were unequivocal: more frequent and more regular contact (which included communication by telephone) was associated with closer, more intense relationships with non-resident fathers (relationships that were both more positive and more conflicted), and fewer adjustment problems in the children.'[19]

1.18   This is plainly an important conclusion, but it does of course beg the question of cause and effect. Indeed, Dunn et al fairly recognise 'that the direction of effects in these patterns of association between contact and relationship quality remains unclear'. It could be, as they recognise, that non-resident fathers enjoyed and encouraged more frequent contact with their children as a result of the positive warm and affectionate relationship that they enjoyed together. Alternatively, it could be that the contact contributed to the children's relationship with their fathers. Maybe both are important. Their own observation is, however, significant:

> 'The correlational analysis suggested that positive relationships between the children and their non-resident fathers were associated over time with more frequent and regular contact rather than vice versa.'[20]

1.19   The authors of this study accept that one has to be cautious about generalising from its findings, not least because the sample of children scrutinised were growing up within a relatively stable community. Nonetheless, this is clearly valuable research. In the context of whether contact between children and their non-resident fathers should be fostered as a matter of policy, the study's primary finding 'that contact with non-resident fathers was, for the sample here, associated with children's wellbeing'[21] is of obvious importance.

1.20   The further key finding of this study relating to the impact on contact of the relationship between the separated parents themselves is considered within our later discussion of what makes for good contact. For now, the immediate question arising is whether this study renders redundant the previous emphasis on quality and not quantity of contact. For our part, we would say not as such, but that it ought to cast it in a new light.

1.21   The difficulty in practice with a concentration on the quality of contact is that parents can have very different views of what constitutes good quality contact. The mantra 'it's the quality of contact that matters' became a shield behind which too many resident parents hid to justify the offer of a manifestly inadequate level of contact. The two concepts of quality and quantity ought not to be mutually exclusive and must in many cases be inter-related. As Buchanan and Hunt[22] observe:

---

19   Ibid, at p 562.
20   Ibid, at p 562.
21   Ibid, at p 564.
22   A Buchanan & J Hunt *Disputed Contact Cases in the Court* in A Bainham, B Lindley, M Richards & L Trinder (eds) *Children and Their Families: Contact, Rights and Welfare* (Hart

'... it is hard to see how active parenting and closeness can be maintained unless contact is relatively frequent and includes overnight stays. Indeed it could be used as an argument for shared residence as the arrangement which is most likely to facilitate high levels of involved and authoritative parenting.'

1.22   It is a statement of the obvious that contact should ideally be of good quality; after all, so should all parenting. But is there a quality threshold that needs to be reached before it takes place? Bringing the research together and placing it within the appropriate rights-based legal framework, we would suggest that the key distinction is between, on the one hand, contact that may potentially harm the child and contact that carries no such risk. We would further suggest that, in judging the value of contact (positive or negative), the views and experiences of the children themselves (especially when independently reported and uninfluenced by parental pressure) should assume particular importance.

Contact and harm

1.23   It is not surprising that contact can have a negative as well as a positive impact on the life of a child. Indeed, in recent years there has been a growing awareness of and insight into the risks to children posed by contact in certain circumstances.

1.24   The clearest cases of harm to children are those where they are subject to direct sexual, physical and emotional abuse[23] or to clear neglect of their needs (whether through adult mental health problems, substance abuse difficulties or otherwise). The harmful consequences for the child of such acts and omissions are self-evident, as are the implications for contact if the risks are not properly assessed. It is important to record the alarming statistic that that in the 10 years between 1994 and 2004 at least 29 children have died during contact visits.[24] Also worthy of note are relatively recent government figures[25] indicating that, of those contact applications where safety was an issue, child abuse and neglect accounted for an estimated 40%. The *Parental Separation:*

Publishing, 2003), commenting in the context of the implications of the Amato and Gilbreth findings that feelings of closeness to and authoritative parenting by the non-resident parent were positively associated with children's academic success and negatively associated with externalising and internalising problems (see P Amato & J Gilbreth *Non-Resident Fathers and Children's Well-Being: a Meta-Analysis* (Journal of Marriage and the Family, 1999)).

23   Emotional abuse of the child can come through the denigration of the child directly or the child's resident carer and through using the contact as a means of continuing or escalating the 'war' with the resident parent – see See J Sturge & D Glaser *Contact and Domestic Violence – the Experts Court Report* [2000] Fam Law 615, at p 618.

24   See H Saunders *Twenty-nine Child Homicides: Lessons still to be Learnt on Domestic Violence and Child Protection* (WAFE, 2000).

25   See the findings of the Consumer Strategy Directorate Court File Analysis for the Department of Constitutional Affairs, recorded in the *Parental Separation: Children's Needs and Parents' Responsibilities* supporting evidence paper available at www.dfes.gov.uk/childrensneeds/downloads.shtml.

Children's Needs and Parents' Responsibilities supporting evidence paper[26] records that 'child abuse and neglect [within the context of private law contact disputes] is … a significant and frequently overlooked issue'. It also highlights the 'important point – that both mothers as well as fathers can be the subject of alleged safety issues in contact cases'.

1.25 For those contact applications where safety was an issue (then amounting to about a third of all contact cases), the same survey indicated that the most commonly cited problem was domestic violence (accounting for some 52% of such cases). A 2002 study showed that, in over a third of cases requiring welfare reports, domestic violence was found or admitted,[27] while it is estimated that 750,000 children witness domestic violence each year.[28]

1.26 In recent years, perceptions about domestic violence and its significance for children and consequently contact have changed markedly.

1.27 The figures above speak to the scale of its prevalence, but the main myth which had to be and has been exploded is that domestic violence only affects the adults involved. In terms of court acceptance of that reality and its resultant widespread dissemination, the real break-through came with the Court of Appeal decision in *Re L; Re V; Re M; Re H*.[29] The legal consequences and implications of that case will be considered in Chapter 6. Its significance for present purposes was the research that the Court of Appeal commissioned and highlighted.

1.28 The Court of Appeal had the Children Act Sub-Committee (CASC) report on parental contact in domestic violence cases[30] and were thus aware of its key findings:

- that domestic violence takes many forms and should be broadly defined;
- that the perpetrator may be female as well as male;
- that involvement may be indirect as well as direct;
- that there needs to be greater awareness of the effect of domestic violence on children, both short-term and long-term, as witnesses as well as victims and also the impact on the residential parent;
- that an outstanding concern of the court should be the nature and extent of the risk to the child and to the residential parent, with the need to put in place proper arrangements to safeguard the child and the residential parent from risk of further physical or emotional harm.

---

26 Available at www.dfes.gov.uk/childrensneeds/downloads.shtml.
27 See Napo *Contact, Separation and the Work of Family Court Staff* (Napo, 2002).
28 Department of Health figures (2003).
29 *Re L (Contact: Domestic Violence); Re V (Contact: Domestic Violence); Re M (Contact: Domestic Violence); Re H (Contact: Domestic Violence)* [2000] 2 FLR 334.
30 *A Report to the Lord Chancellor on the Question of Parental Contact in Cases where there is Domestic Violence* prepared by the Children Act Sub-Committee of the Advisory Board on Family Law (Lord Chancellor's Department, 12 April 2000).

1.29 Additionally, the Court of Appeal commissioned research of its own from two eminent child psychiatrists,[31] Dr Claire Sturge and Dr Danya Glaser, who had access to that CASC report and whose own report was peer approved before submission.

1.30 Their report stressed that domestic violence 'involves a very serious and significant failure in parenting' and agreed with CASC's that there needed to be greater awareness of the effect of domestic violence on children, both short-term and long-term, as witnesses as well as victims. They highlighted the following matters:

● children are affected as much by exposure to violence as to being involved in it – the ongoing fear and dread of it recurring is also emotionally very damaging;

● all children are affected by significant and repeated inter-partner violence even if not directly involved;

● research indicates that, even when children do not continue in violent situations, emotional trauma continues to be experienced, with the memories of the violence continuing as persecutory images;

● the context of the overall situation is highly relevant to decision making;

● the contribution of psychiatric disorders to situations of domestic violence and emotional abuse must be considered – such disorders will have put enormous pressures not only on the child but on the other parent;

● in situations of contact there may be a continuing sense of fear of the violent parent by the child;

● the child may have post-traumatic anxieties or symptoms which the proximity of the non-resident violent parent may re-arouse or perpetuate;

● there may be a continuing awareness of the fear that the violent parent arouses in the child's main carer;

● these situations have a possible effect on the child's own attitudes to violence, to forming parenting relationships and to the role of fathers, with the attitudes in boys particularly affected.

1.31 In terms of the correlation between past domestic violence and present and future contact, Sturge and Glaser did recognise that there could be potential detriment to the child (as in all cases) of having no direct contract with the non-resident parent,[32] but the clear thrust of their expert advice was that 'there should be no automatic assumption that contact to a previously or currently violent parent is in the child's interests'.[33]

---

31 See J Sturge & D Glaser *Contact and Domestic Violence – the Experts Court Report* [2000] Fam Law 615.

32 They listed the deprivation of a relationship with that parent, the loss of the opportunity to know that parent first-hand (with the loss of information and knowledge that will go to the formation of the child's identity), the loss of the opportunity to know grandparents and other relatives on that parent's side of the family, absence of the opportunity for any repair to the relationships or to the harm done and, if that parent is able to provide positive and supportive contact and new and different experiences, the loss of that opportunity (ibid, at pp 624–5).

33 Ibid, at p 623.

1.32 Whilst the Court of Appeal in *Re L; Re V; Re M; Re H*[34] specifically declined from a legal perspective to endorse this approach, it is important to note that the psychiatric opinion that it received was that 'if anything the assumption should be in the opposite direction'.[35]

1.33 Sturge and Glaser listed seven factors without which they saw the balance 'tipping against contact':[36]

'(a) some (preferably full) acknowledgement of the violence;
(b) some acceptance (preferably full if appropriate, ie the sole instigator of violence) of responsibility for that violence;
(c) full acceptance of the inappropriateness of the violence particularly in respect of the domestic and parenting context and of the likely ill-effects on the child;
(d) a genuine interest in the child's welfare and full commitment to the child, ie a wish for contact in which the non-resident parent is not making the conditions;
(e) a wish to make reparation to the child and work towards the child recognising the inappropriateness of the violence and the attitude to and treatment of the [resident parent] and helping the child to develop appropriate values and attitudes;
(f) an expression of regret and the showing of some understanding of the impact of their behaviour on their ex-partner in the past and currently;
(g) indications that the parent seeking contact can reliably sustain contact in all senses.'

1.34 They also added to the list '(h) respecting the child's wishes':

'... while this needs to be assessed within the whole context of such wishes, the older the child the more seriously they should be viewed and the more insulting and discrediting to the child to have them ignored. As a rough rule we would see these as needing to be taken account of at any age; above 10 we see these as carrying considerable weight with 6–10 as an intermediate stage and at under 6 as often indistinguishable in many ways from the wishes of the main carer (assuming normal development). In domestic violence, where the child has memories of that violence we would see their wishes as warranting much more weight than in situations where no real reason for the child's resistance appears to exist.'[37]

1.35 With the recognition of the damaging effects on children of domestic violence has come the dual recognition that violence does not cease on

---

34   *Re L (Contact: Domestic Violence); Re V (Contact: Domestic Violence); Re M (Contact: Domestic Violence); Re H (Contact: Domestic Violence)* [2000] 2 FLR 334. See paras 6.8–6.9 and 6.116.

35   See J Sturge & D Glaser *Contact and Domestic Violence – the Experts Court Report* [2000] Fam Law 615, at p 623.

36   They further saw that, without the first six, there was 'a significant risk to the child's general well-being and his or her emotional development' (ibid, at p 624).

37   Sturge & Glaser make clear that these considerations are specific but by no means exclusive to domestic violence and that other evaluations of how the contact will benefit the child (including in particular the purpose of contact) need to be made (ibid, at p 624).

separation[38] and that contact can be a particular danger-point.[39] Further, it has been noted that there is a strong correlation between domestic violence and child abuse.[40] Sturge and Glaser observe that 'parents who are violent to each other are more likely to be violent to their children', the risks of such said to be between three and nine times greater than in non-violent families,[41] and one study has gone so far as to report that 75% of children ordered to have contact with a violent parent were abused themselves.[42]

1.36 Whilst their study is essentially supportive of the positive power of contact in itself, Dunn et al[43] nevertheless comment:

'... it has to be recognised that there are some family situations where contact may be inappropriate (situations in which children have experienced or are likely to be exposed to domestic violence or child abuse). Some children in the study commented explicitly on the relief they experienced at not having to see their fathers (following violence to their mothers, for instance).'

1.37 Often inter-related with the issue of domestic violence is that of the impact of conflict on the separated child. There is no lack of research on the topic and, as the conclusions and findings below[44] indicate, there is essentially a unanimity of opinion on the issue, which fully justifies the State's concern to avoid or at least reduce the exposure of the separated child to conflict:

- many studies have found an association between the child's exposure to conflict and the child having more long-term problems;[45]

- some conflict is to be expected when relationships end and, especially in the immediate aftermath, may even be seen as both normative and an integral part of the process of psychological uncoupling;[46]

---

38 See C Mirrlees-Black, P Mayhew & A Percy *The 1996 British Crime Study England and Wales* (London, Home Office Research and Statistics Directorate, 1996).

39 See M Hester & L Radford *Domestic Violence and Child Contact Arrangements in England and Denmark* (Bristol Policy Press, 1996).

40 See R Aris, C Harrison & C Humphries *Safety and Child Contact: an analysis of the role of child contact centres in the context of domestic violence and child welfare concerns* (London, LCD, 2002).

41 See J Sturge & D Glaser *Contact and Domestic Violence – the Experts Court Report* [2000] Fam Law 615, at p 621.

42 See L Radford, S Sayer, & AMICA *Unreasonable Fears? Child Contact in the Context of Domestic Violence* (WAFE, 1999).

43 *J Dunn, H Cheng, T O'Connor & L Bridges Children's Perspectives on their Relationships with their Nonresident Fathers: influences, outcomes and implications (*Journal of Child Psychology and Psychiatry, Volume 45:3, 2004, at p 564).

44 Summarised in A Buchanan & J Hunt *Disputed Contact Cases in the Court* in A Bainham, B Lindley, M Richards & L Trinder (eds) *Children and their Families: Contact, Rights and Welfare* (Hart Publishing, 2003).

45 See B Rodgers & J Pryor *Divorce and Separation: The Outcome for Children* (York, Joseph Rowntree Foundation, 1998).

46 See S Day Sclater & C Piper *Undercurrents of Divorce* (Aldershot, Ashgate, 1999).

- Hetherington and Stanley-Hagen suggest that conflict after divorce is even worse for children than conflict within marriage;[47]
- when frequent, intense, physical, unresolved and involving the child, conflict is seen as particularly damaging;[48]
- some parents in high conflict situations can refrain from behaviours that impact on the child – what is key is the extent to which the child feels 'caught' in the conflict;[49]
- where parents were able to agree about access (contact) arrangements, enabling children to have meaningful contact, other aspects of parental conflict did not seem to have the same impact;[50]
- children found conflict which impacts on them to be unacceptable – it can lead to significant unhappiness – children wanted their parents to contain their disputes so that they did not have to be involved or used as emotional props or turned into allies, spies or go-betweens in a parental war.[51]

1.38   Buchanan and Hunt[52] conclude:

'In families where there is significant conflict ... contact may be positively damaging to children, either directly or indirectly through impairment of the parenting capacity of their primary carer. In such circumstances a careful assessment has to be made of the needs of the individual child and the balance of advantage and disadvantage.'

Contact with relatives

1.39   So far, the focus has been on contact between the separated child and the separated parent. It is, however, necessary to consider (albeit briefly) the importance of the child's contact with his or her relatives. In cases of parental separation, there is the risk that the child loses contact not only with his or her parent but also with that side of the family. That can be an additional significant loss for the child.

1.40   Pryor[53] instructively comments:

---

47   See E Hetherington & M Stanley-Hagen *The Adjustment of Children with Divorced Parents: A Risk and Resiliency Perspective* (Journal of Child Psychology and Psychiatry, Volume 40: 129, 1999).

48   See J Grych & F Fincham *The Adjustment of Children from Divorced Families: Implications of Empirical Research for Clinical Intervention* in *The Scientific Basis of Child Custody Decisions* (New York, John Wiley and Sons, 1999).

49   See C Buchanan, E Maccoby, & S Dornbusch *Caught Between Parents: Adolescents' Experience in Divorced Homes* (62 Child Development 1008, 1991).

50   See M McDonald *Children's Perceptions of Access and their Adjustment in the Post-Separation Period* (Sydney, Family Court of Australia, 1990).

51   See C Smart, B Neale & A Wade *The Changing Experience of Childhood: Families and Divorce* (Cambridge, Policy Press 2001).

52   A Buchanan & J Hunt *Disputed Contact Cases in the Court* in A Bainham, B Lindley, M Richards & L Trinder (eds) *Children and Their Families: Contact, Rights and Welfare* (Hart Publishing, 2003).

53   J Pryor *Children's Contact with Relatives* in A Bainham, B Lindley, M Richards & L Trinder (eds) *Children and Their Families: Contact, Rights and Welfare* (Hart Publishing, 2003).

'... at some levels ["relatives"] are relations that are taken for granted and unexamined, perhaps because they are so much a part of the fabric of our emotional landscape. Yet for children they are a powerful and subtle source of identity. They offer unique perspectives on parents and on themselves, in ways that enhance an emerging sense of self within the web of family within which most children develop.'

Conclusion

1.41 The contact canvas is therefore broad. The potential benefits of contact for the child are significant and varied. Recent research suggests that contact in itself can be a positive. Yet there is widespread recognition that contact can in certain circumstances be actually harmful to the child concerned. Factoring in appropriately the perspective of the children themselves, and drawing also the salient distinction between cases where there is and is not a pre-existing relationship between child and parent, Hunt and Roberts[54] summarise the position:

'Most children want to remain in touch. Contact has potential value in terms of developing the child's sense of identity, preserving links with the wider family, and providing an additional source of support for children and even protection from abuse. In ordinary circumstances a parent with an established relationship with the child should not have to prove that contact is in the child's best interests. It does mean, however, that care needs to be taken not to overestimate the presumed benefits of contact either where there is no pre-existing relationship or where there are known risks. Where there is abuse or neglect, exposure to domestic violence or severe parental conflict, contact can be extremely damaging to children.'

1.42 That the position cannot be more easily summarised nor reduced to some more sweeping generalisation in part reflects the reality that no child is the same. It highlights too the variety of circumstances and experiences for the children concerned both before and after separation.

1.43 The essential conclusions to be drawn from this fairly swift trawl through the seas of research may sound trite but are no less important. At the broadest level, they mark up the imperative of ensuring that contact likely to have positive effects for the child (as most contact ought to) should occur, should be encouraged and should be assisted not only to happen but to flourish. However, they also highlight the real significance of safeguarding children from contact that is genuinely likely to be damaging to them.[55]

1.44 The consequent challenge for the State is clear – to shape a system which better serves the child of separated parents and in which those two main goals are more clearly understood and more effectively realised.

---

54   J Hunt & C Roberts *Child Contact with Non-resident Parents* (University of Oxford, 2004).

55   It needs to be borne in mind that safeguarding can take many forms, dependant on the assessment of benefit and detriment for the child in the given case. It can obviously include the prohibition of all contact (or all face-to-face contact), but, short of that, may recognise the need for the contact to be supported or supervised (whether formally or informally). See further J Sturge & D Glaser *Contact and Domestic Violence – the Experts Court Report* [2000] Fam Law 615, at p 626.

THE DEFICIENCIES OF THE SYSTEM

1.45 We use the term 'system' in the broadest sense. When, therefore, we speak of its deficiencies, we do not point the finger at those mostly dedicated and hard-working individuals working inside it. Inevitably, they have to function within the strictures of the law and the confines of resources. Our focus is on the end product, on the overall service provided to the children of separated parents and their families.

1.46 It is particularly important not to see the system (and the room for improvement within it) solely in terms of the court arena. Although an increasing number of disputes are going to court, only around 10% of separating couples with children have their contact arrangements enshrined in court orders. Of the remainder, the arrangements of about 5% have come about through mediation, leaving in the region of 85% making arrangements on an informal basis themselves.[56]

1.47 It is true that, within that 85% (as with the other 15%), there are a significant number of cases where, for whatever reason, there is no meaningful contact between the child and the non-resident parent. But it is telling, though perhaps not that surprising, that those who have undertaken that informal route have on the whole been satisfied (82% of resident parents and 87% of non-resident parents sampled in the 2003 ONS Omnibus Survey)[57] and measurably more satisfied than those who have had recourse to mediation or to the courts.

1.48 The figures (for informal arrangements and for the level of satisfaction about them) are encouraging and accord with one of the key underlying principles of the Children Act 1989 – namely that families should, wherever possible, be encouraged and empowered to sort out problems with their children themselves. However, the figures should not detract from the large number of cases that are subject to the court process.

Contact and the courts

1.49 Bob Geldof writes of his experience of family law as having left him 'feeling criminalised, belittled, worthless, powerless and irrelevant'.[58] Whatever the merits of his particular case, it is important to acknowledge such profoundly adverse reactions and the numbers who share his essentially negative view of the court process.

1.50 Moreover, it is telling that recorded dissatisfaction with the court experience is not only substantial but crosses the divides between mothers and fathers and between resident and non-resident parents. The recent ONS

---

56   See the Office for National Statistics (ONS) Omnibus Survey (2003).
57   Ibid.
58   See his powerful chapter *The Real Love that Dare Not Speak its Name: A Sometimes Coherent Rant* in A Bainham, B Lindley, M Richards & L Trinder (eds) *Children and Their Families: Contact, Rights and Welfare* (Hart Publishing, 2003).

Survey[59] recorded that, of children subject to court contact orders, 57% of non-resident parents and as many as 26% of resident parents were dissatisfied with the resulting contact arrangements. Similarly, the 2001 consumer study by Buchanan et al[60] showed huge dissatisfaction with the court process, with six in ten parents (mothers and fathers, applicants and respondents) being entirely negative.

1.51 That level and spread of dissatisfaction amongst those whose lives, and whose children's lives, were being acutely affected by the court system of itself challenged the system's sustainability. Inevitably, some of that dissatisfaction will have been coloured by personal experience of perceived failure or injustice in court. Plainly, some of the solutions proposed by disaffected litigants[61] could not be justified, either on an objective child welfare basis and/or for reasons of public cost. However, the bulk of the criticism of the court system was dispassionately sound. The principal complaint of those involved in the Buchanan et al study,[62] for example, was delay, with others identified including judicial discontinuity and the stress of court hearings. The need for change was recognised by lawyers, politicians, academics and other professionals involved in the system, as well as from litigants. The demand for change had been building for some time and had reached the point where it could be resisted no longer. The need to do something was clear. The question was what should be done.

1.52 Many of the criticisms of the court system could be seen as non-partisan. The difficulty for the State, however, was that others reflected very much the actual or at least potential tension between the two rival non-resident and resident parent camps – those who decried the system for not doing enough to promote and ensure contact and those who condemned it for promoting and enforcing contact when it was unsafe so to do. This much is apparent when one looks at the various claims, concerns and complaints that are noted within the *Parental Separation: Children's Needs and Parents' Responsibilities* Green Paper[63] (which, for ease of reference, we set out and group below):

Regarding the nature and approach of the courts

- That the lengthy and adversarial nature of court proceedings had the potential to exacerbate rather than reduce acrimony between the parents involved;
- that court decisions were often backward looking rather than focused on reaching workable solutions for the future;
- that the current system of public funding for advice and representation rewarded litigation rather than settlement;

---

59   ONS Omnibus Survey (2003).
60   A Buchanan, J Hunt, H Bretherton & V Bream *Families in Conflict: Perspectives of Children and Parents on the Family Court Welfare Service* (Bristol, Policy Press, 2001). This was a consumer study of families in residence and contact disputes subject to welfare reports.
61   See further at paras 1.59 and 1.63.
62   A Buchanan, J Hunt, H Bretherton & V Bream *Families in Conflict: Perspectives of Children and Parents on the Family Court Welfare Service* (Bristol, Policy Press, 2001).
63   July 2004 – Cm 6273 – available at www.dfes.gov.uk/childrensneeds/.

- that resolution was treated as a one-off event rather than an ongoing process at which parents needed to work over the long term.

Regarding the promotion and enforcement of contact

- That the existing law (or at least its interpretation in practice) did not give the non-resident parent (mostly fathers) the relationship with their child that they ought to have;
- that the courts were biased towards the status quo and favoured the resident parent (most often mothers) and that delays in arriving at decisions worsened this tendency, this being a particular concern of non-resident parents (usually fathers);
- that court ordered contact was poorly enforced;
- that some cases go back to court time and time again, with the courts unable to resolve them;
- that relatives in the wider family (particularly grandparents) lost contact following separation, especially when such was linked to the non-resident parent's contact;
- that some non-resident parents (to the frustration of the corresponding resident parents) had made insufficient effort to keep in touch with their children;
- that there were not enough supervised contact centres.

Regarding safety issues

- That the process for identifying and verifying safety issues was ineffective and slow;
- that the courts allowed contact in a way that put the safety and well-being of the children and their residential parent at risk (something felt by some residential parents).

1.53 A measure of criticism of the court system is probably inevitable. After all, it does have to deal with the most difficult and most protracted of contact disputes. Yet that description certainly does not apply to all residence and contact cases that reach the court door. Nor does it necessarily mean that those cases that do prove difficult and protracted were always destined so to be. Furthermore, it is no more than a reflection of the vagaries of human relationships that there will be complex cases and no more than a statement of the obvious that they have to be dealt with. The simple truth is that historically, for whatever reason, the courts have had limited success at dealing with them.

1.54 The experiences of many family law practitioners, which we summarise below, chime with much that is recorded within *Parental Separation: Children's Needs and Parents' Responsibilities*:[64]

- There are plainly a large number of residence and contact cases which should never have been taken to court. They involved issues which were not hard to resolve, which certainly did not need lawyers to resolve them

---

64   Ibid.

and which could have been resolved had the parents involved been able to communicate in a more objective, effective and above all child-centred way.

- There are a significant number of litigants whose idea of what should be important to the court's decision is at odds with what in law is important to that decision, and who see the court as a forum for pursuing their own agenda.

- Many lawyers genuinely strive to foster compromise. But the lengthy and adversarial nature of the process has the clear potential to polarise positions and raise the temperature in cases. This is manifestly to the detriment of the children whose welfare is at stake and yet who find themselves either drawn into the conflict or the unwitting victims of its repercussions.

- Courts have been too slow and ineffective in dealing with resident parents who have sought to stop or limit contact for no objectively sound reason. In particular, they have not been swift enough to delineate between, on the one hand, genuine issues of harm and, on the other, petty concerns and resistance founded on little more than a difference in parenting style, approach or perception. Whether due to delays in securing appropriate hearing time or to the reluctance of some courts to act decisively early enough, the potential for resident parents to manipulate the system, especially to embed a false status quo, has been far too great.

- The methods for enforcing court orders have been too slow and too cumbersome, and in many a case have proved utterly inadequate. Typically, by the time that the court has lost its patience, the damage has been long done and there is nothing effective then that can be done to undo it.

- The potential for contact in certain circumstances to be harmful to the child (directly and indirectly) has for too long been poorly understood. In particular, there has been a lack of appreciation of the motives of those parents who genuinely do have a sound protective rationale for resisting contact.

- The first headline consequence of the above is that there are far too many children who, for no good reason, have been deprived of a meaningful ongoing relationship with their non-resident parent.

- The second is that, for some children, not enough has been done to protect them from conflict and from contact likely to be harmful to them.

1.55 These observations, drawn from practice, are not out of line with the findings of two important recent research studies, which have looked at the nexus between the court process and private law disputes over children.

1.56 Research by Trinder, Beek and Connolly[65] found that divorced and separated parents who resort to the law to settle chronic disputes over contact with their children risked making matters worse for all concerned. Contrasting the relative success of contact agreements that separated parents reach without legal intervention, their study suggested that lawyers were rarely able to

---

65   L Trinder, M Beek & J Connolly *Making Contact: How Parents and Children Negotiate and Experience Contact after Divorce* (York, Joseph Rowntree Foundation, 2002).

improve their clients' commitment to unwelcome contact arrangements and that applications for court orders tended to fuel rather than resolve conflict.

1.57 Interview-based research by Smart, May, Wade and Furniss[66] was not quite so damning. They mostly looked at high-conflict residence and contact court cases and their findings provide a valuable insight into them – particularly into the reasons why these parents go to court, their expectations and experiences of the court system, their likes and dislikes with respect to it, the consequences of those cases and what those parents actually want from the courts.

1.58 Although the parents involved in this study had genuine child welfare issues that divided them, these issues were not necessarily the driving force behind the conflict. They were often angry about having been mistreated, deceived or abandoned or about the way in which their former partner behaved following separation. Yet, because the courts were unconcerned with these complaints, the parents channelled their anger into the issues of residence and contact in which the court had to take an interest. Smart et al do not suggest that parental concerns for their children were made up or cynically used, rather that the parents were channelled into what the authors call 'a parenting contest' in which the goal was to show the other parent to be inadequate or unworthy – a 'contest' played for very high stakes with the individual's sense of self as a good parent being threatened and even damaged.

1.59 It should come as no surprise that those involved in these disputes had complaints. The parents who felt that the decision had gone against them or rejected their values were not slow to blame the judge and/or the CAFCASS[67] officer for bias, stupidity or lack of insight. Some parents, regardless of the outcome, were unhappy with their court experience. They felt that they had too little time in court, that the CAFCASS officer spent too little time with them, that there was a lack of interest in the things that mattered to them and that the resultant court order was too formulaic when their preference would have been for something more tailor-made to their family's needs. There was real dissatisfaction with the court's failure to enforce orders shown by those in whose favour those orders were made, whilst on the other hand there was strong criticism of those who had gone to court but then did not take up the contact that they were awarded.

1.60 Not that the experiences were entirely negative. Some parents found that the specified nature of a court order provided a certainty that, by obviating the need for communication, thereby reduced the opportunity for subsequent conflict. For fearful parents in cases where there had been violence or threats to abduct the child, a court order was seen as a method by which safety and security could be achieved.

1.61 Interestingly (especially if one bears in mind the Trinder et al conclusions), Smart et al did not feel that their data could answer the question

66 C Smart, V May, A Wade & C Furniss *Residence and Contact Disputes in Court – Volume 2* (London, DCA, 2003).
67 The Children and Family Court Advisory and Support Service.

of whether going to court exacerbated or resolved conflict for parents in general. They felt that it was impossible to isolate 'going to court' as a sole causal factor in what was a complex process of human relationships. They did, however, note that:

* whereas in 10% of the cases that they looked at, the level of conflict had never been high, with the parents said to be on fairly amicable terms, and
* in 30% of the cases, conflict had abated, with an improved parental ability to communicate noted,
* in 60% of the cases that they examined, there was a continuing high degree of conflict that the courts had been unable to resolve (with, for instance, little or no parental communication and/or ongoing hostility that made contact arrangements difficult or unpleasant).

1.62 A further striking feature apparent in most of these high conflict cases was the way in which the parents spoke of their children. They were 'recruits' for their side of the argument. While some parents did speak of their children's stress and unhappiness, this was seen as being the fault of the other parent.

1.63 In the circumstances, it is again not surprising that some parents said that they wanted a more detailed and forensic investigation into the behaviour of their former partner and for such to influence the outcome of the court's decision. Mothers could not understand why withholding or under-payment of child support was treated as immaterial by the courts. Some parents (mothers and fathers) wanted a more substantial opportunity to be heard in court. A common wish was for a more individualised order that fitted better with the specific needs of the children concerned. Parents also said that they wanted more support. They felt that, after the hearing, they were left to get on with matters alone, with the potential for becoming depressed or remaining angry that such entailed. If, on the other hand, the order was not being adhered to, they felt that their only option was to go back to their solicitor and/to court, thereby re-engaging with a cycle of hostility.

1.64 In looking at the pluses and minuses of the court system, it is important to keep a sense of proportion. With the paramountcy principle[68] at the heart of the process, much good work has been carried on within it. But the standards of the family justice system are rightly high and the need for candid self-appraisal is constant. Whatever the merits or demerits of individual complaints, and wherever the roots of its failings lay, three conclusions were inescapable about the court process as it stood, prior to recent reform, in the early years of the twenty-first century:

(1)   that, with court too frequently disappointing rather than meeting the expectations of its litigant users, resort to court, and in particular to contested proceedings, ought to be actively discouraged;
(2)   that a quicker, more consistent, more case-appropriate and more child-focused way of dealing with the variety of cases ending up in court was urgently needed; and
(3)   that there was scope for improvement.

---

68   The principle that, when a court determines any question with respect to the upbringing of a child, the child's welfare shall be its paramount consideration (Children Act 1989, s 1).

THE CONTEXT FOR CHANGE

1.65 Before we look at the State's response to the perceived failings of the system, we consider first the context in which any such response has to be delivered – both in terms of the state of families at the time of parental separation and in the context of the broader societal picture.

The family on separation

1.66 From the outset, it has to be borne in mind that the State is seeking to cater for families at a time when by definition they are subject to change. Each member of the family is having to adjust to a changed role and for each the future to a greater or lesser extent lacks certainty. It is all too easy to preach that separating parents should be responsible, communicative and child-centred and to criticise when objectivity deserts them and they find themselves sucked into conflict. But one should not forget that the experience of many parents at that time of separation makes them ripe candidates for just such consequences. Separation can be an extremely emotional experience. Many parents feel ill-equipped to overcome the conflict between themselves and their former partners such that they can come to an agreement that is in the best interests of their children. Many also feel ill-prepared for the situation ahead, without an understanding of their rights and responsibilities or where to go for help.[69] As for the children experiencing parental separation, most will go through a period of unhappiness and many will experience low self-esteem and behaviour problems.[70]

1.67 If those descriptions demonstrate the challenge of dealing appropriately and effectively with parents and children at the time of separation, the upsides for the future are these:

- that the primary desire of parents, it would appear, whatever their chosen resolution route, is to reach agreement as soon as possible and in a way that subjects both themselves and their family to the lowest possible levels of stress and upset;[71]

- that children at separation are usually helped by good communication with both parents, are assisted by being informed of and involved in decisions about what happens in the family and most settle back into a normal pattern of development;[72]

---

69   See the results of the DCA Consumer Strategy in the *Parental Separation: Children's Needs and Parents' Responsibilities* supporting evidence paper available at www.dfes.gov.uk/childrensneeds/downloads.shtml.

70   See M Maclean's review of research in *Together and Apart: Children and Parents Experiencing Separation and Divorce* (Joseph Rowntree Foundation, 2004).

71   See the results of the DCA Consumer Strategy in the *Parental Separation: Children's Needs and Parents' Responsibilities* supporting evidence paper available at www.dfes.gov.uk/childrensneeds/downloads.shtml.

72   See J Dunn & K Deater-Deckard *Children's Views of their Changing Families* (Joseph Rowntree Foundation, 2001).

● that kin networks, especially grandparents, can play an important part in supporting children and grandchildren at the time of separation.[73]

1.68   If that is what is happening in individual separated families, what are the more relevant trends and features of society as a whole? We look at the significance of three:

(1)   the amount of contact actually taking place and the scope for more;
(2)   the extent to which the more traditional roles of mother and father have changed and are still changing;
(3)   the incidence of parental separation and change for children.

How much contact is taking place?

1.69   One might think this a straightforward question that ought to be capable of a fairly straightforward answer, but the reality is that it depends to a sizeable degree on whichever study or survey is looked at and who the informants are. For example, resident parents typically report less contact than non-resident parents, whilst there is more contact where the parents had been married as opposed to cohabiting or never having lived together.[74]

1.70   Previous studies had indicated 'no contact' levels of up to 40%.[75] However, the recent ONS Survey[76] suggested significantly lower figures, with 24% of children in the resident parent sample and 10% of the children in the non-resident sample reported as having no direct or indirect contact with their non-resident parent. It is to be noted that those figures are in line with the findings of the 2004 study by Dunn et al,[77] where only 29 (18%) out of the 162 children surveyed were found to be having no contact with their non-resident parents.

1.71   Looked at from the alternative perspective – that of the contact that is taking place – the Smith et al study[78] (a representative community sample of stepfamilies in the London area) reported that nearly half the children studied were in regular and frequent (more than monthly) contact with their non-resident parents; whilst a 33% contact level of at least weekly on a regular basis was recorded in the Dunn et al study.[79] Again, these figures broadly

---

73   Ibid.
74   See M MacLean & J Eekelaar *The Parenting Obligation* (Hart Publishing, 1997).
75   See, for example, Bradshaw & Millar *Lone Parent Families in the UK* (DSS Report 6, London HMSO, 1991).
76   ONS Omnibus Survey (2003), involving 649 resident parents and 312 non-resident parents, with 26 falling within both categories, reporting on contact arrangements for 1,506 children.
77   See J Dunn, H Cheng, T O'Connor & L Bridges *Children's Perspectives on their Relationships with their Non-resident Fathers: Influences, outcomes and implications* (Journal of Child Psychology and Psychiatry, Volume 45:3, 2004, pp 553–566).
78   M Smith, J Robertson, J Dixon, M Quigley & Z Whitehead *A Study of Stepchildren and Step-Parenting* (London, Thomas Coram Research Unit, 2001).
79   J Dunn, H Cheng, T O'Connor & L Bridges *Children's Perspectives on their Relationships with their Non-resident Fathers: Influences, outcomes and implications* (Journal of Child Psychology and Psychiatry, Volume 45:3, 2004, pp 553–566).

accord with the results of the ONS Survey,[80] indicating that 43% of children in the resident parent sample and 59% of the children in the non-resident parent sample had direct contact with their non-resident parent at least once a week.

1.72 The analysis of the ONS Survey carried out by Blackwell and Dawe[81] helpfully draws out some interesting underlying features behind some of the survey's more headline statistics:

- there is an apparent correlation between the frequency of direct contact and indirect contact;

- (perhaps predictably) distance between the non-resident parent's home and that of his or her child is an important factor governing the frequency of direct contact between them;

- non-resident parents separated for three years or more were less likely to have direct contact with their child at least weekly than those who had separated within the previous three years;

- further, those children of parents separated for at least three years were also more likely never to have contact with their non-resident parent than those children who had separated more recently;

- the age of the child seems to have little influence over the frequency of contact between child and non-resident parent;

- the majority of children in both the resident and non-resident parent samples were reported to have contact at the home of their non-resident parent – contact centres were used by less than 1% as a contact venue;

- whether the parent was in a new relationship and had further children were influential factors:

  - within the resident parent sample, whilst the frequency of contact with the non-resident parent was unaffected by the resident parent being in a new relationship, where that relationship had produced a child less frequent contact was reported;

  - within the non-resident parent sample, children whose non-resident parent was not currently in a relationship were more likely to have contact of some sort and more likely in particular to have direct contact at least weekly than those children whose non-resident parent was currently in a relationship;

- more than half of all children stay overnight with their non-resident parent (with higher rates for staying contact reported within the non-resident parent sample).

1.73 Blackwell and Dawe also note the correlation between frequency of contact and parental satisfaction with the contact arrangements in place, with high satisfaction rates recorded among both resident and non-resident parents where contact was frequent.

1.74 Most strikingly, they highlight the principal response when parents were asked how the contact arrangements with their child could be improved:

---

80   ONS Omnibus Survey (2003).
81   See A Blackwell & F Dawe *Non Resident Parental Contact* (based on data from the National Statistics Omnibus Survey for the Department of Constitutional Affairs, October 2003).

'The most popular contact improvement, in both sample groups, was that the non-resident parent should have more direct contact with their child. Parents of children in the resident parent group were twice as likely as parents of children in the non-resident parent sample to mention that increased direct contact would improve the current contact arrangements (34% compared with 17%).'[82]

1.75 Those results are actually consistent with the findings of a number of studies[83] and cause Hunt and Roberts[84] to argue that 'there is scope for an increase in contact'. They also show that the stereotypical picture of non-resident father pushing for more contact against reluctant resident parent, whilst true in some cases, cannot and ought not to be generalised. The sad truth is that, whereas some resident parents do seek wholly wrongly to thwart contact, there are children out there who are not having enough or even any contact with their non-resident parent simply by the choice of their non-resident parent – a choice that may be borne out of indifference, emotional avoidance or a bloody-minded insistence on contact on their terms or not at all.

1.76 From the child welfare angle, the indifferent, avoidant or bloody-minded non-resident parent would seem every bit as culpable as the unreasonable resident parent. Whatever the reason for that lack of contact, in cases where contact would not be harmful, it is a tragedy for the children concerned that it does not occur or happen sufficiently often. Whilst properly noting that the general trend is one of more contact taking place, Hunt and Roberts[85] are rightly concerned that:

'... some non-resident parents are still disappearing from children's lives and others having insufficient contact to develop the type of involved parenting likely to yield demonstrable benefits'.

Changing parental roles

1.77 In terms of family status and make-up, time has not stood still for the decade and a half since the coming into force of the Children Act 1989, the statute that provides the framework within which private law children disputes are resolved by the courts.

1.78 The UK census shows that between 1991 and 2001 there was in England and Wales a fall in married couple households and a rise in cohabiting couple households. Interestingly, these changes were particularly marked for households containing dependent children, with the numbers of:

- married couple households with dependent children falling by 13%;
- cohabiting couple households with dependent children rising by 102%;
- lone parent households rising by 21%.

---

82 Ibid.
83 See, for example, J Hunt *Researching Contact* (London: National Council for One-Parent Families, 2003).
84 J Hunt & C Roberts *Child Contact with Non-resident Parents* (University of Oxford, 2004).
85 Ibid.

1.79 Although some 60% of dependent children as of 2001 were living in married couple households, the trend is clearly towards more children being brought up with cohabiting parents or just one parent, with relationships between parents (whether they marry, cohabit or never set up home together) less stable than before.[86]

1.80 If that provides the overview of how families with children are increasingly being made up, which in turn helps to explain the continuingly significant incidence of parental separation, what though of the parental roles within those families?

1.81 If our caseload is in any way representative, then, comparing the situation now with some fifteen years ago, a period in which concepts of parental equality have come increasingly to the fore, the picture is of:

- more fathers taking more involved parenting roles in families prior to separation;
- more families, when intact, having fathers as primary carers or at least in properly shared primary caring roles;
- more fathers, subsequent to separation, having residence and shared residence orders for their children than before;

albeit that, on the whole, it is mothers who still undertake the principal caring role prior to separation and mostly retain the primary caring role after separation (a picture seemingly borne out by the results of the ONS Survey showing 93% of resident parents being female and 89% of non-resident parents being male[87]).

1.82 The suggested change in the nature of the father's role also appears to be borne out by research. Indeed, not only do Shemilt and O'Brien[88] give credence to there being movement, but they seek to explain why the movement has not been greater. They note that British fathers now undertake approximately a third of all childcare and that the amount of time that fathers of children under the age of 5 spend with them on child-related activities has gone up from less than a quarter of an hour per day in the mid 1970s to two hours a day by the late 1990s. They argue that fathers do not get the flexibility that they need at work to help them to do more, with a working culture, where long hours are the norm, preventing fathers from being more involved with their children's lives, as they would like to be.

1.83 Shemilt and O'Brien also emphasise the higher childcare involvement of fathers whose partners work full-time and/or have a high income, recording that, where mothers work, fathers are cited by a third as the main child carer while they are at work. The authors deduce that the 'cash v care' negotiation happens in many a family and note other recent research for the Equal Opportunities Commission (EOC) showing that, because women earn less,

---

86   See the *Parental Separation: Children's Needs and Parents' Responsibilities* supporting evidence paper available at www.dfes.gov.uk/childrensneeds/downloads.shtml.

87   ONS Omnibus Survey (2003).

88   I Shemilt & M O'Brien *Working Fathers: Earning and Caring* (London: Equal Opportunities Commission, 2003).

couples often decide that it makes economic sense for the woman to give up work or cut her hours, so that she can care for the children, and so women continue to earn less and the caring role is still seen primarily as a female one.

1.84 In a 2005 (albeit fairly small sample) study, Lewis and Walsh[89] took a more in-depth look at the nature of the role played by fathers when providing 'childcare'. They saw change, but not quite of the nature and to the extent that some would claim. While they record that the traditional, rather distant, breadwinning father has disappeared, they see in this study no evidence of a shift towards the kind of father who takes equal day-to-day responsibility for his children.

1.85 They did find that fathers were all to a greater or lesser extent committed to and interested in their children, but found that the main forms of such involvement entailed 'a commitment to "be there", often as a jokey, fun dad, alongside a conscious acceptance of macro-responsibilities for guiding, leading and establishing value frameworks', with fathers being perceived favourably by children as well as mothers if able to combine these roles. They note however that:

'... while a small majority of fathers were moderately or highly involved, in almost all cases mothers took the *bulk* of the responsibility for the daily "running" of the family and also for talking to and dealing with children's problems, discipline included.'[90]

1.86 Essentially, what the authors report are more subtle changes in the nature of fathers' involvement with their children, relying to a large degree on an appreciation of the importance of 'passive care' and of co-operative parenting, with mothers often serving 'as the conduit for fathers to "reach" their children about issues such as boundary setting'.

1.87 However, that highlights, they argue, the resultant difficulties when those families fracture – particularly for non-resident fathers who are 'likely to be plunged into contact that requires taking micro-responsibility', whose previous and important provision of 'passive care' (if given) cannot be sustained post-separation and who would probably be resented by the resident mother if they sought still to take macro-responsibility for their children.

1.88 Their findings, Lewis and Welsh contend, have important implications for how the State should act and it will be seen that their recommendations go beyond just the issue of quantum of parental involvement to deal with how that involvement could be better enabled:

---

89   J Lewis & E Welsh *Fathering Practices in Twenty-six Intact Families and the Implications for Child Contact* (International Journal of Law in Context I,I pp 81–99, Cambridge University, 2005).

90   Ibid, at p 94.

'The nature and extent of father involvement in intact families is increasing, albeit slowly, so encouragement of this trend in the hope that it will take root and survive family disruption would seem to be a promising focus for policy development.'[91]

1.89   That, they suggest, puts the focus firmly on family policies designed to 'reconcile' work and family responsibilities for men as well as for women. In that context, they highlight how other Northern European countries have sought to encourage precisely that – the provision of 'daddy leaves' when children are young, as in Scandinavia, and the promotion of a 'combination scenario' of part-time work and part-time care for men and women, as in the Netherlands. They conclude:

'If there is continued movement towards full-time earner couples, and if more non-resident fathers seek contact with their children, then a more equal pattern of involvement for mothers and fathers and a firmer shift towards "new" fathering practices would seem to be necessary.'[92]

The incidence of parental separation and change for children

1.90   We started this chapter by recording the large volume of parents who separate each year and the significant proportion of children who now find themselves the children of separated parents.[93] To a large degree, the scale of those numbers explains the extent of the State's interest in the issue of the child of the separated parent, but it also has repercussions for the approach that the State should adopt.

1.91   Against that numerical backdrop and with an eye to the broader realities of family life, Maclean[94] pertinently comments:

'... we need to move on from categorising the children of divorced and separated parents as having an experience which is essentially different from that of other children. It is time to recognise that all children can be expected to undergo a number of transitions in their family circumstances.'

1.92   She also makes the valid point that, however tempting it is to see parental separation as an event, it actually has to be seen as a process, starting long before the actual departure of one parent and continuing throughout the childhood of the children affected. In terms of when, how and for how long the components of the separating and separated family have a need for support, advice and assistance, that is clearly an important observation.

WHAT MAKES CONTACT WORK

1.93   Before finally setting out in outline how the State has responded to the need for change, we look more closely at what can be gleaned from the research

---

91   Ibid, at pp 95–96.
92   Ibid, at p 96.
93   See para 1.2.
94   M Maclean *Together and Apart: Children and Parents Experiencing Separation and Divorce* (Joseph Rowntree Foundation, 2004).

into the reasons for and factors associated with contact working. In so doing, we draw the distinction between contact that happens and contact that really works and we note the two themes that shine out:

- effective co-operation and communication between parents on issues affecting their children; and
- proper involvement of the children themselves in the process by which arrangements are brought about.

1.94 We have already highlighted the important recent research by Dunn et al[95] and its finding for their sample that contact with non-resident fathers was associated with the well-being of their children. It is, however, as significant to record their allied finding of a correlation between positive non-resident father–child relationships and both:

(1) the quality of the mother–child relationship, a 'close link' being found between the affection, companionship and support children reported within their relationships with their non-resident fathers and the positivity that those children reported in their relationships with their mothers; and

(2) the quality of the relationship between the mother and her former partner – a pattern indicating, in the authors' views, that mothers' relationships with their former partners may indeed function as a 'gateway' for children's continuing contact with their non-resident fathers.

1.95 Commenting on those findings, they draw a conclusion which in the cold light of day may sound simple common sense, but which, as one too easily ignored in the heat of separation and its aftermath, demands continuing prominence:

'This underlines the importance of parents developing a good "working" relationship over children's issues, and of keeping any problems in their own relationship separate from their parenting.'[96]

1.96 Further, and after noting the increasing recognition of the importance of getting children's perspectives on family issues and the research indicating the useful practical suggestions concerning contact arrangements that children can make, Dunn et al assert that 'children's own views of contact should certainly be taken into consideration'.[97] The advantages of involving children appropriately are similarly emphasised by Maclean:[98]

'Researchers ... stress the importance both of making sure that children are told clearly what is happening and of listening sensitively to what children have to say about decisions which affect them.'

---

95   J Dunn, H Cheng, T O'Connor & L Bridges *Children's Perspectives on their Relationships with their Nonresident Fathers: Influences, Outcomes and Implications* (Journal of Child Psychology and Psychiatry, Volume 45:3, 2004, pp 553–566).

96   Ibid, at p 564.

97   Ibid, at p 564.

98   M Maclean *Together and Apart: Children and Parents Experiencing Separation and Divorce* (Joseph Rowntree Foundation, 2004).

1.97   Looking at the issue somewhat more broadly and thematically, Pryor and Rodgers[99] have highlighted a number of factors as being consistently found to be associated with continuing contact. Where the parents had been previously married (rather than cohabiting or never living together), contact was more likely, as it was where the non-resident parent did not have further children. They particularly stressed the following:

- a cooperative post-separation relationship between the parents;
- the child wanting contact;
- proximity between the homes of the resident and non-resident parent;
- the non-resident parent being employed and paying child support.

1.98   The last point is of particular interest. The courts have treated contact and child maintenance as separate issues – the obligation to maintain arises irrespective of contact, whilst compliance with a contact order is not conditional on child support being paid – but, on the ground, the position seems to be different. Where there is contact, child support is more likely;[100] where there is support, it can 'oil the wheels' of contact.[101] On the other hand, payment without contact is resented by non-resident parents and contact without payment is resented by resident parents.[102]

1.99   Trinder et al[103] specifically looked at why some families manage to make contact work and others do not. Defining 'working' contact as:

- that occurring without risk of physical or psychological harm to any party,
- with both adults and children being committed to contact,
- with everyone involved being broadly satisfied with the current arrangements for contact and not seeking significant changes to them, and
- with contact being on balance a positive experience for all parties,

they identified two ingredients as being critical for making contact work – joint parental commitment and role bargain being one, and relationships skills being the other.

1.100   Where contact was working, they saw that everyone (adults and children included) was committed to contact and to making it work, with that commitment being accompanied by an implicit parental agreement or bargain about their respective roles. Non-resident parents did not challenge the status of, denigrate or threaten resident parents, while resident parents actively supported contact, for example by suggesting or organising activities.

---

99   J Pryor & B Rodgers *Children in Changing Families: Life after Parental Separation* (Oxford, Blackwell Publishers, 2001).

100 See G Davis & N Wikeley *National Survey of Child Support Agency Clients – The Relationship Dimension* [2002] Fam Law 522.

101 See J Bradshaw, C Stimson, J Williams & C Skinner *Absent Fathers* (London: Routledge, 1999).

102 See J Hunt & C Roberts *Child Contact with Non-resident Parents* (University of Oxford, 2004).

103 L Trinder, M Beek & J Connolly *Making Contact: How Parents and Children Negotiate and Experience Contact after Divorce* (York, Joseph Rowntree Foundation, 2002).

1.101 They also noted the ability of parents to work through the difficulties that inevitably arose. Contact did not have to be perfect, it was about establishing 'good enough' relationships. The parents who made contact work:

- had a realistic, balanced appraisal of each other, with both strengths and weaknesses recognised;
- accepted that some disagreement would arise, but managed to deal with conflict such that a problem did not escalate into a full-blown dispute;
- assumed the 'good intentions' of the other, accepting differences in parenting style as legitimate and capable, if needs be, of being addressed without contact itself being undermined.

1.102 While this model of 'working' contact provides something to which parents could – and could be encouraged to – aspire, what is as instructive is how these 'working' contact parents arrived at these 'working' contact arrangements. They did it themselves – informed not by legal diktat (none of them mentioned the Children Act 1989) but by general social norms or discourses, by their own personal experiences and circumstances, by the quality of the parental relationship and, to some degree, by the preferences of their children:

> 'Quite simply, parents where contact was working had formulated their own ideas about what was appropriate, and neither solicitors nor the law informed this ... instead what appears to be the case is that it is wider social norms that inform both parental and legal principles rather than the other way around.'[104]

Equal parenting time?

1.103 It is against that background that we consider the topical and contentious issue of whether a child should spend equal amounts of time with each parent.

1.104 It is a debate bedevilled by (understandable) confusion over labels. The concepts of 'shared parenting' and 'shared residence' should not be conflated. Whilst the former is a concept defined not by time but by degrees of emotional support and collaborative working, which does not therefore require the child to spend an equal (or roughly equal) amount of time with each parent, the latter describes that very arrangement. It accordingly follows that it is wrong to assume that the usually laudable goal of shared parenting can only be achieved through such a shared residence arrangement. More confusingly, it is similarly wrong to assume that the making of a shared residence order by the court (an option increasingly favoured by the judiciary[105]) is dependant on having that equal or near equal split of the child's time. Often shared residence orders do reflect that very arrangement but are not confined to that scenario.

---

104 See L Trinder *Working and Not Working Contact after Divorce* in A Bainham, B Lindley, M Richards & L Trinder (eds) *Children and Their Families: Contact, Rights and Welfare* (Hart Publishing, 2003).

105 Such an order can have the benefit of giving the home of each parent an equal status in the eyes of the law and the child. See para 3.48 et seq.

1.105   Insofar as there is research on the benefits of children spending equal or broadly equal time with each of their parents (and there is not enough), it is mixed[106] and perhaps predictably so.

1.106   In certain circumstances, it can work, particularly where the parental relationship is a harmonious one, where the child's two homes are close by, where the work arrangements of each parent allow, where there is flexibility over arrangements (especially as the child gets older) and above all where the needs of the child are prioritised and where the child feels truly at home in both households (as opposed to the parent simply assuming that).

1.107   Equally, however, that very same arrangement can cause a multitude of problems for the child where those factors are absent and where instead it is the needs of the parents that are prioritised, where there is inflexibility over arrangements and where the child does not feel settled in both homes. For the child to share their time between the homes of each parent and to feel truly loved and prioritised in each home is one thing. Doing so because their parents could not reach an amicable arrangement and because one parent could not tolerate the idea that the other parent had more time, leaving the child to feel more like a possession being fought over, is quite another.

1.108   Moreover, and reflecting the wide range of experience and perception of the children who actually lived these arrangements, some factors which could point to success in one home could spell problems in another. Neale et al observe:[107]

> 'Elements that some children found positive – such as a "regular routine", a feeling of being wanted by both parents and a sense of fairness – could be a source of great unhappiness to others. So, for example, a regular routine for some meant they knew exactly what to expect but for others it meant an unbearable and inflexible regime. Some of the children relished the feeling of being loved by both parents and understood shared residence as a manifestation of this, but others felt that this was a terrible burden because they became responsible for the emotional well-being of both their parents. Finally, some children thought the arrangement was excellent because it was fair for their parents, but others thought it was dreadful because it was unfair on them.'

1.109   Thus, while shared residence arrangements can in certain circumstances work, there is no solid research basis to suggest that this ought to be the target to which all families should aspire and for which the State should legislate. As Neale et al conclude, 'shared residence is not a magic solution to a difficult problem'.[108]

1.110   On the contrary, their findings are wholly consistent with the whole body of research that cautions against a 'one size fits all' approach and recognises the centrality of the child:

---

106   See C Smart, B Neale & A Wade *The Changing Experience of Childhood Families and Divorce* (Cambridge, Polity Press, 2001) and B Neale, J Flowerdew & C Smart *Drifting towards Shared Residence?* [2003] Fam Law 904.

107   B Neale, J Flowerdew & C Smart *Drifting towards Shared Residence?* [2003] Fam Law 904, at p 905.

108   Ibid, at p 905.

'Decisions about contact must be child-centred and relate to the specific child in his or her specific situation, now. Every child has different needs and these also alter with the different needs at different stages of development. The eventual plan for the child must be the one that best approximates to these needs.'[109]

1.111   Insofar, therefore, as research provides us with a template for success, it is this – parents, focused on the needs of their children (as opposed to their own), working together and appropriately involving their children so as to formulate the arrangements that in their given circumstances are in the best interests of those children.

THE STATE'S RESPONSE IN OUTLINE

1.112   In the second half of the next chapter, we look at how the response of the State as a whole has evolved – from the vital work undertaken by the Children Act Sub-Committee,[110] chaired by Lord Justice Wall (as he now is), to the publication of the Green Paper *Parental Separation: Children's Needs and Parents' Responsibilities*[111] and the subsequent post-consultative *Parental Separation: Children's Needs and Parents' Responsibilities – Next Steps*,[112] and through to the passing of the Children and Adoption Act 2006. Here we set out what we see as being the essential tenets of that response, the particulars of which we detail and address in Chapters 4, 5, 6 and 7.

1.113   At the heart of the State's response lies the clear and continuing recognition of the impact of parental separation on the child and the importance of handling that process of separation, which inevitably involves making arrangements for any child concerned, as appropriately as possible:

'Where the process of separation is handled well, the adverse impact on children is minimised. When separation goes badly and, in particular, where children are drawn into parental conflict, then the effects can be profoundly damaging for children.'[113]

1.114   What is immediately apparent, in terms of the consequent State aim of encouraging the former and avoiding the latter, is that there is no fundamental legislative change to the principles of the Children Act 1989. No statutory presumption of reasonable contact has been introduced, let alone a statutory presumption of a child having equal time with each parent following their separation.

1.115   The rationale for that outcome will be examined further in Chapter 9. For now, we note that the resistance to a statutory presumption of any sort was

---

109 See J Sturge & D Glaser *Contact and Domestic Violence – the Experts Court Report* [2000] Fam Law 615, at p 616.
110 The Children Act Sub-Committee of the Advisory Board on Family Law.
111 July 2004 – Cm 6273 – available at www.dfes.gov.uk/childrensneeds/.
112 January 2005 – Cm 6452 – available at www.dfes.gov.uk/childrensneeds/.
113 July 2004 HMG Green Paper *Parental Separation: Children's Needs and Parents' Responsibilities* – Cm 6273 – available at www.dfes.gov.uk/childrensneeds/.

built upon the twin contentions that such would compromise the principle of the paramountcy of the welfare of the child and that the formulation upon which the law already works is correct:

> 'The Government believes that the position under current law – that both parents are equal and both should continue to have a meaningful relationship with their children after adult separation, so long as it is safe – is the right position.'[114]

1.116 Yet the absence of major statutory change should not detract either from the clear recognition in Government, in Parliament and within the judiciary that change was needed on a number of fronts or from the measures that have followed in consequence.

1.117 Within this chapter, we have highlighted from a research angle the distinction between safe and potentially unsafe contact and that distinction significantly informs the changes to how contact decisions are to be made by the courts, with:

- statutory measures implemented to help facilitate contact and, where necessary, enforce contact orders; and
- greater statutory clarity about the risks to children and a more effective means by which cases in which those risks are alleged to exist can be identified early and suitably addressed.

1.118 At the same time, and at the broadest level, it is intended that residence and contact cases of all kinds will benefit from more proactive case management, greater judicial continuity and an enhanced ability in the courts to deal with cases more quickly and more appropriately.

1.119 Yet focus on the court process should not mislead. The essential thrust of the State's response is to divert parents away from court, certainly from contested court hearings, towards making sensible, child-centred arrangements themselves (as indeed most parents do). To that end, the agenda for reform sees:

- an emphasis on improving parental access to quality advice, support and information and on enhancing parental understanding of the court process and the impact on the child of parental separation;
- the increased promotion of resolution through mediation and other allied means; and
- a greater encouragement of in-court conciliation, accompanied by a changed, more focused and problem-solving role for CAFCASS.

1.120 Underpinning all of that lies the acknowledgement of what is at stake and the responsibility of society as a whole to act. As the foreword to *Parental Separation: Children's Needs and Parents' Responsibilities – Next Steps*[115] makes clear:

> '... changing social expectations, as well as Government action, are both needed. In time, it needs to become socially unacceptable for one parent to

---

114 Ibid.
115 January 2005 – Cm 6452 – available at www.dfes.gov.uk/childrensneeds/.

impede a child's relationship with its other parent wherever it is safe and in the child's best interests. Equally, it should be unacceptable that non-resident parents absent themselves from their child's development and upbringing following separation. Friends, relatives, the legal profession and the media all have a role to play in emphasising that children require a good and lasting relationship with both their parents wherever it is safe and in the child's best interests to do so'.

Chapter Two

FROM PAST PREJUDICES TO PRESENT PRIORITIES: A BRIEF HISTORY OF PARENTING TIME

2.1   The willingness of the State in modern times to intervene in the lives of fragmented families would have astonished the legislators, judges and parents of the mid-Victorian era, when family law was simply not recognised as a specific area of jurisprudence.[1] In this chapter we chart how the response to the problems of divided families has evolved over time, and chronicle the pressures that have brought about 'the new deal' for contact.

THE LAW BEFORE 1989

Victorian values

2.2   The problems now faced by the courts of how to divide parenting time hardly ever arose in Victorian England. At common law, the father of a legitimate child was exclusively entitled to exercise parental authority and the mother had no legal right to custody, care and control. No doubt many women were able to achieve controlling influence over their families through amicable negotiation with their husbands, but if they failed to do so the law provided no assistance.

2.3   During the nineteenth century, Parliament introduced limited reforms allowing courts to award custody to mothers in certain circumstances, but the father's rights over children during marriage remained supreme. In the words of the Victorian Master of the Rolls, Sir William Baliol Brett:

'The law does not interfere because of the great trust and faith it has in the natural affection of the father to perform his duties ... The rights of a father are sacred because his duties are sacred duties.'[2]

The supremacy of the father even survived his death since he alone had the power to appoint a testamentary guardian.

---

1   For a full historical survey, see S Cretney *Family Law in the Twentieth Century: A History* (OUP, 2003).
2   *Re Agar-Ellis* (1878) 10 Ch D 49.

2.4   In contrast, parental authority over an illegitimate child was vested in the mother.[3] To the modern eye, this might seem to confer some sort of benefit on women. To the Victorians, however, it merely reflected the stigma attaching to illegitimacy. Such children were not permitted to enjoy the benefits of paternal authority enjoyed to children born in wedlock.

Social change

2.5   One of the defining features of the social history of the last century was the fundamental change in the status of women and children:

> 'In the 1870s and 1880s, the married woman was emerging from her chattel existence by reason of the Married Women's Property Acts and ... the tide began to turn against the power and authority of the father, but only gradually ...'[4]

2.6   A similar change occurred in the law's attitude to children. It was in the early years of the last century that the courts, usually sitting in private, developed the principle that a child's welfare was the most important factor when making decisions concerning a child's upbringing. This was finally recognised by the House of Lords in the case of *Ward v Laverty*[5] and shortly afterwards enshrined in statute in the Guardianship of Infants Act 1925.

2.7   Section 1 of the 1925 Act saw the first statutory use of the phrase 'the paramount consideration' as a label to indicate the importance of the child's welfare in the court's decision. Section 2 went further: it provided that a mother had equal rights to apply to the court in respect of any matter affecting her child as were possessed by the father, and further stipulated that a court hearing such an application was not to take into consideration whether the father's rights at common law were superior to those of the mother. But it would be a mistake to regard this reform as sweeping away the father's traditional supremacy entirely. There was no express provision granting the mother any legal authority over her children, and social convention continued to regard the father as the legal master of the home, whilst expecting the mother to carry out the practical chores of child care. Indeed, it was not until 1973 that Parliament expressly enacted that a mother should have the same legal rights over her child as the father.[6]

2.8   The proponents of female emancipation regarded the inequalities suffered by married mothers as unacceptable and a 'monstrous legal fiction'.[7] Yet conservative forces continued to prevail. One argument deployed against change was the impracticality of allowing a child to be subject to 'duality of control'. If mothers were allowed equal rights, the floodgates would be opened for endless disputes about the child's future. Such issues were thought to be beyond judicial resolution. The Permanent Secretary to the Lord Chancellor's

---

3   *Barnado v McHugh* [1891] AC 388.
4   *J v C* [1970] AC 668, per Lord Upjohn at p 721D.
5   [1925] AC 101.
6   Guardianship Act 1973, s 1.
7   E Rathbone *The Disinherited Family* (1924), quoted by Cretney op cit at p 568.

Department, Sir Claud Schuster, pointed out that a court was concerned with the ascertainment and enforcement of rights, not the exercise of a parental discretion:

> 'To take a ridiculous instance, a dispute whether a child is to go to one school or to another school – how on earth is the Court going to deal with that?'[8]

Divorce reform

2.9   The superior position enjoyed by fathers was buttressed by the laws of divorce. The Matrimonial Causes Act 1857, which first empowered the civil courts to grant decrees of divorce, also introduced the power to make orders concerning custody, care and control of children ancillary to decrees of divorce and judicial separation.[9] For most of the eighty years of that Act's life, the restrictive grounds on which a marriage could be dissolved (grounds which were, to modern eyes, manifestly discriminatory against women) were interpreted by the courts in a narrow way. It was the usual practice to award custody to the innocent party in the divorce proceedings, and, as it was much more difficult for a woman to obtain a decree,[10] it was often the father who succeeded in the divorce suit and duly received custody of the children. Furthermore, before the advent of legal aid, divorce was beyond the means of most people. Thus divorce had little social impact during the first third of the last century, and comparatively few children were the subject of court orders as to their custody. Many more children were profoundly affected by the misery engendered by unhappy marriages in which they were trapped together with their unfortunate parents.[11]

2.10   During the course of the twentieth century, the rate of divorce rose, at first steadily after the limited extension of the grounds for divorce enacted in 1937 and the social upheavals caused by the Second World War, then more dramatically as a result of the change of attitudes that characterised the 1960s, leading to the radical relaxation of the divorce laws under the Divorce Reform Act 1969. Throughout that period, both before and after the 1969 Act, the court, after granting a decree, was required to make orders about the future of the children.

2.11   As the divorce rate rose, so did the numbers of children who were the subject of court orders concerning their future care. Reflecting social norms, it

---

8   Quoted by Cretney, op cit, p 570. Nowadays, courts are frequently asked to adjudicate on disputes about choice of education, via applications for specific issues orders under Children Act 1989, s 8.

9   Before 1857, divorce was only attained by undergoing a Byzantine procedure summarised by Cretney, op cit, at p 161, and described in detail by L Stone, *Road to Divorce: England 1530–1987* (OUP, 1990).

10   Until 1923, when women were allowed to petition on the basis of simple adultery. Before then, they (unlike male petitioners) had to prove additional aggravating features.

11   At the end of the nineteenth century, however, magistrates courts were empowered to make orders releasing a wife from the obligation to cohabit with her husband on certain grounds (in short, assault, desertion, persistent cruelty, wilful neglect) and thereupon could make ancillary orders granting the wife custody of any child aged under 16.

gradually became customary to direct that the children should live with their mother whilst seeing their father on a regular basis. For many years, this was expressed through an order for 'custody' to one parent (usually the mother) and 'access' to the other (usually the father). Over time, and reflecting the view that it was important for both parents to remain involved with their children, the courts increasingly adopted the practice of making joint custody orders, under which both parents would retain full legal responsibility for the children, but directing that one parent (usually the mother) should have 'care and control', with access to the other. If it was felt that the parties could negotiate visiting arrangements themselves, the usual order was for 'reasonable access'. If the parties were unable to agree, the arrangements would be defined by the court.

2.12 When required to rule on disputed issues about children's care, the courts would be guided by certain principles and norms that broadly reflected the social consensus of mid twentieth century Britain.

2.13 First, the courts adhered firmly to the principle that the child's welfare was the paramount consideration. Parents were strongly discouraged from seeking to assert any personal 'rights' in respect of their children. The use of the language of 'rights' was deprecated in the family courts. True, the United Kingdom had signed, and Parliament had ratified, the European Convention for the Protection of Human Rights and Fundamental Freedoms 1950, but for fifty years the Convention was not incorporated into English law, and the English family courts paid scant regard to it. Any parent who referred to his or her 'rights' during a hearing about their children was liable to be treated to a judicial homily about the unimportance of such rights and the paramountcy of the children's welfare. 'Access' was said to be the right of the child, not the parent.[12]

2.14 Secondly, despite regular assertions about the equal status of the parents, and the paramountcy of the child's welfare, most judges, expressly or implicitly, continued to apply a number of 'rules of thumb' (as opposed to rules of law) to the determination of disputes about children. These included:

- that young children should live with their mother;
- that siblings should live together;
- that a working parent was prima facie unlikely to look after a child as well as a parent who was not working, and
- that a well-established status quo should be respected unless there was a good reason for departing from it.

2.15 In practice, these rules of thumb tended to favour mothers over fathers when it came to deciding issues of custody and access. It is true that some judges thought that older boys should generally live with their fathers[13] but this was often trumped by another rule of thumb – that the wishes of older children should generally be followed since otherwise they would 'vote with their feet'.

---

12   See, for example, *M v M (child: access)* [1973] 2 All ER 81, per Mr Justice Wrangham at p 86; *Re S (Minors: Access)* [1990] 2 FLR 166, per Lord Justice Balcombe at p 170C.

13   See, for example, Lord Denning, then Master of the Rolls, in *W v W and C* [1968] 1 WLR 1310.

Of course, some older children, of both sexes, chose to live with their fathers, but many did not. Most children of separated parents lived with their mothers.

2.16 Thirdly, whilst joint custody orders were increasingly encouraged, *shared care and control* was not. It was seen as impractical, and contrary to the wider interests of the child, to impose or sanction any arrangement which provided for the child's time to be split equally between his or her parents. It was said that the child's paramount need was for one main home where they could enjoy an element of stability after the emotionally unsettling experience of the divorce: 'to keep a child ... going backwards and forwards each week between mother and father, with no single settled home, is prima facie wrong.'[14] Usually, that meant that the other parent would see comparatively little of the children and, as they grew older, would have to fit in with all the other activities and demands on the children's time.

2.17 Fourthly, much emphasis was placed by judges and the professionals (court welfare officers and psychologists) who advised them on the importance of 'quality time' during access. This meant that courts were inclined, where possible, to order longer periods of staying contact once or twice a month at weekends and during school holidays rather than frequent shorter periods during the week after school. For many judges, staying contact on alternate weekends, half the school holidays and alternate Christmases was regarded as the ideal arrangement. Yet this had the effect of removing the absent parent from the day-to-day life of the child.

2.18 Fifthly, judges, again acting on the advice of professionals, were acutely aware of the risk that enduring bitterness between parties after divorce might infect the child. Particular attention was paid to the adults' conduct at handing over the children at the start and end of each access visit. In many cases, the handover would be the occasion for an argument between the ex-spouses, particularly if, as so often seemed to happen, the fixed deadline for the handover was missed. Rather than expose the children to the traumas of such occasions, the court would often involve third parties to facilitate the handover and take other steps to ensure that the parents did not come into contact with each other, such as directing that the contact should take place at a special venue called a contact centre (staffed by volunteers). By such means the absent parent, usually the father, was at least able to keep in some sort of contact with his children. But overall, it had the effect of removing him from the day-to-day life of the child still further.

2.19 Sixth, the courts made strenuous attempts to persuade and cajole the parties into resolving their disputes by agreement, rather than insist on a full-scale hearing. In doing so, they frequently faced an uphill struggle. Many parents, angered by the circumstances of the marital breakdown, were frustrated by the absence of any opportunity for airing their grievances in the course of the divorce process itself. They resorted to using the proceedings concerning the children as an occasion for extending their personal battles with their former spouses. Invariably the court, and the professionals appearing in

---

14 *Riley v Riley* [1986] 2 FLR 429, per Lord Justice May at p 431G.

the case, warned the parties about the impact on the children of their ongoing animosity. All too frequently, these warnings fell on deaf ears. By the time the dispute arrived at the court arena, the parties' attitudes were too entrenched to allow for rapprochement. Despite the good intentions of the courts and other professionals, they were often inadequately equipped, both in resources and skills, to achieve any resolution. The court had assistance from specialist professionals, 'court welfare officers', who were probation officers who had opted to specialise in this field.[15] But sometimes the laudable determination to reach a consensual outcome failed to identify cases which simply needed to be heard. Judges occasionally used the desire for consensual resolution as a mechanism to impose solutions which did not meet the problem but avoided a trial. Sometimes procrastination proved preferable to concentration on the issues themselves. This left the party in the more powerful position able to manipulate the proceedings, often to the disadvantage of mothers, particularly those who were the victims of serious physical violence or emotional abuse.

2.20 Finally, although the courts were forever making orders about access to children, they were reluctant to deploy the full authority of the law to ensure that such orders were obeyed. In theory, an order directing a mother to allow the father access to children at a certain time and place had to be followed by the parties and needed to be enforced if it was to have any meaning. The normal remedy for breach of a court order was, and remains, committal to prison for contempt of court. In children's cases, however, judges were invariably reluctant to imprison mothers because of the obvious consequences for the children. In one case, a Court of Appeal judge went as far as to say that 'an application to commit for breach of orders relating to access ... [is] inevitably futile and should not be made'.[16] Other judges were less dogmatic, but all were extremely reluctant to impose the ultimate sanction of imprisonment on recalcitrant mothers who disregarded court orders for access.

2.21 Taken together, these practices and principles created a consensus about how courts dealt with disputes concerning access to children. Most children lived with their mothers. It was normally right and proper that they should have access to their fathers, but that access should not disturb the stability and routine of their principal home and should, in the main, be confined to weekends and holidays. Parents were expected to be sensible about sorting out these arrangements, but if not the courts would define the arrangements for them. If, however, the parents chose not to follow these court-ordered arrangements, judges were reluctant to enforce them. All in all, there was a degree of complacency about this area of the law, accompanied by a feeling, common amongst many judges, that it was relatively unimportant work and often a waste of their valuable time.

---

15 At a later date, court welfare officers were subsumed within the Children and Family Court Advisory and Support Service (CAFCASS), the national agency established by the Criminal Justice and Court Services Act 2000 to provide advice and assistance to courts and parties. Since the subsequent creation of the Welsh Assembly, which has assumed responsibility for the services provided by CAFCASS in the principality, CAFCASS's area of responsibility is confined to England.

16 *Churchyard v Churchyard* [1984] FLR 635, per Lord Justice Ormrod at p 638G.

THE CHILDREN ACT 1989

2.22 In 1989, Parliament passed the Children Act, widely regarded as the most successful piece of major legislation in the family law field since the Second World War. It was commended for the clarity of its drafting, the coherence of its underlying policy and the way in which it successfully integrated private law cases (disputes within the family) with so-called public law cases (disputes between the family and the State – specifically care proceedings).

2.23 One of the driving forces behind the Act was the perceived need to reform public law cases where the old law and procedure had proved inadequate for dealing with the growing recognition of the phenomenon of child abuse. The Cleveland Report[17] had exposed fundamental flaws in the systems for investigating such abuse, including the disadvantages faced by parents when the public authorities attempted to remove their children. The Conservative Government, led by Margaret Thatcher and with Lord Mackay of Clashfern as Lord Chancellor, was also keen to champion family values and responded by buttressing the natural family against State intrusion. By integrating public and private law cases within the same statutory framework, the Act extended this policy into disputes between parents.

2.24 Section 1 of the Act sets out the principles to be applied in all cases involving the upbringing of children. Section 1(1) substantially repeated the previous law by providing that:

> '... when a court determines any question with respect to (a) the upbringing of a child or (b) the administration of a child's property or the application of any income arising from it, the child's welfare shall be the court's paramount consideration.'

2.25 Section 1(3) introduced a checklist of factors to be taken into account by a court considering whether to make an order.[18] The checklist was an eminently sensible recital of factors relevant to decisions about a child's future. Parliament was careful not to give one factor precedence over any other. Section 1(3) did not constitute any change in the law or practice, but was merely a codification of those factors which judges had, or should have, applied prior to the Act when making these decisions.

2.26 Section 1(5), however, introduced a new principle:

> 'When a court is considering whether or not to make one or more of the orders under this Act with respect to a child, it shall not make the order or any of the orders unless it considers that doing so would be better for the child than making no order at all.'

Previously, no decree nisi of divorce could be made absolute until the court had held a 'children's appointment' at which the judge was required to satisfy him

---

17 *Report of the Inquiry into Child Abuse in Cleveland 1987*, chaired by Lady Justice Butler-Sloss (as she then was).

18 See para 3.32.

or herself that the arrangements for the children were the best that could be devised in the circumstances and make appropriate orders for custody, care and control, and access. Under section 1(5), however, instead of making orders for custody and access as a matter of course, the court was prevented from making any orders unless satisfied that doing so would be better for the child than making no order at all.

2.27 The underlying assumption was that many parents would be sufficiently sensible to sort out the arrangements for themselves without court interference, and it was no business of the court to intrude in this process. Section 16 of the Act did create 'family assistance orders', designed to provide low-level help to families going through the court system whose circumstances could be categorised as 'exceptional'. But the terms of the section were limited, because of the policy of restricting State interference in the family, and in practice family assistance orders were rarely used by the court, partly because the agencies entrusted with administering them were reluctant to allocate any of their scarce resources to work which had such limited scope for effective intervention.

2.28 The range and nomenclature of available orders were amended. Care and control orders were replaced by 'residence orders'.[19] Access orders disappeared[20] and were reincarnated as 'contact orders'.[21] 'Custody' was abolished altogether. Henceforth, all married parents were endowed with 'parental responsibility' which they retained after divorce and permanently,[22] save in the event of adoption of their children.

2.29 'Parental responsibility' was defined[23] as meaning 'all the rights, duties, powers, responsibilities and authority which by law a parent of a child has in relation to the child and his property'. This was heralded as one of the key reforms of the Act, described by one of its architects as 'the conceptual building block used throughout [the Act]' and representing 'the fundamental status of parents'.[24] By endowing both married parents with this responsibility during and after marriage, it was hoped that many contested disputes would be avoided. It was intended, amongst other things, to signal the continuing role of both parents in the lives of the children after divorce.

2.30 In practice, however, this reform has had limited success in reducing the level of disputes about children. For most parents, the crucial question is: where will the children live? For a parent who had unsuccessfully applied for a residence order, it was often little consolation to be told by their lawyer that they continued to have full legal responsibility for the children. In practice, the parent with whom the child lived continued to hold a decisive advantage. For example, if that parent decided to emigrate with the children, the courts were usually disinclined to prevent them doing so, even though the Act required the

---

19   Children Act, s 8(1). See para 3.14 et seq.
20   Although the term 'access' continued to be used by the general public and media.
21   See para 3.14 et seq.
22   S 2(1).
23   S 3(1).
24   B Hoggett *The Children Bill: The Aim* [1989] Fam Law 217.

court's permission be obtained if the other parent with parental responsibility objected.[25] Provided that the resident parent's plans were well-prepared and apparently bona fide – that is to say, not deliberately designed to cut the children off from the other parent – the courts usually concluded that refusing the primary carer's reasonable proposals for the relocation of their family life was likely to impact detrimentally on the welfare of the children.[26]

2.31 A further limitation on the impact of the new concept of parental responsibility was the steady increase in the proportion of children born outside wedlock. Section 2(1) gave automatic parental responsibility to a father who was married to the child's mother, but not to an unmarried father. In the UK, 12 % of live births were born outside marriage in1989. By 2001, this proportion had risen to 40%.[27] There were perceived to be strong arguments for denying automatic parental responsibility to fathers of such children, who might be conceived after a brief sexual liaison or even rape. Instead, the Children Act 1989[28] provided that such fathers could acquire parental responsibility by agreement or court order.[29] A further distinction between married and unmarried fathers was that the latter, having acquired parental responsibility, could lose it again by court order.[30] In deciding whether to make a parental responsibility order, the child's welfare is the paramount consideration, but case-law established that the court should take into account, amongst other things, the degree of commitment shown by the father to the child, the attachment between father and child, and the father's reasons for applying.[31] In practice, the courts not infrequently refused such applications in the first years after the implementation of the 1989 Act.

THE PRESSURE FOR REFORM

2.32 In the years after the Children Act 1989, a number of factors led to ever-increasing pressure for further reform. Three in particular stand out:

(1) the implementation of the Human Rights Act 1998;
(2) the emergence of a multidisciplinary approach to family law problems; and
(3) the growth of the fathers' lobby.

The Human Rights Act 1998

2.33 One of the first legislative measures of the Labour Government following its return to power in 1997 was the Human Rights Act 1998. This

---

25   S 13(1).
26   See the historical summary of relocation cases in the judgment of Thorpe LJ in *Payne v Payne* [2001] 1 FLR 1052; see further para 3.80 et seq.
27   Source: National Statistics Online at www.statistics.gov.uk.
28   S 4(1).
29   It was not until 2004 that Parliament granted automatic parental responsibility to unmarried fathers and then only to those fathers registered as such: Children Act 1989, s 4(1) and (1)(a) (as inserted by Adoption and Children Act 2002, s 111).
30   S 4(3), now s 4(2A). An unmarried father can still be deprived of parental responsibility by court order even though he may have acquired it automatically by being registered as the child's father.
31   *Re H (Parental Responsibility)* [1998] 1 FLR 885.

finally incorporated into UK law the European Convention for the Protection of Human Rights and Fundamental Freedoms (ECHR). This Convention was drawn up (largely by British lawyers) after the Second World War with the principal aim of establishing a fundamental stratum of rights-based law against which the rules and executive actions of public authorities in the signatory states could be measured and tested. The UK signed and ratified the treaty but did not incorporate it into national law. For fifty years, UK citizens who considered that the actions of UK public authorities infringed their rights under the ECHR were unable to rely on such arguments in English courts and were instead compelled to take their grievance to the European Court of Human Rights in Strasbourg.

2.34 Much speculation greeted the eventual incorporation of the Convention under the 1998 Act, but it was generally considered that the impact in the field of family law would be limited. It was pointed out that the Children Act had been drafted with an eye to the provisions of the ECHR and it was felt that the principal features of the national law in this field would be compatible with the Convention. But at face value, the impact of the most relevant article in the Convention, Article 8, was of great potential significance:

'(1) Everyone has the right to respect for his private and family life, his home and his correspondence.

(2) There shall be no interference by a public authority with the exercise of this right except such as in accordance with the law and is necessary in a democratic society in the interests of national security, public safety or the economic well-being of the country, for the prevention of disorder or crime, for the protection of health or morals, or for the protection of the rights and freedoms of others.'

2.35 Judges, who for years had discouraged parents from thinking in terms of their rights, now had to come to terms with a vocabulary that focused on precisely that concept. Indeed, some commentators speculated that the fundamental principle of the whole Children Act – the paramountcy of the child's welfare – might be incompatible with Article 8.[32] The then President of the Family Division, Dame Elizabeth Butler-Sloss, took advantage of an early opportunity to dismiss such concerns,[33] and judges continued to express the view that in general terms the ECHR had not significantly affected the principles to be applied in Children Act litigation, including contact cases.

2.36 However, although the welfare of the children remained paramount, it was no longer possible to argue that no other factor was relevant. Each member of the family had a right to respect for family and private life. Although, in the ultimate analysis, the rights of the children, as the most vulnerable family members, would take precedence, the court could not completely disregard the rights of others. Indeed, they were obliged to respect

---

32 See, for example, A Vine *Is the Paramountcy Principle Compatible with Article 8?* [2000] Fam Law 827.

33 *Re L (Contact: Domestic Violence); Re V (Contact: Domestic Violence); Re M (Contact: Domestic Violence; Re H (Contact: Domestic Violence)* [2000] 2 FLR 334, at pp 345–346.

them and take them into account. It was no longer acceptable to apply broad rules of thumb. Each case turned on its own facts.

2.37 Of equal importance was the professional and public awareness of the newly-incorporated rights. All professionals working in the field received comprehensive training in the impact of the new human rights law, because they were expected to display the same respect for family life as the courts. Parents going through court proceedings immediately latched onto the potential significance of this reform. The press quickly came to blame the Act for a range of ills that followed in various walks of life, thereby ensuring that the public was aware that it had rights which it could assert.

2.38 One area where the courts re-evaluated the law in the light of the Act concerned applications for the removal of children from the jurisdiction. In *Payne v Payne*[34] the Court of Appeal, whilst insisting that the ECHR had not affected the principles to be applied on such applications, nevertheless concluded, in the words of the then President,[35] that:

'... the implementation [of the ECHR] into English law does ... give us the opportunity to take another look at the way the principles have been expressed in the past, and whether there should now be a reformulation of those principles.'

2.39 The court concluded that there should indeed be a reformulation, and, in the eyes of some, though not all, observers, recast the law in a way that took more account of the position of the parent who did not have residence. Certainly the court now retreated from the view, expressed in some of the earlier cases,[36] that there was a presumption in favour of the parent who presented reasonable proposals to remove the child from the jurisdiction.

2.40 Thus, in subtle ways, the incorporation of the ECHR, with its articulation of the right to respect for family life, strengthened the position of those whose rights had hitherto been undervalued or ignored.

Towards a multidisciplinary approach

2.41 The Cleveland Report had 'strongly recommended ... [t]he development of interagency co-operation'.[37] In the years following the passing of the Children Act 1989, a large number of bodies were set up to meet that need, including the Children Act Advisory Committee, the Family Court Business Committees, the Children Act Sub-Committee of the Lord Chancellor's Advisory Board on Family Law, the President's Interdisciplinary Family Law Committee, the UK Family Law Conference, the Lord Chancellor's Advisory Committee on Judicial Case Management in Public Law Children Act Cases, Family Advice and Information Networks, the Family Justice Council, and many other ad hoc groups, all advised by umpteen university faculties, research

---

34   [2001] EWCA Civ 166, [2001] 1FLR 1052.
35   Ibid, at para [82].
36   *Chamberlain v de la Mare* (1983) 4 FLR 434.
37   Recommendation 8, at p 248.

centres, seminars, conferences, professional bodies, lawyers, sociologists, psychologists, psychiatrists and lobby organisations. To those seeking to follow developments, the sheer amount of multidisciplinary activity was sometimes bewildering. As one judge warned, there was 'a real danger in the area of family law reform that consultation can follow consultation to the point where consultation becomes an end in itself'.[38]

2.42   Nevertheless, it was inevitable that, properly focused, at least some of these bodies would identify areas for change. In the field of contact, the most influential has been the one with the longest name – the Children Act Sub-Committee of the Lord Chancellor's Advisory Board on Family Law (CASC).

2.43   In 2000, CASC produced an important report on the impact of domestic violence on contact disputes.[39] In March 2001, CASC addressed the whole issue of contact in a consultation paper, followed by a final report in February 2002 entitled *Making Contact Work*.[40] Running to a total of 146 pages, the report noted the widespread dissatisfaction with the court system and made a variety of recommendations to deal with a range of issues, notably:

- the provision of better information to separating and divorcing parents and their children;
- improvements in the court process, including additional facilities for in-court conciliation, reduction in delays and judicial continuity;
- the granting to the courts of powers to refer parents to mediation to resolve disputes about contact;
- an extension in the use of family assistance orders (to be operated exclusively by CAFCASS, as opposed to local authorities), with the development of specific programmes to be operated by CAFCASS officers under such orders;
- the proper financing of CAFCASS;
- improved funding for contact centres;
- accreditation of all lawyers engaged in publicly funded children's litigation;
- wider powers for enforcing contact orders, including 'non-punitive' options, such as parenting programmes, as well as a broader range of punitive alternatives, such as community service orders, with the existing remedies of fines and imprisonment kept as a last resort.

These proposals received widespread approval and, as discussed below, most of them were ultimately introduced.

2.44   With a crowded legislative programme, however, it was always going to be difficult for these reforms to force their way onto the Government's agenda, however well-merited, and despite strong support from within the Department for Constitutional Affairs and the judiciary. What was needed was a political

---

38   Mr Justice Wall (as he then was) in a lecture at the conference *Making Contact Work*, 15 February 2003.
39   *A Report to the Lord Chancellor on the Question of Parental Contact in Cases where there is Domestic Violence* (12 April 2000). See Chapters 1 and 6 for further discussion on this topic.
40   Available at www.dca.gov.uk/family/abfla/mcwrep.pdf.

dimension – something to provide extra encouragement to a government closely attuned to popular feeling. This impetus came from the startling growth of the fathers' lobby.

KERPOW!! Fathers fight back

2.45   Over the last twenty years, a number of groups have sprung up, representing aggrieved fathers. The oldest is Families Needs Fathers whose website[41] lists a number of demands, the first five being the following:

- No child shall be denied a full and proper relationship with both of its parents unless it has been shown that such a relationship presents a risk to the child.
- Gender discrimination in social attitudes towards parenting, in policy in relation to the family and the family 'justice' system, should end.
- The 'winner takes all' nature of legal proceedings about children should end. The objective should become the best blend of both parents. Both parents should be given Residence Orders. Demeaning 'Contact Orders' should be replaced by 'Parenting Time Orders' given to both parents.
- Breach of a court order to allow a child a relationship with both parents should become legally and socially unacceptable.
- Fathers' involvement with their children is increasing rapidly. This should be welcomed and encouraged until it equals the care provided by mothers.

2.46   Another group is the Equal Parenting Council, whose website[42] declares that its principal aim is to lead the Government to introduce a legal presumption whereby all separating parents would have the right to parenting time with their children unless it can be shown ('on the basis of credible evidence') that there is some genuine risk to a child's safety. Available parenting time should be divided between fit parents on an equitable, though not necessarily equal, basis.

2.47   The profile of the fathers' lobby was significantly changed by the emergence of another group, Fathers 4 Justice (F4J), who adopted a new tactic of well-publicised direct action. On 17 December 2002, 200 members of F4J, dressed as Father Christmas, invaded the offices of the Lord Chancellor's Department. Further demonstrations followed at a variety of locations, including the High Court in London, Tower Bridge and York Minster. The modus operandi often involved dressing up as superheroes. In May 2004, campaigners threw condoms containing purple flour at the Prime Minister during Question Time in the House of Commons.

2.48   The campaign reached a climax in September 2004, when two campaigners, dressed as Batman and Robin, scaled the wall at Buckingham Palace. Robin was quickly apprehended but the Caped Crusader managed to reach the famous balcony where he remained for some time, long enough for numerous photographs to be taken and transmitted round the world. The fact that he had literally risked death – police sources observed that a split second

---

41   See www.fnf.org.uk.
42   See www.equalparenting,org.

decision had been made as to whether he was a terrorist who would have to be shot – brought condemnation from some quarters, but undoubtedly added to the glamour of a campaign that, prior to the arrival of F4J, had struggled to make itself heard.

2.49 Press reaction was generally hostile to the tactics, but supportive of the general aims. One foreign observer noted that F4J had:

'... managed to spark a sympathetic national dialogue ... striving to recast dads, en masse, as needy and loveable rather than distant and neglectful.'[43]

2.50 For the first time, columnists and leader writers in this country started to pay attention to the issues around contact and parenting, and much criticism was levelled at the time-consuming and secretive procedures of the family courts. Bob Geldof, having endured protracted proceedings in respect of his daughters, continued to draw publicity to the cause by a series of interviews and newspaper articles whereby he attacked the propensity of the courts to devalue the role of the father in children's lives.

2.51 Many judges agreed with much of this criticism. A notable example was Mr Justice Munby in a case[44] in which a father had eventually abandoned an application for contact after the mother had repeatedly sabotaged arrangements over a 5-year period which had seen 43 court hearings and numerous unsuccessful orders. In typically trenchant remarks that received wide publicity in the national media, the judge observed that:

'... when the system fails – and fail it does – it is disproportionately fathers and not mothers who find themselves, as well as the children, the victim of that failure.'[45]

2.52 Earlier in his judgment,[46] Mr Justice Munby delivered this stark warning:

'The melancholy truth is that this case illustrates all too uncomfortably the failings of the system. There is much wrong with our system and the time has come for us to recognise that fact and to face up to it honestly. If we do not we risk forfeiting public confidence. The newspapers ... make uncomfortable reading for us. They suggest that confidence is already ebbing away. We ignore the media at our peril ... Responsible voices are raised in condemnation of our system. We need to take note. We need to act. And we need to act now.'

THE PROCESS OF REFORM

First steps

2.53 Three months after that judicial clarion call from Mr Justice Munby, the Government published its Green Paper *Parental Separation: Children's Needs*

---

43   S Dominus *The Father's Crusade* (New York Times Magazine, 8 May 2005).
44   *Re D (Intractable Contact Dispute: Publicity)* [2004] EWHC 727, [2004] 1 FLR 1226.
45   Ibid, at para [8].
46   Ibid, at para [4].

and Parents' Responsibilities.[47] In their ministerial foreword, the three ministers jointly responsible for the paper[48] referred to the fact that an increasing number of parental disputes about contact arrangements were going to court. The foreword continued:

> 'The current way in which the courts intervene in disputed contact cases does not work well. This is the opinion of both Government and members of the senior judiciary. Some fathers' groups have come to believe that the courts and the law are biased against them. We do not accept this view. However, both the Government and the judiciary consider that major changes are needed so that where it is necessary for the State and the courts to intervene, they are much more effective in helping to secure effective resolutions which are in the interests of the child. We believe that in most cases it is very much in the interests of the child to have an on-going relationship with both parents and so we hope that through improving the system, more non-resident parents will enjoy meaningful ongoing relationships with their children.'

2.54 In the view of the Government, however, such improvements did not extend to any change in the substantive law about parenting after relationship breakdown:

> 'Some have proposed that legislative change is needed to introduce "presumptions of contact", to give parents equal rights to equal time with their child after parental separation. Where such arrangements are best for the child, and are agreed between the parents or determined by a court, such arrangements can and should be put in place. The Government does not, however, believe that an automatic 50:50 division of the child's time between the two parents would be in the best interests of most children. In many separated families, such arrangements would not work in practical terms, owing to living arrangements or work commitments. Enforcing this type of arrangement through legislation would not be what many children want and could have a damaging impact on some of them. Children are not a commodity to be apportioned equally after separation. The best arrangements for them will depend on a variety of issues particular to their circumstances: a one-size-fits-all formula will not work. The assumption that both parents have equal status and value as parents is enshrined in current law. The actual arrangements made by courts start from that position.'[49]

2.55 The detailed proposals[50] in the Green Paper included:

- working with the judiciary to ensure that cases where domestic violence was an issue were identified early and handled effectively through the courts;

---

47   July 2004 – Cm 6273 – available at www.dfes.gov.uk/childrensneeds/.
48   Lord Falconer of Thoroton (Lord Chancellor and Secretary of State for Constitutional Affairs), Charles Clarke (then Secretary of State for Education and Skills) and Patricia Hewitt (then Secretary of State for Trade and Industry).
49   See para 3.14 et seq.
50   See Executive Summary, paras 3–13.

- improved services to ensure that helpful information and support is more widely available and accessible to parents and children;
- the introduction of practical tools – 'parenting plans' – giving guidance about parenting arrangements that are known to work for children and their parents in a range of circumstances;
- improved access to legal advice and practical/emotional advice on how to handle and resolve disputes, by providing it over the telephone and via websites;
- a restructuring of legal aid in order to incentivise early dispute resolution in cases where a solicitor is consulted;
- a new accreditation scheme for expert family lawyers to ensure that the best possible advice is provided to potential clients and thus promote better outcomes;
- an in-court conciliation system designed to put the focus of the courts on problem-solving as an alternative, wherever possible, to full contested court hearings;
- a more intensive supportive intervention model, called the Family Resolutions Pilot Project, which went 'live' from September 2004 with a view to its being rolled out nationally if successful;[51]
- working with the judiciary to develop guidance on case management;
- greater use of family assistance orders to provide more formalised support after orders have been made;
- shifting the emphasis of CAFCASS from writing court reports towards active problem-solving and supporting agreements;
- action to ensure the following of agreements and court orders, with legislation to promote new measures for enforcing court orders, including the power to refer a defaulting parent to information meetings, counselling, or parenting programmes, and impose community-based orders as well as prison sentences or fines.

Next steps

2.56 After a short period of consultation, the Government published *Parental Separation: Children's Needs and Responsibilities – Next Steps*,[52] reporting that 'two points came through loud and clear from the responses', namely that:

- 'everyone wants the best for the children involved'; and
- 'the current system does not always provide this'.

2.57 Behind these perhaps rather generalised comments were a number of detailed proposals:

- *No change to the legal position.* Some 20% of the responses indicated their support for a legal presumption of equal contact; a similar number expressly supported the present legal position, content that each case should be determined on its own facts; significantly, the remaining 60% made no reference to the legal position.[53] The Government stuck to its

---

51   It was not successful – see further at para 4.42.
52   January 2005 – Cm 6452 – available at www.dfes.gov.uk/childrensneeds/.
53   Paras 11–12.

guns, unpersuaded that any fundamental legislative change to the principles of the Children Act 1989 would benefit children.

- *Contact facilitation and enforcement.* There would, however, be legislation introduced in the areas of contact facilitation and enforcement of contact orders, including a greater role for family assistance orders.
- *Domestic violence.* A series of steps were outlined to deal with the issue of the impact of domestic violence in contact disputes.
- *Advice and information.* The Government signalled its intention to improve the availability and quality of necessary advice and information to families.
- *Mediation and dispute resolution.* Although mediation would not be made compulsory, the Government indicated that it would be strongly promoting its use and exploring other methods of dispute resolution.
- *CAFCASS.* The Government adhered to its view that the work of CAFCASS should be re-focused on dispute resolution, with less priority given to report-writing.
- *The court process.* Case management was to be improved and the persisting problem of delay tackled.

The Draft Children (Contact) and Adoption Bill

2.58 Much of the *Next Steps* agenda (to be considered in Chapters 4, 5, 6 and 7) did not require legislative change. To give effect to the main parts that did, the Government, in February 2005, introduced into Parliament a draft Children (Contact) and Adoption Bill.[54]

2.59 There were just four sections dealing with contact. Section 1 amended the Children Act 1989 by introducing new provisions empowering a court to make a 'contact activity direction' prior to making any contact order, or attach a 'contact activity condition' when making a contact order. Section 2 empowered a court to direct a CAFCASS[55] officer to facilitate and monitor contact orders. Section 3 introduced the extension of court powers of enforcement, by empowering courts to make 'enforcement orders' imposing 'unpaid work requirements' or 'curfew requirements'. The latter power included a 'compliance monitoring requirement' (ie electronic tagging). Section 4 empowered the court to order a party to pay compensation for financial loss attributable to breach of a contact order.

2.60 The draft Bill was referred to a Joint Parliamentary Select Committee for consideration and report. The committee's activities were constrained by shortage of time, with a general election imminent. It did, however, manage to hold public evidence sessions over two days at which it heard from a variety of people, including representatives of the specialist family law professional bodies (the Family Law Bar Association and Resolution[56]), Dame Elizabeth Butler-Sloss, the President of the Family Division, and Mrs Justice Bracewell, CAFCASS, the Welfare Accord Centre, the National Association of Child

---

54 The adoption components of this Bill, and its successor, are outside the scope of this book.
55 Or, in Wales, a Welsh family proceedings officer.
56 Formerly known as the Solicitors Family Law Association.

Contact Centres, Relate, the United Kingdom College of Family Mediators, Families Need Fathers, the Grandparents' Association, Both Parents Forever, the Association of District Judges, the NSPCC, Women's Aid and the then Minister for Children.[57] It also received in excess of 60 written submissions from a wide range of organisations and individuals.

2.61 Following these consultations, the committee published a report setting out a number of proposed amendments. It suggested the addition of 'perpetrator programmes', aimed at people who had been violent to their partners, to the list of contact activity directions, and the inclusion of a provision giving the court discretion to refer parties to mediation to explore whether this could be a viable option. Given the proposals about family assistance orders in the Green Paper and in *Next Steps*, the committee observed that the absence of any amendment to section 16 of the Children Act 1989 to make family assistance orders more flexible was surprising. The judiciary (in the persons of the then President, Mrs Justice Bracewell and Mr Justice Wall (as he then was)), in a memorandum to the committee, had described themselves as dismayed at this omission. The committee was also concerned about the feasibility of curfew requirements and tagging as a punishment for breach of an order. There was further concern about the lack of detailed thinking behind some of the provisions, such as the unpaid work requirement and the power to order compensation. The greatest concern, however, was over the level of resources available to achieve the aims of the Bill. Particular concern was expressed about whether sufficient funds would be extended to CAFCASS for its enhanced role, and for the proposed contact activities.

The Children and Adoption Act 2006

2.62 After the election in May 2005, the Government introduced a revised Bill (with the simpler title of the Children and Adoption Bill) that contained a number of amendments in response to some of the criticisms levelled at its predecessor. In particular:

- the definition of 'contact activity' was broadened so that the category of activities that a court could prescribe in a direction or condition was not closed;
- more precise provisions were included as to the burden and standard of proof for making enforcement orders;
- curfew requirements, and the controversial provisions for electronic tagging, were excluded from the list of enforcement orders; and
- section 16 of the Children Act 1989 was amended so as to broaden the scope of family assistance orders.

As with its predecessor, the new Bill contained a separate part covering changes to the law of adoption that fall outside the scope of this book. As before, the Bill was introduced first in the House of Lords.

---

57   The report of the committee, including transcripts of all the oral evidence given at the hearings, can be found at www.publications.parliament.uk – the attendees are recorded in the order set out within the report.

2.63   During the passage of the Bill, the Government supported an important amendment providing for risk assessments to be carried out by CAFCASS officers in any case where there is cause to suspect that the child concerned is at risk of harm. The proponents of the amendment[58] argued that '[t]he link between domestic violence and child abuse is ... not questioned' and claimed that research evidence 'shows that the family justice system does not have adequate proceedings for identifying high-risk cases and assessing and managing risk to ensure that contact is safe'.[59] The Government accepted this criticism and the proposal for risk assessments.

2.64   Other attempts at amendment were less successful. In particular, the Conservative opposition tried on several occasions to introduce a statutory presumption of shared parenting, but on each occasion the Government was able to defeat the proposal, arguing that its implementation would undermine the principle of the paramountcy of the child's welfare. Attempts to make parties attend a compulsory mediation session, and to stiffen the provisions for facilitation and enforcement of contact orders, also foundered in the face of the Government's majority in the House of Commons, leading the Tory front-bench spokesman to describe the resulting statute as a 'toothless fudge' and a 'major missed opportunity'.[60] The Government countered with the proposition that 'its implementation will make a significant difference to many children and families'.[61]

2.65   The Bill received the Royal Assent on 21 June 2006. The Children and Adoption Act 2006[62] will come into force on such day or days as the Secretary of State shall appoint by statutory instrument.[63] At the time of writing, no date has been appointed.

2.66   In striking contrast to the blank canvas of Victorian family law, the picture is now bewilderingly busy and complicated. In the remainder of this book, we seek to analyse the complexities of the family justice system as it relates to the children of separated parents.

---

58   Baroness Gould of Potternewton and Baroness Thornton.
59   Baroness Gould of Potternewton, HL Deb, 14 November 2005, col 887–8.
60   Tim Loughton MP, East Worthing and Shoreham, HC Deb, 20 June 2006, col 1283–4.
61   Beverley Hughes MP, Minister for Children and Families, HC Deb, 20 June 2006, col 1281.
62   The detailed provisions of the Children and Adoption Act 2006 are considered at para 6.44 et seq and in Chapter 7.
63   Children and Adoption Act 2006, s 17(2).

Chapter Three

PRINCIPLES, PRESUMPTIONS, RIGHTS AND RESPONSIBILITIES: AN OVERVIEW OF THE CURRENT LAW

3.1 It is an important finding of research that, at the time of separation, many parents do not know what their rights and responsibilities are and as a result feel ill-prepared for what lies ahead.[1] Most families are able to make arrangements for their children quickly, co-operatively and without recourse to the law, but, for those who cannot, ignorance and misunderstanding of the true legal position and of their 'rights' in particular often provide fertile ground for conflict to grow. The State's strategy is clear – to avoid conflict by stopping it escalating in the first place – and it is part and parcel of that strategy to give those parents who need it a greater awareness of the law in this area and a more realistic expectation of what is likely to happen if they go to court. In this chapter we set out the principles on which the courts act when determining how parenting time shall be arranged, governed by the Children Act 1989, and, since 2000, considered in light of the European Convention for the Protection of Human Rights and Fundamental Freedoms. While the Children and Adoption Act 2006 makes a number of important changes to the process of facilitating and enforcing contact, it leaves untouched those fundamental principles.

3.2 Although rights-based concepts are now relevant again, we do not intend to get too caught in the jurisprudential debate about 'rights' that has raged for centuries and which will doubtless continue for many more to come,[2] nor to provide a comprehensive guide to children law in the private sphere.[3] What we seek to offer is an overview of the central principles governing the way in which courts approach and decide residence and contact disputes over children,

---

1   See para 1.66.
2   For a much more complete and erudite discussion, see A Bainham *Contact as a Right and Obligation* in A Bainham, B Lindley, M Richards & L Trinder (eds) *Children and Their Families, Contact, Rights and Welfare* (Hart Publishing, 2003); N McCormick *Children's Rights: A Test Case for Theories of Rights* in N McCormick (ed) *Legal Right and Social Democracy* (Oxford: Clarendon Press, 1982); J Eekelaar *The Interests of the Child and Children's Wishes: the Role of Dynamic Self-Determinism* [1994] 8 IJLPF 42; C Smith *Children's Rights: judicial ambivalence and social resistance* [1997] 11 IJLPF 103; F Kaganas & A Diduck *Incomplete Citizens: Changing Images of Post-Separation Children* [2004] MLR 959.
3   For that, the reader can do no better than refer to D Hershman & A McFarlane *Children Law and Practice* and the accompanying *Children Act Handbook* (Jordans, regularly updated). See also Judge John Mitchell *Children Act Private Law Proceedings: A Handbook* (Jordans, 2006).

enshrined in the Children Act 1989 and left unchanged by the Children and Adoption Act 2006. In more detail, we look at the particular residence and contact issues that crop up time and time again – the topic of shared residence, the cases where a parent wants to take a child abroad and those disputes where orders for no contact are justified.[4]

'RIGHTS': THE EUROPEAN CONVENTION AND THE UN CONVENTION

3.3   The European Convention is now a firm feature of the legal landscape and the UN Convention on the Rights of the Child is gaining in prominence, but to what extent do 'rights' actually exist and operate in this part of the family law arena? The answer that comes through clearly is that, while parents do have rights, they come with responsibilities, and they are not absolute – they are invariably trumped by the rights of the child and are ultimately subservient to the paramount purpose of promoting the child's welfare.

3.4   The European Convention for the Protection of Human Rights and Fundamental Freedoms 1950[5] (ECHR) was incorporated within English law by the enactment of the Human Rights Act 1998. Whilst there was some largely academic debate around the compatibility of the Children Act 1989 with the ECHR,[6] the impact of the ECHR in private law proceedings has largely been, in practice, to reinforce pre-existing approaches rather than change them.

3.5   The most significant Article incorporated is Article 8,[7] which protects the right to respect for private and family life. In practice, Article 8 forms a 'backdrop' against which contact cases are decided, a factor to be borne in mind when the section 1(3) 'welfare checklist' falls to be applied. It does not create an absolute right: whether or not the right should be overridden (for example, by the making of a 'no contact' order) depends upon a number of factors. When considering an order which might infringe a party's right to private and family life, the principal questions to be asked are:

- Is the proposed order in accordance with domestic law (bearing in mind the 'margin of appreciation' within which domestic authorities are permitted to act)?
- Is it necessary in a democratic society?
- Is it proportionate to the aim it seeks to achieve?

---

4   The important law concerning the treatment of domestic violence in private law cases is considered in Chapter 6.
5   Cm 8969. The Act came into force on 2 October 2000.
6   See para 2.35.
7   Art 8 reads as follows: 1. Everybody has the right to respect for his private and family life, his home and his correspondence. 2. There shall be no interference by a public authority with the exercise of this right except such as is in accordance with the law and is necessary in a democratic society in the interests of national security, public safety or the economic well-being of the country, for the prevention of disorder or crime, for the protection of health or morals or for the protection of the rights and freedoms of others.

3.6   It is not difficult to see how those broad questions can be incorporated into the paramountcy principle[8] and within the application of the 'welfare checklist',[9] and that routinely is how the ECHR applies within contact proceedings.

3.7   The ECHR does, of course, underscore the fundamental importance of contact between children and their natural parents, as recognised by the European Court of Human Rights in many cases.[10] It does not, however, create any inviolable right to contact, either for the parent or for the child. Indeed, the European Court has stressed that, where there is a conflict between a child's Article 8 rights and a parent's, the child's rights must prevail.[11] This can be seen as the European expression of the Children Act's paramountcy principle.

3.8   The United Nations Convention on the Rights of the Child (UNCRC) was adopted by the UN General Assembly on 20 November 1989. Britain ratified the Convention on 16 December 1991 and it was adopted on 15 January 1992. It is one of the most widely accepted international treaties in terms of signatories.[12] The Convention requires signatories to work towards its implementation in the policies of national government, and requires a report from national authorities as to the progress of domestic implementation at regular intervals.[13] For our purposes, it suffices to say that it creates a treaty obligation. It has not been incorporated into English law by enactment of Parliament, unlike the ECHR. It does not therefore create binding, enforceable obligations in individual cases.[14]

3.9   The Convention contains 54 Articles, including the following précised below:

● all the rights guaranteed by the Convention must be available to all children without discrimination of any kind (Article 2(1));

● the best interests of the child must be a primary consideration in all actions concerning children (Article 3(1));

● the child shall have the right from birth to a name, the right to acquire a nationality and, as far as possible, the right to know and be cared for by his or her parents (Article 7(1));

● children capable of forming their own views have the right to express them freely in all matters affecting them, with their views given due weight in accordance with their age and maturity (Article 12(1)).

3.10   Of particular interest, in the context of this book, is Article 9(3):

---

8   Children Act 1989, s 1(1).
9   S 1(3). See para 3.32.
10   See, for example, *Gorgulu v Germany* [2004] 1 FLR 894.
11   See *Hendricks v Netherlands* (1982) 5 EHRR 223; *Johansen v Norway* (1996) 23 EHRR 33; *Yousef v The Netherlands* [2003] 1 FLR 210.
12   The United States and Somalia have not ratified the Convention.
13   The UK Government's first report was made in February 1994; further reports followed in 1999 and 2002.
14   Although it is being cited with increasing frequency in English courts: see, for example, *Mabon v Mabon* [2005] EWCA Civ 634, [2005] 2 FLR 1011.

'States Parties shall respect the right of the child who is separated from one or both parents to maintain personal relations and direct contact with both parents on a regular basis, except if it is contrary to the child's best interests.'[15]

3.11 Again, it can be seen that the 'right'[16] to contact is always subject to a 'best interests' test, which itself depends upon examination of the facts in individual cases. Thus nothing in either Convention fundamentally differs in approach from domestic law: the interests of the child must prevail over the interests of the adult where the two conflict.[17]

3.12 Indeed, the primacy of the child's interests above the 'rights' of a parent find their ultimate expression in orders for no contact.

3.13 It is against that background that we now turn to consider the core principles and presumptions of the current law.

THE CURRENT LAW: PRINCIPLES AND PRESUMPTIONS

Children Act 1989, section 8 – definitions and applications

3.14 The statutory provisions governing contact and residence with respect to children are set out in section 8 of the Children Act 1989.

3.15 A 'contact order' is defined as 'an order requiring the person with whom a child lives, or is to live, to allow the child to visit or stay with the person named in the order, or for that person and the child otherwise to have contact with each other'.

3.16 A 'residence order' is defined as 'an order settling the arrangements to be made as to the person with whom a child is to live'. A residence order need not be confined to one person – section 11(4) provides that: '[w]here a residence order is made in favour of two or more persons who do not themselves all live together, the order may specify the periods during which the child is to live in the different households concerned'.

---

15 UNCRC, Art 9, para 3.
16 In the context of children's rights, and their balancing with the rights of adults, it is interesting also to consider how the courts have approached the issue of corporal punishment. See, for example, *A v United Kingdom (Human Rights: Punishment of Child)* [1998] 2 FLR 959 and *R v Secretary of State for Education and Employment and others* [2005] UKHL 15, [2005] 2 FLR 374. See also now Children Act 2004, s 58.
17 The Children Act 2004 provides for the establishment of a new Children's Commissioner whose role is 'promoting awareness of the views and interests of children in England' (s 2(1)). It is interesting to note that, unlike the Commissioners in Scotland, Wales and N Ireland, the English Commissioner does not have 'children's rights' referred to in any part of his remit. See B Clucas: *The Children's Commissioner for England: The Way Forward?* [2005] Fam Law 290.

Applicants as of right

3.17 Those who may apply as of right for contact and residence orders, and other section 8 orders,[18] are prescribed under section 10 of the Act.[19] They are as follows:

(a)   Any section 8 orders:

- any parent or guardian or special guardian of the child;[20]
- any person who has parental responsibility for a child under section 4A of the Act (a step-parent or civil partner);[21]
- any person in whose favour there is already a residence order with respect to the child.[22]

(b)   Residence and contact orders – in addition to those individuals entitled to apply as of right for any section 8 orders:

- any party to a marriage (whether or not subsisting) in relation to whom the child is a child of the family;[23]
- any civil partner in a civil partnership (whether or not subsisting) in relation to whom the child is a child of the family;[24]
- any person with whom the child has lived for a period of at least three years;[25]
- any person who:
  - in any case where a residence order is in force with respect to the child, has the consent of each of the persons in whose favour the order was made;[26]
  - in any case where the child is in the care of a local authority, has the consent of that authority;[27] or
  - in any other case, has the consent of each of those (if any) who have parental responsibility for the child.[28]

3.18 Although persons falling within those categories are normally entitled to make an application as of right the court has power under section 91(14) to direct that he cannot bring an application without the court's leave.[29]

---

18   The other s 8 orders are specific issue orders and prohibited steps orders. A specific issue order means 'an order giving directions for the purpose of determining a specific question which has arisen, or which may arise, in connection with any aspect of parental responsibility for a child'. A prohibited steps order means 'an order that no step which could be taken by a parent in meeting his parental responsibility for a child, and which is of a kind specified in the order, shall be taken by any person without the consent of the court'.
19   S 10(4)(a) and (b).
20   S 10(4)(a).
21   S 10(4)(aa).
22   S 10(4)(b).
23   S 10(5)(a).
24   S 10(5)(aa).
25   S 10(5)(b).
26   S 10(5)(c)(i).
27   S 10(5)(c)(ii).
28   S 10(5)(c)(iii).
29   See para 3.26 et seq.

Applicants with leave

3.19   Those who are not entitled to apply as of right for a section 8 order may nevertheless apply with the court's leave.[30] In addition to those not entitled to apply as of right, leave is also required where a court has made an order pursuant to section 91(14) preventing a party who would otherwise be entitled to apply from making any further application without the court's permission.

3.20   When an application for leave to apply for a section 8 order is made by a person other than the child concerned (except where leave is required pursuant to section 91(14)), the court must have particular regard to:

- the nature of the proposed application for the section 8 order;

- the applicant's connection with the child;

- any risk there might be of the proposed application disrupting the child's life to such an extent that he would be harmed by it; and

- where a child is looked after by a local authority, the authority's plans for the future care of the child, and the wishes and feelings of the child's parents.[31]

3.21   There has been some confusion surrounding the application of the section 10(9) test. Much of the discussion has surrounded whether in order to succeed on an application for leave a 'good arguable case' or a 'real prospect of success' has to be shown.[32] The settled position appears to be that the application should be considered in light of the section 10(9) criteria rather than through any detailed assessment of the merits of the substantive section 8 application,[33] although in addition it appears that the court will consider:

- whether the application is frivolous, vexatious or otherwise an abuse of the process of the court; and

- whether the prospects of eventual success are so remote that the substantive application is obviously unsustainable.[34]

3.22   The latter part of that test is not to be seen as an evaluation of the positive merits of the case. Instead, it should be seen as a test of whether, irrespective of the positive merits, a particular case is so hopeless that it must fail.[35]

---

30   S 10(1)(a)(ii); (2)(b).

31   S 10(9).

32   See *Re M (Care: Contact: Grandmother's Application for Leave)* [1995] 2 FLR 86; *Re G (Child Case: Parental Involvement)* [1996] 1 FLR 857; *G v F (Contact and Shared Residence: Applications for Leave)* [1998] 2 FLR 799; *Re S (Contact: Application by Sibling)* [1998] 2 FLR 897.

33   See *Re J (Leave to Issue Application for Residence Order)* [2003] 1 FLR 114.

34   See Sumner J in *Re W (Care Proceedings: Leave to Apply)* [2004] EWHC 3342 (Fam), [2005] 2 FLR 468.

35   Query how comfortably this sits with Thorpe LJ's analysis in *Re J* (supra) of the *Re M* (supra) test.

Children as applicants

3.23   As a general rule, children cannot apply for a section 8 order without the court's leave. Such leave may only be granted if the court is satisfied that the child has sufficient understanding.[36] The courts have placed a gloss on that simple test. Even if the child does have sufficient understanding, the court has to consider in all the circumstances that the grant of leave would be appropriate, asking itself:

- whether the child's level of understanding is sufficient for him or her to play a part as a party in the proceedings, coping with the ramifications of that and giving instructions of sufficient objectivity; and
- whether that is so in view of the nature of the proceedings, the elapsed time in the proceedings, the likely future conduct of the proceedings and likely prospective applications.[37]

Ordinarily, children are not allowed to become a party to proceedings or to make an application within them unless represented by a guardian or next friend.[38]

Overview

3.24   Thus it can be seen that a wide range of people connected with a child can apply, under section 8 of the Act, for contact with that child. But the right to apply is not absolute.

3.25   The limits placed upon that right depend, on the one hand, upon statutory enactment (so that on a statutory footing a particular category of potential applicant is deemed to require leave) and secondly upon limits placed upon its exercise by the courts (by an order under section 91(14) requiring leave to apply). So far as the statute is concerned, it appears that the right to apply is (generally) confined to those who are either a natural parent of the child or have been seen as such in the eyes of the child: it is all about 'connection' to the child. So far as the cases are concerned, the broad intention of decisions regulating where leave to apply should be granted is to grant such leave only where such would be concordant with the interests of the child. This is an important example, both in statute and case-law, of the way in which parental 'rights' and responsibilities interact.

Restricting applications: section 91(14)

3.26   Section 91(14) empowers the court to prohibit specified applications without the prior leave of the court. Thus where there is a 'right' to apply for an order under section 8 (a contact order, or for the variation of a contact order), the court may abrogate that 'right', imposing a 'filter' through which an

---

36   S 10(8).
37   See *Re N (Contact: Minor Seeking Leave to Defend and Removal of Guardian)* [2003] 1 FLR 652.
38   See para 3.38 et seq.

application must pass before the 'right' may be exercised. This is usually done in cases where there have been repeated applications to the court, although not exclusively so.

3.27 When considering whether to make such an order, the court will consider the following factors:

- the child's welfare is the paramount consideration (section 1(1) of the Act);

- the power to make an order must be exercised after having considered all relevant circumstances;

- because the power represents an abrogation of a party's right to be heard, it should be used sparingly and only in exceptional circumstances;

- there are circumstances where, even if there is not a long history of unmeritorious applications, a child's welfare will demand the making of an order under section 91(14): in such cases, the order must be proportionate, both in the circumstances and to the harm it seeks to avoid, and should not be made other than exceptionally in cases where, without an order, either the child or the child's primary carers would be subjected to unacceptable strain.[39]

3.28 When considering whether to grant leave to a party following the imposition of an order under section 91(14), the test is whether there is 'an arguable case', not whether there is a reasonable prospect of success. The judge should apply the simplest of tests: namely whether or not the application demonstrates the need for renewed judicial investigation.[40]

3.29 So even where there is a statutory 'right' to apply to court for contact (for example), that 'right' may be subrogated by wider considerations not only of the child's interests directly, but also by consideration of the responding parent's position where that might indirectly affect the child's interests.

Children Act 1989, section 8: general principles and the 'welfare checklist'

3.30 The principle that the child's welfare shall be the court's paramount consideration is central to the Children Act 1989.[41] The so-called paramountcy principle applies when a court determines any question with respect to the upbringing of a child.[42]

3.31 There are three further important provisions in section 1. First, in any proceedings concerning the upbringing of a child, the court 'shall have regard to the general principle that any delay in determining the question is likely to

---

39   See *Re P (Section 91(14) Guidelines) (Residence and Religious Heritage)* [1999] 2 FLR 573;
      Re M (Section 91(14) Order) [1999] 2 FLR 553; *Re F (Children) (Restriction on Applications)* [2005] EWCA Civ 499, [2005] 2 FLR 950.
40   See *Re G (Child Case: Parental Involvement)* [1996] 1 FLR 857.
41   S 1(1).
42   Ibid.

prejudice the child's welfare'.[43] Secondly, where a court is considering whether or not to make an order, it 'shall not make the order ... unless it considers that doing so would be better than making no order at all'.[44]

3.32 Thirdly, in deciding what is in the child's best interests in a particular case (in order to give a structure to the application of the paramountcy principle), the court must have particular regard to a number of factors set out in section 1(3) of the Act – commonly known as the 'welfare checklist'. There is no significance in the order in which they are set out in the statute, which is followed below.

Section 1(3)(a): the ascertainable wishes and feelings of the child concerned (considered in the light of his age and understanding)

It is the duty of the court to place due weight upon the views of the child subject to proceedings, depending upon the child's age and circumstances.[45] In some cases, the views of the child will be determinative; but the significance of a child's views in a particular case will depend upon a number of factors, including the nature of the application and any harm the child might suffer as a consequence of its views being followed.[46] In the end, the decision is always that of the court and not that of the child.

Section 1(3)(b): his physical, emotional and educational needs

'Physical needs' clearly include food, warmth and safety. 'Emotional needs' might include the importance of a loving, family relationship with parents and siblings.[47]

Section 1(3)(c): the likely effect on him of any change in his circumstances

Where there is a satisfactory status quo in relation to the contact and/or residence arrangements for a child, there are stronger reasons for not interfering with it[48] than if the status quo is unsatisfactory. Where small children are involved, there is a 'working rule' that the status quo will not be interfered with without good reason.[49] The basis for the status quo argument is the importance of continuity of care and the harm caused by the disruption of established bonds, especially in younger children.

Section 1(3)(d): his age, sex, background and any characteristics of his which the court considers relevant

Arrangements for contact will vary depending on the age of the child. At one end of the spectrum contact between a father and a young baby may only last a few hours. This is consistent with the commonly held view that a very young

---

43 S 1(2).
44 S 1(5).
45 See *Sahin v Germany; Sommerfield v Germany* [2003] 2 FLR 671.
46 See *Re P (Minors) (Wardship: Care and Control)* [1992] 2 FCR 681; *Re: C (A Minor) (Care: Child's Wishes)* [1993] 1 FLR 832.
47 See *C v C (Minors: Custody)* [1998] 2 FLR 291.
48 See *Dicocco v Milne* (1983) 4 FLR 247.
49 See *Re G (A Minor)(Custody)* [1992] 2 FCR 279.

baby should not be removed from its mother.[50] At the other end, contact arrangements for teenagers have to accommodate their other interests and busy lives. There might also be circumstances where the child's gender, ethnicity, exceptional ability or disability affects the outcome of proceedings.

Section 1(3)(e): any harm which he has suffered or is at risk of suffering

'Harm' means 'ill-treatment or the impairment of health or development, including, for example, impairment from seeing or hearing the ill-treatment of another'.[51]

Section 1(3)(f): how capable each of his parents, and any other person in relation to whom the court considers the question to be relevant, is of meeting his needs

This provision is self-explanatory: the parties will each adduce evidence about relative capacity, and, where necessary, the court will receive evidence of independent observation from CAFCASS or social services.

Section 1(3)(g): the range of powers available to the court under this Act in the proceedings in question

The court will not be constrained by the form of orders sought by the parties. There are a wide range of orders it can make and, irrespective of what the parties are seeking, the court will act in accordance with the child's welfare.[52]

3.33 It should be noted that neither the checklist, nor indeed the Act as a whole, contains any statement to the effect that reasonable contact with a parent is normally in the child's best interests. Attempts during the passage of the Children and Adoption Bill 2006 to amend the checklist to include such a statement were unsuccessful.

COMMENCEMENT AND PARTIES: A PROCEDURAL OVERVIEW

3.34 Although this chapter does not seek to provide a comprehensive guide to procedure, so as to make sense of our subsequent discussion of the new 'Gateway forms' in Chapter 6 and of 'the voice of the child' in Chapter 8, the key procedural points relating to the commencement of proceedings and party status are set out below. An application for a section 8 order must be made in Form C1 if it is a new application or in Form C2 if it is made within ongoing proceedings.[53] If the applicant states on the form a belief that the child concerned has suffered or is at risk of suffering harm through any form of domestic abuse, violence within the household, child abduction or other conduct or behaviour, he or she must also file Form C1A setting out specified

---

50   See *Brixey v Lynas* [1996] 2 FLR 499 (a House of Lords decision in a Scottish case); *Re W (A Minor) (Residence Order)* [1992] 2 FLR 332.

51   S 31(9), as amended by the Adoption and Children Act 2002, s 120.

52   See *Re SW (A Minor) (Care Proceedings)* [1993] 2 FLR 609.

53   Family Proceedings Rules 1991 (SI 1991/1247) (FPR 1991) r 4.4(1), and Family Proceedings Courts (Children Act 1989) Rules 1991 (SI 1991/1395) (FPC(CA 1989)R) 1991, r 4(1), Sch 1.

supplemental information.[54] The applicant must serve the application together with a notice of the proceedings on Form C6 with the date, time and place of the hearing at least two weeks before the date of the first hearing (though, in appropriate circumstances, this period can be abridged).[55] The respondents to the application will be every person whom the applicant believes has parental responsibility for the child, and, if it is an application to vary or discharge an earlier order, the parties to those proceedings.[56] Notice of the proceedings additionally must be given to any person (if they do not fall within the categories above) with whom the child is living at the time that the proceedings are commenced, also any person who is involved in other proceedings in respect of the child or who is named in a court order concerning the child. If an order is being sought against a person who is not either a party, or a person to whom notice of the proceedings must be given, that person should also be served with notice of the application.

3.35 The application plus accompanying documents can be served personally on a respondent who is not known to have a solicitor or by first class post[57] at his last known address. If the respondent or person to whom notice has to be given is represented by a solicitor, then the application can be served upon his solicitor by first class post, document exchange or fax.[58] Service is deemed to have taken place (unless proved otherwise) on the second business day after posting or placing in the document exchange. The applicant has to show that he or she has served the relevant parties at or before the first court appointment by filing a statement setting out the manner, date and time of service, or, if it was effected by post, the date, time and place of posting.[59]

3.36 Where the applicant needs leave to apply, either because he or she does not fall into the category of automatic applicants, or because of a section 91(14) order (barring the applicant from making applications without leave), the procedure is to file an application in Form C2 which must contain reasons for the application and a draft of the proposed application. The court will then either grant the application or direct that the application for leave will be heard on a particular date, with notice to such persons as the court may direct.[60] In very urgent cases, orders can be made without notice to the other parties, but this is very much the exception rather than the rule. An order made without notice will generally only have effect for a short period until it is possible to give notice to the other parties and arrange a hearing.

---

54   FPR 1991, r 4.4(1A), and FPC(CA 1989)R 1991, r 4(1A). Form C1A is also to be used by the respondent when making such allegations and when responding to any made by the applicant.
55   FPR 1991, r 4.4(3), and FPC(CA 1989)R 1991, r 4(1)(b).
56   FPR 1991, r 4.7(1) and r 4.4(3), and FPC(CA 1989)R 1991, r 7(1) and r 4(3).
57   FPR 1991, r 4.8(1)(a), and FPC(CA 1989)R 1991, r 8(1(a).
58   FPR 1991, r 4.8(1)(b), and FPC(CA 1989)R 1991, r 8(1)(b).
59   FPR 1991, r 4.8(7), and FPC(CA 1989)R 1991, r 8(7).
60   FPR 1991, r 4.7(4), and FPC(CA 1989)R 1991, r 3.

3.37 Each respondent to an application must file with the court and serve on the other parties an acknowledgement of the application on Form C7. Once an application has been made it cannot be withdrawn without the leave of the court.[61]

3.38 A child who is the subject of private law proceedings will not usually be a party. The judge may join a child as a party in cases of significant difficulty. *President's Direction (Representation of Children in Family Proceedings Rules 1991, Rule 9.5)* of 5 April 2004, and accompanying CAFCASS Practice Note,[62] set out the likely circumstances where an order joining a child as a party to proceedings will be appropriate. Examples of these are:

- where the child has a standpoint or interests which are inconsistent with or incapable of being represented by one of the adult parties;
- where a CAFCASS officer has notified the court that, in his or her opinion, the child should be made a party;
- where there is an intractable dispute over residence or contact, including where all contact has ceased, or where there is irrational but implacable hostility to contact or where the child may be suffering harm associated with the contact dispute;
- where the wishes and views of the child cannot be adequately met by a report to the court;
- where an older child is opposing a proposed course of action;
- where there are complex medical or mental health issues to be determined or there are other unusually complex issues that necessitate separate representation of the child;
- where there are international complications outside child abduction, in particular where it may be necessary for there to be discussions with overseas authorities or a foreign court;
- where there are serious allegations of physical, sexual, or other abuse in relation to the child or there are allegations of domestic violence not capable of being resolved with the help of a CAFCASS officer;
- where the proceedings concern more than one child and the welfare of the children is in conflict or one child is in a particularly disadvantaged position;
- where there is a contested issue about blood testing.

3.39 Normally, a child who is joined as a party must be represented by a 'guardian ad litem'.[63] Consideration should first be given to appointing an officer of CAFCASS as guardian.

3.40 If CAFCASS is unable to appoint a guardian without delay, or if some other reason makes the appointment of CAFCASS inappropriate, the court may appoint an officer from the National Youth Advocacy Service (NYAS) or a solicitor to act for the child.

---

61   FPR 1991, r 4.5(1), and FPC(CA 1989)R 1991, r 5(1).
62   [2004] 1 FLR 1188 and [2004] 1 FLR 1190. See also the President's Guidance of 25 February 2005 (*The Family Court Practice 2006* (Jordans), at p 2762), which provides that, in the county court, guardians should be appointed by circuit judges. The CAFCASS Practice Note has now been replaced (see www.familylaw.co.uk).
63   FPR 1991, r 9.2 and r 9.5.

3.41   In certain circumstances, a child entitled to defend proceedings may do so without a guardian. These circumstances are

(a)   where he has obtained the permission of the court for that purpose; or
(b)   where a solicitor:
    (i)   considers that the child is able, having regard to his understanding, to give instructions in relation to the proceedings; and
    (ii) has accepted instructions from the child to act for him in the proceedings and, where the proceedings have begun, is so acting.[64]

Where proceedings have already started, with a guardian representing the child, the latter may apply to the court for permission to proceed without the guardian.[65] In considering an application for permission under either of these provisions, the court:

> '... shall grant the leave sought ... if it considers that the [child] concerned has sufficient understanding to participate as a party in the proceedings concerned or proposed without a ... guardian'.[66]

3.42   In *Mabon v Mabon*,[67] the Court of Appeal recognised the growing acknowledgement of the autonomy and consequential rights of children, having regard in particular to Article 12 of the UN Convention on the Rights of the Child. As a result, the courts must, at least in the case of articulate teenagers, accept that their right to freedom of expression and participation in proceedings outweigh the paternalistic view that the child should be represented by a guardian whose role was to advocate the child's welfare.[68] In the light of this authority, it is more likely that older children will be allowed to appear without a guardian in residence and contact cases.[69]

RESIDENCE CASES: SOME PRINCIPLES

3.43   We now turn to consider how the courts have applied the paramountcy principle. Since a contact order is usually made in the context of a residence order, we start by looking at case-law concerning residence.

3.44   A residence order, as already noted, is an order settling the arrangements to be made as to the person(s) with whom a child is to live.[70] The first, largely uncontroversial principle is that a child will be expected to live with a natural parent unless there is a good reason for ordering otherwise.[71]

3.45   As we have observed, following their parents' separation, most children live with their mothers. This has led to accusations that the courts are biased

---

64   FPR 1991, r 9.2A(1).
65   FPR 1991, r 9.2A(4).
66   FPR 1991, r 9.2A(6).
67   [2005] EWCA Civ 634, [2005] 2 FLR 1011.
68   Per Thorpe LJ at paras [25]–[29].
69   For further consideration of this topic, see para 8.44 et seq.
70   S 8(1).
71   See *Re D (Care: Natural Parent Presumption)* [1999] 1 FLR 134; *Re G (Children) (Residence: same sex partner)* [2006] UKHL 43, [2006] 1 WLR 2305.

towards mothers and against fathers. Prior to the implementation of the Children Act 1989, the Court of Appeal in *Re W (A Minor: Residence Order)*[72] said:

> 'Although there is undoubtedly no presumption of law that a child of any given age is better off with one parent or the other, and although the only legal principle involved is that the welfare of the child is the paramount consideration, no court can be ignorant of what would be the natural position if other things were equal. It hardly requires saying that a baby of under four weeks old would normally be with his or her natural mother.'

Lord Donaldson added:

> 'At the risk of being told by academics hereafter that my views are contrary to well established authority, I think that there is a rebuttable presumption of fact that the best interests of a baby are served by being with its mother, and I stress the word "baby". When we are moving to whatever age it may be to describe the baby as having become a child, different considerations may well apply.'

3.46 In the Court of Appeal decision in *Re A (A Minor) (Custody)*[73] Lady Justice Butler-Sloss (as she then was) said:

> 'In cases where the child has remained throughout with the mother and is young, particularly when a baby or toddler, the unbroken relationship of the mother and child is one which it would be very difficult to displace, unless the mother was unsuitable to care for the child. But where the mother and child have been separated, and the mother seeks the return of the child, other considerations apply, and there is no starting point that the mother should be preferred to the father and only displaced by a preponderance of evidence to the contrary.'

3.47 Moving on from the situation involving a very young baby, the fact that most mothers still take on the main caring role for children in families before separation means that they tend to keep doing so afterwards, for the simple reason that the courts tend to be reluctant to change the status quo.[74] There may be some judges who are easier to convince that it was the mother and not the father who carried out most of the care of the children, and that the children 'need' the daily presence of their mother more than their father, but there are probably fewer of them than there once were. Therefore the fact that most children remain with the mother represents not so much a judicial bias towards women but a reflection of how most families choose to operate, and a conservative attitude within society towards changing the children's normal arrangements. Our impression is that, on questions of residence, there is less bias in favour of mothers amongst the judiciary than there was a generation ago.

---

72 [1992] 2 FLR 332, per Balcombe LJ at p 335.
73 [1991] 2 FLR 394, at p 400.
74 See the discussion at para 3.32.

THE MOVE TOWARDS SHARED RESIDENCE

Shared residence generally: shifting perceptions

3.48   Section 11(4) of the Children Act 1989 provides that the court may make residence orders in favour of more than one person, whether living in the same household or not, thus facilitating the 'shared residence order'. A shared residence order need not mean that the child concerned spends equal amounts of time in each household. Before the Children Act 1989, the courts disapproved of orders which gave a child no main, settled home.[75] Since the implementation of the Act, and section 11(4) in particular, this is no longer considered to be good law. Over the years, since the implementation of the Children Act 1989, the courts have increasingly recognised the scope for shared residence in appropriate cases. In *A v A (Minors)(Shared Residence Order)*[76] the Court of Appeal held that, although the conventional order was likely to be a sole residence order, it would be wrong to import an exceptional circumstances test to justify shared or joint residence. It was observed that in cases where there were substantial differences between the parents which had not been resolved, shared residence was unlikely.

3.49   In another case in 1995,[77] Lord Justice Ward noted:

'Orders for shared residence are still unusual orders. They may gradually win more grudging approval from the courts as the judges begin to acknowledge that such orders can reflect practical arrangements made by parents and their children.'

In that case, the court noted that shared residence had a different psychological impact from sole residence in favour of one parent and contact with the other, something which has become more fully recognised in the subsequent decade. Still, however, the courts were emphasising the point that shared residence orders should only really be made when the parents lived close together, and where there was no fundamental disagreement between them.

3.50   The rise of fathers' groups in recent years has put the issue of shared residence on the political agenda. The complaint of many fathers was that it was mothers who were overwhelmingly likely to be given the residence of the children following separation. Although it was never intended that a residence order in favour of one parent should give that parent sole or overriding authority over the children, in practical terms it was difficult to enforce decisions about the children, either about contact or as to other important issues such as schooling or medical treatment in the teeth of opposition from the residential parent. Apart from anything else, the delay involved in bringing a matter to court played into (usually) her hands. Stories about implacably hostile mothers successfully preventing fathers from seeing their children, with the courts helpless to enforce their own orders, began to achieve a wider circulation.

---

75   See *Riley v Riley* [1986] 2 FLR 429.
76   [1994] 1 FLR 669.
77   *Re H (Shared Residence: Parental Responsibility)* [1995] 2 FLR 883.

3.51   The courts responded. In a series of cases,[78] the Court of Appeal stated that it was not necessary to prove exceptional circumstances to achieve a shared residence order. Rather, such orders were appropriate where children were spending significant amounts of time with each parent and where a shared residence order reflected the reality of their lives. After all, a residence order is only an order settling the arrangements with whom the child is to live. It is not a custody order in disguise.

3.52   *In Re F (Shared Residence Order)*[79] the judge at first instance was upheld by the Court of Appeal when she made a shared residence order between one parent living in Scotland and the other in England. In part, this was because it reflected the reality of the children's lives (living in Scotland in the term time, and Hampshire during the holidays), but also because an order for shared residence would be valuable for the children as 'a setting of the court's seal upon an assessment that the home offered by each parent to them [was] of equal status and importance'. Mr Justice Wilson (as he then was) observed:

> 'Speaking for myself, I make no bones about it: to make a shared residence order to reflect the arrangements here chosen by the judge is to choose one label rather than another ... But labels can be very important. The most obvious label to be chosen in respect of any child is surely the name which she or he should bear; and in our courts there is no longer any room for doubting the importance of that.'

3.53   The court, therefore, was showing a willingness to recognise and emphasise the equal status of mother and father by making orders for shared residence even if the children were not spending equal times in each home. There is no doubt that, for many separated parents, particularly fathers, this was a welcome move. The effect of this decision has percolated down. It is now more common for a shared residence order to be made even if the practical arrangements are thoroughly conventional – for example, with father for every other weekend and half of all the school holidays, and with the mother for the remaining time. In a recent case, Lord Justice Wall observed that, in cases where children spend 50% or nearly that with a parent, a shared residence order is most apt to describe what is actually happening on the ground and good reasons are required if such an order is not to be made.[80]

3.54   For some parents, however, this has not been enough. For them, the imposition of unequal parenting time can create an imbalance of power, whatever the name of the order. Many parents (usually fathers) have begun to ask for 'equal time' with their children.

3.55   Until recently, shared residence orders were generally only made in circumstances where there was little fundamental disagreement between the

---

78   See *D v D (Shared Residence Order)* [2001] 1 FLR 495; *Re A (Children) (Shared Residence)* [2001] EWCA Civ 1795, [2002] 1 FCR 177; *Re F (Shared Residence Order)* [2003] EWCA Civ 592, [2003] 2 FLR 397, and those cases in paras 3.53–3.57.
79   [2003] EWCA Civ 592, [2003] 2 FLR 397.
80   *Re P (Shared Residence Order)* [2005] EWCA Civ 1639, [2006] 1 FCR 309.

parents. In the 2004 case of *A v A (Shared Residence)*,[81] however, the order was used in an effort to limit a bitter parental relationship. Unusually, the parties had agreed a more or less equal division of parenting time, despite a long and ongoing history of acrimony, but one party objected to a shared residence order. Mr Justice Wall (as he then was) nevertheless made the order:

'If these parents were capable of working in harmony, and there were no difficulties about the exercise of shared parental responsibility, I would have ... made no order as to residence ... Here, the parents are not, alas, capable of working in harmony. There must, accordingly, be an order. That order, in my judgment, requires the court not only to reflect the reality that the children are dividing their lives equally between their parents, but also to reflect the fact that the parents are equal in the eyes of the law, and have equal duties and responsibilities towards their children.'

3.56 These cases have undoubtedly affected the day to day practice and thinking of the lower courts. Orders for shared residence are becoming more common. The more recent *A v A* case is being used in practice to argue for and obtain shared residence as an effective means of neutralising the power of an undermining parent. The principle that shared residence orders may be appropriate even where the parents have an acrimonious relationship has been reaffirmed by the Court of Appeal in *Re R (Residence: Shared Care: Children's Views)*.[82]

3.57 Orders which allow for equal parenting time are still likely to remain very much the exception, because of the disruption that such constant moving between parental homes is presumed to cause to children's lives. Such a proposition does no more than reflect the primacy of the paramountcy principle over the perceived 'rights' of the parent. It is not an indication that judges are biased against fathers; rather, it is a manifestation of a generally sustainable view of what best serves the interests of children. As Dame Elizabeth Butler-Sloss, then President of the Family Division, observed:[83]

'It is, in my judgment, crucial that the court has the greatest flexibility in deciding on the type and quantum of contact according to the circumstances of each individual case. It has been suggested by parents that there should be a presumption of equality of time spent by a child with each parent. This approach to contact would not be in the best interests of many children whose welfare is the issue before the courts. The court is not and should not be tied to a certain number of days which would be automatically ordered to be spent by the absent parent with the child. Children of all ages and circumstances may be the subject of contact orders and one blanket type of order may inhibit the court arriving at the decision which reflects the best interests of each individual child.'

Shared residence and parental responsibility

3.58 Where the court makes a residence order in favour of the father of a child, it must also make an order giving him parental responsibility (if he

---

81 [2004] EWHC 142 (Fam), [2004] 1 FLR 1195 (not to be confused with the similarly-named case cited at footnote 76).
82 [2005] EWCA Civ 542, [2006] 1 FLR 491.
83 *Re S (Contact: Promoting Relationship with Absent Parent)* [2004] EWCA Civ 18, [2004] 1 FLR 1279, at para [26].

would not otherwise have it). When the court makes a residence order in favour of any person other than a parent, that person has parental responsibility for the duration of the residence order.[84] The courts have been prepared to make a residence order to confer parental responsibility on an individual who would otherwise not be able to apply for a free-standing parental responsibility order (ie someone who was not the natural parent – usually a step-parent or same sex partner[85]). Following the enactment of the Adoption and Children Act 2002,[86] this will no longer be necessary in the case of step-parents, since they will be entitled to apply for parental responsibility. This is also true of same sex partners who have entered into a civil partnership following the passing of the Civil Partnership Act 2004.[87]

CONTACT: RIGHTS AND RESPONSIBILITIES

The 'right' to contact

3.59   Save for the provisions of section 1, the Children Act 1989 does not give any specific guidance as to the practice of the courts in contact or residence cases. There is no presumption as to whether children should live with their mother or their father after separation. There is no presumption of shared parenting. There is no presumption of how much contact there should be between child and parent.

3.60   The courts, however, operate a clear presumption that a child should be entitled to have a relationship with its non-resident parent unless it can be shown that the child would be harmed by doing so. In *Re T (A Minor)(Parental Responsibility: Contact)*[88] Lady Justice Butler-Sloss (as she then was) said:

'It is the general proposition, underpinned undoubtedly by the Children Act 1989 – and indeed the father has correctly reminded us of the importance of continuing relationships between children and their parents – that it is in the interests of a child to retain contact with the parent with whom the child does not reside. The courts generally set their face against depriving a child of such contact and urge reluctant caretaking parents to make contact work, however difficult it may be for that parent who very often does not understand the importance of that continuing contact.'

3.61   Similarly, *in Re O (Contact: Imposition of Conditions)*,[89] Sir Thomas Bingham, then Master of the Rolls, said:

---

84   Children Act 1989, s 12(1) and (2).
85   See *Re G (Residence: Same Sex Partner)* [2005] EWCA Civ 462, [2005] 2 FLR 957 (considered on appeal by the House of Lords in *Re G (Children) (Residence: same sex partner)* [2006] UKHL 43, [2006] 1 WLR 2305).
86   Children Act 1989, new s 4A, inserted by Adoption and Children Act 2002, s 112.
87   Ibid, s 4A(1).
88   [1993] 2 FLR 450, at p 459.
89   [1995] 2 FLR 124, at p 128.

'... it is almost always in the interest of the child that he or she should have contact with the other parent. The reason for this scarcely needs spelling out. It is, of course, that the separation of parents involves a loss to the child, and it is desirable that that loss should so far as possible be made good by contact with the non custodial parent.'

3.62 What will be immediately apparent, however, is that contact to the non-resident parent is nowhere in the authorities, at least in recent years, described in terms of 'rights'.[90] One reason for that is what will already be apparent from the foregoing discussion: perceived 'rights' always have to be balanced with responsibilities and the interests of each individual child.

What does 'contact' mean?

3.63 The description 'contact' encompasses a wide range of practical measures. It does not simply mean face-to-face meetings involving the child, although for most non-resident parents that will be the most desirable form. Face-to-face meetings are usually described by courts as 'direct contact', and may consist of either 'visiting contact', where the child sees the parent but does not stay overnight, or 'staying contact' where the child stays with the non-resident parent for a night or series of nights. Contact can be subject to conditions: it can be supervised, by named supervisors, and at particular venues. Contact can be 'subject to' various conditions designed to regulate parental behaviour where such has caused problems in the past. The law permits of a wide range of conditions to be attached to contact orders[91] above and beyond simple regulation such as the times and locations of contact. The availability and variety of those conditions are a reflection of the law's determination to ensure that contact occurs as well as its pragmatism in an area not well suited to the law's regulation.

3.64 Contact can take many different forms in addition to direct, face-to-face contact. In cases where direct contact would not be in the interests of a child, very frequently 'indirect' contact will be ordered. This is usually for two reasons: first, any contact is more effective than no contact in maintaining a relationship between the child and its non-resident parent; second, indirect contact is very often a 'platform' from which direct contact might, in time, develop. It is very rare indeed that an order for 'no contact' will preclude even some form of indirect contact.

3.65 Courts and practitioners try to be as imaginative as possible when considering the form of indirect contact. Such contact might include, for example, letters and cards, emails, videos, DVDs and any other form of written or visual contact made possible by information technology. The development of the webcam has created new possibilities for indirect contact.

---

90   See *Re S (Minors: Access)* [1990] 2 FLR 166; *Re R (A Minor) (Contact)* [1993] 2 FLR 762; *A v L (Contact)* [1998] 1 FLR 361. The 'right' to contact is almost invariably ascribed to the child, rather than to either parent. See footnote 2 for references to the theoretical debate about 'rights'.

91   Such conditions may be attached pursuant to Children Act 1989, s 11(7).

3.66 Of course, such forms of contact are of limited value in the case of very young children. In addition, they are often dependent for their efficacy upon the goodwill of the parent with care of the child. Frequently, orders for indirect contact will specify that the 'receiving' parent must show the material to the child in question, and it is also common that the court will expect such material to have some form of response from the child. Such indirect contact can be invaluable; but there are obvious difficulties for the 'sending' parent in establishing that the material has been shown to the child, thus making such orders difficult to enforce. The efficacy of indirect contact also depends upon the good faith of the 'sending' parent. Although solicitors are sometimes used as 'letter boxes', in effect 'supervising' indirect contact, the effects of an inappropriate letter or card can be devastating both upon the child and upon what is often a fragile scheme of contact.

How much contact?

3.67 In practice, courts tend to make an order for contact unless there is a good reason for not doing so. But how much contact? A common order, which many judges regard as normal, is that the children should spend every other weekend with their non-residential parent, plus half of the holidays and half-terms. If the parents live quite close to each other, then there may be visiting contact midweek after school. Because of the infinite variability of family life, however, many cases do not conform to this pattern. In the past, courts were often reluctant to order staying contact with respect to a child who was very young – a baby or toddler. The thinking behind this was undoubtedly a reluctance to separate him or her from the mother other than for a short time. Anecdotally, this would appear to be less of an issue now.

3.68 In some cases, the non-resident parent simply lives too far away for contact to be frequent; in others there may have been a break in the relationship between parent and child which needs to be built up again or the children themselves may, for whatever reason, be reluctant to go. Older children have their own lives and will resent arrangements which do not allow them to see friends, play sports, and go to parties. There may be some issues of safety which do not prevent contact but which may limit it. Judges, in dealing with such cases, have a wide discretion as to exactly how much contact there should be, and there are almost no reported cases on the issue of the amount of contact. Most are dealt with in the county courts, and they are rarely appealed. This means that there is little guidance from the higher courts and none from the statutes. The experience of family lawyers is that there will usually be an order for staying contact and holiday contact unless there is a good reason to restrict it. Beyond that – whether, for example, staying contact will be every other weekend, one weekend out of four, three out of four, or whether the weekend will last to Monday morning or end on Sunday evening – the decision will depend very much on the individual circumstances of the case, the opinion of the CAFCASS officer and the particular viewpoint of the judge. In the CAFCASS consultation paper *Every Day Matters: New Directions for*

CAFCASS,[92] it is suggested that 'shared parenting should be positively and actively facilitated where there are no child safeguarding concerns', and that contact levels:

'... should normally be substantial, including overnight and weekend stays, if a relationship between a child and his or her non resident parent is to be maintained and properly developed.'

3.69 Some have pushed for a presumption of a certain level of contact, including staying contact, following separation. It is contended that this would have several effects. First, a resident parent seeking to argue for less contact would have to justify their views; secondly, judicial discretion, which is so difficult to appeal, would be lessened; thirdly, variation between judges would be less common; finally, delays between the commencement of proceedings and trial would be less prejudicial since contact at a certain level might already have been imposed in the interim pursuant to the presumption. In response, it is said that such a presumption would undermine the paramountcy principle, being particularly inappropriate where, as often, allegations are made about the risks presented by contact.

NO CONTACT CASES

3.70 In some cases, the issue before the court is not how much contact there should be, but whether there should be any contact at all.

General principles

3.71 The general principles upon which applications for contact are decided have already been addressed. As can be seen, contact is assumed to be in a child's best interests by virtue of the harm that would be caused to the child were it to be denied.[93] It is at this point that the right of the non-resident parent to family life may achieve greater prominence. Under the ECHR, a severing of the ties between a natural parent and a child can only be justified in the most exceptional circumstances.[94]

3.72 Other than stating that general principle, it is not at all easy to derive many general themes from the reported cases. Many of the authorities involve questions of fact and degree in particular circumstances. It would not assist greatly to indulge in complex analysis of the authorities here.[95] Suffice it to say

---

92   This can be found at www.cafcass.gov.uk/English/Publications/06Jan31EveryDaymatters. pdf.

93   See, for example, *Re H (Minor) (Access)* [1992] 1 FLR 148, at p 153; *Re M (Contact: Welfare Test)* [1995] 1 FLR 274; *Re O (Contact: Withdrawal of Application)* [2003] EWHC 3031 (Fam), [2004] 1 FLR 1258; *Re S (A Child) (Contact)* [2004] EWCA Civ 18, [2004] 1 FLR 1279.

94   Article 8; see also *Gorgulu v Germany* [2004] 1 FLR 894.

95   See the review of the authorities undertaken in J Parker & D Eaton *Opposing Contact* [1994] Fam Law 636, reproduced and regularly updated in D Hershman & A McFarlane *Children Law and Practice* (Jordans).

that there are a number of circumstances where the extreme step of ordering no contact between parent and child is made. This may be because of parental drug or alcohol addiction or mental health problems, and/or risk of sexual, physical or emotional harm to the child.

3.73 A particular question that arises from the authorities is the extent to which so-called 'implacable hostility' from the resident parent towards contact with the non-resident parent affects decisions in relation to contact.

Implacable hostility

3.74 What is 'implacable hostility' in the context of contact applications? The description seems to encompass, at one end of the spectrum, self-serving obduracy and recalcitrance for no reason at all,[96] to, at the other, genuine and sincerely held fears which are found either to be insufficient to displace the presumption of contact or unjustified on the evidence.[97] It is perhaps unfortunate that the label of 'implacable hostility' has developed at all. There is a difference, we would suggest, between, on the one hand, the parent who has no intention of obeying court orders for no reason at all and, on the other, the parent who refuses contact for subjectively good but objectively unjustified reason (or 'no good reason').

3.75 The cases do recognise that it is possible for a parent to have a genuine if irrational belief that contact should not happen, which itself would potentially cause great harm to a child were it to be ignored by the making of a contact order.[98] These are cases in which the hostility towards contact can, of itself, be determinative. Such cases are extremely rare, as indeed they should be, and ought invariably to involve expert (psychiatric or psychological[99]) evidence in relation both to the strength of the alleged fear and the potential harm to the child if, the fear notwithstanding, contact occurs. As Mrs Justice Hale (as she then was) recognised:

> 'It is important to bear in mind that the label 'implacable hostility' is sometimes imposed by the law reporters and can be misleading. It is ... an umbrella term that sometimes is applied to cases not only where there is

---

96   See *Re W (A Minor) (Contact)* [1994] 2 FLR 441; *Re H (A Minor) (Contact)* [1994] 2 FLR 776; *V v V (Contact: Implacable Hostility)* [2004] EWHC 1215 (Fam), [2004] 2 FLR 851; *Re S (Contact: Promoting Relationship with Absent Parent)* [2004] EWCA Civ 18, [2004] 1 FLR 1279; *Re D (Intractable Contact Dispute: Publicity)* [2004] EWHC 727 (Fam), [2004] 1 FLR 1226.

97   See *Re R (A Minor) (Contact)* [1993] 2 FLR 762; *Re F (Minors) (Contact: Mother's Anxiety)* [1993] 2 FLR 830; *Re P (A Minor) (Contact)* [1994] 2 FLR 374.

98   See *Re P (Contact: Discretion)* [1998] 2 FLR 696; *Re L (Contact: Genuine Fear)* [2002] 1 FLR 621. It is interesting to observe that in both of these cases indirect contact was ordered. *Re L* is a particularly good example. In that case, the mother had an irrational 'phobia' of the father, which was found to be deep-seated and genuinely held. The hostility engendered by that 'phobia' was found by Bruce Blair QC (sitting as a High Court Judge) to be determinative of the father's application for contact.

99   See *Re S (Contact: Promoting Relationship with Absent Parent)* [2004] EWCA Civ 18, [2004] 1 FLR 1279.

hostility, but no good reason can be discerned either for the hostility or for the opposition to contact, but also to cases where there are such good reasons. In the former sort of case the court will be very slow indeed to reach the conclusion that contact will be harmful to the child. It may eventually have to reach that conclusion but it will want to be satisfied that there is indeed a serious risk of major emotional harm before doing so.'[100]

One factor for the court to consider in such a case is whether there might need to be formal intervention by child protection agencies, for example pursuant to section 37 of the Children Act 1989.[101] If the court has the picture that 'a parent is seeking, without good reason, to eliminate the other parent from the child's, or children's lives, [it] should not stand by and take no positive action'. Justice both to the children and the deprived parent 'require the court to leave no stone unturned that might resolve the situation and prevent long-term harm to the children'.[102]

3.76 In many ways, for the practitioner, the cases which involve a genuine, if irrational, belief that contact will be harmful to a child are the most difficult and intractable. Where a parent simply refuses to comply with orders out of obduracy alone, where there is another, quite unrelated agenda, the law will treat the offending[103] parent with little sympathy. On the other hand, a parent not complying with orders for deeply rooted psychological reasons (in the sense that the hostility towards contact is psychologically entrenched) is treated as a rather different entity. Whilst the courts have not endorsed the concept of 'Parental Alienation Syndrome' as an entity or type of mental disorder,[104] the latter category of parent is often subsumed within what might be described as a 'therapeutic model'. The problem may be treated as a medical one, with psychiatric or psychological intervention initiated in the hope that contact might be introduced or reinstated.[105] As the then President of the Family Division, Dame Elizabeth Butler-Sloss, said:

> '[32] No parent is perfect but "good-enough parents" should have a relationship with their children for their own benefit and even more in the best interests of the children. It is, therefore, most important that the

---

100 In *Re D (Contact: Reasons for Refusal)* [1997] 2 FLR 48, at p 53.
101 S 37 provides for a report to be prepared by social services into the circumstances of the child: the focus of the report in particular should be on the question of whether the child has suffered or is likely to suffer significant harm (thereby potentially activating Part IV of the Act, and ultimately care proceedings).
102 *Re M (Contact: Long-term Best Interests)* 2005 EWCA Civ 1090, [2006] 1 FLR 627, per Lord Justice Scott Baker at para [41].
103 This is not just a turn of phrase. To breach an order of the court which is sufficiently particularised may be to commit a contempt of court. See further the discussion of enforcement of orders in Chapter 7..
104 See *Re L (Contact: Domestic Violence); Re V (Contact: Domestic Violence); Re M (Contact: Domestic Violence); Re H (Contact: Domestic Violence)* [2000] 2 FLR 334, at p 351.
105 See *Re S (Contact: Promoting Relationship with Absent Parent)* [2004] EWCA Civ 18, [2004] 1 FLR 1279.

attempt to promote contact between a child and the non-resident parent should not be abandoned until it is clear that the child will not benefit from continuing the attempt.'[106]

Such an approach takes time and is not always successful.[107] Such cases quite often form the subject matter of much of the public anxiety around contact with non-resident parents. Much of the danger in this type of case surrounds the risk that the child in question might itself be encouraged to take on a parent's distorted beliefs.[108]

3.77 The decision as to whether a case is simply one of obduracy or one involving a deeply rooted, if irrational, cause is itself a difficult one to assess and take. It sometimes happens, for example, that a resident parent takes the wholly irrational and unsubstantiated view that a child is at risk of sexual harm if contact occurs. What is it in a particular case that leads to the conclusion that such beliefs constitute a psychological problem, and so might be susceptible to treatment, rather than a simple excuse utilised to sabotage contact? Any concerted attempt to answer that question clearly reveals the thorny problem lying in its heart, and the inherent danger of arriving at the wrong decision, confusing what is a straightforward case of obduracy with a case where an irrational fear exists which is susceptible to treatment. If the categorisation of the case is wrong, there might be a lengthy and fruitless attempt to 'cure' a problem which never existed, causing delay and further damage to the prospects for contact. On the other hand, attempts to punish a parent for wilful disobedience of a court order will be inappropriate if the objection is based on irrational but genuine fears which may be amenable to treatment.

3.78 In summary, the term 'implacable hostility' cannot be simply or comprehensively defined. It encompasses a wide range of behaviours, which in themselves might or might not be enough ultimately to lead a court to the conclusion that a child's welfare demands an order for no contact. Cases where there is a simple refusal to comply with court orders or where hostility is founded upon irrational beliefs which are not genuinely held will not be permitted to frustrate contact and will be treated by the courts with little sympathy. Where contact is refused because of a genuinely held but irrational belief, however, the situation is more complicated: in such circumstances, although they are unlikely to attract public sympathy, the courts adopt a 'cajoling' approach, which often includes therapeutic input.

3.79 Of course there are a number of cases in which hostility to contact is objectively justified because there is a risk to the child. Such risks might stem

---

106 Ibid, at para [32].

107 But see *Re S (Uncooperative Mother)* [2004] EWCA Civ 597, [2004] 2 FLR 710: the effluxion of time alone will not be permitted to frustrate contact. This case is a good example of the employment of the 'therapeutic model', albeit with an intention which appears to have been frustrated.

108 Thereby suffering significant harm? In such cases, real consideration needs to be given to whether there should be intervention by a local authority to prevent the occurrence of such harm. The most sinister manifestation of such cases is frequently an irrational belief that contact might expose a child to the risk of sexual harm: in such cases, the child concerned may well be subjected to physical harm by a parent in seeking to prove the existence of that risk. Such behaviour constitutes serious physical, as well as emotional, abuse.

from alcohol or substance misuse, or from physical, sexual or emotional harm. These are not 'implacable hostility' cases at all (although previously some cases were wrongly categorised as such), in the sense that, although there is 'hostility' which is 'implacable', it is not the hostility itself which is determinative of the issue.[109] As an order for no contact is one of last resort, the courts will often wish to consider some input (professional or otherwise) in order to see if contact can be safely managed. Ultimately, however, some cases will end in an order for no contact.[110] An important example of those cases where the option of 'no contact' has to be considered are those involving domestic violence, considered in Chapter 6.

CONTACT AND REMOVAL FROM THE JURISDICTION

Permanent removal from the jurisdiction

3.80 Alongside the endorsement by the courts of better contact and shared parenting (and in some ways at odds with it) has come a policy of permitting resident parents, who wish to relocate to another part of the world, to do so, as long as their plans are reasonable and they are not motivated by a desire to shut the other parent out of the child's life. The applicant parent may be a foreign national who wishes to return home following the breakdown of the marriage or relationship. Alternatively, he or she may have remarried a foreign national, or their spouse has been offered a job abroad. In other cases, there may simply be a desire to start a new life elsewhere. Where a residence order is in force, no person is permitted to take a child out of the United Kingdom without the consent of all those with parental responsibility or the leave (permission) of the court, unless that person is the residence order holder and the period abroad is less than one month.[111] A parent who seeks to do so should either obtain the requisite consent, or make an application to the court. These are always difficult cases, because of the effect on each parent of either making or refusing to make the order. If it is granted, there is likely to be a profound effect on the children's contact with the remaining parent. If it is not, either the applicant parent will go without the children (unusual in the experience of most family lawyers) or he or she will remain behind, distressed and resentful.

3.81 Assuming that the application is made by the parent with the primary care of the children, the Court of Appeal's guidance in the leading case of *Payne v Payne*[112] applies. Lord Justice Thorpe proposed that the following questions should be asked:

(a) Is the application genuine in the sense that it is not motivated by some selfish desire to exclude the other parent from the child's life?

(b) Is the application realistic – ie founded on practical proposals both well researched and investigated?

---

109 See Wilson J (as he then was) in *Re P (Contact: Discretion)* [1998] 2 FLR 696.
110 For a good example of a case in which the risks were such to justify an order for no contact, see *Re H (Contact Order) (No 2)* [2002] 1 FLR 22.
111 Children Act 1989, s 13(1)(b) and (2).
112 [2001] EWCA Civ 166, [2001] 1 FLR 1052.

(c)   Is the opposition of the other parent motivated by genuine concern for
       the future of the child's welfare? What would be the extent of the
       detriment to him and his future relationship with the child were the
       application granted, and to what extent would such detriment be offset by
       extension of the child's relationships with other family members?

(d)   What would be the impact on the applicant, either as the single parent or
       in another relationship, of a refusal of his or her realistic proposals?

3.82 Having asked those questions, the court should then bring the answers
into an overriding review of the child's welfare as the overriding consideration,
directed by the welfare checklist. Lord Justice Thorpe then went on to
emphasise:

> 'In suggesting such a discipline I would not wish to be thought to have
> diminished the importance that this court has consistently attached to the
> emotional and psychological well-being of the primary carer.'

3.83 In the same case, Dame Elizabeth Butler-Sloss, then President of the
Family Division, put the principles this way.

(a)   The welfare of the child is always paramount.

(b)   There is no presumption created by section 13(1)(b) of the Children
       Act 1989 in favour of the applicant parent.

(c)   The reasonable proposals of the parent with a residence order wishing to
       live abroad carry great weight.

(d)   Consequently the proposals have to be scrutinised with great care and the
       court needs to be satisfied that there is a genuine motivation for the move
       and not the intention to bring contact between the child and the other
       parent to an end.

(e)   The effect on the applicant parent and the new child of the family of a
       refusal to leave is very important.

(f)   The effect upon the child of the denial of contact with the other parent
       and in some cases his family is very important.

(g)   The opportunity for continuing contact between the child and the parent
       left behind may be very significant.

3.84 Despite the fact that there is no legal presumption in favour of the
applicant, from a practical point of view, applications are usually granted
unless the applicant has an ulterior motive directed at excluding the other
parent, unless the children are older and do not want to go, or the plans are
inadequate. Examples of cases where permission has been granted or refused
are frequently reported as many of them tend to be heard in the High Court.[113]

3.85 One of the critical factors in weighing whether leave to remove from the
jurisdiction should be granted is the effect of such leave upon contact for the
non-resident parent.[114] Where there is concern about the enforceability of any

---

113   See, for example, *Re A (Leave to Remove: Cultural and Religious Considerations)* [2006]
      EWHC 421 (Fam), [2006] Fam Law 443, *H v F (Refusal of Leave to Remove a Child from the
      Jurisdiction)* [2005] EWHC 2705 (Fam), [2006] 1 FLR 776.

114   See *R v R (Leave to Remove)* [2004] EWHC 2572 (Fam), [2005] 1 FLR 687; *M v M (Minors)
      (Removal from the Jurisdiction)* [1992] 2 FLR 303.

arrangement made for contact, the court may require the departing parent to have a contact order made in the foreign jurisdiction before the permission is given to remove the child.[115]

Holidays and removal from the jurisdiction

3.86   As outlined, a residence order entitles the holder to remove the relevant child from the UK for up to one month,[116] unless there is a prohibited steps order restraining him or her from doing so. Any other person with parental responsibility may not remove the child from the country at all without the consent of every other person with parental responsibility, or the leave of the court. It is a criminal offence for a person 'connected with the child' to remove him or her from the UK 'without the appropriate consent.[117] Therefore, any parent without a residence order wanting to take their child abroad on holiday will have to get consent from the other parent or any other person with parental responsibility or apply for a section 8 specific issue order allowing them to do so.

3.87   In the absence of consent, most courts will grant the non-resident parent their wish to take a child on holiday as long as the plans are sensible and the child is not at risk. If a child is very young and has not spent long periods of time in the care of the non-resident parent, it may be that the court refuses the order or limits the period of time to be away – for example, to one week. What can create more difficulty is where there is a fear of abduction, for example where the other parent is a foreign national with few ties to the United Kingdom. If the country of origin or country to which they intend to take the child is a signatory to the international convention governing child abduction[118] (which broadly operates a policy of returning abducted children), there is usually (but not invariably) less cause for alarm. If the relevant country is not such a signatory, then there will have to be an assessment of the likely risk of abduction before the court is prepared to make the order permitting the holiday. The assessment of risk will include looking at the ties that the applicant parent has with this country – employment, property, family and so on – and/or whether they can give undertakings or provide a bond of money which would be forfeited in the event of a breach of the order requiring them to return the child.[119] The court is likely to need some information about the law relating to children generally in the country of destination, and it can in appropriate cases require the making of an order in that country that will

---

115   See *Re S (Removal from the Jurisdiction)* [1999] 1 FLR 850.
116   See para 3.80.
117   See Child Abduction Act 1984, s 1, for the full statutory provisions, including the meaning of 'connected with the child' and 'without the appropriate consent'. The law as to child abduction is set out in detail in D Hershman and A McFarlane *Children Law and Practice* (Jordans), at Division H.
118   The Hague Convention of the Civil Aspects of International Child Abduction 1980.
119   See *Re K (Removal from the Jurisdiction: Practice)* [1999] 2 FLR 1084.

mirror the orders here so as to create mutual enforcement of the requirement to return the child at the end of the holiday.[120]

3.88   The concern about potential abduction might also arise in the context of the carer parent proposing to take a child abroad for holidays. If that is the case, the non-resident parent would have to apply to the court for a section 8 prohibited steps order which would prevent a removal from the jurisdiction altogether. The court would consider the same principles outlined above when deciding whether or not to make the order.[121]

Temporary relocation abroad

3.89   In a relocation application, if the intention is for the removal to be for a limited period of time, the guidelines set out in *Payne v Payne* should be modified accordingly.[122] The balance to be struck between the effect of refusal of permission upon the primary carer and the effect of the loss of contact to the other parent is obviously a different one from the situation in a case where the removal is permanent.

Contact and removal from the jurisdiction – practicalities

3.90   What in fact happens to the contact between the non-resident parent and child in an emigration case? Before an application to remove is granted, the courts will scrutinise the proposals that the applicant parent is making about contact to ensure that he or she is committed to retaining the relationship between the children and the other parent.

3.91   There are many ways of promoting the relationship despite geographical distance. For example, a fund (which can be created from maintenance payments) can be set aside to pay for visits by the child or children to this country, and to pay for visits by the non-resident parent to the country of destination. If the move is to a country which is very far away (for example, New Zealand or Australia), the non-resident parent might have two lengthy periods of contact a year at least with the children. If the country is closer (for example, in Europe), there can be more frequent, shorter visits, as well as some longer ones. There can be contact by telephone, email and webcam, as well as by letters and cards. If there is thought to be a need, the court in this country can require an undertaking that orders made in this country concerning contact are registered or mirrored in the destination country. There is no doubt that, from the perspective of the non-resident parent, there is the loss of involvement in the day-to-day lives of the children (although non-resident parents by no means always have this when the whole family is in this country), but much can be done to foster and encourage the relationship nonetheless.

---

120   See *Re T (Staying Contact in Non-Convention Country)* [1999] 1 FLR 262; *Re: P (A Child) (Mirror Orders)* [2000] 1 FLR 435.
121   See *Re: D (A Minor) (Child: Removal from the Jurisdiction)* [1992] 1 FLR 637.
122   See *Re (A Temporary Removal from Jurisdiction)* [2004] EWCA Civ 1587, [2005] 1 FLR 639.

Removal from the jurisdiction and shared residence

3.92 Most of the authorities in relocation cases are concerned with an application by a primary carer. With the shift towards making shared residence orders, there are bound to be more cases before the court where the applicant is not the primary carer, but a joint carer in a shared arrangement. The principles of *Payne v Payne*[123] may need to be adjusted. It remains to be seen whether the existence of a shared residence order where the children spend more time with one parent than another will make a successful relocation application harder to achieve, but it seems highly likely that an equal care arrangement will have just that effect, because the potential effect on the child of the loss of contact to one of its parents will be greater.[124]

---

123 See para 3.81 et seq.
124 See *Re Y (Removal from the Jurisdiction)* [2004] 2 FLR 330, where Hedley J chose 'the course of least detriment to the child'.

Chapter Four

ALTERNATIVE ROUTES TO BETTER SOLUTIONS

4.1 Litigation is far from being an ideal way to resolve disputes. It can be expensive, time-consuming and distressing – particularly so for those distressed and angry in the first place. By the time each parent has filed court statements setting out the faults and failings of the other, the temperature will have risen and co-operative parenting will be all the harder in the future. Once parents have faced hostile cross-examination in the witness-box and lawyers have made adversarial submissions to the court, things will be even worse. At the end, there will be a judgment which may be critical of one or both parties and an order that nobody likes. Not surprisingly, court proceedings can leave a legacy of discord between parents which have long-term consequences for their children. No matter how aware the judges are of this, and no matter how hard they try to prevent an escalation of bitterness by the process, it is very difficult to avoid.

4.2 Parents going through this nightmare may console themselves with the thought that it is worth enduring for the benefit of their children. In many cases this is a delusion. The deleterious effects of parental conflict on children have been summarised in Chapter 1. The research carried out by Professor Carol Smart and others[1] is typical. They found that children who had suffered from years of parental conflict:

> '... lost the support of their parents, and the kinds of material, emotional and interpersonal securities which go with it. They saw their parents as impoverishing their lives because they were so intent on pursuing their own grievances ... these young people were rarely in a position to intervene directly in their parents' conflicts; most felt they had to put up with them until they could leave home. Others took sides and saw the other parent as the "enemy" too, while yet others withdrew in various ways.'[2]

The very thing that parents were seeking to preserve – a relationship with their children – was what was most likely to be destroyed.

4.3 The drawbacks of litigation in this field have long been recognised, not least by the people whose careers are devoted to it. Judges often record their

---

1   See C Smart, B Neale & A Wade *The Changing Experience of Childhood: Families and Divorce* (Cambridge, Polity Press, 2001).

2   See C Smart *Parenting disputes, gender conflict and the courts* in *Durable Solutions: The collected papers of the 2005 Dartington Hall Conference* (Jordans, 2006).

regret that more was not done earlier to prevent the escalation of bitter parental disputes. They try hard at various points to encourage the parties to settle, and increasingly court procedures are being designed and modified to facilitate the resolution of litigation by agreement.[3] But in many cases the Rubicon has been crossed long before the case arrives in front of a judge. If a case is going to be settled amicably, the best prospects are often before proceedings are begun, before the parties have embarked upon the process of allegation and counter-allegation, and before they have spent money on lawyers from which they feel compelled to expect results.

4.4   Another reason for favouring early resolution over in-court conciliation is that the former is more likely to lead to a genuinely voluntary agreement. Whilst the distinction between out-of-court and in-court mediation/conciliation may seem artificial from the outside, there is no doubt that parents caught up in a dispute over their children feel the difference. In the 1980s, Professor Gwynn Davis carried out a study of in-court conciliation procedures. He found the results disconcerting. Many parents whom he consulted experienced a loss of authority and control during court-based negotiations. Their cases were repeatedly adjourned and Professor Davis described eventual settlement being arrived at through a 'process of attrition'.[4] What is more, some parents who had been involved in the process could not distinguish between the 'mediation' they had experienced and a full-blown trial, and thought they had undergone the latter. He warned that the language of mediation was being applied to highly coercive procedures. Although there have been undoubted improvements to the system, and much greater awareness of the risks of pushing the reluctant litigant into a settlement in the last twenty years, there is still no doubt that the imminence of litigation and the proximity of the court can be intimidating. Hence a more satisfactory and lasting agreement may be reached by means of both parents voluntarily entering into mediation or other negotiation well away from the court door.

4.5   For all these very good reasons, parents are encouraged to try and reach agreement in respect of their children without recourse to the courts, or, even if they have issued an application and the process is underway, as an alternative to a full-blown hearing. Successive governments have encouraged this process, and it is not surprising to find it at the heart of the latest reforms. In *Parental Separation: Children's Needs and Parents' Responsibilities – Next Steps,*[5] the Government proposed to review relevant rules and Practice Directions so that the:

> '... strongest possible encouragement is given to parties to agree to mediation or other forms of dispute resolution, in order to ensure that all alternative means for resolving family disputes, short of contested hearings, are fully utilised.'

The intention is to advise parents about the kind of arrangements that would in broad terms be expected to pertain in separated families (hence the publication

---

3   See para 5.3 et seq.
4   See G Davis *A Research Perspective* in J Westcott (ed) *Family Mediation: Past, Present and Future* (Jordans, 2004).
5   January 2005 – Cm 6452 – available at www.dfes.gov.uk/childrensneeds/.

of parenting plans); as to the damage that they can cause their children if they are exposed to continuing conflict; and how, if possible, to manage their feelings of distress, loss and anger over the failure of their family relationships. Parents are to be guided towards alternative routes for resolution of their differences – principally, it is hoped, through mediation.

4.6   This chapter is concerned with the process of settling cases outside the court arena and the steps which have been taken to try to help parents to achieve agreement. This may be through agreement between themselves, agreement with the help of solicitors, agreement through mediation or conciliation (with or without solicitors), or agreement through a process known as collaborative law. Conciliation within the confines of the court building and as part of normal court procedure is dealt with in Chapter 5.

THE USE OF PARENTING PLANS

4.7   The majority of separating couples manage to agree arrangements for their children by themselves. By and large, this is much the most satisfactory course, but it carries the risk that, through ignorance and lack of experience, parents may reach agreements that are not in the children's interests or overlook matters that require attention.

The new parenting plan

4.8   The principle of getting parents to agree the arrangements for their children had received encouragement for many years. But there was until recently very little information that could be given to them as to what would be considered a normal arrangement for separated families, to act as a backdrop to their negotiations. Lawyers and welfare officers could tell parents what, in their experience, were the sort of orders that courts would make; but the practice of different courts and different judges in fact varied quite widely. It was not until 2002 that the Government produced a document that was intended not only to give parents information as to what sort of arrangements would be considered 'normal', but also to help them to be aware of the issues concerning their children that might arise in the future and to work out how to tackle them.

4.9   A parenting plan prototype was launched in March 2002. The feedback from parents about the document was welcoming. Most did not physically complete the plans but many of them said that they found it to contain a useful checklist for things that they needed to agree. In 2005, after consultation, the Government launched an updated and more comprehensive version of the 2002 parenting plan. The new plan was longer, with more authoritative advice for parents on the benefits to children of having a relationship with both mother and father. Gone from the 2005 version were references to contact; and gone was this assertion: 'children usually spend more time with one parent than the other for practical reasons. In most cases children will live with one parent and see the other on visits, but this may not suit your children or your circumstances'. Presumably this was because this might be thought to create a presumption that there is a primary and a secondary parent.

4.10   The 2005 version stressed the importance of both parents with the language of parity. It advises that:

'Children are entitled to a relationship with both their parents, whether or not they live together. Research shows that it is normally in the child's best interests if:

- Children are raised by both parents whether or not they live together, as long as it is safe.

- Each parent supports their children to enjoy a positive relationship with the other parent.

- Children are clear about the arrangements for spending time with each parent.

- Children should not be exposed to sudden changes in arrangements unless it is unavoidable.

- Children should not be exposed to continuing conflict as it can harm them.'

Later it advises parents to decide on day-to-day arrangements, asking: 'When will they spend time with each of you?'

4.11   Despite considerable debate on the topic, the parenting plan does not suggest that children should ordinarily spend equal amounts of time with each parent. Like the 2002 version but in more detail, it does give advice and makes suggestions as to the practical matters that separating parents should consider. Matters that parents are advised to discuss over and above the time spent with each parent relate to religion, culture, schooling, health, money and the appointment of a guardian in the event that the parents die before the children have reached the age of majority.

4.12   The advantage of the parenting plan is twofold. First, it sets out broad expectations as to what is in children's interests so far as the involvement of both parents in a child's life following separation. Secondly, it makes it plain that, save in cases where there has been domestic violence and when children or a parent may be at risk from the other parent, there is an expectation of frequent and regular contact. Whilst the courts may have operated on an assumption in favour of contact and involvement of both parents in the past, this was not so explicit as it is now. The plan also encourages parents to communicate at an early stage by demonstrating that there are a number of very important matters they need to consider in the upbringing of their children. There is a clear expectation that these matters are the concern of both parents – not just one of them.

4.13   In accordance with the Government's policy, there is a heavy emphasis in the parenting plan on mediation. The early sections are aimed at helping parents make arrangements for their children. Later on, there is a section for parents who find it difficult to agree. First, parents are advised as to what may be the blocks to agreement:

'When emotions run high around the time of separation, it often feels as if communication between you has broken down completely and there is no possibility of agreeing on anything. This is a normal feeling but it may only be temporary.'

Later on it states:

'... you may need to find some support, such as individual counselling or parenting support to help you come to terms with the situation. You also need to work through some key questions and issues. You will probably find this easier to do if you can talk things through with a third party who is more objective – this could be a family member or friend who you trust, or it could be an organisation.'

4.14 The parenting plan guide sets out a number of case histories which not only promote the importance of parties agreeing arrangements between themselves but also illustrate the wide variety of arrangements that are seen as suitable for families. In some families, there is a shared care arrangement; in others, there is weekend contact, either overnight or visiting. The case histories also illustrate various possible points of conflict and how they have been resolved in that particular instance – for example, the arrival of new partners, new babies, timekeeping and lack of experience of caring for a very young child.

4.15 In the final instance, the parenting plan advises parents that:

'... if you really find there is no scope for compromise between you, parents do have a right to apply to the court for an order.'

There is, in addition, some general advice as to the meaning of parental responsibility, and information about organisations which can help families and children in circumstances of separation and breakdown.

4.16 Parents are expected to consider a parenting plan when separating and the booklets are available from Citizens Advice Bureaux, court offices, family advice services and CAFCASS. The Form C1 (on which any new application to the court concerning children has to be made) now asks at section 15:

- Have you received a Parenting Plan booklet?

- Have you agreed to a Parenting Plan? (If yes, please include a copy of the plan when you send your application to the court)

- If you did agree a Parenting Plan, has the plan broken down? (If yes, please explain briefly why the plan broke down)

4.17 Parenting plans can be used to form the basis of agreement at any stage of the separation process, including at the door of the court, and their use has been specifically commended in a recent high profile case.[6]

---

6   See the comments of Hedley J in *Re Z* (*Shared Parenting Plan: Publicity*) [2006] 1 FLR 405.

RESOLUTION THROUGH MEDIATION

4.18 Parents who are unable to reach agreement by themselves may be more successful if they receive help from others. Mediation is a way of resolving disputes in which parents aim to find solutions to their problems with the help of an independent, trained third party. Mediators are now trained professionals and in many cases are qualified and experienced family lawyers, but, although they can give parties general information about the law, they cannot give legal advice.

4.19 There are several different models for mediation. In family cases the usual model is for face-to-face mediation with the parties and mediator together. Sometimes there are two mediators, although this would usually be reserved for higher conflict cases. The mediator is there to help the parties listen to each other and to try to find a solution. What is said in mediation is confidential (although this does not apply to factual information given in meetings), except if it seems to the mediator from what is said that someone has been seriously hurt or is at risk of being hurt. Agreement through mediation would be expected to take a number of meetings – somewhere between two and six. Although in family mediation it is unusual for solicitors to attend, parties are free to take proposed agreements made in mediation to their solicitors to obtain legal advice, and most do. Agreements made in mediation are not legally binding unless they are incorporated into a court order. People wishing to engage the services of a mediator can contact solicitors local to them who will have the names of mediators in the area, as will the Citizens Advice Bureau. Additionally there are national organisations who can give advice about mediation, the details of which are set out in Appendix 8.

4.20 The advantages of a mediated agreement are that the parties are helped to work out a solution that suits both of them and the children. The circumstances of families vary enormously and it is generally considered that separating couples are the ones best placed to make decisions about their own lives and those of their children. It is easier for a mediated agreement to contain more detail – in relation to practical arrangements, future intentions, consultation – than a court order. Mediation may bring lasting improvement to communication between parents, and can create a process for agreement when future decisions need to be made. By encouraging the parties to focus on the needs of the children, the mediator will try to avoid the parties airing their grievances and bitterness against each other.

4.21 Practical arrangements for mediation will vary from case to case, but in general the procedure is likely to be as follows. First there will be contact between the parties and a mediation organisation (there are several). There will be agreement to use mediation, as to the identity of the mediator and the cost, and the parties will be provided with a proposed mediation agreement which is usually signed before mediation starts. The time and venue will be agreed, as will the length and proposed number of the sessions. At the first mediation meeting, the mediator will clarify the process and set ground rules, identify the issues and work towards an agenda. There is likely to be clarification of the most basic matters – for example, who will speak first, that the other party should remain quiet when the first is speaking, and how long people will be given to set out their positions. Whilst mediators are specifically trained not to take sides, they are also trained to ensure that one party is not able to dominate the agenda, or to control and/or bully the other party. If agreement is reached, then it will be put into writing and signed by all parties. They can seek legal advice on the document if they wish. In respect of financial matters this would almost always be advisable – less so with matters relating to children.

4.22 Most mediators do not see or speak to the children involved in the dispute, unless they are specifically trained to do so and have the agreement of the parents. If sensitively handled, this can also help the children express their views without feeling as if they are being made to choose. Many children who are asked what would have helped them adjust to family breakdown say that they wished they had been given more information. There are some independent mediation services which have introduced a policy of including children in the process – for example the Devon Family Mediators Agency,[7] which offers children whose parents are seeing a mediator the opportunity to meet separately with an independent resource worker (who is an experienced child psychologist in the area supportive of the mediation process). The child's participation is entirely voluntary, and the child has the same rights of confidentiality as the adults do in mediation. Confidentiality will only be broken if there are issues of child protection. The confidentiality gives the child the ability to express views which will not be directly fed back to the parents. The resource worker and the child will decide together what (and in what way) information will be given arising out of the meeting.

4.23 There are other mediation organisations which have a policy (with the agreement of parents and child) of inviting the child to a family meeting at the end of the process where the plans for the children are explained to them with the help of the mediator, and any questions that they have can be answered. The involvement of children in mediation still remains the exception rather than the rule as parents and mediators alike are wary of involving children in the dispute and putting pressure upon them.

The development of mediation

4.24 Mediation has been a feature of the family justice system in England and Wales for over a generation. In 1974 the Report of the Committee on One-Parent Families (Chairman, Sir Morris Finer)[8] pointed the way forward in a number of respects, notably by recommending the creation of a system of family courts, and by proposing that facilities should be provided for 'conciliation' meetings between separated couples. Conciliation was intended to engender 'common sense, reasonableness and agreement in dealing with the consequences of estrangement' and to encourage parties to:

'... wind up their failure with the least possible recrimination, and to make the most rational and efficient arrangements possible for their own and their children's future.'

---

7   See L Parkinson *Child-inclusive Family Mediation* [2006] Fam Law 483.

8   Cm 5629.

A network of local family conciliation services began to develop, starting with the Bristol Family Mediation Service in 1979, followed by others all over the country that then became part of a national network entitled the National Family Conciliation Council. By the mid 1990s the term 'mediation' was being used as well as, or instead of, conciliation, and the National Family Conciliation Council changed its name to National Family Mediation.

4.25 After initial scepticism, mediation has received enthusiastic support from successive governments who see in it not merely a more civilised way of resolving family disputes but also a method of reducing public expenditure on courts and legal aid. Thus the Conservative Government of John Major gave encouragement to the process of out of court mediation through the passage of the Family Law Act 1996. At the same time, changes were introduced to the system of public funding for family proceedings whereunder every application for public funding to the Legal Services Commission for Legal Representation or General Family Help had to be assessed for suitability for family mediation.[9] If suitable, unless an exemption applied, funding will not be granted for litigation until mediation has been tried. Exemptions relate to alleged domestic violence or abuse, inability of the applicant to travel, or if an appointment is not available within 15 working days.[10] Funding is available (subject to means and merit testing) for help with mediation and general family help. The number of publicly funded mediations supported by the Legal Services Commission increased from 400 in 1997/1998 to over 12,000 in 2001/2002.[11] Additionally, privately funded litigants were increasingly drawn to mediation in the hope that they would be spared the trauma and cost of going to court. A further development in this field has been the setting up of the Family Mediation Helpline.[12]

4.26 At the same time, there has been greater emphasis on in-court conciliation. In November 2004, the Private Law Programme was introduced[13] in England and Wales as a framework for managing private law cases in the courts. The Programme emphasises dispute resolution as the first way forward in cases where safety is not in issue, by means of in-court conciliation with the help of a CAFCASS officer, or by referring the parties to outside mediation.

The future of mediation

4.27 Since the aim of mediation is to help parties reach a genuine agreement about the family's future, it must be a wholly voluntary process. There was much discussion in Parliament and elsewhere before the passing of the Children and Adoption Act 2006 as to whether parents should be required to try mediation before having recourse to the courts. To some extent, the voluntary aspect has already been eroded by the element of compulsion for those who seek public funding. Those who are not entitled to such funding have

---

9   Funding Code Procedures, para 27.
10   Funding Code Procedures, paras 28, 29.
11   See the Government's 2004 Response to *Making Contact Work*.
12   At www.familymediationhelpline.co.uk/.
13   See para 5.3 et seq.

no requirement to show that the case is either unsuitable for mediation or that it has been attempted. It was argued by some that a requirement to attend mediation would make agreement between parents more likely at an early stage, with consequent benefits to children. On the other side, experts in mediation argued (successfully) that a willingness to participate (however reluctant) went to the core of the process and that, for there to be any chance of mediation working, there needed to be some motivation on behalf of each party to improve the situation co-operatively, as opposed to competitively, or by imposed solution.[14] Additionally, they argued, compelling individuals to submit to the mediation process might expose weaker parties to coercion, pressure and bullying.

4.28 Eventually, during the passage of the Children and Adoption Bill, a compromise was reached: couples are encouraged but not required to attend mediation before they make any applications to the court. Once the Children and Adoption Act 2006 is in force, the court will, when considering whether to make a contact order, have the power to make 'contact activity directions'. This is an order directing the parties to the case (or one of them), to undertake activities promoting contact. The type of activities may include attending information sessions about mediation, but not mediation itself.[15]

4.29 It is likely that mediation will continue to be the mechanism of first choice for both parents and Government for those family disputes that need active assistance, as it is relatively straightforward and cost-effective. It does, however, have limitations. It is bound to work better in low conflict cases, and there are some cases which either cannot be resolved by agreement or which need more therapeutic and/or educational input to succeed. As already noted, mediation is essentially a voluntary process, so it requires co-operation from each of the parties which may not be forthcoming. Mediation will remain unsuitable for cases where there are serious allegations of domestic violence or abuse. The CAFCASS Domestic Violence Policy and Toolkit[16] makes the following points:

- Family mediation or dispute resolution may increase the vulnerability of the parent who has experienced domestic violence.

- Where there has been intimidation by one party over another, discussion about the child's best interests may become secondary to the management of intimidation between parents.

- In many minority cultures the family and community dynamics can be such that the parent who has experienced domestic violence could be at greater risk of violence because of the process of mediation/dispute resolution.

---

14   See M Roberts *Voluntary participation in Family Mediation* [2006] Fam Law 57.

15   Children Act 1989, ss 11A–11G, as inserted by Children and Adoption Act 2006, s 1; see para 7.17 et seq.

16   The CAFCASS Domestic Violence Policy and Toolkit is available at www.cafcass. gov.uk/English/Publications/policies/FinalversionDomesticVOct.doc. Its final version came out in October 2005. See further at para 6.61 et seq.

In other cases, where parents have psychiatric problems or learning difficulties, mediation may be difficult, although not necessarily impossible. The neutrality of the mediator may mean that, despite their training, imbalances of power between parties are perpetuated or that the agreement reached may not be objectively fair in a way that would be less likely were solicitors involved.

4.30 Another disadvantage of mediation is that it sometimes can lead to delay. If a non-resident parent is not seeing his or her children, or seeing them infrequently, the time taken to mediate, if it is not successful, will add to the considerable time that it takes to get a case into court and then have a full hearing, should that be necessary. This could lead to the parent and child losing many months of valuable and, some would say, irreplaceable time together, and possibly cause long-term damage to their future relationship.

4.31 For the right cases, mediation can be extremely effective. There is even some evidence of it working in the higher conflict cases, although this is likely to be the exception rather than the rule. Neil Robinson, solicitor and Director of the Mediation Centre in Stafford, gives an account[17] of a contact case where there had been repeated applications and court proceedings for four years. Such was the level of conflict that the court appointed a guardian for the children. At a stage in the litigation where contact had tentatively restarted, and the father was seeking an extension, the guardian suggested a referral to mediation – not really to deal with the exact arrangements for contact so much as to help the parties achieve some co-operative parenting and an absence of conflict. The outcome of the mediation was broadly successful, agreement was reached, and the litigation was brought to an end. What is of note is that the case was co-mediated because of the high conflict involved, and that the mediators (particularly the lead mediator) were very experienced professionals. In the case of *Al-Khatib v Masry*[18] parties who had litigated over a number of years and up to the Court of Appeal successfully negotiated a settlement via mediation. Lord Justice Thorpe, supervising Lord Justice in family alternative dispute resolution (ADR), took responsibility for the appointment of mediators (again there were two). One was a retired circuit judge, the other was one of the spiritual leaders of the Muslim community in the UK. Lord Justice Thorpe said:

> 'From the point of view of the Court of Appeal it supports our conviction that there is no case, however conflicted, which is not potentially open to successful mediation, even if mediation has not been attempted or has failed during the trial process.'[19]

COLLABORATIVE LAW

4.32 Recently, a fresh method of resolving disputes without litigation has emerged in the form of collaborative law. The so-called 'collaborative process' was started in the early 1990s in Minnesota and, after spreading across much of

---

17   See N Robinson *Resolving Entrenched Child Litigation Part Two: A New Model of Court-Directed Mediation* [2006] Fam Law 139.
18   [2004] EWCA Civ 1353, [2005] 1 FLR 381. See Thorpe LJ at para [17].
19   Ibid, at para [17].

the United States, it arrived in this country in 2003. In October of that year, the Collaborative Family Law Group was formed and the following year the organisation became affiliated to Resolution (formerly the Solicitors Family Law Association). At the time of writing, more than 500 lawyers have been trained in the process.

4.33　As its name suggests, the collaborative process is based on the principle that a resolution of a legal dispute is most likely to be achieved if the parties refrain from adopting polarised positions at the start of the dispute but rather work together to achieve an agreement. A crucial feature of the process is that each party is represented by a specially trained lawyer whose instructions are exclusively confined to the collaborative process.

4.34　At the outset, the parties and their collaborative lawyers sign a participation agreement, the terms of which may include:

(a)　a statement of the parties' intentions and the principles under which they will work;
(b)　a statement that the negotiations will be conducted in good faith;
(c)　a further statement that the negotiations will be confidential and privileged;
(d)　provision for payment of the lawyers' costs; and
(e)　an explanation of what will happen if the process breaks down, with an important component of this latter provision being that, in the event of a breakdown of the process, neither of the lawyers involved will represent the parties thereafter.

4.35　The process continues with a series of four-way meetings (attended by each party and his or her lawyer). The recommended procedure includes features designed to ensure that the lawyers remain committed to the collaborative nature of the process. For example, they will commonly meet in advance of the four-way meeting to agree the agenda. Each lawyer is given an opportunity to lead part of the meeting so that neither feels excluded. One-upmanship, a regrettable feature of much adversarial litigation, is anathema to the process. Although there is scope for each lawyer to offer advice to their client during the meetings, the emphasis at all times is on working together to achieve a resolution. An illustration of the way that collaborative lawyers work can be found from many of the collaborative law websites, not only from this country, but also from the US and Canada[20] which have a longer history in this regard. For example, according to the website of Collaborative Practice in Alberta, Canada,[21] collaborative lawyers:

- advise on the law;
- advise on fees;
- represent the interests of their clients, but will also listen to the other party's case and consider their interests;
- will guide the Collaborative Family Law meetings;
- will co-operate in sharing all factual information;
- will be honest and respectful;

20　See www.collablaw.org.uk; www.collaborativelaw.org; www.collaborativelawny.com.
21　See www.collaborativelaw.ca.

- will use clear language when speaking and writing;
- will manage emotional situations;
- will point out unreasonable expectations;
- will work hard to help the parties reach an agreement;
- will not go to court before reaching an agreement.

4.36   An important feature of collaborative law is its recognition that lawyers are not blessed with all the professional skills sometimes required to resolve family disputes:

> 'Part of the critical paradigm shift we undergo before becoming successful collaborative lawyers is that of recognising the limitations of our skill-set.'[22]

To that end, the process provides opportunities for the parties to refer aspects of the dispute to a 'family consultant', a professional with appropriate skills in couple and family transition, for example a counsellor, social worker or therapist. Their role will be to offer emotional and psychological support to the parties and/or practical advice in matters arising in the dispute – for example, housing issues, debt counselling or childcare. The consultant may see the parties separately, or sit in during the four-way meetings.

4.37   Collaborative law is in its early stages in this country. To date, there are insufficient practitioners to provide anything like a comprehensive service across the jurisdiction. No research has yet been carried out as to its effectiveness. Although the Legal Services Commission has expressed interest in the process, there is not yet any means of obtaining public funding for using it.

4.38   Potentially, however, it may offer an important alternative method of resolving family disputes without recourse to litigation. It may turn out to incorporate the best features of solicitor led negotiation and of mediation. The disadvantages of solicitor negotiation (that it is adversarial and court driven) are taken away, but the positive features (that the parent has someone representing their own interests and who can give them on the spot legal advice) are retained. Likewise, the disadvantages of mediation (the lack of availability of legal advice and the absence of any individual present who represents the interests of the parent) are taken away, but the advantages (the voluntary intention of two individuals to negotiate an agreement without going to court and without coercion) are retained. That there are likely to be emotional issues that need addressing and which may get in the way of agreement is also recognised and provided for.

4.39   If the process continues to develop successfully in the private sector and thereafter attracts the attention of the Government and the Legal Services Commission, it may provide the best hope yet for a lasting way for some former partners to resolve their differences. It is not to be thought a soft option. As Sherrie Abney (Texas Collaborative Law Council) and Michael Lind (Managing Director, ADR Group UK) have written:[23]

---

22   Steering Committee, Collaborative Family Law Group, May 2005.
23   See www.adrgroup.co.uk.

'Collaborative Law is not for sissies. It is hard work and takes much more creativity and patience than litigation. Nearly one half of the parties who have engaged in the collaborative process and settled their disputes have said that if there had been no withdrawal provision in the participation agreement that they probably would have terminated the process and gone on to litigation. At some point it appeared easier to abdicate their responsibility and let someone else decide their cases. It was only the thought of having to start over with new counsel that kept them working towards settlement. However, these same parties are quick to admit that they probably would not have been satisfied with the results had they gone to litigation and not continued to take an active part in their dispute.'

SETTLEMENT THROUGH SOLICITORS

4.40 With all the emphasis on mediation, it would be easy to overlook the contribution made by specialist family law solicitors to the process of settlement of family disputes.[24] Aside from the innovation of collaborative law, and despite the belief that many hold to the contrary, family law solicitors have for years assisted their clients to come to an agreement with the other party. There are some lawyers (solicitors and barristers) who are inclined to raise the temperature in any dispute, but there are many more who recognise that it is in the interests of their clients to settle away from court. In September 1982, the Solicitors Family Law Association was founded in London with the aim of improving the practice of family law to prevent the legal process increasing acrimony between separating couples. They developed a Code of Practice to be followed by all members with this aim in mind. Couples are encouraged to settle disputes by negotiation wherever possible, with court action being seen as a last resort and parents are urged to deal with each other constructively and to focus on their continuing role in relation to their children. If appropriate, individuals or families may be referred to other professionals – to counsellors, mediators or collaborative lawyers, for example.

4.41 In 2005, the organisation decided to rename itself 'Resolution' in order to broaden understanding of the organisation among the general public, to reflect the fact that not all its members are solicitors, and to describe what separating families wish to achieve. With these principles in mind, many people are encouraged to settle their disputes with the other party, by a combination of advice as to their legal rights, information as to what will be a likely outcome of contested litigation, what happens in other cases and families, and the advantages to their family relationships (as well as to their pockets) of an out-of-court settlement.

EARLY INTERVENTIONS AND THE FAMILY RESOLUTIONS PILOT PROJECT

4.42 For many parents who do need some form of assistance, the combination of the availability of mediation, legal advice and the information

---

24 See J Eeekelaar, M Maclean & S Beinart *Family Lawyers: The Divorce Work of Solicitors* (Oxford, Hart Publishing, 2000).

and checklists contained in the parenting plans are sufficient to enable them to come to an agreement over the arrangements for their children. There are, however, a substantial minority of parents who cannot do so. Divorce or separation are extremely painful events, and to expect people to behave rationally afterwards, even though they know it may damage their children not to do so, is often too much to ask, especially in the early stages. The difficulties that are presented by emotional fall-out are familiar to professionals working in the area, but it is sometimes difficult to know what to do about it. One of the striking features of the system of collaborative law is that it recognises that parents might need therapeutic and emotional support alongside negotiation and provides for parties to be so advised or assisted.

4.43   There was considerable criticism over many years of the manner in which the family justice system handled disputed contact cases. Research has not surprisingly demonstrated that parental management of post-conflict separation and collaboration has a very considerable effect on the well-being of their children.[25] This country had been slow to develop educational and therapeutic programmes to help parents manage conflict.[26] The Family Resolutions Pilot Project[27] was intended to explore the efficacy of combining education with a version of in-court conciliation.

4.44   The Family Resolutions Pilot Project, set up by the Government in March 2004, was a scheme that was designed, if not to provide therapeutic help, then at least to provide parents with information as to how their children would be affected by continuing conflict, and, by means of setting up 'parent groups', to foster a network of support and understanding of parents for each other. The pilot was run in three court centres – in Brighton, in Sunderland and in Inner London. It was a voluntary scheme for those involved in litigation over contact in those areas, although cases involving allegations of domestic violence were not eligible for referral. There were four parts to the scheme – an initial risk assessment at court, parent education groups led by Relate, parent planning meetings held by CAFCASS away from court, and then, where appropriate, meetings with children to ascertain their wishes and feelings. What was new about the scheme was the attempt to put together education and conciliation in the same project. Research on out-of-court mediation[28] and in-court conciliation[29] has demonstrated that reaching an agreement does not automatically mean that parents communicate and/or collaborate effectively thereafter and contain parental conflict in the interests of their children. Therefore any scheme which would assist them to do so, as well as to come to an immediate agreement, could be of long term value.

---

25   See J Pryor & B Rodgers *Children in Changing Families: Life after Parental Separation* (Oxford, Blackwell Publications, 2001).
26   See J Hunt & C Roberts *Child Contact with Non-resident Parents* (University of Oxford, 2004).
27   The Pilot Project ran between September 2004 and August 2005.
28   See J Walker et al *Picking up the Pieces: Marriage and Divorce Two Years after Information Provision* (DCA, 2004) available at www.dca.gov.uk/pubs/reports.
29   See L Trinder, J Connolly, J Kellett, C Notley & L Swift *Making contact happen or making contact work? The process and outcomes of in-court conciliation* (DCA, 2006) – available at www.dca.gov.uk/family/research2006/03_2006.pdf.

Risk assessment

4.45 It was intended that cases of alleged domestic violence, abuse or harm should be excluded from consideration for the project at the earliest stage. The manner in which risk was assessed proved to be a major challenge for the courts involved in the scheme. Professionals in the family justice system were inclined to adopt a narrow definition of 'current risk', whereas Relate adopted a definition which meant that all allegations of fear for safety were taken at face value. The approach that was ultimately adopted by all the courts involved in the pilot was that the issue of risk of harm was considered at a standard first directions appointment in each case, as opposed to a paper assessment when the applications were received.

Parent education groups

4.46 Parents who volunteered for the scheme were invited to attend two parent group sessions. The groups were mixed gender but parents did not attend the same group as the other parent. The groups were run by two facilitators from Relate, one male and one female. The first group focused on raising the awareness of parents of their children's experience of separation and conflict. Parents watched a video and then took part in a group discussion. The second group session involved work and discussion as to how parents manage conflict following separation, with the objective of developing awareness of the child's perspective. Role-play exercises were carried out. The idea was that parents would be assisted not only by the work, but also by the presence of other parents, including those of the opposite sex, resident and non-resident. Several of the parents apparently commented afterwards that it was this very mix of people that helped them to understand things from the perspective of others.

4.47 The feedback from this part of the pilot indicated that parents found the groups a source of support, and that some of the parents did think again about the effect that their disputes would be having on their children.[30] They also indicated that, through group discussion, they learned techniques to manage conflict.

Parent planning

4.48 After the parents attended the group sessions, they were invited to meet jointly with an officer from CAFCASS to try to come to an agreement with respect to contact. The planning meetings were not held at court, and were led by two CAFCASS officers, one male and one female. The intention was that parents would work through the parenting booklet addressing the issues contained therein, although it seemed from the limited number of people who completed the pilot that the booklet was not used very much. It had been the

---

30 See L Trinder, J Connolly, J Kellett & C Notley *Evaluation of the Family Resolutions Pilot Project* (DfES Publications, 2006).

intention that children could be involved at the planning stage of the case, but again very few were involved – in three of the cases only.

Outcome of the project

4.49 The project was marred by the limited numbers of people that took part. There were only 62 referrals in total in the three areas that took part. Of those only two-thirds got as far as the first group session, with a small number of others dropping out later so that only half the original referrals completed the programme. There seem to have been several reasons for the low take-up and completion rate – concern about the length of the process and the effect that would have on a contact application; a lack of communication between various bodies involved in the project such as CAFCASS, Relate, court officials, solicitors and judges; the fact that many cases included allegations of domestic violence, thereby rendering them ineligible; and some difficulties about appointment times. The small sample rate has meant that the authors of the evaluation report[31] have been very cautious in extracting anything other than very tentative conclusions. They did, however, feel that the educational component (the group work) did appear to have a positive impact on the parental relationship beyond the ability to come to an agreement over the current dispute.

4.50 The authors of the evaluation report make a number of recommendations for the family justice system. First, they propose that it develop a range of parenting interventions, including basic parent education and higher conflict education/therapeutic interventions, to work alongside processes for dispute resolution and child involvement. Secondly, they recommend that a small number of demonstration projects addressing both high and low conflict cases should be set up and tested, and/or two or three case management systems. They point out that the content of programmes should follow national and international evidence of what works, that the sites of pilot programmes should be selected with the greatest of care, and that they must have a local core multi-professional group (including the local judiciary) who are enthusiastic and committed.

OUT-OF-COURT RESOLUTIONS – CONCLUSIONS

4.51 With increasing numbers of children living apart from one of their parents, the family justice system has become more conscious of the need to promote agreement between parents as to their relationships with and parental responsibility for their children. That agreement should be encouraged is not a new idea – solicitors, barristers, judges and CAFCASS officers have been involved in brokering agreements between warring couples for many years, often at the court door, but there is now increasing emphasis (and there are better facilities) for doing so away from court and court procedure altogether.

---

31   Ibid.

4.52 The majority of separating parents will be able to work out for themselves a solution which is in the best interests of their children. At one end of the spectrum (the most populated end) are the lowest or no conflict families who need little or nothing new to assist them. At the other end are cases which are so difficult that they never resolve, despite repeated outings to court. It is the cases between the two extremes that are most likely to be assisted by education and alternative dispute resolution, but of course the variations within this group are extremely wide as well. Some cases within it will be resolved with a few sessions of mediation, others will need more. Divorce and separation are deeply emotional events. Some people will recover quickly, some slowly and others not at all. It is a great deal to expect people to act rationally when they are suffering upheaval in every aspect of their lives. They may have had to face losing their partner, their children (at least on a day-to-day basis), their lifestyle and their home. Added to this is the fact that one party to a former relationship may be at a different stage emotionally from the other. They may find themselves (particularly in the early stages) seeking a procedure that will heap blame on the other party and vindication for themselves – a state of mind much better suited to an adversarial system than any other.

4.53 Whilst a combination of mediation, education and the simple passage of time may very well be very effective for most parents, there are cases where the hostility and conflict become entrenched and far less amenable to outside intervention. One party may feel controlled and bullied by the other, one parent (resident or otherwise) may fear not just the loss of the physical company of their children but also of their influence over them to the other parent. It is also not uncommon for one or even both parents to have and develop a distorted view of the other, leading them to misinterpret their actions and motives. These cases need more complex intevention, including not just education and mediation but sometimes some therapeutic intervention as well. The advantage of projects such as the Family Resolutions Pilot Project, and of collaborative law, is that they do not simply look at the mechanics of obtaining agreement but include a process of education and parental support beforehand (Pilot Project) or simultaneous emotional and therapeutic support (collaborative law). If the recommendations of Trinder et al[32] are followed, there may well be future government-sponsored projects which will tackle the wider issues.

4.54 It is clear that mediation and other forms of negotiation and conciliation can be very successful in obtaining agreement between parents, although it is less clear whether those agreements bring with them solutions that are lasting, together with better communication and less conflict in general over the children. One of the most important factors in determining how children respond to separation and divorce is the level of parental conflict and so the importance of this overall cannot be underestimated. This is a salutary lesson indeed.

4.55 It is important, however, not to regard out-of-court resolution as an appropriate process for all cases, and especially for those involving genuine

---

32   Ibid.

safety issues. There is a danger in relying too heavily on it. Professor Gwynn Davis,[33] writing in 2004 about research that he had done in the 1980s, said this:

> 'As far as courts were concerned, settlement was the thing. And why was this? Well there were two reasons, and they still apply today. First, when it comes to disputes about children, the judiciary have no confidence in their own product. Judges themselves believe that courts are a blunt instrument which cannot hope to grapple with the complexity and rival versions of the truth which characterise issues of residence or contact – they think there must be a better way. And secondly there is rationing. This is I think is the main reason: the rationing motif dominates our system of private family law. The principal objective is not to supply a service; it is used instead to restrict access to a service, the service in question being judicial determination.'

4.56 At the outset of this chapter, we observed that litigation is far from the ideal way of resolving disputes. It must be recognised, however, that mediation and other forms of alternative dispute resolution are themselves not ideal, because the family disputes which they address are not concerned with ideal circumstances, but rather with the messy realities of family life. The basic principle behind mediation and out-of-court resolution is, however, undeniably sound – that, wherever possible, families should be encouraged, though not coerced, into reaching agreements about the future that allows them to move forward with their lives.

---

33   See G Davis *A Research Perspective* in J Westcott (ed) *Family Mediation: Past, Present and Future* (Jordans, 2004).

Chapter Five

TOWARDS A BETTER COURT SERVICE FOR CHILDREN

5.1   Whilst the approach of Government, Parliament and judiciary alike is, wherever possible, to keep contact away from the courts, it is recognised that the family court will continue to have an important part to play in the lives of many a child. In some cases, where issues of safety and protection really are entailed, it is entirely proper that it should do so. There will, however, remain a large number of cases which simply reach that forum because one or other parent, or even both, think that it should, in circumstances where objectively the resort to court was unnecessary and likely to be counter-productive.

5.2   Yet, whatever the nature of the case and the rights or wrongs of it being before the court, it has to be dealt with in a way that is appropriate to its circumstances and sensitive to the needs of the child concerned. The courts' approach to private law cases in which domestic violence features properly forms a chapter all of its own. Within this, we look more generally at a number of factors that affect the court experience and the various initiatives aimed at improving that experience for litigants and their children. We begin with the Private Law Programme, which now informs the courts' conduct of residence and contact cases, and focus particularly on its promotion of in-court conciliation. We then examine the new changing role for CAFCASS (the Children and Family Court Advisory and Support Service) and end by looking at how the McKenzie friend process is being encouraged and developed in an attempt to produce a more level playing field for the unrepresented litigant.

THE PRIVATE LAW PROGRAMME

5.3   The centrepiece of the courts' new approach to private law children's disputes is the Private Law Programme.[1] Introduced on 9 November 2004 by Dame Elizabeth Butler-Sloss (then President of the Family Division) and heralded within *Parental Separation: Children's Needs and Parents' Responsibilities – Next Steps*,[2] the Private Law Programme provides guidance geared to improve the resolution of private law family cases in the High Court and county court and is now being widened in its application to the family proceedings court. Whilst very deliberately not championed as a compulsory protocol for private law cases, its foreword explains the intention that:

---

1   Reproduced at Appendix 5.
2   January 2005 – Cm 6452 – available at www.dfes.gov.uk/childrensneeds/.

'... the Programme will be a gradual process involving a national roll out of best practice together with the development of local schemes, having in mind good local initiatives already in place, based upon these principles and key elements.'

5.4 In his speech to the Association of Lawyers for Children 2005 Annual Conference,[3] the new President of the Family Division, Sir Mark Potter, described the overall package promoted by the Programme as representing 'a fundamental change in the way private law cases are handled'.

5.5 The Programme proceeds on the core principle of collaborative working, the aim being to harness the efforts of the judiciary, CAFCASS, the courts . service, the legal profession and the litigants themselves so as to achieve the best outcomes for the children concerned. As will be apparent from its detail, the Programme's overriding characteristic is its emphasis on dispute resolution other than through contested proceedings. That of course reflects the research findings[4] indicating, on the one hand, the greater satisfaction rates associated with non court-based outcomes and, on the other, the damaging consequences for children of being embroiled in their parents' disputes. But it also recognises that the simple act of engaging the court system should not irrevocably set in train a contested (and often lengthy) process. The contested court battle has now been relegated to the option of last resort.

5.6 That is not to suggest that, before the Programme's implementation, there was not encouragement (from the judiciary and, in many cases, from the lawyers as well) to the parties to compromise the proceedings before the court. The effect of the Programme, however, is to place that ethos at the core of the court's function, to prescribe more effectively the means by which compromise can be achieved and to establish an apparent presumption against contested proceedings which bites from the very start of the process.

5.7 Practice suggests that the most intractable cases are the ones which have been allowed to last for too long – time over which acrimony has built up and positions have hardened. The effective presumption in favour of alternative dispute resolution (ADR) is plainly geared to avoiding the onset of the intractable case at source. But, by improving the court's case management functions and its subsequent ability to embed the arrangements that it makes and approves, the Programme shows that the pressure to avoid the most damaging kinds of cases is kept up throughout. To the litigant, a clear message is sent out – that, if there is to be a contest, then it will be properly focused, consistently and appropriately managed, resolved sooner rather than later and with any outcome given the best chance of success.

5.8 Of course, the more the Programme succeeds, the greater will be its prospects for success in the future. What is unlikely to change are the continuing numbers of children enduring parental separation, so the challenge will always be there. But diverting parents away from the court system inevitably frees up court time; as (for those who cannot be so diverted) does

---

3   18 November 2005. See [2006] Fam Law 65.
4   See paras 1.37 et seq.

identifying and limiting the issues, such that contests are focused rather than all-encompassing. If those two objectives can be achieved, then it has to follow that more court time will be freed up to deal – and quickly – with those cases which really do warrant the attention of the courts.

The cardinal principles

5.9 Turning now to the actual content of the Private Law Programme, it begins by recognising that 'the court process exists in the wider context of parental separation and relationship breakdown' and makes clear that 'the court's aim is to assist parents to safeguard their children's welfare'. It expresses the hope that many families will have received out-of-court assistance and early intervention from professionals before or upon making an application, and indicates that the court 'will always investigate' whether the family has had the benefit of these or similar services and whether any available form of alternative dispute resolution can be used.

5.10 The Programme aims to give effect to what is now identified as the overriding objective of the family justice system within the context of private law children disputes. That overriding objective is to enable the court to deal with every children case:

(a)   justly, expeditiously, fairly and with the minimum of delay;
(b)   in ways which ensure, so far as is practicable, that:
      (i) the parties are on an equal footing;
      (ii) the welfare of the children involved is safeguarded; and
      (iii) distress to all parties is minimised;
(c)   so far as is practicable, in ways which are proportionate:
      (i) to the gravity and complexity of the issues; and
      (ii) to the nature and extent of the intervention proposed in the private and family life of the children and adults involved.

5.11 The first respect in which the overriding objective is applied is in the stipulation that there shall in every case be an early First Hearing dispute resolution appointment:

● that identifies immediate safety issues;
● that exercises effective court control so as to identify the aim of the proceedings, the timescale within which that aim can be achieved, the issues between the parties, the opportunities for the resolution of those issues by appropriate referrals for support and assistance and any subsequent steps that may be permitted or required;
● with, wherever possible, a CAFCASS practitioner to be available to the court and to the family whose purpose and priority is to facilitate early dispute resolution rather than the provision of a formal report;
● with the court, save in exceptional circumstances (such as where safety is in issue) or where immediate agreement is possible, directing that the family shall be referred for support and assistance to locally available resolution services.[5]

---

5   The Private Law Programme, as originally drafted, provided also for referral to 'a Family

5.12   The Private Law Programme then provides that the overriding objective shall be furthered by 'continuous and active case management of every case', to include:

- judicial availability – this requires the identification of gatekeeper district judges to undertake early First Hearing dispute resolution appointments;
- judicial continuity – this entails the allocation to the case of private law family judiciary and the identification of dedicated court and CAFCASS practitioners;
- continuous case management – to be undertaken by the allocated judiciary and identified court officers and to include a listing scheme in each hearing centre that describes local listing arrangements to ensure judicial availability, continuity and access to the court for review and/or enforcement;
- the avoidance of unnecessary delay – to be achieved by the early identification of issues and timetabling of the case from the outset;
- maximising Family Court resources – with there to be guidance in place for the flexible transfer of cases between every level of family court so as to make best use of court facilities, judges and Family Proceedings Courts, having regard to availability, urgency and in some cases complexity;
- identifying and achieving the aim of each hearing;
- monitoring and reviewing the outcome (at short notice if needs be);
- enforcing the court's orders (at short notice if needs be);
- controlling the use and cost of resources.

5.13   The third respect in which the Private Law Programme seeks to advance the overriding objective is through what the Programme describes as 'flexible facilitation and referral'. This provides for best interests decisions and agreements to be facilitated by:

- the use of parenting plans to assist parents to agree routine childcare questions;[6]
- the use of a CAFCASS practitioner who, where possible, shall be continuously involved to facilitate and/or supervise the court's orders and the arrangements necessary to make orders and agreements work;
- the flexible use of rehabilitative, training, therapy, treatment and enforcement powers;
- directions that require parties, referral agencies and, where appropriate, the CAFCASS practitioner to report the progress or outcome of any step so that the court might respond by urgent review to safeguard the welfare of the child.

The process in action

5.14   Having set out the court's approach at the various stages of the process in conceptual terms, the Private Law Programme goes into greater detail.

Resolution Pilot Project (where available)': the Project has since ended and has not been extended (see further at para 4.42 et seq).

6   See para 4.7 et seq.

5.15 Recognising the importance of information for all users of the court system, the Programme provides, in the first instance, that in each family hearing centre there will be prepared judicial, listing, parent and child information sheets setting out the procedures, arrangements and facilities that are available to the court and families in each local area.

5.16 The Programme thereafter fleshes out the critical First Hearing dispute resolution appointment, providing:

- that it shall be listed within a target window from the issue of the application of 4 to 6 working weeks;[7]
- that it shall be attended by the parents and, in court centres where the local scheme provides for it, and where resources exist for such to occur, that it may also be attended by any child aged 9 or over.

5.17 Within the Private Law Programme and within *Parental Separation: Children's Needs and Parents' Responsibilities – Next Steps*[8] itself, the concept of in-court conciliation (a form of dispute resolution used in the early stage of proceedings) is clearly promoted.[9] At the time of the Programme's introduction, some courts already had such schemes and the clear intention was for their prevalence to become widespread.

5.18 In those court centres where resources exist to provide in-court conciliation, the Private Law Programme stipulates as follows:

- the First Hearing dispute resolution appointment shall be listed so that a duty CAFCASS practitioner is available to the parties and to the court to facilitate agreements, the identification of issues and any appropriate referrals for assistance;
- where the local scheme provides for it, the detailed content of the conciliation discussions may remain confidential;
- the court may adjourn a First Hearing dispute resolution appointment for further in-court conciliation or a report upon the availability or success of any proposal.

5.19 The Private Law Programme further provides that, in court centres where a duty CAFCASS practitioner is not available, the court will identify the issues between the parties and use its best endeavours to facilitate agreements and referrals for assistance. In appropriate cases where advice is necessary, the court may adjourn the First Hearing dispute resolution appointment for a CAFCASS practitioner to provide oral or short written advice to the parties and the court limited to the facilitation of matters that are agreed and referrals for further assistance.

5.20 Continuing the theme of important information being clear and available to the court user for the present and the future, it is prescribed that, at

---

7   This does not of course prevent cases which, because of their nature, need to come before the court before that target window from being able so to do – see para 5.23.

8   January 2005 – Cm 6452 – available at www.dfes.gov.uk/childrensneeds/.

9   The Programme provides a model scheme for in-court dispute resolution – see paras 5.21–5.33.

the conclusion of the First Hearing dispute resolution appointment and generally at the end of any subsequent hearing required, the court shall identify on the face of the order:

- the issues that are determined, agreed or disagreed;
- the aim of the order, agreement, referral or hearing that is set out in the order;
- any other basis for the order or directions that are made or the agreement that is recorded;
- in respect of issues that are not agreed and that need to be determined so as to safeguard the welfare of the child:
  – the level of court (and where appropriate the allocated judge(s) before whom all future non-conciliation hearings and applications are to be heard);
  – the timetable and the sequence of the steps that are required to lead to any early hearing;
  – the filing and service of evidence limited to such of the issues as the court may identify;
  – whether a CAFCASS practitioner's report is necessary and, if so, the issues to which the report is to be directed;
  – in respect of all orders, agreements and referrals, directions for the facilitation of the same (in particular by a CAFCASS practitioner), for the monitoring of the outcome (including by urgent reserved re-listing before the same court within 10 working days of a request by CAFCASS) and for enforcement.

The model scheme for in-court dispute resolution

5.21   The Private Law Programme provides a model scheme for in-court dispute resolution, the idea being that each hearing centre should formulate its own scheme taking appropriate account of local factors.

5.22   The model scheme provides for a number of practical arrangements to be undertaken before the matter first comes before the court:

- private law applications are to be issued on the date of receipt and to be sent on the same day to CAFCASS;
- information sheets about the FHDRA (the First Hearing dispute resolution appointment), the role of the CAFCASS practitioner[10] and the court are sent to the parties together with the Notice of Hearing;
- prior to the application being listed for the appointment, CAFCASS will carry out their own paper risk assessment, in particular as to safety issues;
- CAFCASS may advise the court that a particular case has risk or safety issues that would best be explored before the judge or magistrates/legal advisor at the FHDRA rather than in discussions between the parties and the CAFCASS practitioner.

5.23   Within the model scheme is the express proviso that, whilst the FHDRA window is 4 to 6 weeks from issue, cases that are very urgent or that involve

---

10   For further information about CAFCASS, see paras 5.52–5.70.

issues of safety or complexity may need to be listed or determined separately and should be referred to a resident judge or magistrates/legal advisor for guidance.

5.24 Once the case is at court, and in the absence of any direction to the contrary (in particular as to safety issues), the FHDRA is listed before a judge or magistrates/legal advisor, with a CAFCASS practitioner available to facilitate early dispute resolution in accordance with the local scheme. Both parents are expected to attend with their representatives (if they have them), with the relevant child or children only attending where a local scheme provides for such attendance and where it can occur in an appropriate child-friendly environment.

5.25 By this stage, the CAFCASS practitioner will already have carried out a paper risk assessment and the model scheme provides that further risk assessment may be undertaken by the CAFCASS practitioner with the child (if appropriate) and each party separately prior to any joint meeting between the practitioner and the parties (the child is not expected to attend this joint meeting unless the CAFCASS practitioner advises that such attendance is in the child's interests and both parties agree).

5.26 Where an agreement between the parties is reached, its terms are considered by the judge or magistrates/legal advisor to decide whether the terms are appropriate and an order is necessary.

5.27 Where full agreement is not reached, the judge (or magistrates/legal advisors) gives directions and provides a timetable for the case to come back to court, dealing in particular with the aim of the next hearing, the issues that need to be determined, the evidence that should be filed for those purposes and any interim provisions. The timetable has always to include the listing of the next, or the full, hearing, 'which should be as soon as is possible consistent with the interests of the child'.

5.28 Annex F of the Private Law Programme sets out a 'Recommended Record of Hearing' and the model scheme suggests that the parties and the court consider drafting orders having regard to its contents 'to provide a better record for subsequent use'. The 'Recommended Record of Hearing', which indicates that the following matters should be addressed and included when setting out the record of what has taken place at court, is self-evidently comprehensive:

- the parties;
- on notice/without notice (this explains whether the respondent to the application had notice of the hearing);
- the application(s);
- representation and attendance;
- the recitals;
- the agreements in principle and as to detail that have been reached and that can be facilitated despite the need for a further hearing on other matters (eg interim provisions);
- the method of facilitation and monitoring of agreed matters (if any);

- the basis for the order/directions that are made or the agreement that is recorded (eg 'on the basis that mother says ... and father says');
- the key ISSUES[11] that remain to be determined, including the issues of fact and any issues relating to safety;
- the AIM[12] of the hearing that is being timetabled (eg to determine the principle/quantum of staying/visiting contact);
- orders and directions;
- any referral to a Family Resolutions Pilot[13] or local ADR schemes;
- the level of court (and if appropriate the allocated judge) before whom all further hearings are to be conducted;
- whether a CAFCASS report or evidence is necessary and, if so, limited to which issues and in what form;
- the case management timetable including directions as to the filing and service of evidence (and specifying the issues upon which the evidence is permitted);
- in the rare cases where independent experts are permitted by the court, the consideration and allocation of the cost of the same;
- the date of the next hearing/the full hearing;
- provisions for facilitation, monitoring and enforcement (including variation and discharge);
- penal notice and guidance;
- schedules (eg of evidence/documents considered).

5.29 Recognising that historically one of the key drivers of delay in private law cases has been the time taken for the CAFCASS practitioner involved to report to the court, the model scheme provides guidance aimed at addressing that problem. It indicates:

- that requests for CAFCASS reports should not be made unless a report is necessary; and
- that, where a report is considered necessary, the key issues, to which the report is to be directed, should be identified, as should the question of whether the issues can be dealt with in a short report so as to minimise the time taken in preparing the report and to allow CAFCASS to maximise its resources to facilitate agreements and orders.

5.30 Traditionally, the court order provided for what should happen but did not provide for the aftermath. It was a static and invariably optimistic statement of intent, which frequently did not (or did not sufficiently) in advance deal with issues of facilitation, monitoring or enforcement. Therein lay the seeds of greater conflict and more delay in those cases where the contact agreed or ordered did not proceed as smoothly as the court had hoped. The thinking behind the model scheme – and indeed the Private Law Programme as a whole – is to try to grasp the nettle from the earliest. Hence the model scheme stipulates that the court order should indicate if a particular agreement or order is to be facilitated or monitored and whether particular arrangements for enforcement are provided for, for example that the first handover for a visiting

---

11   The use of capitals when referring to the issues and to the aim of a hearing would appear to entail a wholly deliberate emphasis on making court hearings more focused.
12   Ibid.
13   See footnote 5.

contact did in fact take place, who is to inform CAFCASS, whether, in what circumstance, and how CAFCASS is to inform the court (eg by email) and whether, how and when the matter is to be listed in the event of non-compliance.

5.31 The model scheme further provides that, where CAFCASS, a party or other agency is asked to inform the court of the success or otherwise of an arrangement, the agreement of that person or agency may need to be sought and the method of informing the court should be specified in the order.

5.32 Local listing and notification arrangements must be included in any local scheme for in-court dispute resolution, so that a party or CAFCASS is able to bring the matter back to court for enforcement within 10 days where an agreement has not been complied with or is not working effectively.

5.33 The model scheme additionally makes the following provisions, all of which are geared to improve the quality of case management and thereby the quality of the outcomes for the subject children:

- it emphasises that the listing of cases is a judicial function;
- it stipulates that all applications for the variation of orders or for enforcement other than in accordance with the terms of an order in an individual case or the local scheme are to be made by separate application, with such applications to be referred to a resident judge or magistrates/legal advisor for a decision as to whether the application should be treated as an urgent enforcement hearing or a separate free-standing hearing; and
- it makes clear that hearings are to be allocated to the judge who dealt with the matter previously so as to maintain judicial continuity, with arrangements to be in place to release the judge or magistrates (as the case may be) for urgent enforcement hearings even if they are sitting at another court.

The annexes

5.34 The Private Law Programme has seven annexes, with the first, Annex A, complementing the Model Scheme for In-Court Dispute Resolution by setting out the following 'key features' to be specified in each local scheme:

- *Venues and facilities* – Where the optimum facilities exist having regard to:
  - the available judiciary;
  - CAFCASS practitioners;
  - safety requirements;
  - the need for interview and/or children's rooms;
  - already existing facilities and schemes.
- *Judges* – The availability of the specialist judiciary:
  - the identity of the ticketed[14] District Judges, Magistrates and Circuit Judges and their sitting patterns;

---

14   Those allowed to deal with private law children's cases.

– the possibility of listing before District Judges (Magistrates' Courts) and Recorders (and their identity and sittings availability);
– the existence and availability of similar schemes in the Family Proceedings Courts.

- *Parenting Plans* – Encouragement to families to consider and make use of the Parenting Plan materials.[15]
- *CAFCASS* – The identity and availability of CAFCASS practitioners.
- *Scheme principles:*
  – Whether the appointment is to be a matter of record or be confidential (ie is it privileged, in which case, unless adjourned for further discussion or referral with a report back to the same judge or magistrate, the matter would then be listed before a different judge/magistrate for any contested hearing).
  – What arrangements can be made for the involvement of children: if they are to attend court or elsewhere, is there an appropriate child friendly environment and what are the specific arrangements that are to be made in each case?
- *Listing* – The local scheme should set out details of the local listing scheme:
  – to give effect to the timetable for the FHDRA and enforcement applications;
  – to indicate whether hearings take place on a dedicated day or days of the week;
  – to indicate too the frequency of lists, the number of judges and magistrates, the number of CAFCASS practitioners and the expected number of hearings in each list and expected estimated length of hearing;
  – to provide for extended discussion after the list is heard (eg during an afternoon when mornings only are listed – in like manner to Financial Dispute Resolution appointments – and to allow mention before the end of the court day);
  – to provide also for adjournment for discussion or to try out an interim agreement but to be re-listed before the same judge or magistrate on another day (and, for example, with the same CAFCASS practitioner being available);
  – to indicate how to obtain a date for the next hearing.

5.35   Annex B is the information sheet that is sent out to the parties about the critical First Hearing dispute resolution appointment. It ensures that, from the off, the parties are aware that, although they are being required to attend court, the aim is clearly to divert them away from contested court proceedings, with the purpose of the FHDRA described in the sheet's first paragraph as being:

'... a preliminary meeting at court to help families resolve disputes about arrangements for children and see if a workable solution can be found without further court proceedings.'

5.36   The information sheet next explains what happens before the date of the FHDRA. It informs the parties that, when an application is first made to the

---

15   See further at para 4.7 et seq.

court, a copy of the application form and the respondent's details and response (the other party's acknowledgement form) are sent to CAFCASS, thereby giving CAFCASS the basic information that they need about the family (to include, where relevant, issues about risk to an adult party and/or a child). It consequently stresses the importance of the parties completing these forms carefully. It also indicates that, if any special risks are identified, then CAFCASS will advise the court about these and that sometimes this will mean that the FHDRA is not the appropriate form of meeting (in which case a judge will decide what form of hearing should take place).

5.37 The information sheet then goes on to explain what happens at court and before the judge. It makes clear that both parties will be expected to attend the FHDRA and that a CAFCASS Family Court Advisor will be there to help the parties reach an agreement that will be in the best interests of the child or children concerned without needing to have a full court hearing. The three possible scenarios that could ensue at the FHDRA and the role of the judge in each are then explained:

- where an agreement is reached, the judge will consider the terms of the agreement and whether a court order is needed to make it work better;
- sometimes the judge will be asked to allow more time so the FHDRA can take longer – this will usually be on the same day but on occasions may include another appointment on another day;
- sometimes it is not possible to reach a full agreement, in which case the judge will decide what happens next, which will include the judge making decisions about whether there should be another court hearing, the date for the case to come back to court, the purpose of the next hearing and the evidence that will be needed (which can include written statements and/or a report prepared by CAFCASS about the current arrangement).

5.38 As to the other five annexes:

- Annex C informs the parties that leaflets are available aimed at their children (to help them make sense of their situation) from the DCA website and from CAFCASS, with the former having a leaflet for each of three age groups (5–8, 8–13 and 13+);[16]
- Annex D is an information sheet for court managers and listing officers;
- Annex E shows what the Notice of Proceedings looks like;
- Annex F is the Recommended Record of Hearing;[17]
- Annex G is a short compendium of useful organisations and links.[18]

IN-COURT CONCILIATION

5.39 The promotion of in-court conciliation lies at the heart of the Private Law Programme. Typically a brief intervention on court premises involving CAFCASS officers and aiming to help parties negotiate an agreement about

---

16   Available at www.dca.gov.uk/family/divleaf.htm and www.cafcass.gov.uk/English/Children/childrenIntro.htm.
17   See para 5.28.
18   See Appendix 8 for a fuller and more up-to-date list of useful organisations and links.

the disputed matter without the need for further legal intervention, in-court conciliation is seen as particularly appropriate for contact cases. Hence the commitment within *Parental Separation: Children's Needs and Parents' Responsibilities – Next Steps*[19] to 'promote and extend in-court conciliation nationwide', which has borne fruit in the number of local schemes which have been either set up or revised since the Programme's introduction.

5.40 As a matter of theory and principle, the encouragement of in-court conciliation seems to be entirely merited; but what do the outcomes of this intervention have to tell us about its efficacy? Does it in fact make contact happen? Does it in fact make contact work? Does it in practice justify the policy focus that is being placed upon it? Having detailed in the preceding section how the Private Law Programme gives practical effect to the concept of in-court conciliation, we now look at the recent research undertaken by Trinder et al[20] that addresses the extent to which in-court conciliation actually does produce better outcomes for the children who are its subject.

5.41 The aim of their study was to identify the overall effectiveness of in-court conciliation in contact cases as well as the relative effectiveness of three contrasting models of conciliation.[21] It entailed interviews with parents, judges, lawyers and CAFCASS officers, with follow-up some 6 to 9 months after the conciliation appointment. In all cases, the families involved in the study were facing significant difficulties, with fraught or tenuous contact, conflicted and distrustful parental relationships, very limited decision-making, high levels of dissatisfaction with arrangements and numerous contact problems.

5.42 Properly recording that conciliation varies widely across the country, the study focused on three different forms:

- the Essex version – there parents attend a scheduled one-hour appointment with the CAFCASS officer then report back briefly to a district judge (described as 'low judicial control');

- that taking place in the Principal Registry of the Family Division – there the District Judge leads negotiations in a court room with lawyers actively negotiating ('high judicial control'); and

- the Suffolk/Cambridgeshire (Cambs) model, in which the District Judge initiates the process in chambers, the parties then go out to negotiate then report back ('mixed').

5.43 The study produces some fairly clear results, indicating that in-court conciliation is on the whole of benefit. In terms of immediate outcomes, the

---

19 January 2005 – Cm 6452 – available at www.dfes.gov.uk/childrensneeds/.
20 See L Trinder, J Connolly, J Kellett, C Notley & L Swift *Making contact happen or making contact work? The process and outcomes of in-court conciliation* (DCA, 2006), available at www.dca.gov.uk/family/research/2006/03_2006.pdf.
21 Effectiveness was measured by agreement rate, satisfaction with the agreement, satisfaction with the process overall and with specific process components, agreement durability, relitigation and further professional intervention, and change (or improvement) in contact patterns, satisfaction with arrangements, contact problems, shared decision-making and parent and child well-being.

'very high' rate of 76% of parents reporting full or partial agreement is notable, as is the revelation that the most satisfied parents are those who have reached full agreement.

5.44 More striking still is the picture at follow-up. Some 6 to 9 months on, only a fifth of agreements had not worked at all, most agreements were intact or had been extended, most cases were closed with low re-litigation rates, many more children were having increased contact, more parents were satisfied with the quantity and quality of contact and children were doing better at baseline. Further, parents whose cases were closed at follow-up scored better on all measures than parents where the court battle was ongoing or had been resurrected.

5.45 Yet, what is also clear from the research is that the benefits of in-court conciliation should not be overstated and have to be placed in context, with the limitations of what it can achieve being recognised.

5.46 Perhaps the most instructive finding of this study reflects the distinction between *contact that happens* and *contact that works*. It is that conciliation is effective in reaching agreement and ensuring that contact occurs, but, regardless of model, has limited impact on the key co-parenting factors that will make contact really work for children. Its authors say that this should not surprise, given that the service that parents receive is very brief and is not designed to address relationship issues – simply providing a dispute resolution process, they observe, does not in itself seem to have further interpersonal or communicative or therapeutic consequences.

5.47 The specific type of conciliation was found to make a difference to both satisfaction with the process and the agreement rate. The 'high judicial control' scheme at the Principal Registry was seen to yield poorer outcomes than the 'low judicial control' or 'mixed' schemes. The extent to which that reflects the difficulty of expecting judges trained to make decisions for others now to help others make decisions for themselves is an issue that clearly needs to be addressed.[22]

5.48 Finally, the study identified significant problems with the conciliation process, regardless again of which model was used. In each area, the courts had adopted a standard case processing approach to achieve agreement and contact. That standard model could be appropriate for 'standard cases', but the one size fits all approach was seen to be ill-suited to dealing with cases raising serious risk issues and could be coercive. The rapid processing of cases and focus on settlement also meant that children were excluded from the process or risked becoming responsible for decisions. Observing that 'all three models struggled to manage risk, to avoid coercion and to involve children appropriately', the authors consider it essential that the development of in-court conciliation occurs only as part of a differentiated case management system and integrated service model. They recommend that the following should be components of the system:

---

22 See further District Judge Stephen Gerlis *Conciliation – Let Battle Commence* [2006] Fam Law 85.

- a triage phase – to entail preliminary screening and risk assessment of all applications, with cases involving serious allegations to be handled in a separate fast-track management system and 'high conflict' or perpetual litigants to be transferred to a specialist programme;
- a dispute resolution process – incorporating features of the low judicial control scheme and/or referral to out of court mediation;
- a child programme – the authors highlight the Australian Children in Focus project,[23] which combines one to two meetings (away from court) between children aged 5 and over and a specially trained child consultant – the consultant then feeds back to parents the child's worldview (and not just the issues concerning the adults), the aim being to support the capacity of the parent to hear the child and focus on that child's needs on a long-term rather than a one-off basis;
- a co-parenting programme – geared to building the capacity of the parent to collaborate,[24] to be available to all parents, alongside a dispute resolution process, with the aim of increasing the prospect of making contact work;
- post-conciliation support – for those families who require ongoing support and trouble-shooting to bed down or adapt an agreement.

5.49   The study accordingly concludes:

'In sum, for a very brief intervention, in-court conciliation does have much to offer as a dispute-resolution process in contact cases. However, in-court conciliation is not suitable for all cases nor is it likely to be sufficient by itself in the majority of cases ... conciliation should be available in all courts but within the context of a differentiated case management system. The Essex or Cambs models are likely to be the most effective, although with more rigorous risk assessment procedures and the appropriate inclusion of children.'

5.50   It is to be hoped that, insofar as resources allow, these messages and recommendations will be taken on board. Clearly there does need to be a realism about what the process of in-court conciliation is capable of achieving and also more work undertaken to improve the effectiveness and sophistication of the local schemes being constructed or revised. Nevertheless, the current correlation between the briefness of this form of intervention and the impact that it can have is remarkable on any basis and of itself justifies the process of in-court conciliation being put into practice nationwide.

5.51   Furthermore, it is not without significance that Trinder et al should have found, perhaps unsurprisingly, that in-court conciliation seems to work best with less entrenched cases. That can only reinforce the imperative of getting hold of cases and steering them away from conflict at the earliest possible stage.

A NEW CHANGING ROLE FOR CAFCASS

5.52   As will be apparent from its mentions in the text thus far, CAFCASS plays a critical part in proceedings concerning children. That much is

---

23   For more information about the project, go to www.childreninfocus.org/index.html.
24   There are already a range of programmes that have been developed in North America and Australia along these lines.

recognised by the Government, Parliament and the judiciary, and key among the measures heralded in *Parental Separation: Children's Needs and Parents' Responsibilities – Next Steps*[25] to improve the outcomes for children of separated parents is what is there described as a 'changing role for CAFCASS'. Yet, before we outline what that changing role entails, it is as well to set out in the first instance what CAFCASS is, what its functions are and how it has been operating.

Background

5.53   CAFCASS was set up on 1 April 2001. It is a national non-departmental public body for England[26] and its creation brought together the services previously provided by the Family Court Welfare Service, the Guardian ad Litem Services and the Children's Division of the Official Solicitor. CAFCASS is independent of the courts, social services, education and health authorities and all similar agencies. Its remit arises 'in respect of family proceedings in which the welfare of children is or may be in question'[27] and its functions are to:

- safeguard and promote the welfare of the child;
- give advice to the court about any applications made to it in such proceedings;
- make provision for children to be represented in such proceedings;
- provide information, advice and support for children and their families.

5.54   CAFCASS becomes involved when social services intervene in families, with the possibility of children being removed for their safety, and where children could be adopted. But, for present purposes, what is in focus is their role when parents are separating or divorcing and have not reached agreement about arrangements for their children.

5.55   In those cases, the CAFCASS officers that will be involved in the court proceedings are either Children and Family Reporters or Guardians ad Litem (described generically as Family Court Advisors). Traditionally the role of the former has been, in the absence of parental agreement, to investigate the issues, write reports for the court and give evidence to it if required. The latter are occasionally appointed in the more difficult private law cases and, where they have been, have comprised those report-writing and evidence-giving functions within the provision of the separate representation of the child's rights and interests. In both guises, the CAFCASS officer will explain the enquiries that they have undertaken and any recommendations that they make as to the future arrangements for the child, such explanations being given in the context of advising the courts to take decisions that are in the best interests of the child

---

25   January 2005 – Cm 6452 – available at www.dfes.gov.uk/childrensneeds/.

26   CAFCASS operates in ten regions throughout England – Eastern, East Midlands, Greater London, North East, North West, South, South East, South West, West Midlands and Yorkshire & Humberside. The operation in Wales has devolved to the National Assembly for Wales and is now CAFCASS Cymru.

27   Criminal Justice and Court Services Act 2000, s 12.

concerned. By way of background, the CAFCASS officer will be qualified in social work and have experience of working with children.

Every Day Matters

5.56 In October 2005, and in a deliberate echo of the *Every Child Matters* agenda,[28] CAFCASS released a consultation paper entitled *Every Day Matters: New Directions for CAFCASS*.[29] The paper entailed and invited comment on a number of proposals for a new professional and organisational strategy for CAFCASS, aimed at improving its service to children and families, most significantly through the provision of 'a guaranteed early intervention service without any delays or backlogs in the allocation of practitioners to cases from April 2007'.

5.57 The rationale for CAFCASS's perceived need to change is set out succinctly in *Every Day Matters: A summary of comments and responses to consultation on a new professional and organisational strategy for CAFCASS*:[30]

> 'Like other public services, our proposed new strategy is set in the context of demanding expectations – that we will deliver improved services within our existing budget. For an organisation such as CAFCASS to achieve this, we need to consider fundamental changes in the way that we work. Our response to these pressures and the changes happening across the family justice system and children's services is to identify opportunities for developing new approaches to our work which are both efficient and produce the outcomes we want to deliver.'

5.58 The consultation paper generated considerable debate both within and outside CAFCASS, engendering some criticism but also (particularly in the private law context) a fair measure of support for what CAFCASS was seeking to achieve and how it was proposing to achieve it. Whilst the changes now being carried forward by CAFCASS extend to organisational as well as practice matters, it is inevitably upon the latter (and particularly by reference to the private law field) that we focus. Having reached a picture of clarity about the form and shape of the way forward, CAFCASS has now published its proposed national standards to put into practice that strategy. Intended, following a short period of consultation as to the detail and a further lead-in period, to operate as from 1 April 2007, they are said to represent 'safe national minimum standards', with which all CAFCASS staff and contractors are expected to comply.

---

28 *Every Child Matters* was the title of a 2003 HMG Green Paper, published alongside the formal response to the report into the death of Victoria Climbié. The Green Paper prompted a large-scale debate about services for children, young people and families and in due course led to the Children Act 2004. *Every Child Matters: Change for Children* was published in November 2004: described as 'a new approach to the well-being of children and young people from birth to age 19', its aim is to provide every child with the support that he or she needs to be healthy, stay safe, enjoy and achieve, make a positive contribution and achieve economic well-being – for more information, go to www.everychildmatters.gov.uk.

29 See www.cafcass.gov.uk/English/Publications/consultation/06Jan31EveryDayMatters.pdf.

30 C Bonehill (published 28 April 2006).

5.59   The proposed national standards begin by setting out a 12-point vision for the service that provides that CAFCASS will:

(1)   put children first;

(2)   keep children as safe as possible;

(3)   ensure that each child has a voice that is heard and listened to;

(4)   start with the child and stay with the child throughout the life of cases;

(5)   articulate and convince others about the needs, wishes and feelings of individual children in family court cases;

(6)   secure the best long-term outcomes for each child;

(7)   respect the importance of family life and family members for each child;

(8)   maintain its independence;

(9)   work within the framework of *Every Child Matters*;[31]

(10) promote an inquisitorial, not an adversarial, family justice system, promoting progress through discussion and agreement;

(11) be passionate about front line services throughout the organisation;

(12) provide a brief expert analysis in each case.

5.60   Appropriately, the first proposed national standard relates to safeguarding. It recognises that CAFCASS's primary role is to safeguard the welfare and promote the interests of each child or young person' referred to by the service and stresses the broadness of CAFCASS's definition of safeguarding which 'can mean safeguarding against abuse, safeguarding important attachments, or promoting a stable and secure future life'. The proposed national standard provides:

- for each CAFCASS assessment, analysis and care plan to be explicit about CAFCASS's safeguarding focus in each case; and

- for the CAFCASS safeguarding policy framework and other policies and toolkits, such as that for domestic violence, to be followed at all times.[32]

5.61   In terms of transforming practice, the most significant aspect of CAFCASS's new strategy is its clear and fixed focus on early intervention, predicated on the belief 'that the most effective intervention is usually achieved through work in the early stages of a case'. Describing early intervention as 'a sequence of work, not a system or structure', the proposed national standard for early intervention includes the following:

- CAFCASS's provision of an early intervention service (based on assessment, analysis and case planning) within the first 6 weeks of every referral;

- the screening of all incoming referrals by a practitioner or service manager on the first working day after receipt;

- the recognition of the importance of practitioner continuity and of continuing to allocate the vast majority of cases to one practitioner with the specialist skills required for the duration of a particular case, with allocation being made at the earliest possible point of a referral;

- requests for checks for initial screening being made within 2 working days;

---

31   See footnote 28.

32   See para 6.52 et seq.

- the intention on behalf of CAFCASS 'to respond at the greatest times of need throughout the duration of a case';
- making the maximum use in private law cases of Family Group Conferences so as to promote early resolution of key issues in a case.

5.62 Continuing the CAFCASS focus on early intervention is the national proposed standard relating to case planning. Case planning is to form the basis of all future work in a case and the proposal is for the following planning work to be completed by CAFCASS within 6 weeks (and more usually within 4 weeks) of each referral:

- an initial risk identification process in all cases;
- an assessment of the needs, wishes and feelings of each individual child;
- basing assessments and analysis on structured interviews with all parties, with parties given prior knowledge of the areas to be explored (for example 'the analysis of power and control issues in a domestic violence case');
- the integration of relevant diversity issues into the analysis, assessment and case plan for individual children, based on culturally competent social work practice;
- carrying out the maximum amount of dispute resolution or dispute management possible and safe for children in private law cases – the emphasis on 'sorting it, not reporting it';
- a short written report or statement analysing the needs, wishes and feelings of each individual child, concluding with a case plan proposing whether there should be further work and, if so, how that work should be taken forward;
- recommendations to the court via the case plan, usually at directions hearings, in the form of action plans for individual parties and, where applicable, for other agencies in the community, on behalf of each child or young person.

5.63 CAFCASS's fourth proposed national standard is intended to mark a shift from descriptive to analytical writing on the part of the CAFCASS practitioner. Predicated on the belief that CAFCASS 'adds most value to family court proceedings through the quality of its analysis in each case, especially its focus on the needs, wishes and feelings of individual children', the following standards are proposed to apply to all CAFCASS court reports, position statements and case notes:

- the writing is to be succinct and analytical, with descriptive writing kept to the essential minimum;
- only facts, evidence, analysis and the basis for a professional judgement are to be recorded;
- the core documents from CAFCASS will be the 'CAFCASS analysis', which will set out the key issues, and integrated needs, wishes and feelings statements about individual children;
- the 'CAFCASS analysis' will be updated where circumstances change;
- the analysis or, where needed, the full report will start with a summary and recommendations, followed by the analysis underpinning those recommendations;
- plain language will be used;

- all records written by CAFCASS will be open, save for where the information is third hand and its provider applies a restriction;
- all third party information used in a court report will be first checked with the person concerned.

5.64 CAFCASS's fifth proposed national standard reflects its desire to integrate its practice, thinking it 'unhelpful to perpetuate distinctions in practice between public and private law work'[33] and believing that 'traditional public law skills, like case management and the independent oversight of a case, can be applied to private law cases'.

5.65 CAFCASS's sixth proposed national standard enshrines its belief that, through active intervention, change can be effected for children. It makes clear that all its work will be based on an active intervention model for each case, whatever its nature or type, with the essential tasks highlighted in each case plan. It proposes the following:

- case plans will contain a list of specific active interventions proposed on behalf of individual children (ie family support, casework, a treatment or therapy programme, if available);
- all interventions will aim to be brief and effective, working to timescales;
- case plans will be regularly reviewed for effectiveness, focusing on what is happening for individual children in real-time ('the passage of time as it is experienced by and impacts upon the child');
- intervention in cases will be proportionate – the less a case needs, the less will be done on it, and vice versa;
- private law cases will be subject to differentiated case management, not a standard filing time for reports, and oral reports as well as short reports and position statements will be used in some cases;
- CAFCASS practitioners will always seek positive engagement at the outset of their work on each case with family members and with other organisations, agreeing both the issues being taken forward and a clear timetable for the work involved;
- intervention by CAFCASS will never duplicate work done elsewhere and it will not take on the responsibilities of other organisations.

5.66 Particularly welcome is CAFCASS's proposed national standard for prioritising cases, recognising that in an environment where 'the demand for services will always outstrip [CAFCASS] resources ... a priority system for cases is essential'. Cases are to be prioritised 'through the discipline of case planning', with case plans ranking the priority for further work. Prioritised will be those cases with immediate high risk issues, where placement stability is in question, which involve the frustration of contact and where residence is contested. By contrast, quantum of contact cases with no welfare issues will only receive a time-limited dispute resolution service or short children's wishes and feelings reports. None of this is meant to detract from CAFCASS's commitment always to respond to emergency needs that arise in cases.

---

33   The proposed national standard does, however, recognise that the roles for the CAFCASS practitioner and the court rules that apply in public and private law cases are different.

5.67 Reflecting the importance of involving children and recognising their rights, CAFCASS's eighth proposed national standard, entitled 'children's active involvement', recognises that 'a service working on behalf of children has to see children and stay connected with what is happening to them during the life of a case'. It promises that children will always be seen, and their active involvement in all aspects of their case will be promoted, within the limits of the child's age and understanding. This is to include in the private law context extended dispute resolution programmes, but there will be exceptions such as short court-based dispute resolution appointments where no further assessment or continuing work are required and where the child is out of the jurisdiction or too ill to be seen. If a child is not seen, the reason for not doing so must be recorded. A further commitment is that all CAFCASS direct work with children and young people be compliant with the United Nations Convention on the Rights of the Child 1989.

5.68 Among the further national standards being proposed by CAFCASS are those relating to:

- resources, promising that every child should receive a prompt and high quality service from CAFCASS, with the level of service provision being the 'minimum necessary, maximum affordable', and setting out the aim of having no backlogs or delays in services from April 2007;
- CAFCASS as a public sector business;
- customer care;
- partnership and multi-agency working; and
- leadership, accountability and governance.

5.69 There can be little doubt that financial exigency has played its part in CAFCASS's attempts to transform itself, with CAFCASS currently having to operate within a standstill budget. The recognition that, with more money, more could be achieved is obvious and has been made explicit throughout the *Every Day Matters* process. But, concentrating (as this book does) on the private law context,[34] and viewing that process as an exercise in reorganisation conducted within the strict parameters of financial constraint, it is hard not to be positive about the changes being carried forward. In particular, the emphasis on early, effective and proportionate intervention, very much the touchstones of the Private Law Programme, is fundamentally sound and welcome in principle.

5.70 Yet, residual concerns have to remain – about the ever increasing burdens on CAFCASS and the effect that such will have on the quality and

---

34   The aim of integrating CAFCASS practice between public and private law proceedings should not obscure the very real differences between public law children's cases (brought by a local authority out of necessity but where the aim, wherever possible, is the reunification of the family) and private law children's cases (brought by a parent essentially out of choice and where the reunification of the family is not an option). It should be noted that there is considerable concern that the proposed changes to the service in the public law context will dilute the impact and influence of the CAFCASS practitioner and reduce the valuable contribution that CAFCASS currently makes in those proceedings.

effectiveness of the service that it can provide.[35] If CAFCASS really is to expand in impact and influence and achieve what it should for the children that it seeks to serve, then the financial straight-jacket has to be loosened and it needs to be given a proper opportunity to realise the aims of its new strategy.

ASSISTING THE UNREPRESENTED LITIGANT

5.71 It is not our aim in this book to comment extensively about the legal representation of adult parties; indeed it would be invidious for four barristers to do so. Suffice it to say that it is critically important that any party to proceedings should have confidence in any lawyer representing them and that the lawyer concerned should have sufficient experience of and expertise in the law relating to children. To that end, two basic rules of thumb are worthy of brief mention:

(1) *The client should beware the non-specialist lawyer.* The law relating to children is increasingly recognised as a specialist field, which requires a mindset and approach that are very different in kind to those apparent in criminal and most other civil proceedings. Any solicitor practising in this field ought to be a member of Resolution[36] and any barrister a member of the Family Law Bar Association (FLBA), whilst many good children lawyers of both descriptions will also be found in the Association of Lawyers for Children (ALC).

(2) *The client should also beware the uncritical representative.* The client may want to be told that they are so right and that their former partner is unreasonableness personified, but the client caught in the maelstrom of separation will need objective, dispassionate and child-centred advice. In cases where genuine safety and protection issues do not arise, any lawyer doing their job properly will seek to steer their client towards a resolution that does not entail contested court proceedings.

5.72 Nor is it proposed within this chapter to look at the issue of the representation of the child within private law proceedings. That highly topical subject will be discussed within the course of Chapter 8.

5.73 What we do wish to focus on here is the unrepresented litigant – the particular problems that they face in private law children's cases, the challenges to the system that those problems pose and how the use of the McKenzie friend process is being encouraged and developed in an attempt to ease those problems and meet those challenges.

5.74 The first point to make is that, with legal representation in such cases ever harder to obtain, it is an increasing feature of court to find one of the parties, and sometimes even both, appearing in person. The growing prevalence of that scenario only reinforces the collective need to deal with the litigant in person with fairness and with courtesy.

---

35 Its new duties and roles under the Children and Adoption Act 2006, including its statutory obligation to carry out risk assessments, are examined in Chapters 6 and 7.

36 Formerly known as the Solicitors Family Law Association.

5.75 A lack of representation places an enormous strain on the litigant in private law children's cases. Bad enough that they are trying to further their case whilst grappling with often alien law and procedure, but what compounds their task is that the goal of retaining a child-focused objectivity is all the harder to achieve when anxious and embroiled in a dispute that affects them so personally.

5.76 How courts and lawyers should respond to such a situation were issues that were addressed head on by the Court of Appeal in the recent case of *In the Matter of the Children of Mr O'Connell, Mr Whelan and Mr Watson*.[37] Indeed, Lord Justice Wall could not have been plainer as to the expectations that the litigant in person should now have of the court and the legal profession.

5.77 In thoroughly reviewing the conduct of three first instance judges whose decisions were subject of appeal, he commented (on behalf of himself and Lord Justice Thorpe):

'The fact that cases are heard in private in order to protect the identities of the children concerned, and the fact that they deal with highly sensitive material are, in our judgment, all the more reason for judges to be astute to ensure that at all times they behave judicially and, in particular, that they remain both courteous and calm ... as a general proposition, the more difficult the litigant, the greater the need for judicial courtesy and calm ... Every judge who has heard cases conducted by litigants in person, whether at first instance or on appeal, knows only too well that they are an extremely diverse cross-section of the population. But two obvious points must be made. The first is that litigants in person are as entitled to a fair hearing as any other litigant. The second is that they are as entitled as everybody else to be treated with courtesy. There is never any excuse for judicial discourtesy.

'Our joint experience, both at first instance and in this court, is that we have only rarely found litigants in person to be discourteous. We have, of course, experienced anger and abuse by litigants in person (notably at the conclusion of judgment), but more commonly litigants in person are nervous, anxious or upset. Sometimes, as a consequence, they are less coherent and less self-controlled than they would be in other circumstances. The corollary to this, in our view, is that any judge hearing a litigant in person is under a particular obligation to remain courteous and to ensure that the litigant in person has a full and fair hearing.'[38]

5.78 So far as the lawyers were concerned, there was only criticism for those members of the legal profession:

'... who do not obey the rules when dealing with litigants in person, and who do not extend to them the normal courtesies they extend to professional opponents.'[39]

---

37   [2005] EWCA Civ 759, [2005] 2 FLR 967.
38   At paras [51]–[55].
39   At para [83].

5.79 Making the same point but in a different way, Anthony Kirk QC (now Chairman of the FLBA), in his evidence to the Joint Parliamentary Committee on the then Draft Children (Contact) and Adoption Bill,[40] said this of the lawyer's role when dealing with the unrepresented parent:

'It is actually quite a privilege to take on that role, because you are there to assist that person, insofar as you can do so within the confines of your instructions, and to make sure that he or she is properly assisted by the judge.'

5.80 Key to assisting the litigant in person in this context and thereby the court has been the development of the McKenzie[41] friend system, which in the *O'Connell* case and elsewhere has been the subject of important and positive recent judicial comment.

5.81 By definition, a McKenzie friend is a layperson who provides reasonable assistance to an unrepresented litigant. The 2005 guidance note issued by the office of the President of the Family Division[42] makes clear that the McKenzie friend may provide moral support for the litigant, take notes, help with case papers and quietly give advice on points of law or procedure, issues that the litigant may wish to raise in court and questions that the litigant may wish to ask witnesses. The McKenzie friend, however, has no right to act on behalf of a litigant in person, to address the court, or to examine witnesses, and the guidance makes clear that it is only in exceptional circumstances that a court, on application, may grant an unqualified person a right of audience.

5.82 Whilst, in proceedings held in open court, the unrepresented litigant can have a McKenzie friend by right, in closed court (in which most first instance children's hearings at present take place) the litigant needs the court's permission at the start of the hearing to be so assisted. The steer given by the guidance as to whether permission should ordinarily be granted again could not be clearer:

'A litigant in person wishing to have the help of a McKenzie friend should be allowed to do so unless the judge is satisfied that fairness and the interests of justice do not so require. The presumption in favour of permitting a McKenzie friend is a strong one.'

5.83 Amplifying the guidance, the Court of Appeal in the *O'Connell* case have set out the following principles:[43]

(1) The purpose of allowing a litigant in person the assistance of a McKenzie

---

40 24 February 2005 – all the oral evidence given to the Joint Committee is available at www.publications.parliament.uk.

41 The name originated in the case of *McKenzie v McKenzie* [1971] P 33.

42 [2005] Fam Law 405.

43 In terms of formalities, Wall LJ added that, where a litigant in person wished to have the assistance of a McKenzie friend in private family law proceedings relating to children, that intention should be made known to the court as early as possible, and stressed that it would always be helpful for the court if a proposed McKenzie friend could produce either a short curriculum vitae or a statement about themselves, confirming that they have no personal interest in the case, and that they understand both the role of the McKenzie friend and the court's rules as to confidentiality.

friend was to further the interests of justice by achieving a level playing field and ensuring a fair hearing. The presumption in favour of allowing a litigant in person the assistance of a McKenzie friend was very strong. A request for such assistance should be refused only for compelling reasons, which if found, must be carefully and fully explained to the litigant in person and the would-be McKenzie friend.

(2) It was not good practice to exclude a proposed McKenzie friend from the courtroom or chambers whilst an application by a litigant in person for such assistance was being made. A litigant was likely to need the assistance of such a friend to make the application for his or her appointment in the first place. It would be helpful for the proposed McKenzie friend to be present so that any concerns about him or her could be raised, and so that the judge could satisfy him/herself that the McKenzie friend fully understood his or her role and would abide by the court's procedural rules.

(3) A litigant in person who sought the assistance of a McKenzie friend should be allowed that assistance unless there were compelling reasons for refusing it. The following, of themselves, did not constitute compelling reasons: that the litigant in person appeared to the judge to be of sufficient intelligence to be able to conduct the case without the assistance of a McKenzie friend; the fact that the litigant appeared to the judge to have a sufficient mastery of the facts and the documentation to enable him or her to conduct the case without the assistance of a McKenzie friend; the fact that the hearing at which the litigant in person sought the assistance of a McKenzie friend was a directions appointment, or a case management appointment; and (subject to (4) below), the fact that the proceedings were confidential and that the court papers contained sensitive information relating to the family's affairs.

(4) There was no reason in principle why a litigant in person should not disclose the court papers to his or her court-sanctioned McKenzie friend. At the same time, the McKenzie friend must appreciate that disclosure was being made for the purpose of enabling the litigant in person effectively to present his or her case and thus to ensure a fair hearing. The documents and information disclosed to the McKenzie friend must not be used by the McKenzie friend for any other purpose. There was a clear responsibility on the part of the McKenzie friend not to disclose the court documents or publish the information they contain to any third party or outside body without the court's permission.

(5) The argument that it was inappropriate for a McKenzie friend to have access to confidential and, in some cases, sensitive family information was best met by the judge ensuring, as a matter of practice, that whenever an application was made by a litigant in person for the assistance of a McKenzie friend, both the litigant in person and the McKenzie friend expressed their clear understanding to the judge of the role of the McKenzie friend and the responsibility of the McKenzie friend to ensure that the documents to which he or she was being given access were to be used solely for the purpose of assisting the litigant in person. There was no need for this expression of understanding to take the form of a formal undertaking.

(6) It should not be considered a contempt of court for a litigant in person to seek advice from a proposed McKenzie friend prior to any application to

the court. In seeking that advice, it would not be a contempt if the litigant in person showed court documents to the person from whom the advice was being sought. The critical point was that those to whom the documents were shown appreciated that they were being shown the documents for the purpose of giving advice, and that wider dissemination of the documents was not permissible.

5.84 Putting those fourth, fifth and sixth principles on a statutory footing, the recently created rule 10.20A(3) Family Proceedings Rules 1991[44] now provides that a party may without the permission of the court communicate to 'a lay adviser or a McKenzie friend[45] any information relating to the proceedings to enable the party to obtain advice or assistance in relation to the proceedings'.

5.85 A further passage of the *O'Connell* judgment is worth noting, if only to disabuse any public perception that judges instinctively take against fathers' groups. With obvious approval, Lord Justice Wall highlighted the comments of the then President of the Family Division (Dame Elizabeth Butler-Sloss) who, in the earlier case of *Re G (Contempt: Committal)*,[46] said of the role of Families Need Fathers in it:

'Again, I have to say, having read many of the communications in question, a great deal of very helpful advice and sound wisdom was provided to the father as a result of his communications in that discussion.'

5.86 With the difficulties faced and posed by the unrepresented litigant now on the up, courts can, on the back of such clear and authoritative guidance, expect to see – and frankly ought to welcome – the presence of more McKenzie friends to assist those that need their help.

CONCLUSIONS

5.87 This chapter has focused on the recent attempts made to improve the court system – and thereby the outcomes for the children with which it deals – through a range of measures, principally through the implementation of the Private Law Programme, and its promotion of in-court conciliation, and through a new changing role for CAFCASS that seeks to frontload and improve its input.

5.88 It is, however, important to see these measures as the start and not the end of the process of change. In-court conciliation is a form of dispute resolution certainly worthy of support but is one which, with more work, has the capacity to become more effective still. The changes to the role of CAFCASS within the private law field are on the whole to be welcomed, but care needs to be taken to ensure that a reluctance to commit resources to the service does not starve it of the success that its new strategy deserves.

---

44   Inserted by SI 2005/1976 – effective 31 October 2005.
45   Defined by Family Proceedings Rules 1991, r 10.20A(5) as 'any person permitted by the court to sit beside an unrepresented litigant in court to assist that litigant by prompting, taking notes and giving him advice'.
46   [2003] EWCA 1055, [2003] 2 FLR 963.

5.89 So far as the Private Law Programme is concerned, the principle of collaborative working upon which it proceeds is surely sound, as are its emphases on early, swift and effective intervention,[47] on improved case management and on discouraging contested court proceedings. But, as the Private Law Programme will in due course be subject to review, we do make some specific comments and suggestions in its regard.

5.90 Placing the existence of safety issues in a case under the banner of 'exceptional circumstances'[48] cannot be right. The prevalence of safety issues within private law proceedings, especially those arising out of domestic violence, is simply far too great to be considered in any way 'exceptional'. Furthermore, the characterisation of 'safety issues' as 'exceptional', even within this limited context, runs the risk of demeaning their importance and discouraging their raising.

5.91 On similar ground, there seems to be a tension which needs to be resolved between the stipulation at the outset of the Programme that 'in every case there shall be an early First Hearing dispute resolution appointment' and the information sheet for the parties (Annex B) which points out that, if any 'special risks' are identified (to be advised to the court by CAFCASS), 'sometimes this will mean that the FHDRA is not the appropriate forum of meeting in which case a judge will decide what form of hearing should take place'.

5.92 Both those comments preface a more general suggestion that a revised Private Law Programme should encapsulate the proper approach not just in those cases where safety is not an issue (which is the current focus of the Programme, albeit that certain aspects are of general application), but also those where safety issues do arise. As will be seen in the next chapter, which deals specifically with contact and domestic violence, good practice guidelines have been formulated for such cases and have not been followed as rigorously as originally hoped. Especially as a time when user-friendliness is key and the amount of unrepresented litigants is a concern, it would seem eminently sensible to have within one booklet the essentials of good practice and procedure whatever the nature of the case.

47　The focus on early intervention should not obscure the importance of conflict management for those cases incapable of resolution. Effective case management has a key role to play in this regard. So too does the CAFCASS practitioner, and it will be important that the proposed policy of frontloading CAFCASS's input is not so rigid as not to recognise those cases where effective CAFCASS involvement after the early stages is vital.

48　See the first section of the Programme, dealing with first hearing dispute resolution (noted at para 5.11).

Chapter Six

DOMESTIC VIOLENCE, CONTACT AND THE COURTS

6.1 Devoting a whole chapter of a book about contact to the issue of domestic violence would, 10 years ago, have seemed surprising. Not to do so today would be unthinkable. That bears testament to the importance of the issue and the determination of those who have campaigned to put it on the political and legal agenda. It reflects also the extent to which the State has developed a greater awareness of the impact, incidence and consequences of domestic violence and has sought to act accordingly.

6.2 In Chapter 1 we highlighted the nexus between contact and domestic violence from a research angle.[1] Within this chapter, we look at how, influenced by that research, the court system now seeks to deal with the issue of domestic violence when it arises within private law disputes about children. A comprehensive guide to the law relating to domestic violence is beyond our scope.[2] Our focus, and this chapter's starting-point, is the relevant law, principles and practice that form the basis for the courts' approach when in private law children's cases the issue of domestic violence arises. Having set that out, we then consider the various more recent statutory and procedural steps that have been put in place – to increase awareness of the impact of domestic violence, to improve the identification of those cases where it is an issue, to provide for a proper assessment of the risks to the children concerned and thereby to assist in the more efficient and informed disposal of such cases. We conclude by outlining the suggestions that have been made for further change in this complex and difficult field.

THE RELEVANT LAW, PRINCIPLES AND PRACTICE

6.3 Perceptions about the impact of domestic violence in contact cases have changed enormously in the last decade. Domestic violence had been seen as an essentially adult problem, with little focus on the consequences for the child. It could be a factor in a case, but would rarely be determinative of it, and it would be an exceptional case indeed where its existence would be considered sufficient to displace the perceived 'presumption' of contact. Many practitioners now look back at advice given before 2000 to parents seeking to refuse or limit

---

1 See para 1.26 et seq.
2 For an authoritative guide, see R Bird *Domestic Violence: Law and Practice* (Jordans, 5th edn, 2006).

contact on the basis of domestic violence with more than a little discomfort in the light of the Court of Appeal's decision in *Re L; Re V; Re M; Re H*[3] and the awareness that it engendered.

6.4 Whilst there had been earlier cases which had addressed the issue of domestic violence in the contact context and which were by no means inconsistent with what the Court of Appeal determined,[4] no case had so comprehensively dealt with the subject nor given such clear guidance. Indeed, it is no exaggeration to say that the *Re L; Re V; Re M; Re H*[5] decision represents a watershed for the treatment of contact cases in which domestic violence is alleged.

6.5 It was also very timely. While the then newly prepared CASC report on parental contact in domestic violence cases[6] stressed that 'the issue of domestic violence in the context of contact applications is seen throughout the Family Justice System as one of considerable importance', it had to recognise the reality outside the court walls:

> 'There is a both a powerful public perception and an acceptance by a significant number of professional organisations that the issue is not being fully addressed by the courts.'[7]

6.6 The research that the Court of Appeal commissioned has already been reviewed in Chapter 1.[8] In setting out the Court of Appeal's response to it, we begin with the important general comments made by Dame Elizabeth Butler-Sloss (then President of the Family Division) in the main body of her judgment:

> 'The family judges and magistrates need to have a heightened awareness of the existence of and consequences (some long term), on children of exposure to domestic violence between their parents or other partners. There has, perhaps, been a tendency in the past for courts not to tackle allegations of violence and to leave them in the background on the premise that they were matters affecting the adults and not relevant to issues regarding the children. The general principle that contact with the non-resident parent is in the interests of the child may sometimes have discouraged sufficient attention being paid to the adverse effects on children living in the household where violence has occurred. It may not necessarily be widely appreciated that violence to a partner involves a

---

3   *Re L (Contact: Domestic Violence); Re V (Contact: Domestic Violence); Re M (Contact: Domestic Violence); Re H (Contact: Domestic Violence)* [2000] 2 FLR 334.

4   See, for example, *Re H (Contact: Domestic Violence)* [1998] 2 FLR 42; *Re M (Contact: Violent Parent)* [1999] 2 FLR 321.

5   [2000] 2 FLR 334.

6   *A Report to the Lord Chancellor on the Question of Parental Contact in Cases where there is Domestic Violence* prepared by the Children Act Sub-Committee of the Advisory Board on Family Law (Lord Chancellor's Department, 12 April 2000), available at www.dca.gov.uk/family/abfla/dvconreport.pdf.

7   Ibid, at sections 4.1 and 4.2.

8   See para 1.29 et seq. For the full report, see J Sturge & D Glaser *Contact and Domestic Violence – the Experts Court Report* [2000] Fam Law 615.

significant failure in parenting – failure to protect the child's carer and failure to protect the child emotionally.'

6.7 From those general comments, the following principles flowed:

- A court hearing a contact application in which allegations of domestic violence were raised should consider the conduct of both parties towards each other and towards the children, the effect of the violence on the children and on the residential parent, and the motivation of the parent seeking contact – is it a desire to promote the best interests of the child or a means to continue violence and/or intimidation or harassment of the other parent?

- On an application for interim contact, when the allegations of domestic violence had not yet been adjudicated on, the court should give particular consideration to the likely risk of harm to the child, whether physical or emotional, if contact were granted or refused. The court should ensure, as far as possible, that any risk of harm to the child was minimised and that the safety of the child and the residential parent was secured before, during and after any such contact.

- In a contact or other section 8 application, where allegations of domestic violence were made which might have an effect on the outcome of the application, those allegations must be adjudicated upon, and found proved or not proved. It will be necessary to scrutinise such allegations which may not always be true or may be grossly exaggerated.

- If however there is a firm basis for finding that violence has occurred, the expert advice on the effects of domestic violence and contact on the child becomes very important.

- There was not, and should not be, a presumption that on proof of domestic violence the offending parent had to surmount a prima facie barrier of no contact. As a matter of principle, domestic violence of itself cannot constitute a bar to contact, but it is one factor in the difficult and delicate balancing exercise of discretion carried out by the judge, applying the welfare principle and the welfare checklist in section 1(1) and (3) of the Children Act 1989.

- In cases of proved domestic violence (as in cases of other proved harm or risk of harm to the child), the court had to weigh the seriousness of the domestic violence, the risks involved and the impact on the child against the positive factors, if any, of contact. The ability of the offending parent to recognise his past conduct, to be aware of the need to change and to make genuine efforts to do so would be likely to be an important consideration when performing that balancing exercise.

- Where there was a conflict between the rights and interests of a child and those of a parent, the interests of the child had to prevail under Art 8(2) of the European Convention for the Protection of Human Rights and Fundamental Freedoms 1950.

6.8 It will be readily appreciated that those principles, which remain good law, largely but do not exclusively follow the expert psychiatric advice that the Court of Appeal had received. Where they departed was in the approach to be adopted where domestic violence was found, with the Court of Appeal seeing the factors listed by Sturge and Glaser[9] as matters to be taken into account in the balancing exercise rather than preconditions to be met before contact could take place.

6.9 Noting that 'it had not been separately categorised in either statute or case-law', and expressing the view that it should not be, Lord Justice Thorpe was keen to emphasise that domestic violence was 'one of a catalogue of factors that may operate to offset the assumption for contact':

> '... the factors that may offset the assumption in favour of contact are probably too legion to be either listed or categorised. Abuse must form the largest compartment: as well as physical abuse of the other parent and/or a child there is equally sexual and emotional abuse within the family. Then there is the self abuse of either drugs or alcohol and the failure to maintain sexual boundaries appropriate to the development of the child. Additionally mental illness or personality disorder may be a dominant factor as may be malign motives prompting the applicant to pursue a seemingly justifiable application for the covert purpose of threatening or dominating the primary carer. This uncomprehensive catalogue only demonstrates that the factor of domestic violence must be kept in proportion and must not be elevated either to reduce the focus on other factors that may counter the assumption in favour of contact or otherwise distort the paramount judicial task.'[10]

6.10 It is hard to argue with Lord Justice Thorpe's view that the factor of domestic violence should be kept in proportion, both in individual cases[11] and generally. But, without in any way detracting from the significance and influence of *Re L; Re V; Re M; Re H*,[12] questions need to be asked of the period following that decision. Did the family justice system, taken as a whole, ensure that the right balance was struck? Was the factor of domestic violence accorded the prominence and weight that it warranted? The fact of subsequent statutory and procedural reform in this context can only raise doubts on both scores.

---

9   See para 1.33.
10 Supra, at p 370. The figures (compiled since) make far clearer the prevalence of domestic violence and show it to be the most commonly cited safety issue in contact cases (see para 1.25). The strong correlation between domestic violence and child abuse (see para 1.35) is also increasingly being stressed. CAFCASS's draft Safeguarding Policy Framework (put out for consultation in May 2006) notes at p 65: 'The risk of harm to children from domestic violence is not a discrete category, separate from other forms of child protection concern. Research is increasingly reporting a significant "cross-over" of concerns.'
11 Thorpe LJ , at p 370, speaks, without in any way condoning the former, of the 'spectrum within the broad categorisation of domestic violence from the slap that may have been provoked to premeditated murder'.
12 Ibid.

The CASC Good Practice Guidelines

6.11 In addressing the issues thrown up by domestic violence in the contact arena, the task of the Court of Appeal in *Re L; Re V; Re M; Re H*[13] was facilitated not just by the expert evidence that it commissioned and received, but also by having access to the freshly completed CASC report on parental contact in domestic violence cases.[14] The guidelines generated by that report,[15] which amplify the core tenets of the Court of Appeal's decision, have since come to be seen as the essential expression of good practice in this area.

6.12 The enduring importance and applicability of the CASC Guidelines cannot be overstated. In a recent Court of Appeal decision,[16] Lord Justice Wall was highly critical of the failure of a first instance judge to adhere to them and in an even more recent report[17] he advocates that those judges who prove themselves incapable of trying cases of this kind appropriately or who deliberately ignore good practice (including the CASC Guidelines) should lose their right to hear such cases. The problem of non-compliance does not seem to be an isolated one, with *Parental Separation: Children's Needs and Parents' Responsibilities – Next Steps*[18] itself recording the concerns raised by many that the CASC Guidelines were not being fully applied.

6.13 That is not to say that the Guidelines should be used slavishly. As Lord Justice Wall recognises, 'not every paragraph applies in every case ... [they] were designed to be applied selectively and intelligently to the facts of the individual case'.[19] But plainly they should not be ignored. Given their continuing significance and the apparent inability of some courts and practitioners still to take on board their full force, the Guidelines are set out in full at Appendix 6.

6.14 The desirability of having early fact-finding hearings in cases where the issue of domestic violence is raised and may influence the outcome of the case, stressed in the CASC Guidelines, has been subsequently emphasised and rationalised:

> 'The court should grasp the nettle. Such allegations should be speedily investigated and resolved, not left to fester unresolved and a continuing

---

13 Ibid.

14 *A Report to the Lord Chancellor on the Question of Parental Contact in Cases where there is Domestic Violence* prepared by the Children Act Sub-Committee of the Advisory Board on Family Law (Lord Chancellor's Department, 12 April 2000), available at www.dca.gov.uk/family/abfla/dvconreport.pdf – see para 1.28.

15 *Guidelines for Good Practice on Parental Contact on cases where there is Domestic Violence* (prepared by the Children Act Sub-Committee of the Lord Chancellor's Advisory Board on Family Law (April 2002)) – reproduced at Appendix 6.

16 *Re H (Contact: Domestic Violence)* [2005] EWCA Civ 1404, [2006] 1 FLR 943. See also *K and S (Children) (Contact: Domestic Violence)* [2005] EWCA Civ 1660, [2006] 1 FCR 316.

17 Lord Justice Wall *A Report to the President of the Family Division on the Publication by the Women's Aid Federation of England Entitled Twenty-Nine Child Homicides: Lessons Still to be Learnt on Domestic Violence and Child Protection with Particular Reference to the Five Cases in which there was Judicial Involvement* (March 2006). Considered at para 6.101 et seq.

18 January 2005 – Cm 6452 – available at www.dfes.gov.uk/childrensneeds/.

19 *Re H (Contact: Domestic Violence)* [2005] EWCA Civ 1404, [2006] 1 FLR 943, at para [142].

source of friction and dispute. Court time must be found – and found without delay – for fact finding hearings. Judges must resist the temptation to delay the evil day in the hope that perhaps the problem will go away ... And allegations which could have been made at an early stage should be viewed with appropriate scepticism. Once findings have been made, everybody must thereafter approach the case on the basis of the facts as judicially found.'[20]

6.15 Another advantage of the early hearing is the recognition that 'the more time passes, the more difficult it will be to make reliable findings'.[21] But there must be a balance, and the need for speed should not in any way obviate the need for proper preparation. This is a hearing of fundamental importance for the children and their parents, with the facts as found at a preliminary hearing serving 'as an enduring foundation for the exercise of the judge's discretion as he determines the future'.[22] The consequences of the court getting it wrong (whether through making findings on inadequate evidence or not making findings where such were warranted) cannot be underestimated. Reflecting that necessity for the court to have the best evidence and in effect amplifying paragraph 1.2 of the CASC Guidelines, the following guidance should also be kept in mind:[23]

- When a finding of fact was sought, the court expected and required the best possible evidence on which to make its decision; this was a particular problem in cases involving allegations of domestic violence, which had to be proved rigorously.
- Full statements by the parties would identify which facts were in issue between them, and therefore needed proof, and which were accepted. Schedules of the allegations made and the responses to them, almost akin to a pleading and most useful in tabular form, would assist in achieving clarity.
- Where first hand evidence was available, either from a witness or in documentary form, it should be presented.
- Attention always had to be given to the issue of evidence that might be corroborative or, alternatively, gave rise to doubt about important allegations. It was normally sensible to give some thought to whether the police had records of reports of domestic incidents and whether there might be material police witnesses, just as consideration should be given to whether there might be medical evidence to corroborate an assertion that a particular assault had taken place and caused injuries.

---

20 Per Munby J in *Re D (Intractable Contact Dispute Publicity)* [2004] EWHC 727 (Fam), [2004] 1 FLR 1226, at para [54].
21 See HHJ John Mitchell in *Children Act Private Law Proceedings: A Handbook* (Jordans, 2006), at p 202.
22 Per Thorpe LJ in *Re H (Contact: Domestic Violence)* [2005] EWCA Civ 1404, [2006] 1 FLR 943, at para [145]. Consistent with the approach in public law proceedings and, in accordance with the emphasis in the Private Law Programme on judicial continuity, the same tribunal should, wherever possible, hear both the preliminary fact-finding hearing and the final hearing.
23 Per Black J in *Re A (Contact: Risk of Violence)* [2005] EWHC 851 (Fam), [2006] 1 FLR 283.

6.16   Taking decisions on good admissible evidence is one respect in which the risks of miscarriages of justice in this area can be reduced, but there remains the anxiety among some that making false allegations of domestic violence carries no downside risk for the maker. The *Next Steps*[24] document records:

'A number of respondents[25] mentioned concerns about ill-founded, or even malicious allegations of domestic violence, which they suggested might be made in order to frustrate and delay proceedings or skew the outcome. Some called for a mechanism to counter these accusations, such as the introduction of a penalty where allegations were proven to have been false.'

6.17   That call has in part been taken up by the Court of Appeal in the recent case of *Re T (Order for Costs)*.[26] The case is interesting not just for the decision of the trial judge (who had found groundless the mother's allegations against the father[27]) subsequently to award residence of the child to him, but for the approach of the Court of Appeal in upholding the judge's award of costs against the mother.

6.18   Whilst the Court of Appeal recognised that irrational behaviour was commonplace in contact disputes and might be exacerbated by the personality of the parent involved, it stressed that there was a limit to any allowance which could be made for a parent who deliberately and unreasonably obstructed contact in circumstances where, on an objective analysis, contact was in the interests of the child. In so doing, it made clear that the mother could not rely on her own irrational anxieties to bring her conduct within the band of reasonable behaviour. Lord Justice Wall added:[28]

'It is for this reason that the judge's findings of fact are so important. Where a judge, as here, carefully investigates the disputed areas of fact which have given rise to a parent's objections to contact, and where the judge, as here, has found in terms that the child enjoys a good relationship with the non-resident parent; that there is no reason for the resident parent to have any concerns; and that there is no reason why contact should not take place, a reasonable parent, even if still anxious, has no proper grounds for failing to implement the order. If, in these circumstances, the resident parent unreasonably fails to implement the order or an agreement as to contact, and if the matter has to return to court, it will be open to the court to find that that parent is acting unreasonably ... We do not think that the orders for costs which we have upheld in the instant case are either likely to or should deter a resident parent from advancing a reasonable opposition to contact which is genuinely based on a proper perception of the child's interests. But those who unreasonably frustrate contact need to be aware that the court has the power to make costs orders in appropriate cases, and

---

24   January 2005 – Cm 6452 – available at www.dfes.gov.uk/childrensneeds/.
25   Families Need Fathers commented: 'At present making false allegations [of domestic violence] is risk free. This should change.'
26   [2005] EWCA Civ 311, [2005] 2 FLR 681.
27   As it is often the cases where judges err that receive most attention, it is proper to note that at paras [29] and [30] the Court of Appeal 'highly commended' HHJ Kushner QC's management of the case – 'a paradigm example of how a difficult contact dispute should be handled'.
28   At paras [51] and [56].

that the consequences of such unreasonable behaviour may well be an order for costs made against the resident parent who has behaved unreasonably.'

DEFINITION AND IDENTIFICATION

6.19   Notwithstanding the Court of Appeal decision in *Re L; Re V; Re M; Re H*[29] and the promulgation of the CASC Guidelines, there remained the belief that more needed to be done if the issue of domestic violence in residence and contact cases was to be properly addressed. Not least was the concern that proper practice was not being universally applied, which in turn fed the need for a greater clarity of definition and for better procedures to identify early those cases where domestic violence was an issue.

6.20   What would not be altered was the fundamental legal position. Having set out the measures designed to meet that need,[30] the *Next Steps*[31] document provided this categorical statement:

'In light of these changes, the Government does not believe that any kind of blanket statutory presumption of no contact would work in cases where allegations of harm were made, it is essential that court-ordered contact should be safe for all involved, but this does not mean that a parent who has been violent may never have contact with their children – but that any contact should be safe and in the child's best interests.'

Clearer definition

6.21   In terms of those changes, it is appropriate to begin by noting the statutory change introduced as from 31 January 2005 by section 120 of the Adoption and Children Act 2002. That section amended section 31(9) of the Children Act 1989, in which the concept of harm was defined. Previously, the definition had extended to 'ill-treatment or the impairment of health or development', with:

– 'development' meaning physical, intellectual, emotional, social and behavioural development;
– 'health' meaning physical or mental health; and
– 'ill-treatment' including sexual abuse and forms of ill-treatment which are not physical.

6.22   Following amendment, the concept of 'ill-treatment or the impairment of health or development' in section 31(9) is now expressly stated as 'including, for example, impairment suffered from seeing or hearing the ill-treatment of another'. Whilst, prior to that amendment, courts were progressively more prepared to construe harm in that way, it is undoubtedly welcome that the consequences for the child of visual or aural exposure to domestic violence should be so explicitly spelt out.

---

29   [2000] 2 FLR 334.
30   Outlined at para 6.21 et seq.
31   January 2005 – Cm 6452 – available at www.dfes.gov.uk/childrensneeds/.

6.23 But what does domestic violence comprise? There is a real debate inside and outside legal circles as to how narrowly or broadly the concept of domestic violence should be defined, with the proponents of a narrower definition concerned especially as to the burdens on the system if too broad a definition is adopted. Given the key role now being played by the CAFCASS practitioner in the identification of domestic violence issues in private law cases and the consequent assessment of risk,[32] it is appropriate here to note the broad definition of domestic violence that CAFCASS now uses:[33]

> 'Any behaviour which is characterised by the misuse of power and control by one person over another within a family context and/or with whom s/he has been in an intimate relationship. This behaviour can be overt as in threatened attempted assault or actual assault or harassment. It can also be subtle, such as the imposition of social isolation on a partner and/or his/her children. It can thus take the form of emotional, financial, physical, psychological or sexual abuse or any combination of these.'

Earlier identification – the 'Gateway forms'

6.24 The further statutory particularisation of the concept of harm was accompanied by the advent of new court forms (described within the *Next Steps*[34] document as 'Gateway forms'). Specifically intended and designed so as to highlight from the start those cases where domestic violence and issues of similar concern were or were alleged to be apparent, the particular purpose of these forms is:

(1) to alert CAFCASS[35] immediately to the possibility of safety issues in the case, allowing the CAFCASS practitioner to undertake any preliminary paper assessment of risk and advise the court accordingly;

(2) to enable the court itself at an early stage to consider the issue of safety and, as appropriate, proceed in accordance with the principles set out in *Re L; Re V; Re M; Re H*[36] and the CASC Good Practice Guidelines.[37]

6.25 In light of the emphasis placed on their introduction and their role in improving the identification of safety issues in private law children's cases, the content of the new 'Gateway forms' is considered in detail.

---

32 Discussed throughout this chapter.

33 Section 2.1.3 of CAFCASS's Domestic Violence Policy & Standards (October 2005), available at www.cafcass.gov.uk/English/Publications/policies/FinalversionDomesticVOct.doc. See also para 6.52 et seq.

34 January 2005 – Cm 6452 – available at www.dfes.gov.uk/childrensneeds/.

35 The Private Law Programme's model scheme for in-court dispute resolution provides for CAFCASS to be sent the forms on the date of issue (see para 5.22). Steps have now been undertaken to make clear to the user of the forms that they will be sent to CAFCASS who may make background safety checks in line with their child protection procedures (see *Harm Checks* [2006] Fam Law 243).

36 [2000] 2 FLR 334. See para 6.6 et seq.

37 See Appendix 6.

6.26   The new Form C1[38] (to be completed when an application for an order under the Children Act 1989 is made) contains a new question 7, to be answered only if the applicant is seeking contact, residence, prohibited steps, specific issue or parental responsibility orders. Headed 'Domestic abuse, violence or harm', question 7 asks whether the applicant believes that the child(ren) subject of the application:

'have suffered or are risk of suffering any harm from any of the following:

- any form of domestic abuse
- violence within the household
- child abduction
- other conduct or behaviour

by any person who is or has been involved in caring for the child(ren) or lives with, or has contact with, the child(ren)?'

6.27   In like fashion:

- Form C2 (to be completed when the application is for leave to commence proceedings, for an order or directions in existing family proceedings or to be joined as or cease to be a party in existing family proceedings) asks the same question at its question 4 (to be answered in the same circumstances);
- Form C7 (by which the respondent to an application acknowledges such) asks the same question at its question 7.

6.28   In all three scenarios, the person filling out the form simply has to tick the Yes or No box (as applicable), but, if the former, is required to complete the Supplemental Information Form (Form C1A). That form has also to be completed by the respondent if the applicant has filled out a C1A and the respondent wishes to comment on any of the statements made within it (question 6 of Form C7).

6.29   Form C1A starts by requiring the personal details and solicitor's details of the person completing the form (section 1), but the Notes for Guidance make clear that, if that person wishes not to disclose their address to the respondent, then they can do so by leaving that space blank and completing instead and filing at the same time Form C8 (the Confidential Address Form).

6.30   Section 2 of Form C1A provides for the respondent's comments on allegations made by the applicant. It should, however, only be completed where the applicant has served a completed C1A with his or her application for an order and the respondent wishes to comment on the applicant's allegations. The comments should be brief, the section making clear that the respondent will have an opportunity to make a more detailed statement later in the proceedings, and should not extend to any other information supplied by the applicant. The guidance indicates that, if the respondent does not wish to comment at this stage, this section may be left blank or the words 'no comments at this stage' may be inserted instead.

---

38   All the forms mentioned in this section are available online at www.hmcourts-service.gov.uk/ HMCSCourtFinder/GetForms.do.

6.31 Section 3 of Form C1A is entitled 'Further Information' and comprises the following eight sub-sections to be completed:

(1)   involvement with outside agencies and organisations;
(2)   incidents of abuse, violence or harm;
(3)   involvement of the child(ren);
(4)   witnesses;
(5)   medical treatment or other assessment of the child(ren);
(6)   abduction;
(7)   steps or orders required to protect you and the children;
(8)   attending the court.

Given the potential for Form C1A to shape the subsequent course of the proceedings, we set out the detail of these subsections and the Notes for Guidance that accompany them (and which begin by setting out the revised section 31(9) definitions of 'harm', 'development', 'health' and 'ill-treatment').[39]

6.32 The first subsection asks the person filling it out to provide certain details if, as a result of any incidence of domestic abuse, other harm or risk of harm to (the person completing it) or the child(ren), there is, has been or there is pending any known involvement with the police, social services, mental health services or other support services in respect of any subject child(ren), any full, half or step sibling of the subject child(ren) and/or a person who is or has been involved in caring for or is having or has had contact with the subject child(ren). The details required (with guidance) are:

- which agency or service has been involved (no further details here required);
- the name of the person who has been the main contact in that agency or service;
- the date(s) of any involvement (in the absence of precise dates being recalled, the month or a date as near as possible should be inserted);
- whether there is any current or continuing involvement (this should be stated in simple terms, the examples given being 'the police are continuing their investigations' or 'the social services are still involved', and all those agencies and services still involved should be included here);
- whether or not the person completing the form has any documents, reports or correspondence relating to the involvement of the agency of service (these should not be enclosed, though the guidance indicates that the court may subsequently ask for this paperwork to be produced if it considers that it may be relevant to the case).

6.33 The second subsection asks, in respect of each alleged incidence of violence, domestic abuse or harm, for the following information in summary form:

- the date(s) on which the incident occurred (as before, in the absence of precise dates being recalled, the month or a date as near as possible should be inserted);

---

39   See paras 6.21 and 6.22.

- the nature and seriousness of the alleged abuse, violence or harm (for example, whether it was physical, mental or sexual and what form it took);
- by whom and against whom it was directed (in considering who the victim of this behaviour was, regard should be had to whether any child saw or heard anything, in which case that child should be named but no further details should be given here);
- how frequently the alleged abuse, harm or violence occurred and the date(s) of the most recent occurrence(s);
- whether any hospital or medical treatment has been sought by the subject child(ren), the applicant or other person in respect of any injuries sustained; and
- whether the person completing the form considers that there is a likelihood of further harm, abuse or violence occurring.[40]

6.34 The third subsection deals with the involvement of the child(ren). If they have seen or heard any of the alleged incident(s) of abuse within the household or been aware of any alleged abuse and its impact on the family, then details should be given. Particularly, it should be stated (in brief at this stage) how it is believed that the children have been affected by this experience.

6.35 The fourth subsection, entitled 'Witnesses', asks whether anyone else has seen, heard or had reported to them any alleged incidence of violence, domestic abuse or harm and, if so, whether that person would be able to provide supporting evidence. The guidance indicates that the witness should be asked whether they are willing, and able, to provide supporting evidence (which could be any paperwork supplied by the police, hospital or any agency to which the incident was reported), and the preparedness of the witness to attend court should also be stated. No evidence should be attached to the form, but its provision may be asked for later in the proceedings.

6.36 The fifth subsection, headed 'Medical treatment or other assessment of the child(ren)', asks for certain details if any of the subject children have been referred for treatment or psychiatric or psychological assessment by any medical or health service relating to their emotional, social or behavioural development (or where any such treatment or referral is pending). The information sought is the following:

- when (or approximately when) and to whom such a referral was made (bearing in mind that the date of referral may not be the same as the date of the appointment);
- details (in summary form) of any treatment or assessment recommended;
- whether there is any continuing involvement with the relevant services in relation to the referral; and
- whether any reports or other correspondence relating to any treatment or

---

40 Although the guidance is silent as to the meaning of 'likelihood' here, it is suggested that it should equate to 'a real possibility, a possibility that cannot sensibly be ignored, having regard to the nature and gravity of the feared harm in the particular case'. This is the definition that case-law has given to 'likely' in the context of the Children Act, s 31(2)(a) (see *Re H and R (Child Sexual Abuse: Standard of Proof)* [1996] 1 FLR 80).

assessment recommended are known of or to hand (though documents should not be included at this stage).

6.37 The sixth subsection deals with 'Abduction', with the guidance defining 'child abduction' as 'the wrongful removal of a child from any person having, or entitled to, lawful control of that child' and 'international child abduction' as 'the wrongful retention away from the country where the child usually lives'. In the event of the person completing the form feeling that the subject child(ren) are at real risk of being abducted, that person should state:

- the reason for such belief;
- whether the child(ren) have previously been the subject of a threatened abduction, an attempted abduction or have been abducted (in which case, dates should be given);
- whether (in this and/or another country) the police or any other organisation (including any private investigators) has been involved in any alleged previous incident identified; and
- whether each child (and if so which) has their own passport and in whose possession that passport is at the moment.

6.38 The person filling out the form is required in the seventh subsection to indicate what steps or orders they believe that the court should take or make to protect the safety of the subject child(ren) and themselves. The guidance reminds that person that they are completing this form because there are allegations that the subject child(ren) may have suffered or be at risk of suffering domestic abuse, violence or harm and they are asking the court to make one or more of five distinct orders available under the Children Act 1989. Helpfully, the guidance also explains each order in the following way:

- Residence: This decides who the child or children are going to live with in the future.
- Contact: This decides how often and for how long the person with whom the child(ren) are living must let the child(ren) visit, stay or otherwise have contact with the person asking for the order.
- Prohibited steps: This prevents a parent from taking a particular action as set out in the order without the permission of the court; this also applies to actions by any other person named in the order.
- Specific issue: This decides specific questions, for example about education, medical treatment or a foreign holiday or visit where parents or those with parental responsibility cannot agree.
- Parental responsibility: This defines all the rights, duties, powers, responsibilities and authority which a parent has in relation to a child and his or her property.

6.39 Finally, the eighth subsection deals with an issue of basic practicalities whose importance is increasingly being recognised – 'attending the court' and the special measures or arrangements to be put in place to ensure that this can be undertaken safely by those alleging domestic violence and their witnesses. The guidance explains:

'If you feel that you are vulnerable or likely to be intimidated when you attend court and would like the court to make special arrangements, please say so on this form. The court will try to supply you and your witnesses with a separate waiting area and, if possible and where available, the use of a video link. For any of these measures to be considered please will you explain why you feel you need them.'

6.40   With the effectiveness of these new forms currently under review, it would seem appropriate to make some observations about them. The first is that it would not be surprising if they were not achieving all that was originally hoped. Three reasons in particular are posited for that view:

(1)   Many victims of domestic violence are simply reluctant to own up to their experiences – whether through feelings of shame, guilt or fear, through a desire to keep the separation as 'normal' as possible or perhaps through a genuine belief that the domestic violence should not impact on the childcare arrangements. The forms will inevitably have a limited impact on those cases.

(2)   While the C1A (when taken together with its Notes for Guidance) is an informative and thorough form, calculated to elicit and convey the level of detail that would allow a reasonable initial assessment of potential risk to be made, the forms triggering it (the C1, C2 and C7) do not make explicit the link between domestic violence and harm to a child, nor do they make clear that harm extends beyond the physical. While any competent lawyer would read the triggering question in those forms with both points in mind, it should not be assumed that the litigant in person would. Incorporating on the face of those forms the revised statutory definition of 'harm'[41] would seem an easy way to address that problem, which may have caused some cases of domestic violence not to be channelled through the C1A Form process.

(3)   Inevitably, the forms are also only as good as those who use them and those who complete them. The CASC Guidelines experience[42] provides a salutary tale of how slow or resistant some lawyers and judges can be to take on board new forms of practice and procedure, and it would not be surprising at all to discover that the new forms are in some quarters either not being used or not being completed as fully and as properly as they should be.

6.41   Yet, even if we are right in those suppositions, it certainly does not mean that the new forms should be considered a failed experiment. Far from it. That some domestic violence cases still get through the net simply means that the system should be alive to and cater for that eventuality;[43] whilst their utilisation and proper completion should be actively encouraged from the highest level with, if appropriate, costs penalties for their non or inadequate use.

6.42   Historically, the late introduction of domestic violence allegations served to delay and derail many a contact case, to the detriment of all. The new forms are now a key part of the process (encompassing also the Private Law Programme, the CAFCASS risk assessment role[44] and the CASC Guidelines), which ought to ensure better and swifter justice for the victim of domestic

---

41   See paras 6.21 and 6.22.
42   See para 6.12.
43   This is something of which CAFCASS is clearly aware – see para 6.56.
44   See para 6.43 et seq.

violence, for the parent wrongly accused of domestic violence and above all for the children who are the subject of such cases.

CAFCASS AND RISK ASSESSMENTS

6.43 The amendment to the statutory definition of harm apart, no other statutory change in this area had been highlighted in *Parental Separation: Children's Needs and Parents' Responsibilities – Next Steps.*[45] None was then intended and consequently none appeared when the Children and Adoption Bill first began its passage through Parliament.

Statutory duty

6.44 However, during the report stage in the House of Lords in November 2005, the Children and Adoption Bill was amended to impose a statutory obligation on the officers of CAFCASS[46] to carry out risk assessments in certain circumstances. That amendment now finds itself enshrined in section 7 of the Children and Adoption Act 2006.[47] As with the provisions relating to contact activity directions and conditions, discussed further in Chapter 7, this is achieved by an amendment to the Children Act 1989.

6.45 Section 7 of the 2006 Act now adds a new section 16A to the 1989 Act, with the substance of the new provision contained in subsection 16A(2):

'If, in carrying out any function to which this section applies, a [CAFCASS officer] or a Welsh family proceedings officer is given cause to suspect that a child concerned is at risk of harm, he must –

(a) make a risk assessment in relation to the child, and
(b) provide the risk assessment to the court.'

6.46 This provision applies to the following functions carried out by CAFCASS officers or Welsh family proceedings officers:

(a) any function in connection with family proceedings in which the court has power to make an order under [Part 1 of the 2006 Act] with respect to a child or in which a question with respect to such an order arises (accordingly including all residence and contact cases);
(b) any function in connection with an order made by the court in such proceedings.[48]

6.47 The meaning of 'risk assessment' in this context is as follows:

'A risk assessment, in relation to a child who is at risk of suffering harm of a particular sort, is an assessment of the risk of that harm being suffered by the child.'[49]

---

45 January 2005 – Cm 6452 – available at www.dfes.gov.uk/childrensneeds/.
46 Or, in Wales, Welsh family proceedings officers.
47 At the time of writing, no provision of the Children and Adoption Act 2006 is yet in force.
48 Children Act 1989, s 16A(1).
49 Children Act 1989, s 16A(3).

6.48 In moving the amendment that founded these new provisions, Baroness Gould of Potternewton explained the rationale for their introduction in the following way:

'[The] evidence shows that the family justice system does not have adequate proceedings for identifying high-risk cases and assessing and managing risk to ensure that contact is safe. That will not do ... the amendment imposes a wide duty on CAFCASS officers to carry out risk assessments. Such assessments will have to be applied consistently whenever there is an issue of harm raised in private law proceedings in which CAFCASS is engaged. That is important because each case must be considered individually with the focus on the well-being of the child. I appreciate that the amendment places greater burdens on CAFCASS officers, but ... anything that enables those working with families to have more clarity about how they proceed is bound to be helpful. I hope that ... this amendment ... will be a part of [the] new CAFCASS domestic violence policy and toolkit. As others have said, the resources will have to accompany this extra duty. I also appreciate that this amendment is not the total answer ... but I believe that it is a major step forward ... It is clear that the present position is not robust enough and that providing guidance is not enough. Risk assessment has to be built into legislation. It is crucial to ensure that contact is safe before it is imposed.'[50]

6.49 This proposed reform was enthusiastically adopted by all sides, including the Government, for whom the minister said:

'The Government are happy to accept those amendments, as we believe that they are a very constructive step forward in ensuring that issues of domestic violence and child abuse are properly addressed as soon as they are raised and before decisions about contact are made, or at any other point in private law Children Act proceedings when they would be relevant.'[51]

6.50 For CAFCASS's part, their Chair, Baroness Pitkeathley, in the same debate observed:

'CAFCASS is concerned about resources, but that does not in any way diminish our enthusiasm for taking on the role of risk assessment. We believe that it will help to focus our practice when under great pressure to broker agreements between warring parents. Sometimes the drive to reach an agreement about contact can mask underlying child protection concerns; at the moment, we have an inadequate statutory base for exploring those concerns. Making risk assessment mandatory will be an alert not just for CAFCASS practitioners but for those agencies from which we ask checks – courts and judges and all agencies in the family justice system.'[52]

---

50 Baroness Gould of Potternewton, HL Deb, 14 November 2005, col 888–9.
51 Lord Adonis, Parliamentary Under-Secretary of State for the Department for Education and Skills, HL Deb, 14 November 2005, col 891.
52 HL Deb, 14 November 2005, col 890.

6.51 It will therefore be readily seen that the aim of this statutory provision is not so much to introduce something new, but to improve the existing process of risk assessment by CAFCASS by formalising it, making it more uniform, ensuring that it is of general application and giving it statutory teeth.

The CAFCASS approach to risk assessment

6.52 With the CAFCASS risk assessment now to be on a statutory footing, it will be important not just for its practitioners to know and understand its procedures and methodology. Judges, magistrates and lawyers will all need to have some familiarity with how CAFCASS goes about this vital role, if they are to be able to gauge the quality of the assessments prepared and, in the case of lawyers, to be able also to advise their clients before, during and after the assessment process.

6.53 In terms of how CAFCASS carries out its risk assessments in private law cases when the issue of domestic violence arises, reference should currently be made to two CAFCASS documents, both of which were introduced in October 2005:[53]

- the CAFCASS policy for section 120 cases, which deals more with the procedure of risk assessment; and
- the CAFCASS Domestic Violence Policy and Standards and Toolkit,[54] which focuses exclusively on the issue of domestic violence.

6.54 It should, however, be borne in mind that CAFCASS is in the process of developing a new Safeguarding Policy Framework, which will be finalised following consultation on its draft. This aims to encompass within one place a whole range of guidance and procedures relating to CAFCASS's statutory duty to safeguard and promote the welfare of the children whom it serves. The finalised Safeguarding Policy Framework will replace, among other documents, the CAFCASS policy for section 120 cases, but the Domestic Violence Policy and Toolkit will form part of the Framework, albeit that it will remain a 'stand alone' document.[55]

The CAFCASS section 120 policy

6.55 As the title of the policy suggests, its prompt was provided by the extension of the statutory definition of harm made by section 120 of the Adoption and Children Act 2002.[56] It is a policy by which CAFCASS recognises the significance of that statutory change and sets out its procedures

---

53 Almost contemporaneously therefore with the amendment to the Bill.

54 Commonly known just as the CAFCASS Domestic Violence Policy and Toolkit, it is available at www.cafcass.gov.uk/English/Publications/policies/FinalversionDomesticVOct.doc. Its final version came out in October 2005.

55 The covering letter introducing the draft Safeguarding Policy Framework for consultation comments that '[CAFCASS] can however take the opportunity offered by this consultation to update the Domestic Violence Policy and Toolkit if necessary'.

56 See paras 6.21 and 6.22.

for dealing with the new court forms designed to identify those cases where a child has been harmed or is at risk of suffering harm by reason of any form of domestic abuse, violence within the household, child abduction or other conduct or behaviour.

6.56 The key procedural aspects of the policy can be summarised as follows:

- CAFCASS will receive copies of all applications for orders under section 8 of the Children Act 1989, regardless of whether or not an in-court dispute resolution scheme is operating in the court concerned.
- All applications must be scrutinised by CAFCASS for allegations of harm.
- In situations where a child has in the past been exposed to domestic abuse but there is insufficient information to require a child protection referral, no formal section 47[57] (child protection) referral will be made to the local authority. If, however, domestic abuse has been an issue within the family at any time, a formal notification must be made immediately to the local authority.[58]
- While it is unlikely that any inter-agency checks (police, local authority, child protection register) will be available at this immediate stage, this information will form part of CAFCASS's further work in the case and, for some families, this further assessment will lead on to a child protection referral. The immediate notification should not be delayed pending receipt of this information.
- The notification will inform the local authority of CAFCASS's concern and the most usual format for notification will be, where derived from the forms, to send through a copy of the relevant ones. It will also inform the local authority of the level and time limits of CAFCASS's involvement in the family.
- If there appears to be immediate, current risk to a child, then a section 47 (child protection) referral should be made as it would be in any other circumstances.[59]
- The responsibility to assess whether there appear to be current risks to the safety of the child continues throughout CAFCASS's work with the family.
- In particular, CAFCASS staff should continue to explore the possibility of domestic abuse, even if it is not recorded on the court papers – cultural issues, fear or accepting behaviours as 'normal' may mean that parents do not disclose concerns at the formal stage of making an application.
- Referrals to the local authority should also be made at any stage of

---

57 Children Act 1989, s 47, provides for a local authority in certain circumstances to investigate to decide whether 'they should take any action to safeguard or promote the child's welfare'. Those circumstances include the local authority having reasonable cause to suspect that the child in their area is suffering, or is likely to suffer, significant harm.

58 The rationale for notification rather than referral in these circumstances is explained in the draft Safeguarding Policy Framework, at p 57: 'This is because in many CAFCASS private law cases, family separation has changed the context within which the previous harm allegedly occurred.'

59 The process for the referral is currently set out in section 3 of the CAFCASS Child Protection Procedures. This too will be replaced by the finalised CAFCASS Safeguarding Policy Framework.

involvement with a case where it becomes apparent that the child /young person needs assessment for services as a 'child in need'. Parental consent is required for such a referral.

- In all situations where CAFCASS has been in contact with the local authority about a family, the local authority should be informed when CAFCASS's involvement has ended and be told the outcome of the case.
- CAFCASS should be told about the final outcome of the court process in all cases where the C1, C7 and C1A forms were provided at the outset.
- If CAFCASS has not been directed to prepare a section 7 report[60] in the proceedings, then agency checks can *only* be made without the subject's consent if something particular in the papers indicates that the checks are necessary. This means that:
  - where allegations in the C1 indicate a current risk to the child from domestic abuse, then agency checks should be carried out plus internal checks for any previous knowledge of the family, and a section 47 referral should also be made to the local authority (as this is a current child protection concern);
  - where the form indicates that domestic abuse has occurred but there is insufficient information at this stage to require an immediate child protection referral, internal checks within CAFCASS and external agency checks should still be carried out (because the child may have suffered harm in the past and the checks are necessary to ascertain whether the child remains at risk), and the local authority should be notified (as the previous domestic abuse indicates child protection issues relating to the family of which the local authority should be aware).
- Where concerns arise for any other reason, or at a later stage in a case, then it will be important for the CAFCASS practitioner to inform the parents that notifications or referrals are made to the local authority. Where such concerns arise, if the CAFCASS practitioner believes that agency checks are necessary then the checks should be carried out and, unless there is good reason not to do so, the subject of the checks should be informed.
- It is good practice to share the result of agency checks with the party or other adult who has been checked, as this will allow him/her to comment on the accuracy of the information that has been provided to CAFCASS by the other agency. This practice should be followed unless there is very good reason not to do so.
- Where allegations in the C1A relate specifically to domestic abuse, but there is no allegation or direct link to the child having witnessed the violence, then the policy records that 'CAFCASS does not currently have the authority to make automatic full agency checks at this stage'.

6.57 Whilst recognising the increased work demand caused by the extension of the statutory definition of harm and the routine provision to CAFCASS of all applications in private law cases, the CAFCASS section 120 policy ends positively with this conclusion:

---

60 A report directed by the court, under Children Act 1989, s 7, 'on such matters relating to the welfare of that child as are required to be dealt with in the report'.

'We believe that this is time well spent because it provides the opportunity to conduct a fuller risk assessment where allegations of harm to children exist and to protect children from harm at an earlier stage in the proceedings.'

6.58 Under its draft Safeguarding Policy Framework,[61] CAFCASS proposes to speed up the process of inter-agency checking and plug the procedural gaps through which some cases with safety issues inevitably fell. The proposal is for the screening of all applications notified by the court to CAFCASS, with, as an initial stage of any subsequent risk assessment, checks being made with the police,[62] the local authority[63] and the child protection registers to ascertain what (if any) information is already held about the family.

6.59 The rationale for a policy of screening in all cases is simply expounded within the body of the draft:[64]

'As a safeguarding agency, CAFCASS needs to be as sure as we can be, that children are safe within their current living arrangements, and will continue to be safe in any proposals for change to those arrangements. This is only a first step in a range of complex processes undertaken by CAFCASS staff, in the overall task of safeguarding and promoting the welfare of children. 'Being safe' is the start of a process not the end of the story.'

6.60 CAFCASS's aim is to implement the policy of total screening by 1 April 2007; however, it stresses that, while such screening is 'a vital first step ... it is not an adequate risk and safety assessment tool in isolation from other assessment'.

The CAFCASS Domestic Violence Policy and Toolkit

6.61 CAFCASS's Domestic Violence Policy and Toolkit is a comprehensive document that stretches to 71 pages. It starts with this clear policy statement:

'The purpose of the policy is to make clear our position on how we approach and work with cases of domestic violence. The professional standards are the minimum requirements that staff are expected to follow. The standards referred to in this policy are set out in full in the accompanying toolkit. The knowledge and good practice can be drawn on and referred to as staff consider the materials useful and relevant.

'CAFCASS is committed to the promotion of good outcomes for the children which are safe and sustainable. For most children this will involve positive relationships with parents, family members and other important relationships. Children are entitled to receive a service from CAFCASS

---

61 Available at www.cafcass.gov.uk/English/Publications/consultation/06May02ConsultSub Framework.pdf.

62 The information required from the police relates to criminal records, domestic violence incidents and any MAPPA (Multi-Agency Public Protection Arrangements) or MARAC (Multi-Agency Risk Assessment Conferencing) involvement.

63 The information required from the local authority relates to any relevant child protection or children in need concerns.

64 Supra, at p 42.

which is informed by a good assessment of their needs, including an assessment of any risk associated with alleged domestic violence.

'In all cases CAFCASS practitioners will screen for issues of domestic violence and conduct an appropriate and proportionate risk assessment.'

6.62 The stated policy aims and objectives reflect that general policy statement:

- to safeguard children and their parents or carers;
- to ensure that allegations of domestic violence are taken seriously and receive an appropriate and proportionate response;
- to ensure that appropriate child focused services are put in place;
- to establish clearly the agreed standards to be adopted in relation to domestic violence;
- to promote use of the good practice toolkit provided;
- to support the development of appropriate training for identifying domestic violence and assisting those affected by it;
- to ensure appropriate safety planning for all family members and staff;
- to provide standards of practice which can be consistently applied across all regions.

6.63 The remainder of Part I of the Domestic Violence Policy and Toolkit deals with CAFCASS's policy and standards in relation to a number of important areas:

- *Diversity* – CAFCASS sets out its commitment 'to providing a service that recognises the difference and uniqueness of all families and their individual circumstances'.
- *Children's rights* – CAFCASS sets out its commitment 'to ensure that the wishes of an individual child, subject to their age and understanding, will be sought as part of [the CAFCASS] assessment'.
- *Standards for routine enquiries* – The policy in this respect covers the following matters:
  - being routinely alert to the possibility of domestic violence in all private and public law family proceedings even when it has not been alleged, and the need for appropriate screening;
  - in private law cases, complying with the CAFCASS section 120 Policy;[65]
  - giving attention to any indication on the papers from the court, parties or solicitors that the address of one party should not be disclosed;
  - routinely asking parents about domestic violence separately, and in privacy at the first meeting or interview;
  - if there are concerns regarding interim orders or arrangements that appear to place a child and/or parent at risk, requesting more time from the court to assess the risk, or referring the matter back to

---

65   See paras 6.55–6.57.

court for further directions and/or consideration of whether a
finding of fact hearing is necessary.[66]

- *Standards for safety planning* – The policy makes clear that, if enquiries
  about domestic violence indicate that it may be a feature, CAFCASS's
  'work will be structured so as to protect children, families and staff' – two
  features are highlighted:
  - giving careful thought to the safety of bringing family members
    together and to making appropriate arrangements in such regard;
  - CAFCASS's holding of all personal information in confidence, with
    additional care to be taken in all cases where domestic violence is
    alleged to ensure that no information is disclosed that could prove
    dangerous to the adult victim or children.

- *Standards for assessment* – The standards here in large part mirror the
  requirements of the CAFCASS section 120 policy:
  - CAFCASS practitioners must continually assess potential risk
    arising from domestic violence throughout family proceedings and
    work closely with other agencies, particularly the police and the local
    authority, to ensure appropriate and proportionate enquiries about
    families are carried out to inform the assessment;
  - the child should be met with separately to discuss their wishes and
    feelings without the influence of parents or siblings;
  - in cases where the professional assessment concludes that the
    allegations of domestic violence could present a continuing risk of
    harm from a violent parent, a child protection referral to the local
    authority should be made in accordance with the child protection
    procedures;
  - if the allegations of domestic violence are such that a child could be
    in imminent danger from a violent parent, the immediate and urgent
    priority is to secure the safety of the child.

- *Standards for post order safety planning* – Two matters are emphasised:
  - where the assessment indicates ongoing issues of risk, the CAFCASS
    practitioner should discuss safety issues with the child and parents to
    ensure that they are able to make safety plans for future
    arrangements (for example, arranging for someone other than the
    parent to drop off or pick up a child from a contact visit);
  - the practitioner should also make sure that a vulnerable child or
    parent is made aware of and is able to access appropriate local
    support services and, when safety concerns are a feature, notify
    social services that CAFCASS's involvement with the children or
    family has ended.

6.64   Part II of the Domestic Violence Policy and Toolkit is the toolkit itself,
which is introduced with the following exposition:

'The toolkit is grounded in an understanding that a child[67] will differ in
her/his ability to cope with difficult family circumstances and with
separation from a parent. A child's ability to cope and adjust is influenced

---

66   The policy here makes direct reference to the CASC Guidelines for 'further information on
     interim orders'. See Appendix 6.
67   The toolkit makes clear that the term is intended to refer to all children and young people.

by a number of factors including: gender and age; personality; intellectual and other personal resources; the child's experience of an abusive environment; the nature and duration of the abuse; how aware the child is of what is or has taken place and what it means; the levels of attachment to the parents or carers; and the availability of support from family members and others.'

6.65 The wider context for the CAFCASS practitioner is also acknowledged, with a recognition that 'the political climate of this work is becoming increasingly pressured for practitioners'. This is seen as resulting from the 'polarisation' of 'views amongst some stakeholders' between a pro-safety approach and a pro-contact approach, which is regarded as having 'a significant impact on the issue of children and domestic violence'.

6.66 The toolkit is described as 'a flexible resource that can be used to assist staff to work through these difficult issues'. It sets out a research knowledge base, examples of evidenced based practice and some minimum professional standards for safeguarding and promoting the well-being of a child who has experienced domestic violence. It is divided into five sections:

- Definitions and Collaborative Practice;
- Understanding the Child's Experience of Domestic Violence;
- The Impact of Domestic Violence on Child Development;
- Good Practice for Assessment;
- Identifying and Reducing Risk.

6.67 One of the most significant features of the toolkit – CAFCASS's definition of 'domestic violence' – has already been recorded.[68] We highlight also the following aspects.

6.68 Within the section entitled 'Understanding a child's experience of problems at home', the context for the child is powerfully set out:[69]

'A child living with domestic violence is in an impossible situation in which her/his needs cannot be met. There may be an atmosphere of unpredictability and fear. The child may be hyper-vigilant for any signs of tension, raised voices and where it is a factor, signs for alcohol or drug abuse. What happens in the family may be kept secret and a child may feel at risk should they choose to disclose it or fear the wider consequences of family instability.'

6.69 The toolkit then observes[70] that 'a child will react in different ways to the violence they have witnessed or experienced depending on their personal resilience and support' and that among the complex mix of emotions which the child may experience are the following:

- a sense of guilt about the abuse between their parents;
- difficulties with their sense of identity;
- blaming parents and modelling inappropriate behaviour;

---

68   See para 6.23.
69   See section 3.2.1.
70   Sections 3.2.4 and 3.2.5.

- difficulty understanding parenting and a sense of divided loyalty between their parents.

6.70   Having identified that 'lack of effective communication can be a major barrier for a child to get the help s/he needs' and recorded that children who had participated in studies on domestic violence had 'stressed in particular that they wanted their parents to talk to them more',[71] the toolkit recognises the 'challenging task' for the CAFCASS practitioner 'to find a balance between enabling a child to discuss her/his wishes and feelings and asking them to re-visit upsetting thoughts'.[72] In terms of the CAFCASS practitioner achieving that task, the following pointers are provided:

- It is important to ensure that the environment chosen to interview a child is appropriate for the particular child and as non-threatening as possible (for example, if a child is present at court, it is unlikely to be appropriate to question him or her then and there about their experience of family violence).

- Before meeting the child, gather as much relevant information as possible from other agencies about their involvement and understanding of the child's experience, and any welfare concerns they may have.

- A child should not be treated as a witness to domestic violence. The focus of assessing the child's wishes and feelings will be to understand 'his/her reality' of the situation.[73]

- A child should be encouraged to discuss his or her feelings without the influence of parents or siblings and in an environment in which they can feel safe.

- When communicating with a child it is helpful for the CAFCASS practitioner to reflect on their own assumptions about a child or parent and to try to understand the child's experience through discussion with the family. Wider family networks, and even the community to which they belong, may be part of the problem. When making a critical professional judgment it is important for the CAFCASS practitioner to make a realistic and informed appraisal of the strengths and resources in the family and the relative weight that should be afforded to each.

- When talking to a child about his or her experience of domestic violence, it may help communications between the CAFCASS practitioner and the child for the former to identify and acknowledge with the child any barriers to communication that may exist because of the differences between them (such as age, gender, ethnicity, faith, culture, sexuality). It may also help for the practitioner to recognise the relationship of power that they have, and understand that this may reinforce the child's sense of vulnerability: this can be lessened through allowing the child the time to 'tell their story' in a way comfortable to them and by providing the child

---

71   Section 3.4.1.
72   Section 3.5.
73   This is amplified at section 5.10.5: 'It is important to keep in mind when interviewing a child that the purpose of the interview is not to identify whether or not the domestic violence has happened, but to determine the child's reality of the situation and to assess the impact on the child. It will usually be necessary to ask some questions to assess the impact.' Suggested child assessment questions are set out at section 5.10.8.

with the support he or she may need to communicate (eg interpreters) and the time to demonstrate their feelings through play and drawing.

• The complex nature of some of these communications may require a practitioner to suggest to the court that the child would benefit from separate legal representation under rule 9.5 of the Family Proceedings Rules 1991.

6.71 Section 4 of the toolkit provides in matrix form a guide to considering the impact of domestic violence on the child in five identified stages of childhood – the unborn child to two years; child(ren) aged 3–4 years; child(ren) aged 5–9 years; child(ren) aged 10–14; child(ren) 15 years and older. For each age range, and in respect of each area of development – health, intellectual development, identity, family and social relations, and emotional/behavioural development – the matrix outlines the impacts of domestic violence and suggests both protective factors and some warning signs. Whilst commending the potential helpfulness of the matrix, the toolkit stresses that 'the response to children who have experienced domestic violence needs to be sensitive and not overly prescriptive'.[74]

6.72 Section 5 of the toolkit sets out points of good practice for the CAFCASS practitioner, with the aim that their following 'will ensure that potential or actual harm posed by domestic violence is identified, assessed and minimised for all children and their families'. These points of good practice, which are intended to support (and in some cases reiterate) the minimum professional standards set out in Part I of the policy, provide guidance on routine enquiries for domestic violence, safety planning (for meetings and in court) and for initial assessment for domestic violence.

6.73 Good practice on the part of CAFCASS includes the following:

• report writing that moves beyond citing domestic violence as a feature and attempts to explore the nature of the violence or abuse that has occurred and to analyse its likely impact;[75]

• being aware when assessing a parent's statement that it is common for a parent to have involvement with many agencies before they disclose the occurrence or extent of the abuse – a parent may be unaware of the effects of the abuse on their children and so not include issues of domestic violence in their statements, or those disclosed may only represent the 'tip of the iceberg';[76]

• following, where appropriate, the CASC Guidelines, remembering that 'the key point is whether a finding [of fact] might affect the issue of contact';[77]

• where early screening identifies domestic violence as a feature which could indicate a risk of abuse, alerting the court to the need for further enquiries, with consideration of the following options: informing the court that domestic violence has been raised as an issue, requesting a

---

74 Section 4.1.1.
75 Section 5.3.4.
76 Section 5.5.4.
77 Section 5.9.3.

directions appointment if domestic violence is only raised after the first directions appointment, and preparing an interim report (if time allows);[78]

- where domestic violence is a feature, being alert to emerging risks associated with all interim arrangements that could place a child at risk of harm while awaiting a finding of fact hearing (a speedy referral of the case back to court may be required).[79]

6.74 Section 5.9.7 deals with report-writing for the fact-finding hearing, providing as follows:

> 'In private law proceedings the practitioner can invite the court to order a report for a finding of fact hearing. Any report for a finding of fact hearing should be restricted to information on the alleged facts relating to the issue before the court, i.e. domestic violence. If the court wishes the report to address any other issues, the practitioner should invite the court to clarify what is being requested, bearing in mind the difficulties that the practitioner will have in making a welfare recommendation before any findings have been made as to the domestic violence. A decision as to whether the child should be interviewed, as part of the preparation for the report for the finding of fact hearing should only be taken following discussion with the service manager to assess the implications and risk to [the] child of using her/his evidence.'

6.75 Section 5.9.9 requires the CAFCASS practitioner to consider putting before the court the issue of separate representation for the child[80] where 'the allegations of domestic violence are very serious or the case has considerable levels of complexity'.

6.76 The role of the domestically violent parent in the future life of their child is probably the most contentious issue in this area. We have noted the subtle but important differences in approach to that issue in *Re L; Re V; Re M; Re H*[81] between Drs Sturge and Glaser on the one hand and the Court of Appeal on the other.[82] What of the CAFCASS approach?

6.77 In addressing that issue, the toolkit (in its section entitled 'the implications of domestic violence for parenting assessments'[83]) refers the CAFCASS practitioner to (it is said) two aspects of the decision *Re M (Contact: Violent Parent)*.[84] It does so, however, with a degree of inaccuracy in citation.

6.78 First, it describes the Court of Appeal as having held in that case that 'as a matter of principle domestic violence of itself cannot constitute a bar to contact. It is one factor in the difficult and delicate balancing exercise of

---

78   Section 5.9.4.
79   Section 5.9.5.
80   See para 8.44 et seq.
81   Supra.
82   See paras 6.7–6.9.
83   Sections 5.9.10–5.9.11.
84   [1999] 2 FLR 321.

discretion'. In fact, *Re M* was not a Court of Appeal authority, it is a first instance decision of Mr Justice Wall (as he then was). Further, the citation, while accurate, comes not from *Re M* but from the later Court of Appeal decision of *Re L; Re V; Re M; Re H.*[85]

6.79 Secondly, and of more importance is the following passage, with the CAFCASS practitioner directed (at section 5.9.11 of the toolkit) to comments (again said to be from *Re M*):

'... that too little weight had been given to the need for the father to change. He suggested that the father should demonstrate that he was a fit person to exercise contact and should show a track record of proper behaviour. Assertions without evidence to back it up will not be sufficient.'

6.80 Again, the passage is from *Re L; Re V; Re M; Re H*[86] (paraphrasing the comments of Mr Justice Wall in *Re M*), but it is not accurately recited. Between the first two words ('that' and 'too') lies the qualification: 'often in cases where domestic violence had been found'. Further, the true coda ('Assertions, without evidence to back it up, may well not be sufficient') has seen 'may well not' hardened into 'will not'. In a line of work where clarity of emphasis is important and where inaccuracy can breed mistrust, it is to be hoped that this section of the toolkit is corrected if and when updated.

6.81 In terms of guidance within this section other than through law report citation, the toolkit directs the CAFCASS practitioner as follows:[87]

'Where domestic violence is a feature, the questions are around what role a parent should play in the future of the children's life ... In undertaking this difficult balancing exercise, the practitioner should consider whether the nature and scope of the abuse or violence by one parent against the children's main carer can be regarded as a failure in their parenting capacity.

'... If there is evidence that the children have been exposed to traumas, an assessment should be made as to the abusive parent's ability to recognise the impact of their conduct on the children and their partner. The obligation is on the abusive parent to demonstrate that he or she can be a positive and constructive influence on the children's life in the future.'

6.82 Sections 5.10.1–5.10.18 set out good practice in relation to the assessment of children and their families. Some aspects of that good practice have already been highlighted in the earlier parts of the policy and toolkit; the following should also be borne in mind:

● The CAFCASS practitioner should try to analyse critically the behaviour and emotions demonstrated by the children such as sadness, guilt, illness,

---

85	[2000] 2 FLR 334, at p 342. The same principle was enunciated, albeit with slightly different words, in the earlier Court of Appeal decision of *Re H (Contact: Domestic Violence)* [1998] 2 FLR 42, at p 56.

86	[2000] 2 FLR 334, at p 342.

87	Sections 5.9.10–5.9.11 of the toolkit.

and depression to assess the possible causes. Attention will need to be given to the possibility that domestic violence and/or other abusive situations are the cause.

- When preparing to talk to a child about domestic violence the practitioner may wish to allow extra time and care to provide the right circumstances for this to take place. It is important to keep in focus how terrifying adult anger can be for a child, and how different the child's perception of threat to life can be from that of an adult. It is good practice for a child who has experienced domestic violence to be interviewed alone and given the opportunity to share his or her feelings about what has happened and what they wish the future solution to be.

- Effective early planning is recommended. The meeting is likely to evoke difficulties and pain for the child and the difficulty of being part of this process should be thought through ahead of the meeting.

- If a child has sufficient understanding, a balance should be sought between encouraging the child to participate in finding a solution and ensuring that they do not feel the weight of responsibility. The overriding priority to consider is the safety of the children or that of any other children in the family.

- It is important for the CAFCASS practitioner to reassure the child at the outset and to validate their wishes and feelings.[88]

- It is important that the child is seen in all cases, particularly so in cases where domestic violence is a feature. In most circumstances, one interview with a child will not be enough to assess fully their wishes and feelings.[89]

- Whether or not the couple are still together, an assessment of their relationship should also take place, and this should include an awareness of any power and control issues. The dynamics in the relationship are relevant to the violence and to the couple's ability to give due attention to the needs of their child. Sometimes abused parents can be so consumed by their need for survival that this need is prioritised above all else.

- It is important to discuss with parents their understanding and reaction to any allegations of abuse that have been made, and the likely impact upon the child.

- For parents who have separated and are in dispute about contact arrangements, the assessment should include consideration of the following:
  - whether the violence is denied or minimised by the parent, and/or minimised by the parent who has escaped from the domestic violence;
  - the increased risk period for the most severe violence (including murders) often being post-separation;
  - whether there are anger management issues;[90]
  - whether the separation is likely to be sustained – a pattern can often

---

88   This is because, whilst children's accounts of receiving professional help vary, many report negative experiences (see section 5.10.7).

89   Section 5.10.8 sets out some sample questions that could be asked of a child when assessing the child's experience of domestic violence.

90   Section 5.10.13 makes the point that 'anger management and domestic violence should not be confused – the exertion of power and control in domestic violence makes it very different, however, the two can sometimes co-exist'.

be found where the couple repeatedly separate only to reverse their decision if the partner swears to reform or, through violent threats, persuades the parent to re-consider.

- The child should be observed with each of his or her parents or carers and the quality and nature of the attachment assessed, though the toolkit directs the practitioner, when observing contact, to be alert to the risk of harm and to refer the case back to court for directions if the risks associated with contact are too great.[91] However, it is also important to remain child focused when observing contact and use this opportunity to understand how the child feels about the situation.
- The ability of the parent to understand the consequences of his or her actions should be assessed as well as their potential to change.
- A judgement based on an initial assessment of risk must be made as to whether a referral to dispute resolution or mediation will be appropriate.

6.83 Amplifying guidance from earlier parts of the toolkit, sections 5.10.19–5.10.24 set out the factors for the CAFCASS practitioner to consider when assessing possible contact arrangements in circumstances of domestic violence. In terms of considering the possible contact options, it is recommended that an assessment should be made of:

- what is happening to a child in the context of his or her family and the wider community;
- the nature of the interactions between the child, the child's family and environmental factors; and
- how his or her learning and development have been affected.

6.84 This assessment should aim to identify both positive and negative influences for the child, with the practitioner invited to consider:

- in relation to positive influences:
  - the history of relationships within the family;
  - the potential for change in the child and family;
  - how well the child is doing; and
  - the likelihood of a parent building on and developing positive experiences for the child;
- in relation to negative influences:
  - the level and type of abuse, neglect, domestic violence;
  - the possible collusion of others family members in the domestic violence, with analysis to be undertaken of all those involved in proposed contact arrangements; and
  - the child and family response to intervention.

6.85 Additionally, the CAFCASS practitioner should be satisfied that contact is not being sought on the following grounds:

- to allow a parent to continue to abuse or threaten the child and/or the other parent;
- to gain access to the parent who has experienced the violence or abuse;
- to obtain that parent's new address; and

---

91 Although not explicitly spelt out, this must mean that the guidance to observe is not universal and must give way where such observation would not be safe and in the child's best interests.

- to use friends or relatives to achieve any of the above.

6.86 Directing the CAFCASS practitioner to the research indicating the potential risks associated with contact handovers,[92] the toolkit recommends that the dangers of assaults, threats and verbal abuse arising at such should be discussed with the parent and a safety plan identified as part of agreed contact arrangements.[93]

6.87 At section 5.10.22, the CAFCASS practitioner is invited, 'when balancing the sometimes conflicting needs of the child and parent in contact arrangements', to consider the following possible implications for the child:[94]

- a continuing sense of fear of the violent parent;
- anxieties when close to the violent parent;
- a continuing awareness of the fear a violent parent arouses in the child's main carer;
- that the child's experience of the climate of conflict could:
    - undermine his or her general stability and sense of emotional well-being;
    - cause tugs of loyalty and a sense of responsibility for the conflict;
    - continue the unhealthy example of parental relationships (ie dominant, bullying and controlling behaviour);
    - bring about unreliable patterns of contact causing the child to feel frequently let down or unwanted and of little importance to a parent; and
    - continue the physical, sexual or emotional abuse of the parent;
- the child's own attitudes to parenting and relationships, including the potential for the child to behave violently to other children and adults;
- the child being at risk from direct physical abuse, with parents who are violent to each other being more likely to be violent to their child; and
- the child trying to act as a peacemaker in the family and feeling responsible for the family.

6.88 In the context of assessing contact options available to the court, the toolkit also stresses the following:

- It is important to distinguish between the implications of an order for no contact, supported contact arrangements (which are typically not closely supervised), and an order for full-supervised contact arrangements.
- The CAFCASS practitioner should be cautious about supporting an application to withdraw a case from court. It could be a safer outcome if the court makes an order for no contact and it may also be appropriate to recommend that an order under section 91(14) of the Children Act 1989 be made 'to prevent an abusive parent making repeat applications that aim to continue to harass and abuse through the court system'.
- Where contact is felt to be in the best interests of the child, the issue of

---

92　See M Hester & L Radford *Domestic Violence and Child Contact in England and Denmark* (University of Bristol Policy Press, 1996).

93　Section 5.10.21.

94　These factors are drawn from the report by J Sturge & D Glaser *Contact and Domestic Violence – the Experts Court Report* [2000] Fam Law 615.

safety should remain central to discussions at all times, with it being increasingly recognised that, in families where domestic violence is a concern, effective child protection is provided through ensuring the safety and protection of an abused parent.

6.89 Section 6 of the toolkit 'provides guidance on the complex exercise of identifying and reducing the risk of domestic violence for a child'. Introducing that exercise, section 6.1.2 provides as follows:

'Risk assessment in situations of domestic violence means trying to identify the child or adult who is most at risk of experiencing violence in the future. Routine enquiries are the first stage of this process, if information about domestic violence emerges from the initial enquiry it will be necessary to try to assess the level and type of risk and decide how, or, if it can be managed.'

6.90 This section of the toolkit in particular:

- gives examples of the types of behaviour that may indicate situations of domestic violence;[95]
- suggests how to facilitate a discussion about domestic violence;[96]
- gives examples of some evidenced based risk indicators and some risk assessment models;[97] and
- addresses the issue of post order reduction of risk, marking the importance especially of the following matters:
  - the risks of violence post separation;
  - the need to include as an element in risk assessments and future safety planning the parent's perception of risk;
  - discussing safety planning with the abused parent.[98]

6.91 It should be noted that, within CAFCASS's draft Safeguarding Policy Framework,[99] the following 18 key elements for CAFCASS risk and safety assessments are identified:

(1) If the screening process has revealed a cause for concern, then wherever possible the relevant professionals (eg health, local authority children's social care, education, probation) should be spoken to and file records seen.

(2) The level of involvement of these other relevant agencies must be identified, along with their own assessments of risk and safety features in the family.

(3) A chronology of previous contacts and concerns should be prepared, co-ordinating information from all sources.

(4) Account should be taken of safety issues for staff and other adults, as well as for the child.

---

95 Section 6.2.
96 Section 6.3.
97 Section 6.4. Appendix 1 of the toolkit comprises a model risk assessment tool. Appendix 2 is the 'Model from Cardiff Women's Safety Unit & South Wales Police – Victim Initial Risk Indicator'.
98 Section 6.5.
99 Supra, at p 48.

(5)   The CAFCASS practitioner should differentiate between risk factors determined by the behaviour and circumstances of the perpetrator, and those determined by the circumstances of the victim.

(6)   The practitioner should consider whether the child is able and confident enough to give a view about the court application.

(7)   Where there are domestic violence issues, the views of the victim must be ascertained about the current perceived level of risk and whether this is getting worse.

(8)   The victim's views should also be ascertained about the applications being considered by the court.

(9)   Where the perpetrator of any alleged harm is a family member, the alleged perpetrator's views should be ascertained about the harm, about the perceived impact on the victim and about the applications being considered by the court.

(10)   Where there are domestic violence concerns, there should be a consideration of what needs to change for a perpetrator to be considered safe.[100]

(11)   The assessment must always cover issues about the safety of others who are important to the child, especially adult and child family members. This is a core part of the child's own assessment.

(12)   The practitioner should identify the specific factors which are making matters better or worse.

(13)   The practitioner should identify too the impact of race, culture or any other diversity factors.

(14)   The practitioner should also identify in detail what would make matters safer, and what would increase the risk.

(15)   The practitioner needs to plan ahead: what needs to happen at home for this child to be safe?

(16)   Consideration has to be given to what needs to happen at court for the safety plan to be effective.

(17)   The longer term future also needs to be considered – are there risks to the child's safety that may need a child protection referral?[101]

(18)   The practitioner should use the CAF (Common Assessment Framework)[102] form to identify needs beyond immediate safety issues.

FURTHER REFORM

6.92   For doubtless too long, the focus in contact cases involving domestic violence issues has been predominantly on law and procedure. What, however, has become increasingly apparent is the significance of other aspects of the court process and the consequent need for all participants in that process to have a greater breadth of knowledge and understanding.

---

100   Reference is there made to the report by J Sturge & D Glaser *Contact and Domestic Violence – the Experts Court Report* [2000] Fam Law 615.

101   The draft urges the practitioner to 'remember, for example, that almost all prisoners come out …'.

102   The CAF is a mechanism for use by all children's agencies for gathering information at the start of work with families. More information and a copy of the current form can be found at www.everychildmatters.gov.uk.

The HMICA Report

6.93 That much is clear from the important recent report prepared by HMICA (HM Inspectorate of Court Administration).[103] Published on 11 October 2005, *Domestic Violence, Safety and Family Proceedings*[104] entails the review that HMICA undertook of how domestic violence issues are addressed by CAFCASS and administered by HMCS (Her Majesty's Courts Service).

6.94 The HMICA inspection looked at the handling of these issues by the family courts in their administrative arrangements, particularly from the perspective of court users. It reported also on CAFCASS's strategic management and its frontline practice when dealing with such cases. In his foreword to the report, Eddie Bloomfield, Chief Inspector of HMICA, summarised its thrust:

'This report finds an inherent danger arising from the current policy emphasis on seeking mediated agreements between parents in ever larger numbers of disputed family proceedings. We conclude that ensuring the safety of both children and adults receives insufficient consideration – this was a strong and consistent message from the women survivors of domestic violence who we consulted. We consider that arrangements for assessing the risks associated with allegations of domestic violence need markedly strengthening.

'I am pleased to report examples of good practice in both Services. But, the overall picture is far less satisfactory. Both HMCS and CAFCASS need significantly to improve safety within their service delivery and the report's eleven recommendations are designed to assist that process.

'We also need to recognise how emotionally wearing it is for the wide range of professionals who have to deal with domestic violence on a near daily basis. As this inspection shows, there is a risk that individuals within agencies sometimes find it easier to down-play or even ignore the presenting signs of domestic violence. Its seriousness, and corrosive effects on both survivors and children, require that HMCS and CAFCASS implement robust strategies to guide staff in how to handle cases where domestic violence is alleged, or is proven to be an issue, in the context of family proceedings. These are essential steps towards achieving improved sensitivity and effectiveness in service delivery for some of society's most vulnerable people.'

6.95 The HMICA report, which came out during the course of the Children and Adoption Bill's passage through Parliament, provided a prompt for the amendments that now see the CAFCASS risk assessment placed on a statutory

---

103 HMICA describes itself as 'an independent inspectorate, reporting directly to ministers on the services provided for those who have come to court'. This does not include inspecting or commenting on judicial decisions.

104 The full title of the report is *Domestic Violence, Safety and Family Proceedings – Thematic review of the handling of domestic violence issues by the Children and Family Court Advisory and Support Service (CAFCASS) and the administration of family courts in Her Majesty's Courts Service (HMCS)* (October 2005) – available at www.hmica.gov.uk.

footing. It also had the desired effect on HMCS and CAFCASS who, to their credit, responded quickly and constructively to its proposals.

6.96   On behalf of HMCS, its Chief Executive, Sir Ron de Witt, commented:

> 'Domestic violence is a feature of many family proceedings cases. Victims deserve to receive the best possible support from the family courts so they can take a full part in the legal process. I am pleased this report praises our work in the criminal courts and highlights examples of good practice at a local level in the family courts. However, we need to do better and have prepared an action plan in response to the recommendations. We will develop a national strategy for dealing with family cases where domestic violence is a factor, ensure we have systems in place to identify these cases and publicise the special facilities we can offer, such as video conferencing. These changes will help to ensure that family courts address the experiences and fears of victims of domestic violence.'

6.97   For CAFCASS, Anthony Douglas, its Chief Executive, responded in a similarly positive way:

> 'CAFCASS recognises the need to safeguard and support victims of domestic violence, including children, more rigorously. Our recently launched Domestic Violence Policy and Toolkit, which was commended in the report, is key to achieving consistent standards of practice in this work. The report highlights many areas of concern for us and an action plan has been prepared in response to the recommendations. The findings of this report will be built into our practice and into our quality assurance programmes, and the lessons for ourselves and our partner agencies will be taken on board and given the highest priority.'

6.98   As highlighted in its foreword, the HMICA report makes 11 recommendations (five to CAFCASS and six to HMCS), which are aimed at improving service delivery to the public. In the case of CAFCASS, the particular emphasis is on putting in place national standards and competencies, providing training in risk assessment and improved safety planning. In the case of HMCS, it is on developing and implementing policies (including staff training) that safeguard vulnerable people, and making information about court facilities available to them before they attend court.

6.99   For ease of reference, these specific recommendations, of which all family court users should be aware, are set out in Appendix 7, with the responses and actions plans of CAFCASS and HMCS respectively italicised under each recommendation.

6.100   Suffice to say that, if those action plans are fully carried out, then considerable improvements will have been made to the way in which domestic violence issues arising in private law children's cases are addressed by the court system as a whole.

The Wall Report

6.101   The same can also be said of the recommendations made by Lord Justice Wall in a report that he prepared for the President of the Family Division in March 2006.

6.102   *A Report to the President of the Family Division on the Publication by the Women's Aid Federation of England Entitled Twenty-Nine Child Homicides: Lessons Still to be Learnt on Domestic Violence and Child Protection with Particular Reference to the Five Cases in which there was Judicial Involvement*[105] by its title summarises and reflects the importance of its subject matter.

6.103   In introducing his report, in which he examines the cases highlighted by WAFE which had court involvement, Lord Justice Wall makes this initial point:

'... whilst I by no means agree with everything in it, I welcome WAFE's initiative in publishing *29 Child Homicides*. However painful they are, practitioners in the Family Justice System need regular reminders of the evils of domestic violence. The document provides one such reminder.'[106]

6.104   Having thoroughly examined the court files relating to the five cases subject to court proceedings (in which 11 children were killed by their fathers) and sought and obtained the views of the judges involved, Lord Justice Wall starts his conclusions with these general observations:

'Nothing in what follows is intended, or should be read, as seeking in any way to minimise the appalling human tragedies represented by each of the 29 homicides identified by WAFE. Equally, nothing in what follows should be read as indicating that there are no lessons to be learned from the cases under discussion or that the system operating in the Family Courts does not require constant vigilance, re-examination and improvement. It is, however, only fair to the Family Justice System to make the following points.'[107]

6.105   He first emphasises that *29 Child Homicides* deals with a 10-year period and that 18 of the 29 children who were murdered were not subject to any form of court proceedings.

6.106   Of the 11 children who were the subject of court proceedings, Lord Justice Wall expresses himself satisfied that eight:

'... died as a result of parental actions which could not have been reasonably foreseen or prevented by the court, and in which no criticism can be made of the judges who made the respective contact orders.'[108]

6.107   As to the remaining three children, he concludes that:

'... it is arguable that the court should have taken a more proactive stance and refused to make a consent order for contact. On the other side of the argument, however, is the case put forward by the judges for making the contact orders, and the fact that the orders were made in what the judges concerned genuinely believed to be in the best interests of the children.'[109]

6.108   Lord Justice Wall adds:

---

105   The report is now available in full at www.family-justice-council.org.uk/docs/report_family. pdf.
106   Ibid, at para 1.13.
107   Ibid, at para 8.1.
108   Ibid, at para 8.3.
109   Ibid, at para 8.4.

'It must, I think, always be remembered that the responsibility for murdering a child lies fairly and squarely on the murderer. The function of the Family Justice System is to protect children and to make contact safe. The system cannot, however, be foolproof, and parents who are determined to murder their children will find the means to do so whether or not an order is in place.

'These cases, therefore, tragic as they are, represent a tiny proportion of the many thousands of contact orders which are made each year.

'Furthermore, I am in no doubt that all the contact orders in the cases concerned were made in good faith and that the judges did their best conscientiously to apply section 1 of the Children Act 1989.'[110]

6.109 Following on from those observations and case conclusions, Lord Justice Wall expresses himself:

'... quite satisfied that it would be wrong to hold any of the judges "responsible" or "accountable"[111] for the deaths of any of the children, nor would it be appropriate for any form of disciplinary action to be instituted.'[112]

6.110 He is very keen, however, to emphasise that such a conclusion 'does not of course mean that there are no lessons to be learned' and he is equally swift to highlight that three of the five cases involved consent orders for contact. He explains:

'Applications for such orders, in my judgment, pose a difficult challenge for the court. On the one hand, as the judge in the case NS and JS pointed out, the philosophy of the Children Act is non-interventionist, and encourages settlements. Section 1(5) of the Act provides in terms that the court must not make an order "unless it considers that doing so would be better for the child than making no order at all". So if parents come into court with a consent order, the judicial instinct is to welcome it. As the judge in the same case pointed out, if he had refused to make the order, there was nothing to stop the parents implementing their agreement without reference to the court.

'It has, however, to be remembered that the responsibility for making an order remains that of the judge, and judges can only make orders in relation to children if they consider that the order is in the best interests of the child. A judge cannot therefore abnegate responsibility for an order because it is made by consent. Judges have the responsibility to scrutinise proposed consent orders and satisfy themselves that the particular order is in the interests of the child.

---

110 Ibid, at paras 8.5–8.7.
111 Lord Justice Wall comments, at paras 8.8 and 8.9, that, while he sees as apt six of the seven questions posed by WAFE, he expresses the view that there is a non sequitur in the first – 'Did the court knowingly grant unsupervised contact or residence to a violent parent – and, if so, has anyone been held accountable?' He also describes the wording of WAFE's second recommendation as 'unhelpful'.
112 Ibid, at para 8.15.

'In my judgment, the question of making consent orders in contact and residence proceedings involving domestic violence needs to be further considered. It may be that in such cases judges need to be more proactive, and that good practice should require a more interventionist and robust approach to such orders. At the same time, it is, in my judgment, essential that the court satisfies itself that each party had entered into the consent order freely and without pressure being placed upon them. It is a frequent complaint that because of what is perceived as the court's bias towards contact, lawyers pressurise reluctant mothers into consent orders for contact which they do not believe to be safe for their children.'[113]

6.111 Those observations form the first of three specific recommendations made by Lord Justice Wall:

'That ... the Family Justice Council[114] [be invited] to consider and to report, in a multi-disciplinary context, on the approach which the courts should adopt to proposed consent orders in contact cases where domestic violence is in issue. Possible terms of reference would be those set out by the judge in the case of TB, namely:

'This tragic case raises a difficult question. When is it appropriate for a judge to refuse to approve a consent order agreed between well represented parents as to arrangements for their children, in circumstances when the court has not made any findings as to cross-allegations of domestic violence? I think the lesson to be learned is that there are some cases when the court should decline to approve an agreed order until it has heard evidence, and made findings.[115] The difficulty is spotting such cases, particularly if the family court advisor is neutral, or largely supportive of contact.

'In addition, any investigation by the Family Justice Council could consider the allegation that parties (and particularly mothers) are sometimes pressurised by their lawyers into reaching agreements about contact which they do not believe to be safe.'[116]

6.112 His second recommendation relates to those cases where violence is directed to the mother but not the child. Having been 'concerned to read at a number of places in the files that reliance was being placed on the proposition that it may [in those circumstances] be safe to order contact'[117], he states that:

'... reinforcement needs to be given to the lead provided by Drs Sturge and Glaser (and accepted by the Court of Appeal in *Re L; Re V; Re M; Re*

---

113 Ibid, at paras 8.19–8.21.

114 The primary role of the Family Justice Council is to promote an inter-disciplinary approach to the needs of family justice, and through consultation and research, to monitor the effectiveness of the system and advise on reforms necessary for continuous improvement. For more information, see the Council's website at www.family-justice-council.org.uk.

115 For the court's power to take this course and, for the relevant factors to be applied when considering such course in public law proceedings, see *A County Council v DP, RS, BS (by the Children's Guardian)* [2005] EWHC 1593 (Fam), [2005] 2 FLR 1031.

116 The Wall Report (supra), at para 8.27.

117 Ibid, at para 8.22.

H[118]) that it is a non-sequitur to consider that a parent who has a history of violence to the other parent of their children is, at one and the same time, a good parent. This needs to be considered in all cases where there is domestic violence and would ensure a more rigorous approach to safety in these cases.'[119]

6.113   Prefacing that second recommendation, Lord Justice Wall comments:

'It is, in my view, high time that the Family Justice System abandoned any reliance on the proposition that a man can have a history of violence to the mother of his children but, nonetheless, be a good father.'[120]

6.114   The third recommendation of the report relates to training and reflects its particular importance in this field:

'... no judge should sit for the first time in private law proceedings without having undergone training which includes multi-disciplinary instruction on domestic violence. It is also imperative that all refresher courses contain updating on domestic violence issues.'[121]

CONCLUSIONS

6.115   The discussion of the HMICA and Wall reports highlights the key tension in this area – between the long-standing policy focus on settlement (with its assumed benefits of avoiding further conflict) and the necessity of keeping the child safe. In many private law children's cases, those objectives will not be in conflict, but in some they clearly will. At the time of writing, the Family Justice Council is responding to the invitation contained in Lord Justice Wall's first recommendation and their multi-disciplinary consideration will be welcome.

6.116   But that identified tension may mask another, which may in some part be responsible for it – the tension between what, in *Re L; Re V; Re M; Re H*,[122] the experts contended should be the approach to future contact when domestic violence has been found and what the Court of Appeal itself found should be the approach. This is important because of the significance attached to this decision and to the continuing references to the expert advice that it contained. Whilst one frequently reads of the expert advice having been accepted or endorsed by the Court of Appeal, that of course is not entirely correct; and it may actually be far more productive to consider the possible consequences of this tension than unconsciously glossing over its existence:

●   Is this a problem in practice for the CAFCASS practitioner, whose critical and soon-to-be statutory role it is to assess risk? Do they, in the circumstances of a finding of domestic violence, form their recommendation on the basis of the outlined considerations (the ability of the offending parent to recognise their past conduct, to be aware of the

118   [2000] 2 FLR 334.
119   The Wall Report (supra), at para 8.28.
120   Ibid, at para 8.22.
121   Ibid, at para 8.29.
122   [2000] 2 FLR 334.

need to change and to make genuine efforts to do so) being in effect preconditions for contact (the Sturge/Glaser approach) or just factors (albeit important ones) in the discretionary balance (the Court of Appeal approach)?

- Did the Court of Appeal's reluctance to endorse the approach of the experts, whose views they commissioned and otherwise entirely endorsed, send out (inadvertently) a message that was too ready to countenance contact where domestic violence was found? If so, has this reverberated in practice in a way that, maybe in some cases, has seen consent orders arrived at in the belief that the court would still look to order some form of contact, notwithstanding the findings that it has made? To what extent have some judges generally and in the individual cases concerned contributed to that belief?[123]

- What are the parent – and in particular the victim parent – perceptions of this tension? Are they aware of it? Do they understand it?

6.117 Of course, the issue identified by Lord Justice Wall potentially has far broader ramifications. As he noted, most of the 29 child homicides occurred in cases unknown to the courts. They would have been part of the vast majority of children whose parents are able, without outside intervention, to agree childcare arrangements. This is the broad band of the parenting public held up as the ideal and shown to have far higher satisfaction rates than those families who have engaged either in mediation or in court proceedings.[124] If, as it should, the safety of the child is to trump the advantages of compromise, should the State not be sending out the message to all families on separation to consider carefully the arrangements for their children in situations where safety issues arise (particularly where there has been domestic violence)? Should these families not be encouraged to seek advice and, if needs be, to bring their cases to court where the court's decision may see their children better protected than otherwise? These are questions which, at some stage, will have to be properly addressed.

6.118 Again, in this chapter, as in the last, CAFCASS has heavily featured. Within the preceding chapter, we expressed the concerns at the increased burdens on CAFCASS and cautioned that, without sufficient resources, they might not be able to be borne. Particularly accounting for the extent and importance of their role in this specific area, the point warrants repetition.

6.119 Delayed assessments defeat the laudable aim of early intervention, leave children in limbo and foster anxiety. Inadequate assessments undermine the collaborative approach, encourage contested litigation, breed a lack of confidence in the system and may put the child at risk. In neither scenario are the interests of the child served and, in both, there are obvious increased costs implications, which would make the upfront reluctance to commit further resources seem like a very false saving.

---

123 Certainly, this was a view held in Parliament by the proponents of the amendment that saw the CAFCASS risk assessment put on a statutory footing (see para 6.48). The reference in the Private Law Programme to 'safety issues' constituting 'exceptional circumstances' (see para 5.90) provided grist to their mill.

124 See paras 1.46–1.47.

6.120 Nobody is suggesting that the officers of CAFCASS will do anything other than their utmost to discharge the key duties incumbent on them, but this line of work is important, complex and voluminous,[125] demanding on time and requiring a high level of skill and care. It cannot be done effectively without proper training and can only be done appropriately if the CAFCASS officers concerned have manageable workloads.

6.121 Many well-intentioned changes in public administration over the past 10 years have foundered through an unrealistic assessment of the level of resources required; and it is striking in this context that concern about the adequate resourcing of CAFCASS should be quite so widespread. At the very least, a careful eye will need to be kept on the frontline to see whether their risk assessments are being completed in timely and competent fashion. If not, action will need to be taken, and quickly, to enable that to occur.

6.122 Talk of resources, however, leads to mention of the welcome identification within *Parental Separation: Children's Needs and Parents' Responsibilities – Next Steps*[126] of £3 million and £4.5 million of additional government funding in 2006/7 and 2007/8 to help support contact, to include support delivered through contact centres. Especially in this area, where the safety of the child must be paramount, contact centres serve a very useful purpose; and it may well be a consequence of recent reforms and developments that there is more call for their use. It remains to be seen whether the additional funding identified will go far enough.

6.123 Whilst many of the changes that we have outlined in this chapter are applicable to safety issues as a whole, it is right that our focus has been on domestic violence, for it is that issue above all else that has driven those reforms and initiatives and raised and kept in the limelight the issue of child safety in the private law sphere.

6.124 It is also right to conclude on a positive note. The chapter ends where it began, with a comparison between the position today and that pertaining 10 years ago. There can be no doubt that the proper treatment of domestic violence in private law children's cases remains even now very much a work in progress, with more change to come and much for all the participants in the system still to learn and take on board. Nevertheless, and without seeking to engender any degree of complacency, the system has come on a long way in a relatively short period of time and the continuing determination in so many quarters to improve that system yet further can only augur well for the future.

---

125 From the outset, the Government indicated that risk assessments would be carried out in all cases where domestic violence is alleged (see Lord Adonis, Parliamentary Under-Secretary of State for the Department for Education and Skills, HL Deb, 14 November 2005, col 892).

126 January 2005 – Cm 6452 – available at www.dfes.gov.uk/childrensneeds/.

Chapter Seven

MAKING CONTACT HAPPEN: THE IMPACT OF THE CHILDREN AND ADOPTION ACT 2006

7.1 Many separated parents are able to agree the arrangements for their children with little or no assistance. Some need more help and guidance and are able to gain such from parenting plans and through mediation. For those who come to court, the process of in-court conciliation has fostered countless successful childcare arrangements. However, there will always be cases where the court is clear that contact is in the best interests of the child concerned, but the implementation of that 'best interests' decision requires more than a simple contact order alone. The passing of the Children and Adoption Act 2006 reflected the widespread recognition that more could and should be done to facilitate and enforce contact. With the new measures brought in by the Act in mind, we consider in this chapter the tools that the courts can now use to make sure that contact which should happen does happen.

7.2 Much of this chapter is taken up with a detailed consideration of some of the new provisions of the Children and Adoption Act 2006. That Act is concerned with two different areas of the law – orders with respect to children in family proceedings (Part 1) and adoptions with a foreign element (Part 2). The latter provisions are outside the scope of this book. The scheme of Part 1 is to insert various additional sections into the Children Act 1989, namely new sections 11A–11O, new section 16A[1] and new Schedule A1. Section 15 and Schedules 2 and 3 provide for minor and consequential amendments and repeals, and section 16 makes provision for the exercise of regulatory powers and for commencement.[2] At the time of writing, no date has been appointed for the commencement of any of the provisions in Part 1.

7.3 The overall effect of the new provisions is to extend the scope for court involvement in the management of parental contact where parents are unable to agree or resolve disputes through mediation. This approach is considered appropriate in order to achieve the social objective of enabling children to grow up with a close relationship with both parents. One result of these reforms is to make Part II of the Children Act a less accessible piece of legislation. The

---

1   S 16A, which introduces new provisions for risk assessments, is dealt with at para 6.44 et seq.

2   The relevant provisions of the Children Act 1989, as amended by the Children and Adoption Act 2006, are set out in Appendix 1. The full text of the 2006 Act, plus the relevant provisions of the Criminal Justice Act 2003, are set out in Appendix 2.

original provisions about section 8 orders, set out in relatively clear and concise prose, will hereafter be afflicted by a cumbersome set of 15 new sections.

7.4   Before setting out these new provisions, we consider the law governing enforcement of contact orders as it existed prior to the passing of the 2006 Act. That law is still highly relevant because the old remedies – contempt proceedings leading to imprisonment or fine, and/or orders changing the residence of the child – remain available, but are now supplemented by the much wider and, it is hoped, subtler and more effective powers provided by the 2006 Act. This chapter will therefore consider the law governing the facilitation and enforcement of contact in the following order:

- enforcement prior to the 2006 Act;
- contact activities under the 2006 Act;
- monitoring contact under the 2006 Act;
- family assistance orders following the amendments introduced by the 2006 Act;
- enforcement under the new law.

ENFORCEMENT OF CONTACT: LAW AND PRACTICE BEFORE 2006

7.5   For years, the courts have struggled to square the circle of enforcing orders for contact without damaging the welfare of the child. Even though a judge would usually conclude that it was in the child's interest to have contact with the non-resident parent, he or she would frequently draw back from enforcing his or her order because to do so would involve taking steps against the resident parent that might inflict harm on the child out of all proportion to the benefit to be derived from enforced contact. Typically, the emotional harm caused to a child if its mother is sent to prison has been thought to outweigh the advantages of any contact that may thereby follow. As a result, the process of enforcing contact was often long and drawn-out, and frequently unsuccessful.

7.6   The first stage in the process is to frame the contact order in a way which allows it to be enforced by court sanction. An order for 'reasonable contact' is not enforceable by contempt proceedings.[3] What is required is a clearly defined order directed at one or both of the parties,[4] for example, an order that the mother do make the child available for contact by delivering him or her to the father's address at a certain time.

7.7   Under the old law, the next stage was to attach a penal notice to the order, that is to say, a notice in the following terms: 'You must obey the directions contained in this order. If you do not you will be guilty of contempt of court and you may be sent to prison.' In the case of orders under section 8 of the Children Act 1989, however, the decision whether to attach a penal notice to such an order has hitherto been a matter for the discretion of the judge.[5] Until

---

3   *D v D (Access: Contempt: Committal)* [1991] 2 FLR 34.
4   *Re H (Contact: Enforcement)* [1996] 1 FLR 614.
5   FPR r 4.21A.

recently, judges would not infrequently decline to attach a notice if they felt that the process of enforcement would jeopardise the child's welfare.

7.8   If a parent continued to flout a contact order, notwithstanding the attachment of a penal notice, the court was placed in a difficult position, as described vividly by Mrs Justice Bracewell in *V v V (Contact: Implacable Hostility).*[6] Speaking of the situation prior to the passing of the Children and Adoption Act 2006, she said:[7]

> 'At present, enforcement of contact orders creates insuperable problems for the courts. Currently, there are only four options available to the court and each is unsatisfactory: one, send the parent who refuses or frustrates contact to prison, or make a suspended order of imprisonment. This option may well not achieve the object of reinstating contact; the child may blame the parent who applied to commit the carer to prison; the child's life may be disrupted if there is no one capable of or willing to care for the child when the parent is in prison; it cannot be anything other than emotionally damaging for a child to be suddenly removed into foster care by social services from a parent, usually a mother, who in all respects except contact is a good parent. Two, impose a fine on the parent. This option is rarely possible because it is not consistent with the welfare of a child to deprive a parent on a limited budget. Three, transfer residence. This option is not necessarily available to the court, because the other parent may not have the facilities or capacity to care for the child full-time, and may not even know the child. Four, give up. Make either an order for indirect contact or no order at all. This is the worst option of all and sometimes the only one available. This is the option which gives rise to the public blaming the judges for refusing to deal with recalcitrant parents. This option results in a perception fostered by the press that family courts are failing in private law cases and that family judges are anti-father.'

7.9   Notwithstanding the disincentives to imposing custodial sentences identified by Mrs Justice Bracewell, the courts have on occasions sent contemnors to prison for failing to comply with contact orders. Examples include *C v C (Access Order: Enforcement)*[8] and *A v N (Committal: Refusal of Contact).*[9] In other cases, the courts pass suspended sentences – see, for example, *Re S (Contact Disputes: Committal).*[10] Despite judicial determination to take a tougher stand when faced with breaches of contact orders, there are still many cases where the courts have drawn back from a custodial sentence (for example, see *M v M (Breaches of Orders: Committal).*[11] In determining a

---

6   [2004] 2 FLR 851.
7   Ibid, at para [10].
8   [1990] 1 FLR 462.
9   [1997] 1 FLR 533.
10   [2005] 1 FLR 812.
11   [2005] EWCA Civ 1722, [2006] 1 FLR 1154. See also *Re M (Contact Order)* [2005] EWCA Civ 615, [2005] 2 FLR 1006, in which the Court of Appeal discharged a suspended sentence imposed in lieu of a fine which the judge at first instance had concluded the contemnor would be unable to pay.

committal application in such cases, the child's welfare is relevant to the exercise of the discretion but is not the paramount consideration.[12]

7.10 An application to commit a party to prison for contempt of court must follow the procedure set out in RSC Order 52 (Schedule 1 to the Civil Procedure Rules) in the High Court and CCR 29 (Schedule 2 to the Civil Procedure Rules) in the county court. The family proceedings court has the power to commit for breach of a court order under section 63 of the Magistrates Court Act 1980. Alternatively, the High Court or a county court may make a committal order of its own motion, although the same judge should not normally both initiate the proceedings and sit in judgment.[13] Any parent appearing at a hearing at which their liberty is at stake is entitled to have legal representation under Article 6 of the European Convention for the Protection of Human Rights and Fundamental Freedoms.[14]

7.11 In other cases, despite the problems highlighted by Mrs Justice Bracewell, the courts have been willing to transfer residence if such a solution is consistent with the child's welfare – see, for example, *A v A (Shared Residence)*[15] and *Re S (Contact Disputes: Committal)*[16] (on an interim basis).

7.12 In *Re M (Intractable Contact Dispute: Interim Care Order)*[17] Mr Justice Wall (as he then was) achieved the same result by a different course. After repeated breaches of a contact order, he concluded that the children's situation was so serious that it might be appropriate for a care or supervision order to be made, and therefore made a direction under section 37 of the Children Act 1989 requiring the relevant local authority to undertake an investigation of the children's circumstances. Subsequently, after the local authority had concluded that the children were suffering significant harm in their residential parent's care and started care proceedings, the children were removed from home under interim care orders. Thereafter, 'within a very short space of time, and freed from the need to accommodate the residential parent's false belief system, the children rapidly resumed their relationship with the non-residential parent'[18] and the judge subsequently made a residence order in his favour.

7.13 Mr Justice Wall was at pains to stress that this option would not be suitable in all circumstances and that his judgment therefore came with 'a series of strong health warnings'. A number of important factors were identified[19] as being relevant when considering this option:

- The court must be satisfied that the statutory criteria for making a section 37 order are met.
- The action contemplated (removal of the children from the residential parent's care whether for an assessment or with a view to a change of

---

12   *Re M (Contact Order: Committal)* [1999] 1 FLR 810.
13   *Re M (Contact Order: Committal)*, supra.
14   *Re K (Contact: Committal Order)* [2002] EWCA Civ 1559, [2003] 1 FLR 277.
15   [2004] EWHC 142, [2004] 1 FLR 1195.
16   [2005] 1 FLR 812.
17   [2003] EWHC 1024 (Fam), [2003] 2 FLR 636.
18   Ibid, at para [5].
19   Ibid, at para [11].

residence) must be in the children's best interests. The consequences of the removal must be thought through. 'There must, in short, be a coherent care plan of which temporary or permanent removal from the residential parent's care is an integral part'.

- Any significant factual issues must be resolved by a hearing at which findings are made.

- In its judgment, the court must spell out its reasons carefully and arrange for a transcript to be prepared for the benefit of the local authority.

- The children should be separately represented.

- Preferably, the section 37 report should be supported by professional or expert advice.

- Judicial continuity is essential, undue delay must be avoided, and the case must be kept under review.

These requirements are likely to discourage many hard-pressed judges from choosing this option and are sufficiently onerous to ensure that transfer of residence occurs only in a small minority of cases.[20]

7.14 For a number of years, the courts had voiced their frustration at the inadequacy of their powers. Amongst many, the most striking examples are the comments of Lord Justice Wall (as he had by then become) in a 2005 article, *Enforcement of Contact Orders*,[21] drawing on the CASC report, *Making Contact Work*, and the observations of Mrs Justice Bracewell in *V v V*.[22] In the latter case, the judge, after outlining the limited powers available to the courts, in the passage already cited,[23] drew this pertinent conclusion:

'The truth, however, is that without the weapons to use against what is in essence a small group of obdurate mothers, the ability of judges to do better for fathers is strictly limited. It is not commonly recognised by the public that, in order to have enforcement procedures which are effective, legislation by Parliament is necessary.'

7.15 It was in response to these views, as well as the other pressures identified in Chapter 2 above, that the Government proposed and introduced the reforms that eventually found their way onto the statute book in the Children and Adoption Act 2006.

7.16 The new measures are designed to provide a series of remedies for the problems that beset contact arrangements. When the Act is in force, there will be more extensive methods of facilitating contact, both during and after the proceedings, with the aim of removing some of the impediments at an earlier stage in the litigation process. In addition, there are new orders available to the court to deal more constructively with breaches of contact orders.

---

20 Wall J himself declined to follow this course in *A v A (Shared Residence and Contact)* [2004] EWHC 142 (Fam), [2004] 1 FLR 1195. For a recent example of a case in which the court declined to order a s 37 investigation, see *Re F (Family Proceedings: Section 37 Investigation)* [2005] EWHC 2935 (Fam), 1 FLR 1122.

21 [2005] Fam Law 26.

22 [2004] 2 FLR 851.

23 See para 7.8.

CONTACT ACTIVITIES

7.17   A major innovation introduced by the 2006 Act is the power granted to the court to compel parents at various stages in the litigation process to take part in 'contact activities'. A contact activity is an activity that promotes contact with the child concerned.[24]

Contact activity directions

7.18   Under the new section 11A of the Children Act 1989,[25] whenever a court is considering whether to make, vary or discharge a contact order, it may make a 'contact activity direction' directing an individual to take part in a contact activity.

7.19   An individual can only be the subject of a contact activity direction if he or she is a party to the proceedings.[26]

7.20   The categories of activities that may be required under a contact activity direction are, in theory at least, not closed, but are said to 'include, in particular', the following:

(a)   programmes, classes and counselling or guidance sessions of a kind that:
     (i)   may assist a person as regards establishing, maintaining or improving contact with a child;
     (ii) may, by addressing a person's violent behaviour, enable or facilitate contact with a child;
(b)   sessions in which information or advice is given as regards making or operating arrangements for contact with a child, including making arrangements by means of mediation.[27]

7.21   However, no individual may be required by a contact activity direction to undergo medical or psychiatric examination, assessment or treatment.[28]

7.22   Similarly, although an individual may be directed to attend information or advice sessions about mediation, no individual may be required by a contact activity direction to take part in mediation.[29]

7.23   The following further provisions apply to contact activity directions:

•   In deciding whether to make a contact activity direction, the welfare of the child is to be the child's paramount consideration.[30]

---

24   Children Act 1989, ss 11A(3) and 11C(2), as inserted by Children and Adoption Act 2006, s 1.
25   Inserted by Children and Adoption Act 2006, s 1.
26   Children Act 1989, s 11A(3).
27   Children Act 1989, s 11A(5).
28   Children Act 1989, s 11A(6)(a).
29   Children Act 1989, s 11A(6)(b).
30   Children Act 1989, s 11A(9). On a broad interpretation, a decision whether to make a contact activity direction is determining a question relating to the child's upbringing. If so, s 1 of the Children Act 1989 applies and s 11A(9) is superfluous. It is not repeated under the provisions dealing with contact activity conditions.

- The direction must ('is to') specify both the activity and the person providing it.[31]
- A court cannot make a contact activity direction at the same time as it makes a 'final' contact order ('disposes finally of the proceedings as they relate to contact with the child concerned').[32]
- A court cannot make such a direction unless there is a dispute about a contact order ('a dispute as regards the provision about contact that the court is considering whether to make in the proceedings').[33]
- A child cannot be directed to take part in a contact activity unless he or she is a parent of the child in respect of whom the court is considering provision about contact.[34]
- A contact activity direction cannot be made when the court is considering making, varying or discharging a contact order in adoption cases as defined by s 11B(4), (5) and (6) (save in adoptions by a couple one of whom is the child's natural parent, or by the partner of a natural parent).[35]
- Before making a contact activity direction, the court must satisfy itself
  (a) that the activity proposed is appropriate in all the circumstances;[36]
  (b) that the proposed provider is suitable to provide the activity;[37] and
  (c) the proposed activity is provided in a place to which the individual can reasonably be expected to travel.[38]

A CAFCASS officer[39] may be asked to provide information about these matters.[40]

- Before making a contact activity direction, the court must obtain and consider information about the individual who would be subject to the direction and its likely effect on him or her,[41] including information as to any conflict with his or her religious beliefs and any interference with the times (if any) at which he or she normally works or attends an educational establishment.[42] Again, a CAFCASS officer may be asked to provide information about these matters.[43]
- A contact activity direction can only be made in relation to an individual who is habitually resident in England and Wales, and ceases to have effect if he or she ceases to be habitually resident in those countries.[44]
- Where a court stays proceedings on the grounds that (a) other

---

31   Children Act 1989, s 11A(4).
32   Children Act 1989, s 11A(7).
33   Children Act 1989, s 11B(1).
34   Children Act 1989, s 11B(2).
35   Children Act 1989, ss 11B(3)–(6).
36   Children Act 1989, s 11E(1), (2).
37   Children Act 1989, s 11E(1), (3).
38   Children Act 1989, s 11E(1), (4).
39   Or, in Wales, a Welsh family proceedings officer.
40   Children Act 1989, s 11E(7).
41   Children Act 1989, s 11E(5).
42   Children Act 1989, s 11E(6). It is unlikely that any judge would have made such a direction that conflicted with such commitments.
43   Children Act 1989, s 11E(7).
44   Children Act 1989, s 11B(7).

proceedings with respect to the matters in dispute are continuing outside the jurisdiction of England and Wales, or (b) it would be more appropriate for those matters to be determined in proceedings outside the jurisdiction, the court may also suspend any contact activity direction made in the proceedings.[45]

- A contact activity direction is automatically discharged if the child concerned is made subject to a care order under s 31 of the Children Act 1989,[46] or a placement order under section 21 of the Adoption and Children Act 2002.[47] If a special guardianship order is made with respect to the child, but an existing contact order is not discharged, any contact activity direction already in force is not automatically revoked, but the court must consider whether it should be discharged.[48]

Contact activity conditions

7.24   As already outlined, a contact activity *direction* may be made when the court is considering whether to make, vary or discharge a contact order. In the event that the court actually makes or varies a contact order, it may impose a 'contact activity *condition*'.

7.25   The provisions as to contact activity conditions are similar, though not identical, to those governing contact activity directions.

7.26   The individuals on whom such conditions may be imposed are:

(1)   the person with whom the child lives or is to live;
(2)   the person whose contact with the child concerned is provided for in the order; and
(3)   any person upon whom the order imposes a condition under section 11(7)(b) (which in practice means, in addition to those covered by (1) and (2) above, any parent or other person with parental responsibility).[49]

7.27   The categories of activity which may be imposed under a contact activity condition are the same as may be required under a contact activity direction.[50] Similarly, no condition may be imposed obliging any individual to undergo medical or psychiatric examination, assessment or treatment, nor to take part in mediation.[51]

---

45   Family Law Act 1986, s 3(2A), inserted by Children and Adoption Act 2006, Sch 2, para 3(2). If the stay is subsequently removed under s 3(3) or (3A) of the 1986 Act, the court may also bring to an end the suspension of the contact activity direction: Family Law Act 1986, s 3(3B), inserted by Children and Adoption Act 2006, Sch 2, para 3(3).
46   Children Act 1989, s 91(2A), inserted by Children and Adoption Act 2006, Sch 2, para 9. All s 8 orders are automatically discharged by the making of a care order: Children Act 1989, s 91(2).
47   Adoption and Children Act 2002, s 26(1), as amended by Children and Adoption Act 2006, Sch 2, para 13 and 14.
48   Children Act 1989, s 14B(1)(d), inserted by Children and Adoption Act 2006, Sch 2, para 8.
49   Children Act 1989, s 11C(2) and (3).
50   Children Act 1989, s 11C(5); and see para 7.20.
51   Children Act 1989, s 11C(5).

7.28   The following further provisions apply to contact activity conditions:

- The condition must ('is to') specify both the activity and the person providing it.[52]
- A contact activity condition cannot be imposed on a child unless he or she is a parent of the child concerned.[53]
- A contact activity condition cannot be imposed under any contact order in adoption cases as defined by section 11B(4), (5) and (6) (save in adoptions by a couple one of whom is the child's natural parent, or by the partner of a natural parent).[54]
- A contact activity condition can only be imposed on an individual who is habitually resident in England and Wales, and ceases to have effect if he or she ceases to be habitually resident in those countries.[55]
- Before imposing a contact activity condition, the court must satisfy itself:
  (a)   that the activity proposed is appropriate in all the circumstances;[56]
  (b)   that the proposed provider is suitable to provide the activity;[57] and
  (c)   the proposed activity is provided in a place to which the individual can reasonably be expected to travel.[58]

As with contact activity directions, a CAFCASS officer[59] may be asked to provide information about these matters.[60]

- Before making a contact activity direction, the court must obtain and consider information about the individual who would be subject to the direction and its likely effect on him or her,[61] including information as to any conflict with his or her religious beliefs and any interference with the times (if any) at which he or she normally works or attends an educational establishment.[62] Again, a CAFCASS officer may be asked to provide information about these matters.[63]

Financial assistance

7.29   Section 11F makes provision for regulations to be introduced to authorise the giving of financial assistance to individuals who are required by a contact activity direction, or ordered under a contact activity condition, to take part in an activity promoting contact with a child. The regulations:

- may require the individual to comply with certain conditions as regards his or her financial resources;[64]

---

52   Children Act 1989, s 11C(4).
53   Children Act 1989, s 11D(1).
54   Children Act 1989, s 11D(2).
55   Children Act 1989, s 11D(3).
56   Children Act 1989, s 11E(1), (2).
57   Children Act 1989, s 11E(1), (3).
58   Children Act 1989, s 11E(1), (4).
59   Or, in Wales, a Welsh family proceedings officer.
60   Children Act 1989, s 11E(7).
61   Children Act 1989, s 11E(5).
62   Children Act 1989, s 11E(6). It is unlikely that any judge would have made such a direction that conflicted with such commitments.
63   Children Act 1989, s 11E(7).
64   Children Act 1989, s 11F(6)(a).

- may make provision as to the maximum amount of assistance payable to or in respect of any individual;[65]
- may make provision for how the amount of assistance is to be determined where that amount may vary according to the individual financial resources;[66]
- may authorise payments to be made directly to an activity provider.[67]

Monitoring contact activities

7.30 Section 11G gives the court power, on making a contact activity direction or making or varying a contact order so as to impose a contact activity condition, to ask a CAFCASS officer[68] to monitor, or arrange for the monitoring of, the individual's compliance with the direction or condition, and to report to the court on any failure to comply. The officer is under a duty to comply with any such request.[69]

Discussion

7.31 At first sight, these comprehensive, indeed complex, provisions appear to grant new powers to the court to take practical steps to promote contact both before making a contact order, via contact activity directions, and when making or varying a contact order, via contact activity conditions. It is arguable, however, that a court could have made contact activity directions and conditions under its existing powers provided by section 11 (7) of the Children Act 1989, whereunder:

'... a section 8 order may

(a) contain directions about how it is to be carried into effect;
(b) impose conditions which must be complied with by any person
    (i) in whose favour the order was made;
    (ii) who is a parent of the child concerned;
    (iii) who is not a parent of his but who has parental responsibility for him, or
    (iv) with whom the child is living, and to whom the conditions are expressed to apply;
(c) be made to have effect for a specified period, or contain provisions which are to have effect for a specified period;
(d) make such incidental, supplemental, or consequential provision as the court thinks fit.'

Hitherto, the section 11(7) powers have been used to particularise the arrangements for contact, rather than the sort of activities suggested by the new section 11A(5) – 'programmes, classes and counselling or guidance sessions'. The wording of section 11(7) is, however, sufficiently broad to

---

65   Children Act 1989, s 11F(7)(a).
66   Children Act 1989, s 11F(7)(b).
67   Children Act 1989, s 11F(7)(c).
68   Or, in Wales, a Welsh family proceedings officer.
69   Children Act 1989, s 11G(3).

encompass such activities. Indeed, in *Parental Separation: Children's Needs and Parents' Responsibilities*, the Government had suggested that it would indeed use section 11(7) to achieve its aims.

'The Government will legislate to ensure that section 11(7) … is sufficiently flexible to allow courts to make a requirement to attend relevant parenting classes or programmes, including information meetings or meetings with a counsellor, a condition of a contact order being made.'

If it was felt that clarification of section 11(7) was required to achieve this flexibility, a short additional subsection might have been sufficient.

7.32 Of course, one reason why section 11(7) has not to date been used to direct or impose such activities has been the lack of any resources for programmes and classes. At present, however, it is far from clear whether such resources will be extensively available. It remains to be seen whether the proposed programmes and classes will be popular with judges and parties, and whether they will achieve the stated aim of promoting contact.

7.33 It is also arguable that the new law is unnecessarily complicated by providing for both contact activity directions and contact activity conditions. In most cases, the court will make some form of interim contact order at an early stage of the proceedings, and in such cases it will be able to impose contact activity conditions. It would surely have been simpler to provide one instrument, whether it be called a direction or a condition, rather than two with similar though not identical provisions.

MONITORING CONTACT

7.34 Section 2 of the 2006 Act amends the 1989 Act further by adding a new section 11H headed 'Monitoring Contact'.

7.35 The powers granted are in addition to those introduced by the new section 11G[70] which enables the court to ask a CAFCASS officer or Welsh family proceedings officer to monitor compliance with contact activity directions or conditions. Section 11H is concerned with ensuring compliance with other terms of a contact order.[71]

7.36 Where a court has made a contact order, or an order varying such an order, the court may ask a CAFCASS officer[72] to monitor whether an individual complies with the order and to report to the court on such matters relating to the individual's compliance as the court may specify in the request.[73] It is the duty of the officer to comply with any such request.[74]

7.37 An 'individual' may fall within this section if the order:

---

70   See para 7.30.
71   Children Act 1989, s 11H(4).
72   Or, in Wales, a Welsh family proceedings officer.
73   Children Act 1989, s 11H(1), (2).
74   Children Act 1989, s 11H(7).

(a)   requires him or her to allow contact with the child;

(b)   names him or her as having contact with the child; or

(c)   imposes a condition under section 11(7) on him or her.[75]

The request may be made by the court on making the contact order (or the order varying the contact order) or at any time during the subsequent course of the proceedings as they relate to contact with the child concerned.[76]

7.38   The court must specify in the request the period of time over which the officer is to monitor contact. That period must not exceed 12 months.[77]

7.39   The court may order any individual falling within the section to take such steps as may be specified in the order with a view to enabling the CAFCASS officer to comply with the court's request,[78] but no such order may be made against a child unless he or she is a parent of the child in respect of whom the contact order was made.[79]

7.40   The power to request CAFCASS to monitor contact does not apply to contact orders made in adoption cases as defined by section 11B(4), (5) and (6) (save in adoptions by a couple one of whom is the child's natural parent, or by the partner of a natural parent).[80]

Discussion

7.41   As with a number of other new provisions introduced by the 2006 Act, the power to direct that compliance with a contact order be monitored by a CAFCASS officer has the potential to cause a significant increase to the service's workload. There are many contested cases in which the court may be attracted by the idea of using CAFCASS to keep an eye on the arrangements, without wishing to impose a family assistance order. Of course, 'monitoring' is not the same as 'supervision', and it is unlikely that a CAFCASS officer would be expected to attend every contact visit in order to ensure compliance. But one can foresee circumstances in which, in order to comply with the request, the CAFCASS officer is obliged to attend a series of contacts over the period covered by the request, possibly lasting for the full 12 months allowed in the section.

7.42   The power to request a further report as to the extent of compliance with the contact order is also potentially burdensome, and might be seen as contrary to the declared aim of cutting back on the amount of report-writing to be expected of CAFCASS officers.[81]

---

75   Children Act 1989, s 11H(3).
76   Children Act 1989, s 11H(5). Once the proceedings have come to an end, it would seem that the power to ask CAFCASS to monitor contact lapses.
77   Children Act 1989, s 11H(6).
78   Children Act 1989, s 11H(8).
79   Children Act 1989, s 11H(9).
80   Children Act 1989, s 11H(10).
81   See para 5.56 et seq.

7.43 Further, by allowing for monitoring to continue for as long as 12 months, with the option of a further report thereafter, this new provision increases the chances of litigation continuing for longer than might be thought desirable.

FAMILY ASSISTANCE ORDERS

7.44 The 2006 Act significantly alters the scope of family assistance orders under section 16 of the Children Act 1989.

7.45 As originally conceived, family assistance orders were a short-term remedy with a maximum term of 6 months. Prior to the passing of the Children Act 1989, the court had had wider powers to make a supervision order in private law proceedings placing the children under the supervision of a local authority. As part of the scheme of the 1989 Act to restrict the scope of local authority intervention in family life, supervision orders became a purely public law remedy available only where the section 31 threshold is crossed.[82] Although the local authority does not have parental responsibility, it may be granted the power to impose certain requirements on the parents and child and thus exercise an element of control.[83] Thus the supervision order is 'designed for the more serious cases, in which there is an element of child protection involved, and access to the local authority's facilities and services may be particularly important'.[84]

7.46 The change in the function of supervision orders left a need for a lower-level remedy. This was the rationale for the family assistance order which 'aims simply to provide short-term help to a family, to overcome the problems and conflicts associated with their separation and divorce'.[85] In theory they provided a useful option for the courts when there were concerns about the family's capacity to arrange matters concerning the children, in particular contact with the non-resident parent. In practice, courts found that they were often not a viable option because the agencies entrusted with delivering the service – local authorities and the court welfare section of the probation service (later CAFCASS) – were chronically under-funded and obliged to prioritise more urgent demands. A legal justification for avoiding family assistance orders was available in the hurdle in section 16(4) of the original 1989 Act whereby no court could make such an order unless satisfied that the circumstances of the case were 'exceptional'.

7.47 The 2006 Act widens the scope of family assistance orders in four respects. First, it extends the maximum length of the order from 6 to 12 months. Secondly, it removes the statutory requirement that such orders may

---

82 To cross the threshold, the local authority must prove that the child is suffering, or is likely to suffer, significant harm, attributable to either (i) to the care given to the child, or likely to be given to him if the order were not made, not being what it would be reasonable to expect a parent to give him, or (ii) the child being beyond parental control.

83 Children Act 1989, Sch 3.

84 *The Children Act 1989 Guidance and Regulations, Vol 1 Court Orders,* at para 2.50.

85 Ibid.

only be made in exceptional circumstances.[86] Thirdly, it specifically provides that the order may direct the officer to focus advice and assistance on the issue of contact. Fourthly, whereas the original section merely permitted the officer charged with implementing the family assistance order to refer back to court the question whether an existing section 8 order should be varied or discharged, the new law empowers the court to direct the officer to report back to court 'on such matters relating to the section 8 order as the court may require'.[87]

7.48 A family assistance order is defined in the 1989 Act as 'an order requiring (a) [a CAFCASS officer] to be made available, or (b) a local authority to make an officer of the authority available, to advise, assist and, where appropriate, befriend any person named in the order'.[88] The slightly quaint use of the word 'befriend' is a hangover from the old language used for pre-Children Act supervision orders.[89] The Act empowers the court to make a family assistance order in any family proceedings[90] where the court has power to make an order under Part II of the 1989 Act, whether or not it makes such an order.[91]

7.49 The persons who may be named in a family assistance order are:

(a)   any parent or guardian of the child;

(b)   any person with whom the child is living or in whose favour a contact order is in force with respect to the child; and

(c)   the child him/herself.[92]

No such order can be made unless the court has obtained the consent of every person to be named in the order other than the child.[93]

7.50 A family assistance order may direct some or all of the persons named in the order to take such steps as may be specified in the order, with a view to enabling the officer concerned to be kept informed of the address of any person named in the order and to be allowed to visit any such person.[94]

7.51 If the family assistance order is to be in force at the same time as a contact order made with respect to the same child, the family assistance order may direct the officer concerned to give advice and assistance as regards

---

86   Children and Adoption Act 2006, s 6(2), Sch 3.
87   Children Act 1989, s 16(6), substituted by Children and Adoption Act 2006, s 6(5).
88   Children Act 1989, s 16(1).
89   It is also retained for supervision orders under the Children Act – see s 35(1). The phrase dates back to the early days of the probation service: see the Probation of Offenders Act 1907.
90   As defined by Children Act 1989, s 8(3), to include any proceedings under the inherent jurisdiction of the High Court and under a list of statutory provisions set out in s 8(4).
91   Children Act 1989, s 16(1).
92   Children Act 1989, s 16(2).
93   Children Act 1989, s 16(3). If one family member refuses to be named in the order, there would seem to be no objection to making the order naming the other members of the family, although the purpose of the order may be defeated if there is a lack of co-operation from the refusenik.
94   Children Act 1989, s 16(4).

establishing, improving and maintaining contact to such persons named in the order as may be specified in the order.[95]

7.52   Unless it specifies a shorter period, a family assistance order shall now have effect for a period of 12 months beginning on the day on which it is made.[96] When the maximum period was 6 months, it was almost unheard of for a shorter period to be specified. It is likely that some orders may now specify a period less than the new maximum, given the ongoing constraints on CAFCASS and local authority resources.

7.53   If the family assistance order is to be in force at the same time as a contact order made with respect to the same child, the family assistance order may direct the officer concerned to report to the court on such matters relating to the section 8 order as the court may require (including the question whether the section 8 order ought to be varied or discharged).[97] As already stated, this is a stronger power than under the previous wording, although it is puzzling why Parliament chose not to introduce a simpler power to direct the officer to report back on any matter concerning the child's welfare.

7.54   Section 16 allows the court to select a local authority as the more appropriate agency to implement the order, but it cannot do so unless the authority agrees or the child concerned lives or will live within the authority's area.[98]

Discussion

7.55   The broadening of the scope of the family assistance order will be widely welcomed by courts and practitioners. In the past, the possibility of making such orders was frequently floated in contested contact proceedings, but rejected because of objections from local authorities and CAFCASS that their resources were insufficient, and that the circumstances were not 'exceptional'. Now that the latter objection has been removed by Parliament, it remains to be seen whether the former will carry any weight with the courts. Potentially, the increased scope for family assistance orders, and the doubling of the maximum duration, may represent a significant additional demand on the agencies' resources. There may in consequence be more cases where there is a disagreement between CAFCASS and a local authority as to which of them should be saddled with the order.

7.56   During the debates on the Children and Adoption Bill, it was suggested that family assistance orders might become the norm, and that the Government had not made appropriate allowances for the resource implications. Not surprisingly, the Government rejected this view.[99] Time will tell if its optimism is

---

95   Children Act 1989, s 16(4A).
96   Children Act 1989, s 16(5), as amended.
97   Children Act 1989, s 16(6), as amended.
98   Children Act 1989, s 16(7).
99   See the comments of Jeremy Wright MP and Maria Eagle MP, Parliamentary Under-Secretary for Education and Skills, HC Deb, 21 March 2006, cols 149–151.

justified. It should be noted, however, that the extension of family assistance orders is not confined to contact disputes. It applies to cases where a court is considering making any section 8 order, and thus extends to residence, prohibited steps and specific issues orders. Many judges will surely be tempted to make an order whenever resolving any difficult private law case.

ENFORCEMENT: THE NEW PROVISIONS UNDER THE 2006 ACT

7.57   Prior to the passing of the Children and Adoption Act 2006, there was, as described above,[100] much frustration felt by judges and parents at the limited powers available to courts to enforce orders for contact. In response to criticism from many quarters, the Government was determined from the outset to extend the range of these powers. The provisions that have ultimately found their way onto the statute book are certainly complex, but are somewhat less radical than those originally proposed. Notably, the powers to make curfew orders accompanied with electronic tagging, which were included in the Children (Contact) and Adoption Bill introduced into Parliament before the 2005 election, are absent from the 2006 Act.

7.58   In this section we shall consider:

(a)   the new statutory provisions about warning notices to be attached to contact orders;
(b)   the extensive new range of methods of enforcing contact; and
(c)   the new powers to order compensation for financial loss caused by breaches of contact orders.

Warning notices

7.59   Section 3 of the 2006 Act inserts a new section 11I into the 1989 Act providing that, where the court makes (or varies) a contact order, it is to attach to the order a notice warning of the consequences of failing to comply with the contact order.

7.60   Under the previous law, the court had a discretion whether or not to add a so-called penal notice to contact orders. This almost invariably caused ill-feeling. The aggrieved party, usually the father, seeking to enforce a contact order, would have to apply to the court for a penal notice as a preliminary step before starting enforcement proceedings. Thus an extra court hearing would be required at which the parties could air their differences. Frequently, judges would refuse to add a penal notice on the basis that they did not believe that the prospect of proceedings for contempt of court would advance the child's welfare. As a result, many contact orders were unenforceable and rendered meaningless.

7.61   Henceforth, all contact orders made after the coming into force of the 2006 Act will carry a warning about the consequences of breach. Although this

---

100   See para 7.5 et seq.

provision does not apply automatically to every contact order in existence before the coming into force of the 2006 Act, the transitional provisions stipulate that a court must attach a notice to an existing order on the application of any person entitled to apply for an enforcement order.[101] In addition, the court must also attach a warning notice to a contact order where a question arises with respect to the order in any family proceedings.[102] It appears, therefore, that, after the 2006 Act comes into force, the court must attach a warning notice to any existing contact order whenever it has cause to consider that order. If a warning notice is attached to a pre-existing contact order, and served on the other party, the court has power to make an enforcement order or a compensation order if that party breaches the contact order.[103]

7.62   The Government believes that this stricter regime for warning notices will improve the rate of compliance with contact orders. But that rate will only be improved if the courts show themselves willing to use their new enforcement powers, to which we now turn.

Making enforcement orders

7.63   Prior to the implementation of the reforms enacted in the 2006 Act, the courts' powers to enforce contact orders were limited to contempt proceedings, for which the sanction was either a financial penalty, often unrealistic, or imprisonment of the resident parent, with almost invariably adverse consequences for the child's welfare. Another option, transfer of residence, was available and advocated in certain cases[104] but as any decision as to residence had to be determined in accordance with section 1 of the Children Act 1989, and in particular the paramountcy principle, the circumstances in which a change of residence could be used following a breach of a contact order were rare.

7.64   The provisions of the new sections 11J–11N of the 1989 Act, inserted by section 4 of the 2006 Act, create an important new procedure designed to broaden the courts' powers to secure compliance with contact orders without infringing the child's welfare. The new weapon in the court's armoury is the 'unpaid work requirement'.

7.65   If the court is satisfied beyond reasonable doubt that a person has failed to comply with a contact order, it may make an 'enforcement order' imposing

---

101   Children and Adoption Act 2006, s 8(2)(a). The categories of persons so entitled are defined in the Children Act 1989, s 11J(5): see para 7.67. Under the Children and Adoption Act 2006, s 8(3), and Children Act 1989, s 11J(6), the child concerned can only apply for a warning notice with the court's permission, but, as a court considering whether to grant permission to the child would be considering 'a question ... with respect to the contact order', it seems that the notice would have to be attached automatically under s 8(2)(b) of the 2006 Act.

102   Children and Adoption Act 2006, s 8(2)(b).

103   Children and Adoption Act 2006, s 8(4).

104   See para 7.12.

on the person an unpaid work requirement.[105] However, the court may not make an enforcement order if the person alleged to be in breach proves on a balance of probabilities that he had a reasonable excuse for failing to comply.[106]

7.66 The different standards of proof in subsections 11J(2) and (4) should be noted. The higher, criminal, standard of proof is required to establish a breach. The lower, civil, standard is needed to prove a reasonable excuse. How this works out in practice remains to be seen. It can be foreseen that a person alleged to be in breach will either (a) deny the breach altogether, (in which case the person alleging breach will have to prove the breach to the higher standard), or (b) admit the breach and claim reasonable excuse, which he or she will have to prove to the lower standard. It seems that this difference in the standard favours the person against whom a breach is alleged. It is also important to note that, even if the court is satisfied that a breach has occurred without reasonable excuse, its power to make an enforcement order is discretionary ('may') rather than mandatory.[107]

7.67 The categories of persons entitled to apply for an enforcement order are defined by subsection 11J(5), namely:

- the person who is, for the purposes of the contact order, the person with whom the child lives or is to live;
- the person whose contact with the child concerned is provided for in the contact order;
- any individual subject to a condition under section 11(7)(b) or a contact activity condition[108] imposed by the contact order; or
- the child concerned, (provided he has obtained the leave of the court,[109] which may only be granted if the court is satisfied that the child has sufficient understanding to make the proposed application[110]).

7.68 The amended law contains a number of further provisions about the making of enforcement orders:

- The court may not make an enforcement order against a person unless, before the failure to comply occurred, he or she has been given (in accordance with rules of court) a copy of, or otherwise informed of the terms of, a warning notice under section 11I.[111]
- An enforcement order cannot be made against a person in respect of a failure to comply with a contact order occurring before that person attained the age of 18.[112]
- An enforcement order cannot be made in respect of any breach of a contact order in adoption cases as defined by section 11B(4), (5) and (6)

---

105 Children Act 1989, s 11J(2).
106 Children Act 1989, s 11J(3), (4).
107 For the statutory provisions governing the exercise of that discretion, see s 11L and para 7.69.
108 For contact activity conditions, see para 7.24 et seq.
109 Children Act 1989, s 11J(6).
110 Children Act 1989, s 11J(7).
111 Children Act 1989, s 11K(1). For warning notices, see para 7.59 et seq.
112 Children Act 1989, s 11K(2).

(save in adoptions by a couple one of whom is the child's natural parent, or by the partner of a natural parent).[113]

- An enforcement order can only be made against an individual who is habitually resident in England and Wales, and ceases to have effect if he or she ceases to be habitually resident in those countries.[114]

- The court may suspend an enforcement order for such period as it thinks fit.[115]

- Where a court under section 5 of the Family Law Act 1986 stays proceedings for an order under section 8 of the Children Act 1989, or under the High Court's inherent jurisdiction for care of, or contact with, a child, on the grounds that (a) other proceedings with respect to the matters in dispute are continuing outside the jurisdiction of England and Wales, or (b) it would be more appropriate for those matters to be determined in proceedings outside the jurisdiction, the court may also suspend any enforcement order made in the proceedings.[116]

- Where matrimonial proceedings in England and Wales are stayed in favour of concurrent proceedings in another jurisdiction, and a contact order is in force in the stayed proceedings, the court may not make an enforcement order in relation to the contact order.[117]

- The court can make more than one enforcement order in relation to the same person on the same occasion.[118]

- The provisions of section 11(1) and (2) of the 1989 Act apply so that the court is under an obligation to take active case management steps to ensure that the matter is determined without delay.[119]

- When the court makes an enforcement order, it must attach a notice warning of the consequence of failing to comply.[120]

- Unless revoked[121] the enforcement order imposing an unpaid work requirement remains in force until the person subject to the order has worked for the number of hours specified in the order.[122]

7.69 As already observed, the court's power to make an enforcement order upon proof of a breach of a contact order without reasonable excuse is discretionary. The factors governing the exercise of that discretion include amongst others the following matters set out in section 11L:

---

113 Children Act 1989, s 11K(3).

114 Children Act 1989, s 11K(4).

115 Children Act 1989, s 11J(9).

116 Family Law Act 1986, s 5(2A), inserted by Children and Adoption Act 2006, Sch 2, para 3(2). If the stay is subsequently removed under s 3(3) or (3A) of the 1986 Act, the court may also bring to an end the suspension of the enforcement order: Family Law Act 1986, s 5(3B), inserted by Children and Adoption Act 2006, Sch 2, para 3(3).

117 Domicile and Matrimonial Proceedings Act 1973, Sch 1, para 11(4A) and (4B)(a), as inserted by Children and Adoption Act 2006, Sch 2, para 1(2).

118 Children Act 1989, s 11J(10).

119 Children Act 1989, s 11J(11).

120 Children Act 1989, s 11N.

121 For revocation of enforcement orders, see para 7.80 et seq.

122 Criminal Justice Act 2003 s 200(3), as applied to enforcement orders by Children Act 1989, Sch A1, inserted by Children and Adoption Act 2006, Sch 1.

- The court must be satisfied that making the proposed enforcement order is necessary to secure the person's compliance with the contact order.[123]

- The court must be satisfied that the likely effect of the enforcement order on the person against whom it is to be made is proportionate to the seriousness of the breach.[124]

- The court must be satisfied that provision for the person to work under an unpaid work requirement can be made in the area where the person lives.[125]

- Before making an enforcement order, the court must obtain and consider information about the person against whom it is proposed the order should be made, and the likely effect of such an order on him or her,[126] including information as to any conflict with the person's religious beliefs and any interference with his times of work or education.[127] The court may ask a CAFCASS officer[128] to provide such information, and the officer must comply with such a request.[129]

- It should be noted that the court must take the child's welfare into account when considering whether to make an enforcement order,[130] but the child's welfare is not the paramount consideration.

7.70   There is a risk that the long list of the statutory factors identified as relevant to the exercise of the court's discretion as to whether or not to make an enforcement order may discourage the court from making the order in many cases. One-off breaches may well not lead to enforcement orders. In all probability, it will be only where there is a series of breaches amounting to a clear course of conduct that the court is likely to act. There will be cases where a parent will seek to come back to court after one or two breaches and the court will decline to make an enforcement order. One can foresee that in some cases the dissatisfaction that arose when a court refused to attach a penal notice to contact orders under the old law will resurface.

7.71   It should be noted that, under transitional provisions,[131] the new power to make enforcement orders will be applicable to contact orders made prior to the coming into force of the 2006 Act provided a warning notice under section 11I of the Children Act 1989 (as amended) has been attached to the order and duly served on the party against whom enforcement is sought.

---

123   Children Act 1989, s 11L(1)(a).
124   Children Act 1989, s 11L(1)(b).
125   Children Act 1989, s 11L(2).
126   Children Act 1989, s 11L(3).
127   Children Act 1989, s 11L(4). Unlike the provisions governing requirements (including unpaid work requirements) imposed under community orders under the Criminal Justice Act 2003, the court is not specifically obliged to ensure as far as practicable that the requirements imposed avoid conflict with religious beliefs or attendance at educational establishments – cf Criminal Justice Act 2003, s 217, expressly omitted from the rules relating to enforcement orders by Children Act 1989, Sch A1, para 3(5). Any orders that conflicted with religious beliefs might, however, be vulnerable to a challenge under the Human Rights Act 1998.
128   Or, in Wales, a Welsh family proceedings officer.
129   Children Act 1989, s 11L(5), (6).
130   Children Act 1989, s 11L(7).
131   Children and Adoption Act 2006, s 8(4).

Unpaid work requirements

7.72 The detailed provisions governing unpaid work requirements under enforcement orders are set out in Part 1 of the new Schedule A1 inserted into the 1989 Act by Schedule 1 to the 2006 Act. The scheme of these detailed provisions is to apply with modifications the relevant provisions of the criminal law governing unpaid requirements in community orders, namely Chapter 4 of Part 12 of the Criminal Justice Act 2003. Thus paragraph 2 of the new Schedule A1 provides that references to 'an offender' in the Criminal Justice Act 2003 are to be treated as including references to a person subject to an enforcement order. It may come as a surprise to someone who breaks a contact order and is placed under an enforcement order to find that he is treated like a criminal offender.

7.73 The management of a person subject to an unpaid work requirement is delegated under the Criminal Justice Act 2003 to the 'responsible officer'. In the criminal code, the identity of the responsible officer depends on the nature of the community order, but in the case of enforcement orders under the amended Children Act 1989 it will mean a local probation officer.[132] The duties of the responsible officer under an enforcement order are (a) to make any arrangements that are necessary in connection with the requirements imposed by the order and (b) to promote the offender's compliance with those requirements.[133] In addition, the responsible officer is required to comply with any request from the CAFCASS officer,[134] who has been asked by the court under section 11M of the Children Act 1989 to monitor compliance with the unpaid requirement, to report to him or her on such matters relating to the order as he or she may require for the purpose of making a report under section 11M(1)(c) or (d).[135]

7.74 An offender in respect of whom an unpaid work requirement of an enforcement order is in force must perform for the number of hours specified in the order such work at such times as he or she may be instructed by the responsible officer.[136] The number of hours which a person may be required to work under an unpaid work requirement must be specified in the enforcement order and must not be less than 40 or more than 200.[137] Where on the same

---

132 Criminal Justice Act 2003, s 197(1)(c) and (2)(b). The provisions in the Criminal Justice Act 2003 relating to offenders under the age 18 do not apply to enforcement orders which, by virtue of s 11K(2), cannot be made against a person in respect of a failure to comply with a contact order occurring before that person attained the age of 18. The definition of 'responsible officer' may be changed by the Secretary of State: Criminal Justice Act 2003, s 197(3).

133 Criminal Justice Act 2003, s 198(1)(a) and (b). The duty imposed under s 198(1)(c) in criminal cases, namely, where appropriate, to take steps to enforce the requirements, is excluded by Children Act 1989, Sch A1, para 3(2)(a)(ii) (as amended). Instead there is a separate procedure for breaches of enforcement orders provided by Sch A1, paras 8 and 9.

134 Or, in Wales, a Welsh family proceedings officer.

135 Criminal Justice Act 2003, s 198(1A), as inserted by Children Act 1989, Sch A1, para 3(2)(b). For the provisions governing the monitoring of enforcement orders, see para 7.78 et seq.

136 Criminal Justice Act 2003, s 200(1).

137 Criminal Justice Act 2003, s 199(2) as modified by Children Act 1989, Sch A1, para 3(3)(a).

occasion, and in relation to the same person, the court makes more than one enforcement order imposing an unpaid requirement, the court may direct that the hours of work specified in any of those requirements is to be concurrent with or additional to those specified in any other of those orders, but so that the total does not exceed the above statutory maximum.[138]

7.75 Subject to the provisions of paragraphs 7 and 9 of Schedule A1 to the Children Act 1989, (which deal respectively with amendment and breaches of enforcement orders[139]), the work required to be performed under an unpaid work requirement imposed by an enforcement order must be completed during a period of 12 months,[140] although the statute specifies that the time is not to run for any period when the enforcement is suspended under section 11J(9) of the Children Act 1989.[141] During the currency of the enforcement order, the offender must keep in touch with the responsible officer in accordance with such instructions as he or she may from time to time be given by that officer and must notify him or her of any change of address.[142]

7.76 Section 222(1) of the Criminal Justice Act 2003, as applied to enforcement orders by Schedule A1, paragraph 3(9), to the Children Act 1989, empowers the Secretary of State to make rules for regulating the supervision of persons who are subject to such orders, the functions of responsible officers, and the arrangements to be made by local probation boards for the performance of work under unpaid work requirements, including provisions (a) limiting the number of hours of work to be done on any one day, (b) as to the reckoning of hours and the keeping of work records, and (c) for the payment of travelling and other expenses in connection with the performance of work.

7.77 It will be interesting to see the impact of this scheme. Given that the courts have hitherto been reluctant to imprison resident parents, the deterrent effect of the prospect of committal proceedings has been limited. If courts show a greater inclination to impose the new enforcement orders, recalcitrant parents may be more readily deterred from infringing court orders. The concept of community work as a punishment could also be seen as reflecting the greater recognition that breaking contact orders runs the risk of damaging society as a whole and therefore deserves an order for some form of personal reparation.

Monitoring enforcement orders

7.78 On making an enforcement order, the court is obliged to ask a CAFCASS officer[143] to monitor, or arrange for the monitoring of, compliance

---

The Secretary of State may by order amend the maximum number of hours of work that may be imposed under an unpaid work requirement: Criminal Justice Act 2003, s 223(1)(a), expressly applied to enforcement orders by Children Act 1989, Sch A1, para 3(9).

138 Criminal Justice Act 2003, s 199(5), as modified by Children Act 1989, Sch A1, para 3(3)(c).
139 See, respectively, paras 7.82 and 7.84.
140 Criminal Justice Act 2003, s 200(2), substituted by Children Act 1989, Sch A1, para 3(4).
141 Criminal Justice Act 2003, s 200(2A), substituted by Children Act 1989, Sch A1, para 3(4).
142 Criminal Justice Act 2003, s 220(1).
143 Or, in Wales, a Welsh family proceedings officer.

with the unpaid requirement imposed by the order.[144] The officer is under a duty to comply with such a request.[145] This adds yet another task to the lengthening list of new duties imposed on CAFCASS by the 2006 Act.

7.79 The request may include asking the officer to report to the court if the person is reported for non-compliance by the responsible officer,[146] or if he or she 'is, or becomes unsuitable to perform work under the requirement, or on other matters relating to compliance as may be specified under the request'.[147]

Revocation and amendment of enforcement orders

7.80 Part 2 of the new Schedule A1 to the Children Act 1989 gives the court power to revoke an enforcement order. Paragraph 4(2) empowers the court (either on application by the person subject to the order, or of its motion[148]) to revoke such an order if it appears that either:

(a) the order should not have been made;
(b) it would be appropriate for it to be revoked, having regard to all the circumstances which have arisen since the order was made, taking into account the extent to which the person subject to the enforcement order has complied with it and the likelihood that he will comply with the contact order;[149] or
(c) it would be appropriate for the enforcement order to be revoked, having regard to the person's satisfactory compliance with the contact order, and taking into account the likelihood that he will comply with the contact order in the absence of an enforcement order.[150]

7.81 This latter provision highlights the distinction between the criminal and civil powers to impose unpaid work requirements. It demonstrates that the fundamental purpose of the requirement in contact cases is to secure compliance with the contact order. Once that has been demonstrated, the unpaid work can, with the court's consent, be effectively abandoned.

7.82 Part 2 of Schedule A1 also contains power to amend an enforcement order, in three separate circumstances:

- where the person subject to the enforcement order changes residence, in which case the court, either on the application of the person subject to the order, or of its motion, may substitute one justice area for another;[151]
- where it appears to the court that, having regard to the circumstances that have arisen since the enforcement order was made, it would be appropriate to reduce the hours specified in the order (though not below the minimum specified in section 199(2)(a) of the Criminal Justice

---

144 Children Act 1989, s 11M(1)(a).
145 Children Act 1989, s 11M(2).
146 See para 7.73.
147 Children Act 1989, s 11M(1)(b)–(d).
148 Children Act 1989, Sch A1, para 4(3).
149 Children Act 1989, Sch A1, para 4(4).
150 Children Act 1989, Sch A1, para 4(5).
151 Children Act 1989, Sch A1, para 5.

Act 2003), provided that the court is satisfied that the effect on the person subject to the amended order is no more than is required to secure compliance with the contact order;[152]

- where it appears appropriate to extend the period of 12 months stipulated in section 200(2) of the Criminal Justice Act 2003.

The provisions relating to the making of enforcement orders in section 11L(2)–(7) inclusive and as to monitoring of enforcement orders in section 11M apply to orders amending enforcement orders.[153]

7.83 If a special guardianship order is made with respect to the child, but an existing contact order is not discharged, any enforcement order already in force in relation to that contact order is not automatically discharged, but the court must consider whether it should be discharged.[154]

Breach of enforcement orders

7.84 Part 2 of Schedule A1 also contains provisions dealing with a breach of an enforcement order.

7.85 Paragraph 8 provides that, if the responsible officer is of the opinion that the person subject to the enforcement order has failed without reasonable excuse to comply with the unpaid work requirement imposed by the order, the officer must give a warning (and record that he has done so[155]), describing the circumstances of the failure, stating that the failure is 'unacceptable' and informing the person that, if within the next 12 months he or she again fails to comply with the requirement, the warning and the subsequent failure will be reported to the appropriate person,[156] defined[157] as the CAFCASS officer,[158] required under section 11M to report on matters relating to enforcement. In the event that the responsible officer is of the opinion, within 12 months of the date of the warning being given, that the person has again failed without reasonable excuse to comply with the unpaid work requirement imposed by the order, the officer must report the failure to the appropriate person. A warning under paragraph 8(2) need not be given if the person subject to the order has previously been given a warning in the previous 12 months, or if the responsible officer reports the failure to the appropriate person.

7.86 If the court is satisfied beyond reasonable doubt that the person subject to the enforcement order has failed to comply with the unpaid work requirement, it may either amend the order so as to make the requirement more onerous,[159] or make a second enforcement order and direct that the second

---

152 Children Act 1989, Sch A1, para 6.
153 Children Act 1989, Sch A1, para 10.
154 Children Act 1989, s 14B(1)(c), inserted by Children and Adoption Act 2006, Sch 2, para 8.
155 Children Act 1989, Sch A1, para 8(4).
156 Children Act 1989, Sch A1, para 8(2) and (3).
157 Children Act 1989, Sch A1, para 8(7).
158 Or, in Wales, a Welsh family proceedings officer.
159 If it does so amend the order, the court must again comply with the provisions as to making

order is to have effect either in addition to or in substitution therefor.[160] Once again, however, the court cannot exercise these powers if the person alleged to be in breach proves on a balance of probabilities that he had a reasonable excuse for failing to comply,[161] nor may it do so unless satisfied that the person had been served with, or otherwise informed of the terms of, a notice under s 11N. The provisions as to who may apply to the court for exercise of these powers are similar to those governing applications for an enforcement order under s 11J.[162]

7.87   If it elects to make the order more onerous, the court:

- may extend the period of 12 months and increase the hours of unpaid work, though not above the maximum allowed under section 199(2)(b) of the Criminal Justice Act 2003 (as substituted by Schedule A1, paragraph 3[163]);
- must be satisfied that, taking into account the extent to which there has been compliance with the requirement imposed by the first enforcement order, the effect of the proposed exercise of its powers is neither any more than required to secure compliance with the contact order, nor any more than is proportionate to the seriousness of the failures to comply with the contact order and the first order.[164]

7.88   The provisions of sections 11K(4) (habitual residence),[165] 11L(2)–(7) (information required before making an order),[166] 11M (monitoring)[167] and 11N (warning notices)[168] apply to the making of second enforcement orders under Schedule A1, paragraph 9(2).

7.89   Where a contact order has been made in connection with matrimonial proceedings, and an enforcement order in relation to that contact order has been made, the court may not exercise its powers under Schedule 2, paragraph 9(2) in relation to the enforcement order if the matrimonial proceedings are stayed in favour of concurrent proceedings in another jurisdiction.[169]

Compensation

7.90   One of the complaints most frequently heard from parents in contact disputes is that they have suffered financially as a result of the failure of the

---

enforcement orders under Children Act 1989, s 11L(2)–(7) inclusive, and monitoring such orders under s 11M: Sch A1, para 10.
160   Children Act 1989, Sch A1, para 9(2).
161   Children Act 1989, Sch A1, para 9(3), (4).
162   See para 7.67.
163   Children Act 1989, Sch A1, para 9(9).
164   Children Act 1989, Sch A1, para 9(10).
165   See para 7.68.
166   See para 7.69.
167   See para 7.78–7.79.
168   See para 7.68.
169   Domicile and Matrimonial Proceedings Act 1973, Sch 1, para 11(4B)(b), as inserted by Children and Adoption Act 2006, Sch 2, para 1.

other parent to comply with agreed or ordered arrangements. Marriage or relationship breakdown is almost invariably a time of relative financial hardship and the waste of money on abortive contact plans increases the pressure on parties who may be experiencing stress for a variety of reasons. The courts try strenuously to keep arguments about money separate from disputes about the children, but grievances over losses arising out of broken contact arrangements bring these two issues closer together.

7.91 The 2006 Act addresses this problem by introducing a new statutory scheme for awarding compensation for broken contact orders. Whilst it is arguable that the court could have ordered redress under the old law, in practice it rarely did so.

7.92 Under the new section 110[170] of the 1989 Act, if a court is satisfied that:

(a) an individual has failed to comply with a contact order; and
(b) a person falling with one of the categories laid down in the Act has suffered financial loss by reason of the breach,

it may make an order requiring the individual in breach to pay the person compensation in respect of his financial loss.[171]

7.93 The new section provides that such an order may only be made on an application by the person who claims to have suffered financial loss,[172] and thus not on the application of any other person nor, it seems, by the court of its own motion. The categories of persons in favour of whom such an order may be made, and who are therefore entitled to make an application, are defined[173] as:

- a person who is, for the purposes of the contact order, the person with whom the child concerned lives or is to live;
- the person whose contact with the child concerned is provided for in the contact order;
- an individual subject to a condition under section 11(7)(b) or a contact activity condition imposed by the contact order; or
- the child concerned (provided the child has first obtained the leave of the court before making the application[174] – such leave can only be granted if the court is satisfied that the child has sufficient understanding to make the proposed application[175]).

7.94 The following points should be noted about this new power:

- The court has a discretion whether or not to order compensation.
- In exercising that discretion, the court is required to take into account the welfare of the child concerned,[176] but the child's welfare is not

---

170 Inserted by Children and Adoption Act 2006, s 5.
171 Children Act 1989, s 110(2).
172 Children Act 1989, s 110(5).
173 Children Act 1989, s 110(6).
174 Children Act 1989, s 110(7).
175 Children Act 1989, s 110(8).
176 Children Act 1989, s 110(14).

paramount. Presumably the court will, when exercising its discretion, take into account the welfare of any other child.

- The court is not allowed to make a compensation order if it satisfied that the individual in breach had a reasonable excuse for failing to comply with the contact order.[177] The burden of proving this lies on the person claiming to have had a reasonable excuse.[178]

- The new section is silent as to the standard of proof both as to the standard required when proving loss and when providing reasonable excuse.

- The court is also precluded from making a compensation order unless, before the breach occurred, the person alleged to be in breach has been given a copy of, or otherwise informed of, an appropriate warning notice under section 11I.[179]

- A compensation order under section 11O cannot be made against a person in respect of a failure to comply with a contact order occurring before that person attained the age of 18.[180]

- A compensation order cannot be made in respect of any breach of a contact order in adoption cases as defined by section 11B(4), (5) and (6) (save in adoptions by a couple one of whom is the child's natural parent, or by the partner of a natural parent).[181]

- The provisions of section 11(1) and (2) of the 1989 Act apply so that the court is under an obligation to take active case management steps to ensure that the matter is determined without delay.[182]

- Where a contact order made in another part of the United Kingdom is registered in England and Wales under the provisions of section 27 of the Family Law Act 1986, a court in England and Wales (which, under section 29 of the 1986 Act, has the same powers of enforcement as if it had itself made the order), may make a compensation order under section 11O of the 1989 Act.[183]

7.95 The amount of compensation awarded is a matter for the court, but must not exceed the applicant's financial loss.[184] Thus, this power cannot be used to award compensation for other non-financial losses, such as stress or

---

177   Children Act 1989, s 11O(3).
178   Children Act 1989, s 11O(4).
179   Children Act 1989, s 11P(1). For warning notices, see para 7.59.
180   Children Act 1989, s 11P(2).
181   Children Act 1989, s 11P(3).
182   Children Act 1989, s 11O(13).
183   Family Law Act 1986, s 29(1), as amended by the Children and Adoption Act 2006, Sch 2, para 4. Although an application may be made under s 30 of the 1986 Act to stay proceedings to enforce an order registered under s 27 on the basis that other proceedings have been, or are going to be, taken elsewhere, there is no power to stay an application for a compensation order under Children Act 1989, s 11O(2), in respect of the registered order: Family Law Act 1986, s 30(1A), inserted by Children and Adoption Act 2006, Sch 2, para 5. Similarly, the power under s 31(1) of the 1986 Act to dismiss proceedings to enforce an order registered under s 27 on the basis that the order has ceased to have effect in the part of the UK in which it was made does not extend to applications for an order under Children Act 1989, s 11O(2): s 31(1A) of the 1986 Act, inserted by Children and Adoption Act 2006, Sch 2, para 6.
184   Children Act 198, s 11O(9).

waste of time. In calculating the level of compensation payable, the court must take into account the financial circumstances of the individual in breach of the contact order.[185]

7.96 Once ordered, compensation due under section 11O can be recovered by the applicant as a civil debt[186] using all the relevant debt recovery powers available under the civil law.

7.97 These new powers will be welcomed by those many parents who have grievances about losses sustained as a result of breaches of contact orders by their former partners. Whether they will be welcomed by courts is another matter. The fear is that satellite litigation may distract the parties and the court from other issues more directly relevant to the child's welfare. It should be noted that the new compensation orders can be made against either parent – that is to say, the resident parent and/or contact parent. One can foresee that some cases will be taken up with claim and counterclaim, stoking up ill-feeling between the parties and undermining the efforts by the court and professionals to introduce greater harmony into contact arrangements. Much will depend on the case management skills of the judges to ensure that these new powers are used fairly and sensibly.

7.98 It should be noted that, under transitional provisions,[187] the new power to make compensation orders will be applicable to contact orders made prior to the coming into force of the 2006 Act provided a warning notice under section 11I of the Children Act 1989 as amended has been attached to the order and duly served on the party from whom compensation is sought.

Discussion

7.99 Overall, the new powers to enforce contact orders mark a considerable extension of the remedies available to judges trying to make contact happen. Some apprehension may, however, be felt about the extent to which the ramifications of the reforms have been fully realised.

7.100 To apply these new provisions effectively will involve a significant amount of court time and resources. There will probably be an increased number of court hearings. Each hearing may take longer as the court struggles to apply the detailed provisions as to enforcement, monitoring and compensation. There is a dangerous opportunity for 'satellite' litigation, about the details of the unpaid requirements to be imposed, and the appropriate level of compensation, which risks distracting attention from the issues concerning the child's welfare.

7.101 At the heart of the new enforcement orders lies an assumption that the imposition of unpaid work is an apposite way of addressing the problem of recalcitrant parents who refuse to comply with contact orders. Community

---

185 Children Act 1989, s 11O(10).
186 Children Act 1989, s 11O(11).
187 Children and Adoption Act 2006, s 8(4).

orders in the criminal justice system are imposed to reflect society's disapproval of delinquent behaviour, allow offenders to repay society in a positive way, and instil in them a greater understanding of social responsibility. They are not designed to effect an instant change of attitude to a specific issue. Presumably it is hoped that being forced to undergo unpaid work will teach parents who breach contact orders to refrain from similar actions in future. Yet many parents who fail to comply with contact orders are genuinely convinced that their actions are in the best interests of the child. It is open to question whether such people will change their minds as a result of bring forced to do unpaid work. There is surely a risk that, in some cases, their attitudes will become ever more entrenched. If so, judges in such cases will continue to be faced with the same inadequate options as identified by Mrs Justice Bracewell in *V v V*.[188]

FACILITATION AND ENFORCEMENT OF CONTACT: CONCLUSIONS

7.102   Much of the publicity surrounding the Government's reforms have understandably focused on the proposals about taking contact disputes out of the court arena altogether. It is likely that, as a result of new initiatives in this field such as in-court conciliation, many cases will now be resolved without contested litigation. Yet there will continue to be a sizeable proportion of cases that prove insoluble without greater court involvement. The challenge to Parliament, as identified by Mrs. Justice Bracewell amongst many judges, has been to devise more effective ways of facilitating and enforcing contact. As a result, judges will now have the new range of powers outlined above. On paper, the new powers to direct parties to undertake contact activities, to monitor contact arrangements closely through CAFCASS, and to subject recalcitrant parents to do unpaid work and pay compensation if they breach contact orders, significantly extend the range of options available to judges in their efforts to make contact work.

7.103   There are, however, concerns as to whether adequate resources will be made available to allow them a fair opportunity to be effective. Parents will be given every chance and encouragement to settle disputes without litigation. If they cannot settle, they may find themselves caught up in a court process that is rather more interventionist and protracted than hitherto. If the hopes that more cases will settle before proceedings are started prove optimistic, the volume of litigation in this area will surely increase. It is doubtful that the court service will have the resources to meet this extra demand. There are further concerns about the level of resources that will be made available to CAFCASS. The Government's stated aim has been to unshackle CAFCASS officers from their burdensome obligations to write reports and attend court so that they can be more available to provide direct assistance to families. Yet the new procedures for facilitating and enforcing contact impose a series of new duties on CAFCASS which threaten to channel its officers back into the court arena. The combined effect of their new duties to provide information about, and monitor, contact activities and unpaid work requirements, and administer the

---

188   [2004] 2 FLR 85. See footnote 7.

more extensive family assistance orders, will require considerable extra
resources. Experience shows that such resources are not always forthcoming in
the modern overstretched public sector. There is a risk that public expectations
will be disappointed again.

Chapter Eight

BEYOND THE NEXT STEPS

8.1 The primary focus of this book has been the collection of reforms and initiatives outlined in *Parental Separation: Children's Needs and Parents' Responsibilities – Next Steps*,[1] many of which are geared directly to improve practice and procedure for those residence and contact disputes that reach the court arena. But it would be wrong to limit our analysis of court-based change in this sphere simply to those measures.

8.2 Within this chapter we look at three topics, none of which made the *Next Steps* agenda, all of which have been the subject of much attention and debate since the *Next Steps* document was first published:

- the opening up of the family court;
- the creation of a single family court; and
- the hearing of the voice of the child.

These are all areas where action is being contemplated and, in each case, the consequences of action are likely to bear significantly on how private law children's cases are to be conducted and perceived in the years to come.

OPENING UP THE FAMILY COURT

Introduction

8.3 Public interest in perceived and actual miscarriages of justice has never been greater than at present. Such actual and perceived miscarriages of justice and the public interest in them are not confined to the workings of the criminal justice system. The overlap between the substance of criminal cases such as the trial of Angela Cannings and family proceedings involving alleged abuse of children leads inevitably to public curiosity about and scrutiny of the work of the family justice system. The question for the press and the public is this: if Angela Cannings was wrongly convicted, how many parents have lost their children wrongly in the family courts?

8.4 This curiosity and criticism is not confined to public law children's cases, where there are obvious parallels between the criminal and family justice systems. The work of groups like Families Need Fathers and Fathers 4 Justice has brought clearly and unforgettably into the public gaze the work of the

---

1   January 2005 – Cm 6452 – available at www.dfes.gov.uk/childrensneeds/.

family justice system where issues of residence and contact are in dispute between private citizens. In many ways, it is the very public campaigning of groups such as these that has forced the family justice system to face up to what are perceived to be its shortcomings. It is not an exaggeration to observe that these campaigns have played a significant role in driving forward some of the reforms that this book seeks to describe.[2]

8.5   There can be little doubt that the secrecy surrounding the work of the family courts is part of the reason for and cause of these campaigns and scrutiny. There is an obvious danger that, where decisions are made in an environment shielded from public comment and accountability, principles and conventions develop which might not reflect the wider views of society as a whole. There is also a danger that a vigorous and fair system becomes the target of misdirected and partisan criticism, and is unable to defend itself because of its own culture of confidentiality. There is an argument that the rules by which the family justice system attempts to shield the interests of the children it seeks to protect have become the most potent weapons in the armoury of those who seek to attack it. It is important to observe that this culture of confidentiality is statute-based: the judges simply apply the rules provided by Parliament.

8.6   There is an urgent need for reform of the rules and procedures by which the family justice system is hidden from public view. Such reform would serve two important purposes: first, it might increase public confidence in the decisions and procedures of the family courts; second, it would provide an important and instant public accountability. More transparency, it is argued, would lead to greater understanding, and greater understanding would lead to greater confidence.

The 'curtain of privacy'[3] or the 'cloak of secrecy'?

8.7   The vast majority of cases involving children and heard in the family courts are heard in private. Rule 4.16(7) of the Family Proceedings Rules 1991 provides that, unless the court otherwise directs, hearings under the Children Act 1989 shall be heard in chambers. In practice, that rule amounts to a total prohibition on access to the court save in the case of the parties and their legal advisors. In addition, a CAFCASS officer will usually be present. The court is entitled, under the rule, to direct otherwise; but in reality, that discretion is simply not exercised beyond applications made on behalf of people such as professional supporters (for example, an advocate for a party with learning disabilities) or professional supervisors (for example, a social worker or the manager of a health visitor). Occasionally the spouse or partner of a party is allowed to attend, provided no other party objects. Beyond those sorts of examples, it is a discretionary exception so rarely exercised that it is almost forgotten.

---

2   See para 2.45 et seq.
3   *Re Manda (Wardship: Disclosure of Evidence)* [1993] 1 FLR 205, per Balcombe LJ at p 215.

8.8   Even where access to the court is permitted (either because of party status or because of the discretionary exception to the rule), there are stringent and comprehensive prohibitions on the 'reporting' of family proceedings. Until very recently, the term 'reporting' covered not just the 'publication' of family proceedings, but also the dissemination of material between private individuals, for example a party and his or her brother or sister or parents. Section 97 of the Children Act 1989 makes it a criminal offence to publish to the public at large or sections of the public any material intended, or likely, to identify:

- any child as being involved in court proceedings in which any power under the Children Act 1989 or the Adoption and Children Act 2002 may be exercised with respect to that, or any other, child, or;
- an address or school as being that of such a child.[4]

8.9   In addition, section 12(1)(a) of the Administration of Justice Act 1960 makes it a contempt of court to publish 'information relating to proceedings before any court sitting in private' including proceedings involving the inherent jurisdiction relating to minors, proceedings brought under the Children Act 1989 or Adoption and Children Act 2002 and any other proceedings relating 'wholly or mainly' to the upbringing of a minor.

8.10   Exceptions have always been allowed so as to permit disclosure to certain narrow categories of person.[5] Following a widely publicised case in which a solicitor inadvertently infringed these provisions,[6] there has been an important extension of these exceptions. It is now permissible for a party to communicate information about proceedings without the court's permission to other specific persons for certain specific purposes. Those persons include (amongst others):

- a lay adviser or McKenzie friend;
- the party's spouse, cohabitant or close family member;
- a person or body providing counselling for children or their families;
- a mediator;
- an elected representative or peer (an MP for example);
- a police officer or the Crown Prosecution Service.[7]

8.11   Rule 10.20A also sets out the purposes for which information communicated pursuant to it may be used. Different purposes are specified for different categories of person.[8] The result is that litigants will now be free to disclose information about proceedings for most legitimate purposes, although it must be stressed that all parties and their lawyers should check the rules before disclosing information relating to proceedings. This is an important step in the right direction which seems to iron out some of the more bizarre practical anomalies created by the statutory provisions. However, the primary statutory provisions[9] still amount to a comprehensive prohibition on the

---

4   See Children Act 1989, s 97(2). See para 8.12 for a recent re-interpretation of s 97.
5   Under the former Family Proceedings Rules 1991, r 4.23, now superseded by the new rule 10.20A (brought into force on 31 October 2005).
6   *Re B (A Child) (Disclosure)* [2004] EWHC 411 (Fam), [2004] 2 FLR 142.
7   For the full list of persons, see FPR 1991, r 10.20A.
8   See para 5.84 in relation to lay advisers and McKenzie friends.
9   Children Act 1989, s 97; Administration of Justice Act 1960, s 12.

publication of any accounts of children's proceedings, whether in the form of summaries of the evidence, excerpts from the documents, documents filed in the proceedings, transcripts of the evidence, or notes from the hearing. This total restriction applies irrespective of whether or not the documents or notes or summaries have been anonymised.

8.12 The Court of Appeal has considered the proper ambit of section 97 of the Children Act 1989 in the recent case of *Clayton v Clayton*.[10] The court held that the prohibition on publication in section 97 ceased when the Children Act proceedings came to an end. However, this construction did not dilute the provisions of the Administration of Justice Act 1960, so that the limitation under section 12 on reporting information relating to the proceedings remained. The court also stressed that its construction of section 97 did not preclude the making of an injunction to prevent further disclosure in appropriate circumstances. As a consequence of this decision, judges in individual cases will have to consider, at the conclusion of proceedings, whether the child's welfare demands any further orders designed to ensure continuing confidentiality. It is particularly interesting, in the context of the wider debate about openness in family courts, that the court was keen to emphasise that such restrictive orders would be '... unlikely to be made in many cases ...'.[11] It may well be that this decision paves the way for a fresh approach to the issue of confidentiality.

8.13 Thus, the statutory provisions do not represent the limit of a judge's powers to restrict the dissemination of information relating to children's cases. A High Court Judge has even wider powers to meet the justice of a particular case.[12]

8.14 In a free society, such an extraordinary restriction on the freedom of expression can only be justified in compelling circumstances. That justification, as discerned from the cases decided prior to the implementation of the Human Rights Act 1998,[13] amounts to the proposition that the interests of justice would be compromised were it not for this level of restriction. The arguments for restricting publication include:

- the child involved in proceedings has an interest in keeping his or her proceedings confidential;
- litigants in such proceedings are entitled to expect that the intimate details of their lives will be kept from the public arena lest they should be deterred from bringing proceedings in the interests of their children;
- witnesses in such proceedings (whether or not they are parties) must feel able to give their evidence frankly without fear that their evidence will be

---

10　[2006] EWCA Civ 878, [2006] 2 FCR 405.
11　Wall LJ, at para [145].
12　See, for example, *Re S (Identification: Restrictions on Publication)* [2004] UKHL 47, [2005] 1 FLR 591; *Thompson and Venables v News Group Newspapers Ltd and Others* [2001] 1 FLR 791; *A Local Authority v W, L, W, T and R (By the Children's Guardian)* [2005] EWHC 1564 (Fam), [2006] 1 FLR 1.
13　For discussion of the case-law, see *Re Z (A Minor) (Freedom of Publication)* [1996] 1 FLR 191; *Re X (Disclosure of Information)* [2001] 2 FLR 440.

exposed to the public arena (and this includes, for example, the perpetrator of abuse, who must be able to admit it without the pressure of public opprobrium);

- where evidence has been given in a children's case on the assumption that it would remain confidential, that belief should be preserved.

8.15 In *Re S (A Child) (Identification: Restriction on Publication)*,[14] the House of Lords held that, as a consequence of the enactment of the Human Rights Act 1998,[15] the scope and extent of the jurisdiction to restrain publicity derived from the rights under the European Convention for the Protection of Human Rights and Fundamental Freedoms 1950 (ECHR). The earlier case-law remained relevant, but the competing interests at the heart of an application to restrain publicity were the rights of the child under Article 8 of the ECHR and the right to freedom of expression under Article 10.

8.16 In balancing those competing interests, the following propositions[16] apply:

- neither Article 8 nor Article 10 has (as such) precedence over each other;
- where the values under the two articles are in conflict, an intense focus on the comparative importance of the specific rights being claimed in the individual case is necessary;
- the justification for interfering with or restricting each right must be taken into account;
- the proportionality test must be applied to each (in what might be called the 'ultimate balancing test' – the earlier authorities prior to the implementation of the Human Rights Act 1998 might be of relevance here).

8.17 Thus it can be seen that there is a panoply of jurisprudence, statutory and otherwise, through which the courts have wide powers to protect the confidentiality of children's proceedings. Do these restrictions and their justification amount to a veil of justified and necessary privacy? Or do they amount to a rather more dangerous cloak of secrecy?

Visible justice

8.18 As we have seen, the restrictions on access to and publication of the work of the family courts are both subject to judicial discretion. The arguments deployed where the discretion is in issue demonstrate the weaknesses and tensions in the justification behind these restrictive rules. An application for exceptions to the restrictions on publicity might rehearse the following arguments:

---

14 [2004] UKHL 47, [2005] 1 FLR 591.
15 See Appendix 3.
16 As summarised by Lord Steyn in *Re S (Identification: Restrictions on Publication)* [2004] UKHL 47, [2005] 1 FLR 591, at para [17].

- the right of a parent to tell his or her story to the world where there is a feeling of injustice, which might engage Articles 6, 8 and 10 of the ECHR;[17]
- the right on the part of the press to tell a story which is perceived to be in the public interest, engaging Article 10;
- the right of the child concerned to protecting private life by maintaining confidentiality (Article 8, Article 6);
- the right of the public as a whole to maintain freedom of expression.

These are powerful and often conflicting considerations.

8.19   Perhaps the most compelling consideration, however, particularly at the present time, is the importance of maintaining public confidence in the family justice system. As Mr Justice Munby points out, framing the debate in the context of the ECHR:

> '... of great importance, as it seems to me, in the present context is what I have referred to as the public interest in maintaining the confidence of the public at large in the courts. Article 6 is intended, among other things, to promote confidence in the judicial process. This is a point that has repeatedly been stressed by the Strasbourg court.'[18]

8.20   The media attention generated by criminal cases such as Angela Cannings's leads inevitably to the question of how such cases are dealt with in the family justice system. It is not easy to understand why a parent accused of abusing a child in criminal proceedings may 'use' the media to stimulate public debate about controversial medical issues, whereas a parent accused of the same act in the family courts runs the risk of criminal charges and imprisonment for attempting to stimulate debate in the same way. Similarly in the private law sphere, issues such as shared residence and the handling of intractable contact disputes are matters of public interest which are ripe for public scrutiny and debate. Yet the parent involved in such proceedings cannot participate in any specific debate without risking imprisonment.

8.21   In those circumstances, it is understandable that the public might perceive the confidentiality rules as being protective of a 'secret' justice system: 'secret' because it is in some way corrupt or 'loaded' against one interest or another (for example, the common argument that the system is 'loaded' against fathers). Whether or not it is 'loaded', the 'secrecy' prevents any public scrutiny and feeds a sense of unease. It is also the case that, conspiracy theories apart, sometimes the system fails. In those cases, it could be contended that the public is entitled to know about the failure. As matters stand, those who seek to portray the family justice system as corrupt or biased can themselves hide behind the very rules of 'secrecy' that they seek to exploit; and the public is suspicious that what it knows or suspects about the failings of the system is the thin end of a large wedge.

8.22   Thus, it can be argued, the rules of confidentiality in children's proceedings strike at the heart of public confidence in the family justice system, and feed that lack of confidence.

---

17   See Appendix 3.

18   See Mr Justice Munby *Access to and Reporting of Family Proceedings* [2005] Fam Law 945.

The road to reform

8.23 In its report, *Family Justice: the operation of the family courts* (published in February 2005), the House of Commons Constitutional Affairs Committee recognised the need for greater transparency in the workings of the family courts. In its recommendations, the Committee proposed greater access to family courts, in the form of the press and the public, subject to reporting restrictions and the judge's discretion to exclude the public. It is a perverse feature of the existing system that, while the High Court and county courts are closed to press and public, the press have a statutory right to attend hearings in the family proceedings court (subject to the court's power to exclude them),[19] while the Court of Appeal sits in public. This recommendation, if implemented, would iron out these anomalies.

8.24 In addition, the Committee recommended that judgments should 'normally' be delivered in public, subject to the names of the parties being kept anonymous.

8.25 In line with the Committee's recommendations, although independently of them, there is a growing recognition amongst judges and practitioners that the rules and procedures designed to protect the privacy of family proceedings are in fact causing it to be attacked.[20] In a recent Court of Appeal authority,[21] Lord Justice Wall expressed the view that, where the court was dealing with issues which had attracted media attention or controversy, there was a strong argument for the preparation by the judge of a short written summary of his conclusions and reasons which could be made publicly available when judgment was delivered.[22]

8.26 On 11 July 2006, the Department for Constitutional Affairs published its Consultation Paper, *Confidence and Confidentiality: Improving Transparency and Privacy in Family Courts*.[23] It outlines the fundamental changes in the 'certainties' of family life which have taken place as a consequence of changing social attitudes, which themselves have significantly altered the work of the family courts. As a consequence of these changing times, the paper continues, there needs to be a review of the need for greater openness in the family courts for the purpose of greater public scrutiny of its work; in addition, there is a need for greater openness in the form of more information about the process for those involved in family litigation.

8.27 The paper rightly identifies the central issue as the balancing of the need for confidence in the system against the need for confidentiality of those

---

19   See Magistrates Courts Act, 1980, s 69(2)(c). For the discretion to exclude, see s 69(4) and Family Proceedings Courts (Children Act 1989) Rules 1991, r 16(7).

20   See Mr Justice Munby *Access to and Reporting of Family Proceedings* [2005] Fam Law 945; see also *Re D (Intractable Contact Dispute: Publicity)* [2004] EWHC 727 (Fam), [2004] 1 FLR 1226; *Re B (A Child) (Disclosure)* [2004] EWHC 411 (Fam), [2004] 2 FLR 142.

21   *Re H (Freeing Orders: Publicity)* [2005] EWCA Civ 1325, [2006] 1 FLR 815.

22   A view repeated by the judge at the Association of Lawyers for Children *Hershman/Levy Memorial Lecture*, 29 June 2006.

23   CP 11/06, Cm 6886: see www.dca.gov.uk/consult/confr.htm.

involved in it. The current law (as we have identified) is complex and sometimes inconsistent. There is an interesting review of the approaches of other jurisdictions: in particular, both New Zealand[24] and British Colombia take a much less restrictive approach towards media attendance at and reporting of family proceedings.

8.28   Five principles are identified as the basis for any change in approach:

(1)   Ensuring public confidence in the system through public scrutiny: in other contexts (for example, the criminal law), the public relies upon the media as a proxy through which it can scrutinise the operation of public institutions, including the courts. It must follow that the media has an important role to play in ensuring public confidence in the workings of the family courts.

(2)   Improving understanding of the courts' decisions: publication of the decisions and proceedings of family courts would promote understanding of how and why decisions have been made. This is of particular importance to the parties involved in the proceedings, and the child subject of them. In private law cases, children are reliant upon their often warring parents to explain how and why decisions about them have been made: greater access to decisions and the reasons for them would promote a child's objective understanding in such circumstances. In cases where children are adopted, published decisions might help the child or later an adult understand why they have not been cared for by their natural families.

(3)   Protecting the privacy of children and their families: it is possible and crucial to publish decisions and proceedings without infringing the privacy of the parties and the children. Only that which might be in the public interest should be published.[25] At the same time, there might be a need for greater privacy in certain circumstances, for example, in relation to adoption proceedings where any publication might disrupt adoptive placements.

(4)   Ensuring effective sanctions for breaches of privacy: there needs to be a single statutory offence covering all breaches of blanket anonymity. Any further reporting restrictions in any particular case would be enforced by the existing law relating to contempt of court.

(5)   The need to consider the practical implications of any changes: any significant change would have implications for security in courtrooms, the size of courtrooms and potentially delay in proceedings whilst applications dealing with publicity are made and determined.

8.29   The consultation paper ends with proposals for:

●   changes to the attendance and reporting restrictions across all family proceedings (with the exception of adoption proceedings) giving the media a right to attend, subject always to a judicial power to exclude or restrict reporting;

---

24   Primarily as a consequence of the recent Care of Children Act 2004.
25   A specific example is the judgment of McFarlane J in *Re X (Emergency Protection Order)* [2006] EWHC 510 (Fam), (2006) *The Times*, 21 April.

- permission for other members of the public to attend family proceedings either by application or of the court's own motion;
- imposition of a blanket provision of anonymity in reporting, with a judicial discretion to increase or decrease restrictions in any particular case;
- primary legislation creating a single statutory offence for all breaches of blanket anonymity, and the retention of the other statutory powers to deal with any breaches of reporting restrictions; and
- the need to consider practical arrangements, taking into account matters of security and potential delay caused by applications in connection with reporting restrictions and/or attendance.

The consultation period is due to end on 30 October 2006.

8.30 There can be no doubt that the consultation period will uncover a number of significant difficulties with the proposals. Amongst the most obvious potential problems are these:

- There is the danger that greater publicity within a child's community will have a detrimental effect upon the child's welfare. It may well be easier than the Government anticipates for neighbours, school friends and the like to identify a particular child and family even where publicity remains anonymised.
- Greater publicity might impact upon the willingness of witnesses to co-operate in circumstances where their evidence, if it is to be of maximum value, must be given without any fear of the consequences.
- Although the press is obviously a valuable proxy for the general public in the context of criminal proceedings, that has not prevented often grossly distorted and inaccurate reporting. It is not easy to see how greater opportunities for publicity in children's cases can carry any guarantee that the publicity will be accurate and balanced.

8.31 These are thorny problems, and it will be interesting to see whether and how they can be solved at the end of the consultation period.

Conclusions

8.32 What is the way forward? There can be absolutely no doubt that the present rules which restrict access to the family courts and reporting from them, whilst attempting to serve the public interest, in fact operate to stifle public debate about matters of public interest. Worse still, those very rules can sometimes promote not only a distortion of the debate, but a shield behind which perceived and actual injustices are sometimes hidden. Even were that not the case, it is difficult in today's society to justify the position with any argument sufficiently compelling to support such a fundamental restriction on freedom of expression.

8.33 Judges will always need the discretion to exclude the press and the public in certain, exceptionally sensitive cases. At the same time, it is becoming increasingly obvious that public confidence in the family justice system needs to be better promoted, and the work of the family courts better understood. A relaxation of the rules against reporting is an obvious way forward, but it creates its own problems which need careful consideration and analysis before they can be adequately solved. It is to be hoped that the consultation document will stimulate a lively debate which will assist those charged with the immensely difficult task of implementing a more open family justice system. In that exercise, it is critical that the welfare of children at the heart of the system does not become obscured.

THE SINGLE FAMILY COURT

8.34   On 3 February 2005, the Department for Constitutional Affairs issued a consultation document, *A Single Civil Court? The scope for unifying the civil jurisdictions of the High Court, the County Courts and the Family Proceedings Courts.*[26] The consultation had at its root a feeling that the multi-tiered system (family proceedings court, county court and High Court) was overly complex and cumbersome. Previous reviews had mooted the idea of unified family courts,[27] and the idea had received popular support. A system of unified courts was felt, in some corners, to be the logical 'next step' in the reform of the civil justice system, following the Woolf Reforms of 1999, and the unification of the courts' administration.[28]

8.35   The consultation document identifies, broadly, three potential advantages of a unified civil court:

(a)   *User benefits:* A less complex and cumbersome system would reduce actual and apparent complexity, reducing cost to the administration and therefore the consumer, and encouraging the use of a simplified court structure.

(b)   *Assisting with the appropriate allocation of work:* The removal of geographical and jurisdictional barriers would facilitate early allocation to the 'lowest appropriate tier' of the judiciary.

(c)   *Improved central administration of the courts:* A unified court facilitates a unified administration, leading to increased efficiency and reduced cost.

8.36   The central proposal for consultation was that the county courts should be abolished, leaving the High Court as the single unified court. A suggestion made in the document is that the family proceedings courts should form part of the unified structure, thus expanding its jurisdiction to include all types of family case which could then be allocated in accordance with procedural rules. One of the major issues for consultation was whether and if so how jurisdiction should be limited and conferred in a unified system; another was the question of whether there should be a unified family court standing alongside a separate, unified court for all other civil cases.

8.37   The consultation period closed on 27 April 2005, and on 19 October 2005 the response was published.[29] 131 consultees responded. One of the more

---

26   CP 06/05; see www.dca.co.uk/consult/civilcourt/civilcourt_cp0605.pdf.
27   See *The Finer Report on One-Parent Families* (1974*); The Review of Family and Domestic Jurisdiction Consultation Paper* (1986).
28   With the establishment of HM Courts Service in April 2005.
29   CP(R) 06/05; see www.dca.co.uk/consult/civilcourt/response_civilcourt_cp0605.pdf.

controversial areas, interestingly, was the question of whether any of the benefits hypothesised by the consultation document would in fact be likely to accrue from a unified court structure. Of the 131 consultees, only 77 were prepared to speculate about the likely benefits. 58% felt that the hypothesised benefits were likely to accrue, but 42% (including the then Vice-Chancellor of the Chancery Division, Sir Andrew Morritt) felt that some or all of the hypothesised benefits would in fact be illusory.

8.38 Specifically in relation to the family jurisdiction, there was also some controversy over the proposal to unify the family courts. Just under 50% of consultees responded to this issue, of whom 65% favoured a unified family court standing alongside the single civil court. Only one consultee favoured a single court unifying the whole civil jurisdiction, but 34% favoured neither suggestion. There was a strong feeling amongst consultees that the family jurisdiction was specialist and distinct from the general civil jurisdiction, requiring different skills and different rules and procedures.

8.39 In conclusion, and as a consequence of the consultation, the Government has decided that the creation of single but separate civil and family courts with unified jurisdictions would be beneficial and desirable. The long-term goal of primary legislation to realise these reforms seems some time away; in the interim, the Government and judiciary will be working on the rules governing allocation of work in an effort to smooth the progress of any primary legislation when it arrives.

8.40 Partly in response to the Lord Chancellor's announcement that there would be no increases in the number of High Court judges, the Judicial Resources Review considered in particular the structure of allocation of work to the judiciary, and worked on the basis of the unified structure. On 19 October 2005, the Review issued its consultation document, *Focusing Judicial Resources Appropriately – The Right Judge for the Right Case*.[30] The proposals (the responses are as at the time of writing yet to be published) are designed to ensure that cases 'cascade down' to be heard at the lowest appropriate tier of the judiciary.

8.41 In his speech to the Association of Lawyers for Children 2005 Annual Conference,[31] Sir Mark Potter, President of the Family Division, shared his vision of the single family court and how it might be attained. He made it clear that greater use of the family proceedings courts was not only an inevitable consequence of the 'cascading down' of cases and the single family court, it was also a pre-requisite for the implementation of reforms. Pilot schemes for the more effective use of the family proceedings court were already in place in Birmingham and Barnet. He favoured a more specialist, confident and pro-active role for lay magistrates, akin to that of county court judges, and brought about by more training in and experience of specialist family work. In addition, work is underway to produce a single set of procedural rules for family proceedings, to be applied irrespective of level of court. It is significant

---

30   CP 25/05; see www.dca.co.uk/consult/focus/focus_cp2505.pdf.
31   18 November 2005. See [2006] Fam Law 65.

that the President expressed a real determination to reverse what he saw as a decline in the use of the family proceedings court.

8.42   It seems that primary legislation to achieve the single family court is some way off. In the meantime, we can expect policy tailored to the ultimate aim of the single family court. In particular, we have seen and will continue to see a 'cascading down' of work to the family proceedings courts, more active consideration at every stage of the lowest appropriate tier for any particular case, and greater utilisation of district judges and specialist lay magistrates.

8.43   Many practitioners will be extremely anxious at the prospect of a wide expansion in the jurisdiction of the family proceedings court. As the President mentioned in his speech to the ALC[32] there is a perception amongst some practitioners that the family proceedings court is inferior to the higher tier courts (and not just in hierarchical terms). Some feel that the family proceedings court is slower, less interventionist in its approach and less specialised in its knowledge and experience. On a practical note, the 'squeeze' on public funding for legal costs in family cases is most keenly felt at family proceedings court level. As the President indicated, what is of crucial importance in any policy intended to widen the jurisdiction and work-load of the family proceedings courts is a commitment to fully trained and experienced benches of specialist magistrates as well as a commitment to adequate funding for the lawyers. Without that commitment, there is a danger that the perception of the family proceedings court as an 'inferior' tribunal will continue.

THE VOICE OF THE CHILD

8.44   Section 1(3)(a) of the Children Act 1989 provides that, when the court is considering any application made under section 8, it shall have regard in particular to the wishes and feelings of the child concerned, so far as they are ascertainable, and considered in light of the child's age and understanding.

8.45   Our purpose here is to examine the role of the voice of the child in private law children's proceedings. Is the child's voice sufficiently represented or heard in our system of family justice? What are the mechanisms by which a child can be heard or represented? Are those mechanisms sufficiently well developed to serve their purpose? How can they be improved? These are the questions that we seek to address as part of the topical debate on the proper role that children themselves should play in proceedings about them.

International law

8.46   The UN Convention on the Rights of the Child 1989 (UNCRC)[33] provides that a child capable of forming views has the right freely to express its views in relation to all matters affecting it.[34] Those views, it continues, should

---

32   Ibid.
33   See Appendix 4.
34   UNCRC, Art 12, para 1.

be given due weight in accordance with the child's age and maturity. In particular, the Convention provides for children to be heard whether directly or through a representative or an appropriate body in any proceedings affecting them.[35] The Convention also provides children with the right to freedom of expression.[36]

8.47 The focus of the ECHR is, on its face, different. Originally intended to defend adults from State interference, it has tended to retain that emphasis on the rights of the adults as it has become more used in the context of conflict between the rights of individuals. Thus it is that children's 'rights' can sometimes be seen to be analysed in terms of violations of adult rights. In *Sahin v Germany*,[37] the European Court was invited (amongst other things) to consider whether the national court was right to decide a father's contact application without hearing directly from the child (who was about 5 years old), or whether such failure constituted a violation of the father's Article 8 right. The national court had taken evidence from a psychologist, who advised that ascertaining the child's views directly would not be in its interests. The court held that:

'... the German courts' failure to hear the child reveals an insufficient involvement of the applicant in the access proceedings. It is essential that the competent courts give careful consideration to what lies in the best interest of the child after having had direct contact with the child.'[38]

8.48 That decision was challenged by the German authorities, and the case was revisited by the Grand Chamber in 1993. The Chamber held:

'It would be going too far to say that domestic courts are always required to hear a child in court on the issue of access to a parent not having custody, but this issue depends on the specific circumstances of each case, having due regard to the age and maturity of the child concerned.'[39]

It is worth adding that, in this case, the court accepted the expert opinion that hearing from the child would be likely to cause harm and that no sufficiently protective special arrangements could be implemented at court to minimise that harm.

8.49 Whether the UN Convention confers a right which goes much further than the European Court's analysis is a moot point. What both Conventions and the cases establish, however, is that the 'voice of the child' is an important component of the decision making process in family proceedings Europe-wide. In some European countries, it is routine for judges to speak directly to children in the context of disputes relating to them; in the Commonwealth, at least one country automatically provides for the representation of the child in its proceedings.[40]

---

35   UNCRC, Art 12, para 2.
36   UNCRC, Art 13.
37   *Sahin v Germany; Sommerfield v Germany; Hoffmann v Germany* [2002] 1 FLR 119.
38   Ibid, at para [47]. Compare the approach taken in *Yousef v The Netherlands* [2003] 1 FLR 210.
39   *Sahin v Germany; Sommerfield v Germany* [2003] 2 FLR 671, at para [73].
40   New Zealand has ss 6 and 7 of its Care of Children Act 2004.

Domestic law: the position before the Adoption and Children Act 2002

8.50   Although the Children Act 1989 provides that the court should have regard to the wishes and feelings of the child concerned, it does not create any right for the child to be represented in private law proceedings. In practice, the wishes and feelings of the child have been expressed through the welfare report (which would be prepared generally either by a CAFCASS officer or a representative of the local authority, if relevant).[41] In such cases, the report has followed the statutory scheme[42] (namely, the considerations enshrined in section 1 of the Children Act 1989) and set out the ascertainable wishes and feelings of the child concerned. Such reports are not, however, invariably ordered: it depends on the nature of the proceedings and the stage that they reach. Such a reporting process is not the same as affording an opportunity for the child freely to express his or her views, by him or herself or through representation. On the face of it, then, the primary statutory scheme does not appear fully compliant with the UN Convention, in particular Article 12.[43]

8.51   The position for children in public law proceedings is different. There, as a general rule, the child participates in proceedings as a party and is represented by both a solicitor and a guardian (although the nature of that representation is paternalistic in the sense that its purpose is to safeguard the child's interests rather than simply represent his or her views).[44]

8.52   The question of representation of the child in private law proceedings is addressed in the secondary legislation. The two central provisions are rules 9.2A and 9.5 of the Family Proceedings Rules 1991.[45] Rule 9.5 provides for the appointment of a guardian on behalf of the child where it appears to the court that it is in the best interests of the child to be made a party to the proceedings.[46] Once that direction is made, the child, through its guardian[47] and appointed solicitor, is to be treated procedurally in the same way as any other party. This mechanism is sometimes described as the 'tandem system' and is highly regarded, having recently been described as a 'Rolls-Royce' procedure.[48] The guardian's primary duty, however, is to advance the child's 'best interests'; his or her duty to ascertain and advance the wishes and feelings of the child is secondary to that. Rule 9.2A provides that a child may conduct proceedings as a party without a guardian either with the court's leave or where

---

41   See Children Act 1989, s 7.

42   See para 5.63 for how the report-writing function of CAFCASS officers is set to change.

43   Section 64 of the Family Law Act 1996 does give the Lord Chancellor power to make regulations for the representation of children in cases involving domestic violence and disputes over the family home. The section has never been brrought into force.

44   See Children Act 1989, s 41.

45   SI 1991/1247.

46   Family Proceedings Rules 1991, r 9.5(1).

47   Either a CAFCASS Officer, or the Official Solicitor (subject to his consent) or 'some other proper person'.

48   See *Mabon v Mabon* [2005] EWCA Civ 634, [2005] 2 FLR 1011, per Thorpe LJ at para [25].

a solicitor instructed by the child considers that the child is able to give instructions in relation to the proceedings having regard to the child's understanding.[49]

8.53 This paternalistic approach to 'the voice of the child' remains dominated by adult perceptions of the child's interests as opposed to the child's expressions of his or her desires. It is certainly a distant echo of the UN Convention's right of a child 'freely ... to express [its] views ...',[50] whether or not it is technically compliant on a purposive construction.

8.54 In view of those provisions, it would not be unfair to describe domestic law's approach to the question of representation of the child or 'hearing the child's voice' as somewhat cautious. Indeed, the older authorities seem to advocate a restrictive interpretation of the Rules, in particular rule 9.2A.[51]

8.55 The precise reason for this apparently restrictive and cautious approach towards the question of representation of children is not easily discerned. One suggestion is the adversarial nature of children's proceedings within the civil justice system, which would create obvious pressures and risks were a child participant in proceedings to be treated as any other witness.[52] Another is a greater sense of paternalism, born out of a historical social conservatism, in contrast to other European jurisdictions. The cost of the legal representation of the child may well be a factor as well.

The pressure for reform

8.56 In recent years, there has been significant pressure from a number of directions (as Lord Justice Thorpe puts it) to:

> '... reflect the extent to which, in the twenty-first century, there is a keener appreciation of the autonomy of the child and the child's consequential right to participate in decision-making processes that fundamentally affect his family life.'[53]

8.57 In 2002, the Children Act Sub-Committee of the Advisory Board on Family Law demonstrated that 'keener appreciation' when, in *Making Contact Work*,[54] it recommended separate representation of children in appropriate private law proceedings. The Government's final response to that report (in March 2004) did not go that far. Instead, it contained a promise to keep 'under review' the question of extending the scope of separate representation for

---

49   Family Proceedings Rules 1991, r 9.2A(1).
50   UNCRC, Art 12.
51   See *Re S (A Minor) (Independent Representation)* [1993] 2 FLR 437: the court should be 'slow' to conclude that a child's understanding is sufficient to merit separate representation. See also *Re N (Contact: Minor Seeking Leave to Defend and Removal of Guardian)* [2003] 1 FLR 652, and the then President in *Re W (Contact: Joining Child as Party)*[2001] EWCA Civ 1830, [2003] 1 FLR 681: r 9.5 guardians should only be appointed in 'exceptional cases'.
52   See Wall LJ in *Mabon v Mabon* [2005] EWCA Civ 634, [2005] 2 FLR 1011, at paras [37] and [38].
53   In *Mabon v Mabon* [2005] EWCA Civ 634, [2005] 2 FLR 1011, at para [26].
54   Available at www.dca.gov.uk/family/abfla/mcwrep.pdf.

children in private law proceedings. Of course, as most children would qualify for assistance from the Legal Services Commission, this reform would involve significant further public expenditure.

8.58   In April 2004, there was renewed optimism that separate representation of children in private law proceedings should become more widespread with the issuing of the *President's Direction (Representation of Children in Family Proceedings Pursuant to Family Proceedings Rules 1991, Rule 9.5)*.[55] At the same time, the President's Office also issued a CAFCASS Practice Note[56] on the same topic. In the *President's Direction*, the circumstances in which a rule 9.5 appointment was envisaged included: 'where the child has a standpoint or interests which are inconsistent with or incapable of being represented by any of the adult parties',[57] and:

> '... where there is an intractable dispute over residence or contact, including where all contact has ceased, or where there is irrational but implacable hostility to contact or where the child may be suffering harm associated with the contact dispute.'[58]

8.59   In a sense, this guidance remained cautious, but there can be little doubt that, amongst practitioners, it signalled a clear intention that rule 9.5 should be used more frequently. There can be few practitioners specialising in this field who do not have, at any given time, at least one case in which 'the child may be suffering harm associated with' an intractable dispute over residence or contact, thereby bringing the case within the terms of the *President's Direction*.

8.60   Although practitioners could hardly be criticised for interpreting the *President's Direction* as a signal to expand their use of rule 9.5, it appears that such an expansion was not its intention. On 25 February 2005, the President's Office issued guidance on *The Appointment of Guardians in Accordance with Rule 9.5 and the President's Practice Direction of 5 April 2004*.[59] In its opening paragraph, the guidance complains that an 'unanticipated effect' of the *President's Practice Direction* has been a 'dramatic increase' in the number of guardians appointed in private law cases, which has had a 'major impact' on the Community Legal Services Fund and placed an 'intolerable strain' on the resources of CAFCASS. The guidance itself amounts to little more than procedural guidelines, but the reader can be left in little doubt that, in so far as the Practice Direction increased the number of guardians in private law cases, that was probably never the intention, and certainly not the intention by the time of this guidance. Furthermore, on 16 March 2005, CAFCASS issued its internal guidance[60] which reflected a feeling that guardians were being appointed unnecessarily.

---

55   [2004] 1 FLR 1188.
56   *Practice Note (Representation of Children in Family Proceedings Pursuant to Family Proceedings Rules 1991, Rule 9.5)* [2004] 1 FLR 1190. The Practice Note has now been replaced (see *www.familylaw.co.uk*).
57   See para [3.2].
58   See para [3.3].
59   Reproduced in *The Family Court Practice 2006* (Jordans), at p 2762.
60   *CAFCASS Guidance to Regional Directors and Service Managers: Implementing the President's Guidance to her Practice Direction on the Appointment of Guardians in Accordance with Rule 9.5 of 5 April 2004.*

8.61   The practitioner could be forgiven for feeling that, in the year following the issuing of the *President's Direction*, there must have been a massive rise in the appointment of rule 9.5 guardians, which placed an almost catastrophic strain upon the resources of the family justice system. That is certainly the impression conveyed by the guidance. Whether in fact the statistics justified this strong response has been questioned.[61]

8.62   The impact of the *President's Direction* has also been minimised in other ways. It is arguable that the joint Protocol produced by CAFCASS and NYAS[62] in December 2005[63] is not always consistent with the Practice Direction. Paragraph 5.2 of the Practice Direction provides for a guardian other than CAFCASS (for example from NYAS) where either a CAFCASS appointment would cause delay, or where such an appointment would be inappropriate for 'some other reason'. The joint protocol, however, records that NYAS 'may' provide a guardian where the family involved can 'no longer work with CAFCASS despite best efforts having been made'. It is at least arguable that this 'gloss' placed upon the Practice Direction restricts the involvement of NYAS in a way which was not obviously intended by the text of the Practice Direction itself.[64]

8.63   Furthermore, it would appear that the Legal Services Commission has also placed a restrictive 'gloss' upon the Practice Direction. From its perspective, there are costs implications if a guardian is appointed from NYAS rather than CAFCASS.[65] In the LSC's Manual (guidance on public funding provided to solicitors), the Commission suggests that NYAS will only be appointed to act as guardians in 'very exceptional circumstances and after careful consideration'.[66] This goes very much further than what the Practice Direction envisaged, namely appointment of a guardian other than from CAFCASS where such an appointment is either more appropriate or where a CAFCASS appointment would cause delay.

8.64   It could be argued that these events of 2004–2005 represent a missed opportunity to reform the treatment of representation of children from within the family justice system. More positively, The Private Law Programme[67] provides that, 'where the local scheme provides for it and where resources exist', children over 9 'may' attend the First Hearing dispute resolution appointment of proceedings concerning them. This again reflects, in a limited way, a

---

61   See the interesting article by Judge Clifford Bellamy *Rule 9.5: Further Reflections* [2006] Fam Law 298. He appears to suggest that the statistics must be incomplete, and questions the quality of the evidence upon which the proposition that there had been a 'dramatic increase' in rule 9.5 appointments was based.

62   NYAS, the National Youth Advocacy Service, is a charity providing advice and advocacy services to children and young people up to the age of 25. See www.nyas.net.

63   The purpose of which was to clarify the respective roles of these organisations in representing children in court proceedings.

64   See further Judge Clifford Bellamy *Rule 9.5: Further Reflections* [2006] Fam Law 298.

65   Where a CAFCASS officer is appointed to act as a guardian under rule 9.5, the CLS meets the cost of his or her solicitor. Where a NYAS appointment is made, the LSC must meet not only the solicitor's costs, but also those of the guardian.

66   Para 20.32(15).

67   See para 5.3 et seq.

continued desire more effectively to empower children in cases involving them. That pressure for reform, felt keenly amongst the lawyers and judiciary, remains, as does the justification for it. The Practice Direction seemed to be an expression of the need to reform; the response to it could be seen as a realisation that, without adequate resources and political will, reform must be frustrated.

The Adoption and Children Act 2002

8.65   Section 122 of the Adoption and Children Act 2002 inserts a new subsection (6A) into section 41 of the Children Act 1989. Section 41(6) lists those proceedings – 'specified proceedings' – in which the court must appoint a CAFCASS officer[68] to represent the child. Prior to the 2002 Act, that list did not include applications for a section 8 order. The category of 'specified proceedings' is not closed because it includes proceedings 'which are specified for the time being, for the purposes of this section, by rules of court'.[69] The new subsection (6A) expressly provides that the proceedings which may be specified by rules of court 'include (for example) proceedings for the making, varying or discharging of a section 8 order'. If, as clearly anticipated, such rules of court are made, section 8 proceedings will no longer be 'non-specified' family proceedings, in which the court has the discretion under rule 9.5 to appoint a guardian. Instead, they would be specified proceedings, in which such an appointment would be obligatory unless the court was satisfied that it was unnecessary to safeguard the child's interests.[70]

8.66   This important amendment to the Children Act 1989 was brought into force on 7 December 2004.[71] At the time of writing, some 18 months later, we still await the procedural rules which govern the amendment's operation, and, until those rules are enacted, subsection (6A) remains entirely without effect.

8.67   In 2003, the Department for Constitutional Affairs commissioned Cardiff University to undertake research directed towards ascertaining whether children who were or had been separately represented by CAFCASS under rule 9.5 felt the experience to be satisfactory. In that context, it is perhaps surprising that in *Parental Separation: Children's Needs and Parents' Responsibilities*,[72] there is no mention at all of the issue of separate representation. Similarly, the report of the House of Commons Constitutional Affairs Committee, *Family Justice: the operation of the family courts*,[73] is completely silent on the issue.

8.68   Notwithstanding a number of Parliamentary questions on the topic, the Government remained determined to await the outcome of the Cardiff research before acting.

---

68   Or, in Wales, a Welsh family proceedings officer.
69   Children Act 1989, s 41(6)(i).
70   Children Act 1989, s 41(1).
71   Adoption and Children Act 2002 (Commencement No 7) Order 2004 (SI 2004/3203).
72   July 2004 – Cm 6273 – available at www.dfes.gov.uk/childrensneeds/.
73   March 2005, HC 116-I.

Time to act: research into the operation of rule 9.5 of the Family Proceedings Rules 1991

8.69 Cardiff University published its final report, *Research into the Operation of Rule 9.5 of the Family Proceedings Rules 1991*[74] at the beginning of May 2006. The report's recommendations include:

- the need for the potential advantages of rule 9.5 appointments to be identified and appointments secured earlier in proceedings;
- the need for greater judicial continuity in cases;
- the need for children involved in proceedings to have clear, reliable and accurate information about the separation and divorce of their parents from the outset of proceedings;
- the need for children to be actively supported by an independent 'passage agent' particularly in cases of intractable disputes;
- the need for early identification of features likely to cause intractable behaviour on the part of parents;
- the need for automatic separate representation of children in enforcement proceedings brought under the forthcoming Children and Adoption Act 2006;
- the need to improve the system ('FamilyMan') for recording statistics in relation to children's cases.

8.70 The research revealed (perhaps unsurprisingly) that at present rule 9.5 is invoked as a 'last resort' in cases of perceived 'exceptional difficulty'. In the context of that finding, it is interesting (but perhaps no more surprising) that both the children and parents interviewed felt that separate representation was a good idea, which ought to be more frequently directed.

8.71 As a consequence of the way in which rule 9.5 appears to be used by judges as a weapon of 'last resort' in particularly intractable or unusual cases, the Cardiff research was faced with formidable research difficulties. It must be borne in mind that the research and its findings are not necessarily representative of the whole population subject to rule 9.5. That said, the findings drawn from the 'closed files' of children subject to rule 9.5 were broadly supported by the wider survey of solicitors having experience of rule 9.5 cases.

8.72 Of particular interest are the views of the children forming the basis of the research. It was a clear and consistent message that children liked the idea of someone appointed by the court to help them have their say in proceedings. They also felt the need for someone neutral to help them with their thoughts and feelings, and with the passage of the litigation, separate from their parents and independent of the court. Although some children felt that the guardian and CAFCASS adequately fulfilled this role, there were a significant number who felt that they had nobody to help them and that they were lost within an intimidating family justice system.

---

74   G Douglas, M Murch, C Miles & L Scanlan *Research into the Operation of Rule 9.5 of the Family Proceedings Rules 1991* (Cardiif University, 2006). Available at www.dca.gov.uk/family/familyprocrules_research.pdf.

8.73 A number of children felt entirely ignorant about the litigation and the process, imagining for example that judges were 'scary', with the power to imprison their parents. One of the strongest criticisms levelled at guardians or CAFCASS was the perception that material expressed by children to be 'confidential' later found its way into reports. Some children also felt that they were not kept fully informed of the progress of their case by their solicitors or guardians. There was sometimes a feeling that the only information that the children were getting was from obviously partisan parents.

8.74 All of these findings underpin one of the key recommendations: that children, subject of intractable disputes, should be actively supported by an independent 'passage agent' through proceedings. Furthermore, the report recommends the need for skilled and specialist training for solicitors and guardians in representing children to ensure the requisite skill, experience and aptitude. Solicitors and guardians must explain and ensure that the child understands the differing roles of guardian, reporting officer and solicitor, and also the distinction between the family court and the more punitive role of the criminal court.

8.75 The views of the parents interviewed largely reflected the children's views. They also favoured separate and independent representation, and emphasised the need for such representation to be accurate and impartial.

8.76 Other central findings, reflected in the views of children and their parents, related to case management. It was felt that a failure to identify the need for separate representation until late in the day, when it was clear that a case was in some way 'unusually difficult' caused unacceptable delay and associated anxiety for parents and children. That finding underscores the recommendation that assessment of the need for separate representation should take place at the First Hearing dispute resolution appointment. The assessment should not only encompass the question of risk where domestic violence is alleged, but should also take account of any risk to the child's education, social development and mental health arising from the parents' dispute. To assist in this assessment, CAFCASS officers should be trained in the administration of simplified psychometric measures. The question of what sort of separate representation should be used (the guardian model or child solicitor model) should be a judicial decision based on this assessment at the First Hearing. A Practice Direction should ensure that, when undertaking this assessment, judges should state clearly their reasons for directing separate representation and their reasons for directing a particular model of that representation.

8.77 The second major finding in relation to case management is the need for judicial continuity. It was of particular concern to all parties to the research that a lack of judicial continuity contributed to the lack of 'child-friendliness' perceived in the system and to unacceptable delay. The report recommends an inquiry into judicial continuity and continuing monitoring of it.

The future

8.78 Any practitioner in the family justice system will immediately recognise that, if the recommendations of the Cardiff research are to be implemented, there will be a significant cost. The report's implementation would demand far greater involvement from CAFCASS in individual cases, as well as (potentially) the provision of an independent 'passage agent'. Coming on top of the increased demands on CAFCASS consequent on the provisions of the Children and Adoption Act 2006, there is a danger that the service will become seriously overburdened and stretched. 'Judicial continuity' demands optimum use of judicial resources. There can be no question that, as is often the case, the provision of adequate resources, whether in the form of finance or man-power, remains key to the implementation of these recommendations. As for the recommendations themselves, few within the family justice system will be in any doubt, upon reading the report, that they are fundamentally sound and likely to advance the welfare of children who, through no fault of their own, find themselves enmeshed in painful and confusing litigation.

8.79 If the response to the *President's Direction* of 2004 is any indicator, it is difficult not to feel pessimistic about the prospects for what the Cardiff research proposes. It may well be that the apparent crisis of resources caused by the *President's Direction* will be dwarfed by the likely demands of these recommendations. The Government delayed formulating the rules for the implementation of section 41(6A) of the Children Act 1989 on the basis that it was awaiting the results of the Cardiff research. Now that the research is to hand, it will be interesting to see the approach that it takes..

8.80 At the time of writing, there is still no timetable for the formulation of these rules, even after publication of the research. In her announcement of the publication of the research, the Minister of State for the Department for Constitutional Affairs said that it would 'inform' the formulation of the rules alongside other research and statistics.

8.81 Another, more direct suggestion has been made by Sir Mark Potter, President of the Family Division.[75] In a key note address, he pondered whether we should in fact review our reluctance to permit children to speak to judges in private. We have touched upon the reasons why that has not generally been favoured in this jurisdiction.[76] The President wondered whether it was time for our system of family justice to trust the judiciary to talk directly to children and to 'hold the balance' between the child's confidence in so doing and the right to a fair trial for the adults. Would such an approach unduly burden the child concerned, or would it be empowering? Would it operate to erode a parent's right to a fair trial, or would it enhance the child's right to the same? It certainly appears that family justice systems elsewhere in Europe have less difficulty in holding these particular balances than ours.

Conclusion

8.82 Notwithstanding the recognised importance of hearing 'the voice of the child', our domestic family justice system lags behind others in providing a

---

75   At the Children Law UK *Voice of the Child* Conference held in December 2005. See [2006] Fam Law 150 and 170.

76   See para 8.55.

procedural mechanism for the expression of that voice. Our current procedures reflect an inherent conservatism and paternalism, which in many ways continue to favour adult perceptions of the voice of the child. The pressure for reform is widely recognised, and the benefits of a different approach are keenly felt well beyond the most intractable and difficult cases. Unfortunately, the benefits continue to be confined to those cases.

8.83   The costs implications of the Cardiff research recommendations, taken together, have been acknowledged. What, however, can and should happen – and what may well lead to savings in the long run – is the ending of the process whereby rule 9.5 appointments are seen as options of last resort. Consistent with the approach enshrined in the Private Law Programme, the cases likely to benefit from such appointments should be identified at the earliest possible stage. That would maximise the contribution that the child's guardian and lawyers could make to the proceedings. It would also provide a good chance of avoiding the protracted, conflictual and costly cases that bedevil the system and cause so much distress to the families concerned.

Chapter Nine

DEAL OR NO DEAL?

9.1 The Children Act 1989 revolutionised the law relating to children for private as well as public law cases. A decade and a half on, the time was right to reconsider the deal that the State was providing for the children of separated parents.

9.2 We have written this book with a degree of envy for those who wrote the guides for that ground-breaking measure. The beauty of reviewing an Act as comprehensive as the Children Act 1989 was that everything was all in one place, set out in a logical structure that had clearly been the product of considerable thought. The reviewer could start with section 1 and carry on seamlessly through until the schedules ran out and be fairly confident that nothing of relevance had been ignored.

9.3 We have had no such luxury. What we have termed 'the new deal' encompasses a range of changes, reforms, initiatives and developments. They have straddled both the court and the non-court arena; they have in part troubled the statute book but have mostly left it untouched; they have come about at different times and in differing ways; and nowhere are they to be found handily and logically set out. Trying to identify them all and bring them sensibly together in one place has not been an easy task, but it has been an illuminating process in its own right.

9.4 The idea of this book was conceived when *Parental Separation: Children's Needs and Parents' Responsibilities – Next Steps*[1] was produced in January 2005. The contents of that document have proved to be the tip of a very large iceberg. Below the surface of its commitments lay already a vast amount of research, thought and effort that had preceded and continued through the consultation exercise that informed its shape. In the 18 months since, there has been no let up in activity. Quite apart from the battles in and out of Parliament about the proper ambit of the Children and Adoption 2006, the period has seen countless reports, research papers, policy documents and consultation drafts that have all contributed in larger or lesser part to the various aspects of 'the new deal' that we have analysed. Nor is there any sign that the activity will

---

1   January 2005 – Cm 6452 – available at www.dfes.gov.uk/childrensneeds/.

cease; and indeed one of our other major problems has been knowing where to draw the line in what is a continually moving process.[2]

9.5   That provides the basis for our first conclusion. Whatever may be felt about what has resulted, it is frankly staggering how much work has gone into the process and its end product. It is also an eye-opener to appreciate the extent of the canvas on which that work has been carried out. As lawyers, we tend to focus on the law and the courts, but what is truly striking is the importance of the role played by those with no legal qualification, likewise the value of what takes place outside the court-room.

9.6   In an area where emotions inevitably run high, it is also right to make this observation. It is unfortunate that the debate has to a large degree been polarised into 'pro-contact' and 'pro-safety' camps. What unites all the time, thought and effort that we have already commended, and which includes that emanating from both lobbies, is the drive and determination of all those involved to do what is right for the children of separated parents. There is consensus about the ultimate objective, so why should the two camps be in conflict? Can anyone dispassionately contend for contact that is not safe for the child concerned? Equally, can anyone objectively argue with the proposition that a child should know the love, company and influence of both its parents, save where such endangers its safety?

9.7   It is a given in this area that no system will please everyone and that there will be cases that will defeat even the best of designs. The challenge is to try to structure the system such that it gets the overall balance as right as possible, keeps the insoluble cases to the barest minimum, and deals with the problem areas and issues without disturbing or undermining what has been seen to work before. What makes the challenge harder is to achieve all that with limited resources.

9.8   It is against those criteria that we seek to assess the efforts made by the State in its various guises to improve the deal for the children of separated parents.

9.9   At its broadest level, what we have termed 'the new deal' actually represents quite an interventionist agenda. For it reflects the State's recognition of the need to deal appropriately and effectively with the impact of parental separation on the life of a child. Private problems for the children and families concerned, they have, when not properly addressed in-house, the potential to be problems for the community at large. When a child is wrongly denied a relationship with a parent, that child suffers. When a child is forced into childcare arrangements that are not safe, that child suffers too. When a child is exposed to continuing parental conflict, that child suffers as well. In all three scenarios, the consequences are potentially far broader than the child's immediate suffering. Dysfunctional families are seen as a cause of social malaise, and problems created by this generation, if left unaddressed, will likely

---

2   That Fathers 4 Justice has, over the course of the writing of this book, both disbanded and reformed neatly encapsulates just how changeable is the landscape that we have attempted to cover.

spawn more for the next. Whatever the importance of getting it right for the individual children and families involved, it is the ramifications of getting it wrong, when seen in the context of the sheer numbers of children enduring parental separation, that explains the extent of the State's concern.

9.10 But within those parameters, 'the new deal' seems to be consistent with the fundamental principles enshrined in the Children Act 1989. It has at its core the paramountcy of the welfare of the child; it is informed by the need for speed; and, above all, it reflects the necessity for any intervention to be proportionate.

9.11 What, however, is significant and indeed new about this 'new deal' is the more proportionate way in which it responds to different scenarios and different kinds of problems.

9.12 It rightly holds up as the ideal the majority of parents who manage safely and successfully to sort out their childcare arrangements without the need for active intervention, whether through mediation or through the court process. As with the parents who follow those routes, some of them may find guidance and ideas in the updated and now widely available 'parenting plans', but this is not really intervention at all. This is not the State telling them what to do, merely giving them some concept of what has worked for others.

9.13 The parents who now come to court can be broadly categorised into those who should be there and those who should not. For the latter, who would in previous times have had their childcare arrangements ordered by the court (possibly after contested proceedings), there is the clear steer away from that form of intervention. They are encouraged to attend mediation, a far less conflictual process, or, if they have already reached the court arena, to participate in in-court conciliation. In both scenarios, the aim is to divert them from a less satisfactory path of potential conflict and to empower them by providing them with the means and encouragement to agree their own arrangements.

9.14 That leaves the cases that should be in the court arena. For them, 'the new deal' recognises that the heavier touch is required where the lighter touch has failed before. It is no coincidence that the longest chapter in this book is that about domestic violence. For the effective addressing of safety issues in private law children's cases presents a huge challenge to the system, not least where the emphasis on compromise comes into conflict with that on safety. For those cases, it is recognised that there needs to be far more proactive, more considered and more wide-ranging forms of intervention.

9.15 Similarly, the passing of the Children and Adoption Act 2006 entailed an acceptance that the more difficult kinds of case were being failed by a lack of effective options. Those that existed were either too onerous or too ineffectual and, on paper at least, the Act allows for a more proportionate and creative response to the problems thrown up by these cases, and will likely signal greater intervention in them.

9.16 If the principle of proportionality can be seen as a recognition of the truism that no child, family or case is the same, then the most proportionate aspect of 'the new deal' lies not in what has done but in what it chose not to do.

9.17 The absence of a statutory presumption of reasonable contact or equal parenting is perhaps its most newsworthy aspect. There are understandable arguments both for and against, but, in our view, the case has not as yet been compellingly made for the introduction of such a presumption now. We say that for a number of reasons.

9.18 In the first place, there seems no need for it. The balance currently struck in law, which sees an assumption in favour of contact, to be displaced only if the child's interests indicate otherwise, is manifestly correct, readily understood and incapable of better exposition.

9.19 As the attempts to reduce the position into some meaningful statutory presumption have shown, there is the risk of interfering unnecessarily and unjustifiably with the principle that the welfare of each and every child is paramount. This can be seen when one considers the lead amendment that was proposed during the Third Reading Debate of the Children and Adoption Bill. It sought to insert after section 1(1) of the Children Act 1989 the following:

'In respect of subsection (1)(a)[3] the court shall, unless a contrary reason be shown, act on the presumption that a child's welfare is best served through residence with his parents and, if his parents are not living together, through residence with one of them and through both of them being as fully and equally involved in his parenting as possible.'[4]

9.20 At a stroke, the amendment would create in the private law context a 'presumption' that the welfare of the child of separated parents is best served 'through residence with one of them'. But where is the research basis to underpin the extent of that proposition? Certainly, the norm is for the child of separated parents to have a primary residence. However, as research has shown,[5] shared residence arrangements can in certain circumstances work; so why should the concept per se be presumed to be contrary to the best interests of the child? Sole residence should be the outcome where consistent with the best interests of the child; shared residence should be the result when the very same test so dictates. There should be no presumption one way or another. The welfare of the child should be allowed, without qualification, to be paramount.

9.21 As for the proposed presumption in favour of both parents having 'full and equal involvement in parenting', perhaps it takes lawyers to point out what is likely to raise expectations and consequently provide fertile ground for further and future litigation.

9.22 Finally, it is sometimes said that a statutory presumption in favour of reasonable contact would somehow send the right message to those charged with making the decisions. Perhaps no other point more forcibly makes the case for opening up the family courts. Whilst judges and magistrates have been hampered by the inadequacies of the system in which they have had to operate, our collective seventy years' experience of the family courts shows no such universal anti-contact bias on the part of those who administer justice in this

---

3   'Where a court determines any question with respect to the upbringing of a child.'
4   Moved by Tim Loughton MP, HC Deb, 20 June 2006.
5   See para 1.105 et seq.

area. Of course, there will be cases which may seem unjust or which can be made to sound so, but to equate that with a lack of enthusiasm on the part of the courts as a whole for the principle of contact, when (if anything) the bias is the other way, is a proposition without foundation.

9.23 Accordingly, and albeit that our standpoint conflicts with our own self-interest, we think it right on balance that the Children and Adoption Act 2006 contains no statutory presumption in favour of reasonable contact or equal parenting.

9.24 In saying that, we have no doubt that the issue will be revisited in the future, and it will be important at that stage to take stock, on the evidence then available, of the advantages and disadvantages of any such statutory presumption being introduced.

9.25 So far as 'the new deal' as a whole is concerned, it is hard not to see it as a genuine and well considered attempt to improve a system that has to address a multitude of different problems.

9.26 The emphasis on keeping cases that do not involve safety issues away from court and, in particular, from contested court proceedings is plainly sensible, and the allied restructuring of the system to promote less conflictual, more consensual solutions (including the changes to the role of CAFCASS) is to be welcomed.

9.27 Equally, the developments affecting cases that do have safety issues, particularly those where the issue of domestic violence appears, reflect a sound and timely commitment to deal with such cases with greater proactivity and effectiveness.

9.28 The Children and Adoption Act 2006 focuses on a statistically narrow band of cases, which also tend to be the most difficult – ones where problems arise in the implementation of 'best interests' decisions by the court. As such, one has to be cautious about the Act's likely success. What is right is its implicit recognition that, in this context, more needed to be done to facilitate and enforce contact. As a matter of principle, therefore, an Act that allows the court more flexibility and gives it more ways of seeing its 'best interests' decisions implemented can only be seen in a positive light. How it will work in practice, we await to see.

9.29 In an area where it is very easy to criticise, it is right to give praise where it is due. In our view, 'the new deal' for contact improves on the system that pre-existed, provides for more proportionate and effective ways of dealing with the variety of problems and issues thrown up when parents separate and firmly keeps the paramountcy of the child's welfare at the core of the process.

9.30 But, if this new improved system is to succeed, then it needs time (to bed in and to be shown to work) and it needs adequate resourcing. We do not call for a blank cheque, nor do we say that no improvement is possible within a limited budget. But there has to be a realistic acknowledgement of what is needed to make this system work. This is particularly true of CAFCASS. Placing the service at the heart of the system makes sense. However, expecting it to shoulder ever more burdens, whilst confining it to a financial straitjacket, runs the real risk of undermining the very edifice that 'the new deal' has sought to build. It is short-sightedness of the worst sort, for it fails to recognise that money well spent now should entail a significant saving down the line. It also fails to see that a system frustrated by under-resourcing might in time be misinterpreted as not having been the right system in the first place. What is needed is a confidence in what 'the new deal' has created and could achieve for the sons and daughters of separated parents, and an appreciation that there is no more worthwhile investment than that in the future of children.

APPENDICES

Appendix 1

CHILDREN ACT 1989 (MATERIAL PARTS, INCORPORATING PROSPECTIVE AMENDMENTS INTRODUCED BY THE CHILDREN AND ADOPTION ACT 2006)[1]

PART I

INTRODUCTORY

1 Welfare of the child[2]

(1) When a court determines any question with respect to–

(a) the upbringing of a child; or
(b) the administration of a child's property or the application of any income arising from it,

the child's welfare shall be the court's paramount consideration.

(2) In any proceedings in which any question with respect to the upbringing of a child arises, the court shall have regard to the general principle that any delay in determining the question is likely to prejudice the welfare of the child.

(3) In the circumstances mentioned in subsection (4), a court shall have regard in particular to–

(a) the ascertainable wishes and feelings of the child concerned (considered in the light of his age and understanding);
(b) his physical, emotional and educational needs;
(c) the likely effect on him of any change in his circumstances;
(d) his age, sex, background and any characteristics of his which the court considers relevant;
(e) any harm which he has suffered or is at risk of suffering;

---

1 Information: Act reference: 1989 c 41. Royal assent: 16 November 1989. Long title: An Act to reform the law relating to children; to provide for local authority services for children in need and others; to amend the law with respect to children's homes, community homes, voluntary homes and voluntary organisations; to make provision with respect to fostering, child minding and day care for young children and adoption; and for connected purposes.

2 Provision details: Commencement: 14 October 1991 (SI 1991/828).

(f)   how capable each of his parents, and any other person in relation to whom the court considers the question to be relevant, is of meeting his needs;

(g)   the range of powers available to the court under this Act in the proceedings in question.

(4) The circumstances are that–

(a)   the court is considering whether to make, vary or discharge [a special guardianship order or]³ a section 8 order, and the making, variation or discharge of the order is opposed by any party to the proceedings; or

(b)   the court is considering whether to make, vary or discharge an order under Part IV.

(5) Where a court is considering whether or not to make one or more orders under this Act with respect to a child, it shall not make the order or any of the orders unless it considers that doing so would be better for the child than making no order at all.

   Amendments—Adoption and Children Act 2002, s 115(2), (3).

2 *Parental responsibility for children*⁴

(1) Where a child's father and mother were married to each other at the time of his birth, they shall each have parental responsibility for the child.

(2) Where a child's father and mother were not married to each other at the time of his birth–

(a)   the mother shall have parental responsibility for the child;

(b)   the father [shall have parental responsibility for the child if he has acquired it (and has not ceased to have it)]⁵ in accordance with the provisions of this Act.

(3) References in this Act to a child whose father and mother were, or (as the case may be) were not, married to each other at the time of his birth must be read with section 1 of the Family Law Reform Act 1987 (which extends their meaning).

(4) The rule of law that a father is the natural guardian of his legitimate child is abolished.

(5) More than one person may have parental responsibility for the same child at the same time.

---

3   Amendment: Words inserted: Adoption and Children Act 2002, s 115(2), (3), with effect, for certain purposes, from 7 December 2004 (SI 2004/3203), for remaining purposes, from 30 December 2005 (SI 2005/2213).

4   Provision details: Commencement: 14 October 1991 (SI 1991/828).

5   Amendment: Words substituted: Adoption and Children Act 2002, s 111(5), with effect from 1 December 2003 (SI 2003/3079).

(6) A person who has parental responsibility for a child at any time shall not cease to have that responsibility solely because some other person subsequently acquires parental responsibility for the child.

(7) Where more than one person has parental responsibility for a child, each of them may act alone and without the other (or others) in meeting that responsibility; but nothing in this Part shall be taken to affect the operation of any enactment which requires the consent of more than one person in a matter affecting the child.

(8) The fact that a person has parental responsibility for a child shall not entitle him to act in any way which would be incompatible with any order made with respect to the child under this Act.

(9) A person who has parental responsibility for a child may not surrender or transfer any part of that responsibility to another but may arrange for some or all of it to be met by one or more persons acting on his behalf.

(10) The person with whom any such arrangement is made may himself be a person who already has parental responsibility for the child concerned.

(11) The making of any such arrangement shall not affect any liability of the person making it which may arise from any failure to meet any part of his parental responsibility for the child concerned.

Amendments—Adoption and Children Act 2002, s 111(5).

3 *Meaning of 'parental responsibility'*[6]

(1) In this Act 'parental responsibility' means all the rights, duties, powers, responsibilities and authority which by law a parent of a child has in relation to the child and his property.

(2) It also includes the rights, powers and duties which a guardian of the child's estate (appointed, before the commencement of section 5, to act generally) would have had in relation to the child and his property.

(3) The rights referred to in subsection (2) include, in particular, the right of the guardian to receive or recover in his own name, for the benefit of the child, property of whatever description and wherever situated which the child is entitled to receive or recover.

(4) The fact that a person has, or does not have, parental responsibility for a child shall not affect–

(a)   any obligation which he may have in relation to the child (such as a statutory duty to maintain the child); or

(b)   any rights which, in the event of the child's death, he (or any other person) may have in relation to the child's property.

---

6   Provision details: Commencement: 14 October 1991 (SI 1991/828).

(5) A person who–

(a) does not have parental responsibility for a particular child; but

(b) has care of the child,

 may (subject to the provisions of this Act) do what is reasonable in all the circumstances of the case for the purpose of safeguarding or promoting the child's welfare.

4 Acquisition of parental responsibility by father[7]

(1) Where a child's father and mother were not married to each other at the time of his birth [, the father shall acquire parental responsibility for the child if–

(a) he becomes registered as the child's father under any of the enactments specified in subsection (1A);

(b) he and the child's mother make an agreement (a 'parental responsibility agreement') providing for him to have parental responsibility for the child; or

(c) the court, on his application, orders that he shall have parental responsibility for the child.][8]

[(1A) The enactments referred to in subsection (1)(a) are–

(a) paragraphs (a), (b) and (c) of section 10(1) and of section 10A(1) of the Births and Deaths Registration Act 1953;

(b) paragraphs (a), (b)(i) and (c) of section 18(1), and sections 18(2)(b) and 20(1)(a) of the Registration of Births, Deaths and Marriages (Scotland) Act 1965; and

(c) sub-paragraphs (a), (b) and (c) of Article 14(3) of the Births and Deaths Registration (Northern Ireland) Order 1976.

(1B) The [Secretary of State][9] may by order amend subsection (1A) so as to add further enactments to the list in that subsection.][10]

(2) No parental responsibility agreement shall have effect for the purposes of this Act unless–

(a) it is made in the form prescribed by regulations made by the Lord Chancellor; and

(b) where regulations are made by the Lord Chancellor prescribing the manner in which such agreements must be recorded, it is recorded in the prescribed manner.

---

7 Provision details: Commencement: 14 October 1991 (SI 1991/828).

8 Amendment: Words substituted: Adoption and Children Act 2002, s 111(1), (2), with effect from 1 December 2003 (SI 2003/3079).

9 Amendment: Words substituted: Transfer of Functions (Children, Young People and Families) Order 2003, SI 2003/3191, art 3(a), with effect from 12 January 2004.

10 Amendment: Subsections inserted: Adoption and Children Act 2002, s 111(1), (3), (7), with effect from 1 December 2003 (SI 2003/3079).

[(2A) A person who has acquired parental responsibility under subsection (1) shall cease to have that responsibility only if the court so orders.

(3) The court may make an order under subsection (2A) on the application–

(a)   of any person who has parental responsibility for the child; or
(b)   with the leave of the court, of the child himself,

 subject, in the case of parental responsibility acquired under subsection (1)(c), to section 12(4).][11]

(4) The court may only grant leave under subsection (3)(b) if it is satisfied that the child has sufficient understanding to make the proposed application.

   Amendments—Adoption and Children Act 2002, s 111(1), (2), (3), (4), (7); SI 2003/3191.

[4A   Acquisition of parental responsibility by step-parent

(1) Where a child's parent ('parent A') who has parental responsibility for the child is married to[, or a civil partner of,][12] a person who is not the child's parent ('the step-parent') –

(a)   parent A or, if the other parent of the child also has parental responsibility for the child, both parents may by agreement with the step-parent provide for the step-parent to have parental responsibility for the child; or
(b)   the court may, on the application of the step-parent, order that the step-parent shall have parental responsibility for the child.

(2) An agreement under subsection (1)(a) is also a 'parental responsibility agreement', and section 4(2) applies in relation to such agreements as it applies in relation to parental responsibility agreements under section 4.

(3) A parental responsibility agreement under subsection (1)(a), or an order under subsection (1)(b), may only be brought to an end by an order of the court made on the application –

(a)   of any person who has parental responsibility for the child; or
(b)   with the leave of the court, of the child himself.

(4) The court may only grant leave under subsection (3)(b) if it is satisfied that the child has sufficient understanding to make the proposed application.][13]

   Amendments—Adoption and Children Act 2002, s 112(7); Civil Partnership Act 2004, s 75(1), (2).

---

11   Amendment: Subsections substituted for subsection (3): Adoption and Children Act 2002, s 111(1), (4), with effect from 1 December 2003 (SI 2003/3079).
12   Amendment: Words inserted: Civil Partnership Act 2004, s 75(1), (2), with effect from 30 December 2005 (SI 2005/3175).
13   Amendment: Section inserted: Adoption and Children Act 2002, s 112(7), with effect from 30 December 2005 (SI 2005/2213).

7 *Welfare reports*[14]

(1) A court considering any question with respect to a child under this Act may–

(a)   ask [an officer of the Service][15][or a Welsh family proceedings officer][16]; or

(b)   ask a local authority to arrange for–

   (i)   an officer of the authority; or

   (ii)   such other person (other than [an officer of the Service][17] [or a Welsh family proceedings officer][18]) as the authority considers appropriate,

   to report to the court on such matters relating to the welfare of that child as are required to be dealt with in the report.

(2) The Lord Chancellor may[, after consulting the Lord Chief Justice,][19] make regulations specifying matters which, unless the court orders otherwise, must be dealt with in any report under this section.

(3) The report may be made in writing, or orally, as the court requires.

(4) Regardless of any enactment or rule of law which would otherwise prevent it from doing so, the court may take account of–

(a)   any statement contained in the report; and

(b)   any evidence given in respect of the matters referred to in the report,

   in so far as the statement or evidence is, in the opinion of the court, relevant to the question which it is considering.

(5) It shall be the duty of the authority or [officer of the Service][20] [or a Welsh family proceedings officer][21] to comply with any request for a report under this section.

---

14   Provision details: Commencement: 14 October 1991 (SI 1991/828).

15   Amendment: Words substituted: Criminal Justice and Court Services Act 2000, s 74, Sch 7, paras 87, 88(a), with effect from 1 April 2001 (SI 2001/919).

16   Amendment: Words inserted: Children Act 2004, s 40, Sch 3, paras 5, 6, with effect from 1 April 2005 (SI 2005/700).

17   Amendment: Words substituted: Criminal Justice and Court Services Act 2000, s 74, Sch 7, paras 87, 88(a), with effect from 1 April 2001 (SI 2001/919).

18   Amendment: Words inserted: Children Act 2004, s 40, Sch 3, paras 5, 6, with effect from 1 April 2005 (SI 2005/700).

19   Amendment: Words inserted: Constitutional Reform Act 2005, s 15(1), Sch 4, Pt 1, paras 203, 204(1), (2), with effect from 3 April 2006 (SI 2006/1014).

20   Amendment: Words substituted: Criminal Justice and Court Services Act 2000, s 74, Sch 7, paras 87, 88(b), with effect from 1 April 2001 (SI 2001/919).

21   Amendment: Words inserted: Children Act 2004, s 40, Sch 3, paras 5, 6, with effect from 1 April 2005 (SI 2005/700).

[(6) The Lord Chief Justice may nominate a judicial office holder (as defined in section 109(4) of the Constitutional Reform Act 2005) to exercise his functions under subsection (2).][22]

Amendments—Criminal Justice and Court Services Act 2000, s 74, Sch 7, paras 87, 88; Children Act 2004, s 40, Sch 3, paras 5, 6; Constitutional Reform Act 2005, s 15(1), Sch 4, Pt 1, paras 203, 204(1), (2), (3).

PART II

ORDERS WITH RESPECT TO CHILDREN IN FAMILY PROCEEDINGS

General

8 Residence, contact and other orders with respect to children[23]

(1) In this Act–

'a contact order' means an order requiring the person with whom a child lives, or is to live, to allow the child to visit or stay with the person named in the order, or for that person and the child otherwise to have contact with each other;

'a prohibited steps order' means an order that no step which could be taken by a parent in meeting his parental responsibility for a child, and which is of a kind specified in the order, shall be taken by any person without the consent of the court;

'a residence order' means an order settling the arrangements to be made as to the person with whom a child is to live; and

'a specific issue order' means an order giving directions for the purpose of determining a specific question which has arisen, or which may arise, in connection with any aspect of parental responsibility for a child.

(2) In this Act 'a section 8 order' means any of the orders mentioned in subsection (1) and any order varying or discharging such an order.

(3) For the purposes of this Act 'family proceedings' means [-][24] any proceedings–

---

22 Amendment: Sub-section inserted: Constitutional Reform Act 2005, s 15(1), Sch 4, Pt 1, paras 203, 204(1), (3), with effect from 3 April 2006 (SI 2006/1014).

23 Provision details: Commencement: 14 October 1991 (SI 1991/828).

24 In view of the Government's decision not to implement (and in due course to repeal) Part II of the Family Law Act 1996, the prospective amendments to Children Act 1989, s 8(3), introduced by Family Law Act, Sch 8, have been omitted.

(a)   under the inherent jurisdiction of the High Court in relation to children; and

(b)   under the enactments mentioned in subsection (4),

but does not include proceedings on an application for leave under section 100(3).

(4) The enactments are–

(a)   Parts I, II and IV of this Act;

(b)   the Matrimonial Causes Act 1973;

[(ba) Schedule 5 to the Civil Partnership Act 2004;][25]

(c)   ...[26]

[(d)   the Adoption and Children Act 2002;][27]

(e)   the Domestic Proceedings and Magistrates' Courts Act 1978;

[(ea) Schedule 6 to the Civil Partnership Act 2004;][28]

(f)   ...[29]

(g)   Part III of the Matrimonial and Family Proceedings Act 1984;

[(h)   the Family Law Act 1996;][30]

[(i)   sections 11 and 12 of the Crime and Disorder Act 1998.][31]

[...][32]

> **Amendments**—Family Law Act 1996, s 66(1), Sch 8, Pt III, para 60; Crime and Disorder Act 1998, s 119, Sch 8, para 68; Adoption and Children Act 2002, s 139(1), Sch 3, paras 54, 55; Civil Partnership Act 2004, s 261(1), Sch 27, para 129(1), (2), (3). Prospectively amended by Family Law Act 1996, s 66(1), Sch 8, para 41(3).

---

25   Amendment: Paragraph inserted: Civil Partnership Act 2004, s 261(1), Sch 27, para 129(1), (2), with effect from 5 December 2005 (SI 2005/3175).

26   Amendment: Paragraph repealed: Family Law Act 1996, s 66(1), Sch 8, Pt III, para 60, with effect from 1 October 1997 (SI 1997/1892).

27   Amendment: Paragraph substituted: Adoption and Children Act 2002, s 139(1), Sch 3, paras 54, 55, with effect from 30 December 2005 (SI 2005/2213).

28   Amendment: Paragraph inserted: Civil Partnership Act 2004, s 261(1), Sch 27, para 129(1), (3), with effect from 5 December 2005 (SI 2005/3175).

29   Amendment: Paragraph repealed: Family Law Act 1996, s 66(1), Sch 8, Pt III, para 60, with effect from 1 October 1997 (SI 1997/1892).

30   Amendment: Paragraph inserted: Family Law Act 1996, s 66(1), Sch 8, Pt III, para 60, with effect from 1 October 1997 (SI 1997/1892).

31   Amendment: Paragraph inserted: Crime and Disorder Act 1998, s 119, Sch 8, para 68, with effect from 30 September 1998 (SI 1998/2327).

32   In view of the Government's decision not to implement (and in due course repeal) Part II of the Family Law Act 1996, the proposed new Children Act 1989, s 8(5), introduced by Family Law Act, Sch 8, has been omitted.

9 Restrictions on making section 8 orders[33]

(1) No court shall make any section 8 order, other than a residence order, with respect to a child who is in the care of a local authority.

(2) No application may be made by a local authority for a residence order or contact order and no court shall make such an order in favour of a local authority.

(3) A person who is, or was at any time within the last six months, a local authority foster parent of a child may not apply for leave to apply for a section 8 order with respect to the child unless–

(a)   he has the consent of the authority;

(b)   he is relative of the child; or

(c)   the child has lived with him for at least [one year][34] preceding the application.

(4) ...[35]

(5) No court shall exercise its powers to make a specific issue order or prohibited steps order–

(a)   with a view to achieving a result which could be achieved by making a residence or contact order; or

(b)   in any way which is denied to the High Court (by section 100(2)) in the exercise of its inherent jurisdiction with respect to children.

(6) [Subject to section 12(5)][36] no court shall make any section 8 order which is to have effect for a period which will end after the child has reached the age of sixteen unless it is satisfied that the circumstances of the case are exceptional.

(7) No court shall make any section 8 order, other than one varying or discharging such an order, with respect to a child who has reached the age of sixteen unless it is satisfied that the circumstances of the case are exceptional.

> **Amendments**—Adoption and Children Act 2002, ss 113(a), (b), 114(2), 139(3), Sch 5.

10 Power of court to make section 8 orders[37]

(1) In any family proceedings in which a question arises with respect to the welfare of any child, the court may make a section 8 order with respect to the child if–

---

33   Provision details: Commencement: 14 October 1991 (SI 1991/828).

34   Amendment: Words substituted: Adoption and Children Act 2002, s 113(a), with effect from 30 December 2005 (SI 2005/2213).

35   Amendment: Subsection repealed: Adoption and Children Act 2002, s 113(b), 139(3), Sch 5, with effect from 30 December 2005 (SI 2005/2213).

36   Amendment: Words inserted: Adoption and Children Act 2002, s 114(2), with effect from 30 December 2005 (SI 2005/2213).

37   Provision details: Commencement: 14 October 1991 (SI 1991/828).

(a)   an application for the order has been made by a person who–
     (i) is entitled to apply for a section 8 order with respect to the child; or
     (ii) has obtained the leave of the court to make the application; or
(b)   the court considers that the order should be made even though no such application has been made.

(2) The court may also make a section 8 order with respect to any child on the application of a person who–

(a)   is entitled to apply for a section 8 order with respect to the child; or
(b)   has obtained the leave of the court to make the application.

(3) This section is subject to the restrictions imposed by section 9.

(4) The following persons are entitled to apply to the court for any section 8 order with respect to a child–

(a)   any parent[, guardian or special guardian]³⁸ of the child;
[(aa)   any person who by virtue of section 4A has parental responsibility for the child;]³⁹
(b)   any person in whose favour a residence order is in force with respect to the child.

(5) The following persons are entitled to apply for a residence or contact order with respect to a child–

(a)   any party to a marriage (whether or not subsisting) in relation to whom the child is a child of the family;
[(aa)   any civil partner in a civil partnership (whether or not subsisting) in relation to whom the child is a child of the family;]⁴⁰
(b)   any person with whom the child has lived for a period of at least three years;
(c)   any person who–
     (i) in any case where a residence order is in force with respect to the child, has the consent of each of the persons in whose favour the order was made;
     (ii) in any case where the child is in the care of a local authority, has the consent of that authority; or
     (iii) in any other case, has the consent of each of those (if any) who have parental responsibility for the child.

[(5A) A local authority foster parent is entitled to apply for a residence order with respect to a child if the child has lived with him for a period of at least one year immediately preceding the application.]⁴¹

---

38   Amendment: Words substituted: Adoption and Children Act 2002, s 139(1), Sch 3, paras 54, 56(a), with effect from 30 December 2005 (SI 2005/2213).
39   Amendment: Paragraph inserted: Adoption and Children Act 2002, s 139(1), Sch 3, paras 54, 56(b), with effect from 30 December 2005 (SI 2005/2213).
40   Amendment: Paragraph inserted: Civil Partnership Act 2004, s 77, with effect from 5 December 2005 (SI 2005/3175).
41   Amendment: Subsection inserted: Adoption and Children Act 2002, s 139(1), Sch 3, paras 54, 56(c), with effect from 30 December 2005 (SI 2005/2213).

(6) A person who would not otherwise be entitled (under the previous provisions of this section) to apply for the variation or discharge of a section 8 order shall be entitled to do so if–

(a) the order was made on his application; or
(b) in the case of a contact order, he is named in the order.

(7) Any person who falls within a category of person prescribed by rules of court is entitled to apply for any such section 8 order as may be prescribed in relation to that category of person.

[(7A) If a special guardianship order is in force with respect to a child, an application for a residence order may only be made with respect to him, if apart from this subsection the leave of the court is not required, with such leave.][42]

(8) Where the person applying for leave to make an application for a section 8 order is the child concerned, the court may only grant leave if it is satisfied that he has sufficient understanding to make the proposed application for the section 8 order.

(9) Where the person applying for leave to make an application for a section 8 order is not the child concerned, the court shall, in deciding whether or not to grant leave, have particular regard to–

(a) the nature of the proposed application for the section 8 order;
(b) the applicant's connection with the child;
(c) any risk there might be of that proposed application disrupting the child's life to such an extent that he would be harmed by it; and
(d) where the child is being looked after by a local authority–
    (i) the authority's plans for the child's future; and
    (ii) the wishes and feelings of the child's parents.

(10) The period of three years mentioned in subsection (5)(b) need not be continuous but must not have begun more than five years before, or ended more than three months before, the making of the application.

Amendments—Adoption and Children Act 2002, s 139(1), Sch 3, paras 54, 56; Civil Partnership Act 2004, s 77.

11 *General principles and supplementary provisions*[43]

(1) In proceedings in which any question of making a section 8 order, or any other question with respect to such an order, arises, the court shall (in the light of any rules made by virtue of subsection (2))–

(a) draw up a timetable with a view to determining the question without delay; and

---

42 Amendment: Subsection inserted: Adoption and Children Act 2002, s 139(1), Sch 3, paras 54, 56(d), with effect from 30 December 2005 (SI 2005/2213).
43 Provision details: Commencement: 14 October 1991 (SI 1991/828).

(b)   give such directions as it considers appropriate for the purpose of ensuring, so far as is reasonably practicable, that that timetable is adhered to.

(2) Rules of court may–

(a)   specify periods within which specified steps must be taken in relation to proceedings in which such questions arise; and
(b)   make other provision with respect to such proceedings for the purpose of ensuring, so far as is reasonably practicable, that such questions are determined without delay.

(3) Where a court has power to make a section 8 order, it may do so at any time during the course of the proceedings in question even though it is not in a position to dispose finally of those proceedings.

(4) Where a residence order is made in favour of two or more persons who do not themselves all live together, the order may specify the periods during which the child is to live in the different households concerned.

(5) Where–

(a)   a residence order has been made with respect to a child; and
(b)   as a result of the order the child lives, or is to live, with one of two parents who each have parental responsibility for him,

  the residence order shall cease to have effect if the parents live together for a continuous period of more than six months.

(6) A contact order which requires the parent with whom a child lives to allow the child to visit, or otherwise have contact with, his other parent shall cease to have effect if the parents live together for a continuous period of more than six months.

(7) A section 8 order may–

(a)   contain directions about how it is to be carried into effect;
(b)   impose conditions which must be complied with by any person–
      (i)   in whose favour the order is made;
      (ii) who is a parent of the child concerned;
      (iii) who is not a parent of his but who has parental responsibility for him; or
      (iv) with whom the child is living,
and to whom the conditions are expressed to apply;
(c)   be made to have effect for a specified period, or contain provisions which are to have effect for a specified period;
(d)   make such incidental, supplemental or consequential provision as the court thinks fit.

[11A Contact activity directions

(1) This section applies in proceedings in which the court is considering whether to make provision about contact with a child by making–

(a) a contact order with respect to the child, or

(b) an order varying or discharging a contact order with respect to the child.

(2) The court may make a contact activity direction in connection with that provision about contact.

(3) A contact activity direction is a direction requiring an individual who is a party to the proceedings to take part in an activity that promotes contact with the child concerned.

(4) The direction is to specify the activity and the person providing the activity.

(5) The activities that may be so required include, in particular–

(a) programmes, classes and counselling or guidance sessions of a kind that–
    (i) may assist a person as regards establishing, maintaining or improving contact with a child;
    (ii) may, by addressing a person's violent behaviour, enable or facilitate contact with a child;

(b) sessions in which information or advice is given as regards making or operating arrangements for contact with a child, including making arrangements by means of mediation.

(6) No individual may be required by a contact activity direction–

(a) to undergo medical or psychiatric examination, assessment or treatment;

(b) to take part in mediation.

(7) A court may not on the same occasion–

(a) make a contact activity direction, and

(b) dispose finally of the proceedings as they relate to contact with the child concerned.

(8) Subsection (2) has effect subject to the restrictions in sections 11B and 11E.

(9) In considering whether to make a contact activity direction, the welfare of the child concerned is to be the court's paramount consideration.

11B *Contact activity directions: further provision*

(1) A court may not make a contact activity direction in any proceedings unless there is a dispute as regards the provision about contact that the court is considering whether to make in the proceedings.

(2) A court may not make a contact activity direction requiring an individual who is a child to take part in an activity unless the individual is a parent of the child in relation to whom the court is considering provision about contact.

(3) A court may not make a contact activity direction in connection with the making, variation or discharge of a contact order, if the contact order is, or would if made be, an excepted order.

(4) A contact order with respect to a child is an excepted order if–

(a)   it is made in proceedings that include proceedings on an application for a relevant adoption order in respect of the child; or

(b)   it makes provision as regards contact between the child and a person who would be a parent or relative of the child but for the child's adoption by an order falling within subsection (5).

(5) An order falls within this subsection if it is–

(a)   a relevant adoption order;

(b)   an adoption order, within the meaning of section 72(1) of the Adoption Act 1976, other than an order made by virtue of section 14 of that Act on the application of a married couple one of whom is the mother or the father of the child;

(c)   a Scottish adoption order, within the meaning of the Adoption and Children Act 2002, other than an order made–

(i)   by virtue of section 14 of the Adoption (Scotland) Act 1978 on the application of a married couple one of whom is the mother or the father of the child, or

(ii)   by virtue of section 15(1)(aa) of that Act; or

(d)   a Northern Irish adoption order, within the meaning of the Adoption and Children Act 2002, other than an order made by virtue of Article 14 of the Adoption (Northern Ireland) Order 1987 on the application of a married couple one of whom is the mother or the father of the child.

(6) A relevant adoption order is an adoption order, within the meaning of section 46(1) of the Adoption and Children Act 2002, other than an order made–

(a)   on an application under section 50 of that Act by a couple (within the meaning of that Act) one of whom is the mother or the father of the person to be adopted, or

(b)   on an application under section 51(2) of that Act.

(7) A court may not make a contact activity direction in relation to an individual unless the individual is habitually resident in England and Wales; and a direction ceases to have effect if the individual subject to the direction ceases to be habitually resident in England and Wales.

11C Contact activity conditions

(1) This section applies if in any family proceedings the court makes–

(a)   a contact order with respect to a child, or

(b)   an order varying a contact order with respect to a child.

(2) The contact order may impose, or the contact order may be varied so as to impose, a condition (a 'contact activity condition') requiring an individual falling within subsection (3) to take part in an activity that promotes contact with the child concerned.

(3) An individual falls within this subsection if he is–

(a)   for the purposes of the contact order so made or varied, the person with whom the child concerned lives or is to live;

(b) the person whose contact with the child concerned is provided for in that order; or

(c) a person upon whom that order imposes a condition under section 11(7)(b).

(4) The condition is to specify the activity and the person providing the activity.

(5) Subsections (5) and (6) of section 11A have effect as regards the activities that may be required by a contact activity condition as they have effect as regards the activities that may be required by a contact activity direction.

(6) Subsection (2) has effect subject to the restrictions in sections 11D and 11E.

11D Contact activity conditions: further provision

(1) A contact order may not impose a contact activity condition on an individual who is a child unless the individual is a parent of the child concerned.

(2) If a contact order is an excepted order (within the meaning given by section 11B(4)), it may not impose (and it may not be varied so as to impose) a contact activity condition.

(3) A contact order may not impose a contact activity condition on an individual unless the individual is habitually resident in England and Wales; and a condition ceases to have effect if the individual subject to the condition ceases to be habitually resident in England and Wales.

11E Contact activity directions and conditions: making

(1) Before making a contact activity direction (or imposing a contact activity condition by means of a contact order), the court must satisfy itself as to the matters falling within subsections (2) to (4).

(2) The first matter is that the activity proposed to be specified is appropriate in the circumstances of the case.

(3) The second matter is that the person proposed to be specified as the provider of the activity is suitable to provide the activity.

(4) The third matter is that the activity proposed to be specified is provided in a place to which the individual who would be subject to the direction (or the condition) can reasonably be expected to travel.

(5) Before making such a direction (or such an order), the court must obtain and consider information about the individual who would be subject to the direction (or the condition) and the likely effect of the direction (or the condition) on him.

(6) Information about the likely effect of the direction (or the condition) may, in particular, include information as to–

(a)   any conflict with the individual's religious beliefs;

(b)   any interference with the times (if any) at which he normally works or attends an educational establishment.

(7) The court may ask an officer of the Service or a Welsh family proceedings officer to provide the court with information as to the matters in subsections (2) to (5); and it shall be the duty of the officer of the Service or Welsh family proceedings officer to comply with any such request.

(8) In this section 'specified' means specified in a contact activity direction (or in a contact activity condition).

11F Contact activity directions and conditions: financial assistance

(1) The Secretary of State may by regulations make provision authorising him to make payments to assist individuals falling within subsection (2) in paying relevant charges or fees.

(2) An individual falls within this subsection if he is required by a contact activity direction or condition to take part in an activity that promotes contact with a child, not being a child ordinarily resident in Wales.

(3) The National Assembly for Wales may by regulations make provision authorising it to make payments to assist individuals falling within subsection (4) in paying relevant charges or fees.

(4) An individual falls within this subsection if he is required by a contact activity direction or condition to take part in an activity that promotes contact with a child who is ordinarily resident in Wales.

(5) A relevant charge or fee, in relation to an activity required by a contact activity direction or condition, is a charge or fee in respect of the activity payable to the person providing the activity.

(6) Regulations under this section may provide that no assistance is available to an individual unless–

(a)   the individual satisfies such conditions as regards his financial resources as may be set out in the regulations;

(b)   the activity in which the individual is required by a contact activity direction or condition to take part is provided to him in England or Wales;

(c)   where the activity in which the individual is required to take part is provided to him in England, it is provided by a person who is for the time being approved by the Secretary of State as a provider of activities required by a contact activity direction or condition;

(d)   where the activity in which the individual is required to take part is provided to him in Wales, it is provided by a person who is for the time being approved by the National Assembly for Wales as a provider of activities required by a contact activity direction or condition.

(7) Regulations under this section may make provision–

(a) as to the maximum amount of assistance that may be paid to or in respect of an individual as regards an activity in which he is required by a contact activity direction or condition to take part;

(b) where the amount may vary according to an individual's financial resources, as to the method by which the amount is to be determined;

(c) authorising payments by way of assistance to be made directly to persons providing activities required by a contact activity direction or condition.

11G Contact activity directions and conditions: monitoring

(1) This section applies if in any family proceedings the court–

(a) makes a contact activity direction in relation to an individual, or

(b) makes a contact order that imposes, or varies a contact order so as to impose, a contact activity condition on an individual.

(2) The court may on making the direction (or imposing the condition by means of a contact order) ask an officer of the Service or a Welsh family proceedings officer–

(a) to monitor, or arrange for the monitoring of, the individual's compliance with the direction (or the condition);

(b) to report to the court on any failure by the individual to comply with the direction (or the condition).

(3) It shall be the duty of the officer of the Service or Welsh family proceedings officer to comply with any request under subsection (2).

11H Monitoring contact

(1) This section applies if in any family proceedings the court makes–

(a) a contact order with respect to a child in favour of a person, or

(b) an order varying such a contact order.

(2) The court may ask an officer of the Service or a Welsh family proceedings officer–

(a) to monitor whether an individual falling within subsection (3) complies with the contact order (or the contact order as varied);

(b) to report to the court on such matters relating to the individual's compliance as the court may specify in the request.

(3) An individual falls within this subsection if the contact order so made (or the contact order as so varied)–

(a) requires the individual to allow contact with the child concerned;

(b) names the individual as having contact with the child concerned; or

(c) imposes a condition under section 11(7)(b) on the individual.

(4) If the contact order (or the contact order as varied) includes a contact activity condition, a request under subsection (2) is to be treated as relating to the provisions of the order other than the contact activity condition.

(5) The court may make a request under subsection (2)–

(a) on making the contact order (or the order varying the contact order), or
(b) at any time during the subsequent course of the proceedings as they relate to contact with the child concerned.

(6) In making a request under subsection (2), the court is to specify the period for which the officer of the Service or Welsh family proceedings officer is to monitor compliance with the order; and the period specified may not exceed twelve months.

(7) It shall be the duty of the officer of the Service or Welsh family proceedings officer to comply with any request under subsection (2).

(8) The court may order any individual falling within subsection (3) to take such steps as may be specified in the order with a view to enabling the officer of the Service or Welsh family proceedings officer to comply with the court's request under subsection (2).

(9) But the court may not make an order under subsection (8) with respect to an individual who is a child unless he is a parent of the child with respect to whom the order falling within subsection (1) was made.

(10) A court may not make a request under subsection (2) in relation to a contact order that is an excepted order (within the meaning given by section 11B(4)).

11I Contact orders: warning notices

Where the court makes (or varies) a contact order, it is to attach to the contact order (or the order varying the contact order) a notice warning of the consequences of failing to comply with the contact order.

11J Enforcement orders

(1) This section applies if a contact order with respect to a child has been made.

(2) If the court is satisfied beyond reasonable doubt that a person has failed to comply with the contact order, it may make an order (an 'enforcement order') imposing on the person an unpaid work requirement.

(3) But the court may not make an enforcement order if it is satisfied that the person had a reasonable excuse for failing to comply with the contact order.

(4) The burden of proof as to the matter mentioned in subsection (3) lies on the person claiming to have had a reasonable excuse, and the standard of proof is the balance of probabilities.

(5) The court may make an enforcement order in relation to the contact order only on the application of–

(a) the person who is, for the purposes of the contact order, the person with whom the child concerned lives or is to live;

(b)   the person whose contact with the child concerned is provided for in the contact order;

(c)   any individual subject to a condition under section 11(7)(b) or a contact activity condition imposed by the contact order; or

(d)   the child concerned.

(6) Where the person proposing to apply for an enforcement order in relation to a contact order is the child concerned, the child must obtain the leave of the court before making such an application.

(7) The court may grant leave to the child concerned only if it is satisfied that he has sufficient understanding to make the proposed application.

(8) Subsection (2) has effect subject to the restrictions in sections 11K and 11L.

(9) The court may suspend an enforcement order for such period as it thinks fit.

(10) Nothing in this section prevents a court from making more than one enforcement order in relation to the same person on the same occasion.

(11) Proceedings in which any question of making an enforcement order, or any other question with respect to such an order, arises are to be regarded for the purposes of section 11(1) and (2) as proceedings in which a question arises with respect to a section 8 order.

(12) In Schedule A1–

(a)   Part 1 makes provision as regards an unpaid work requirement;

(b)   Part 2 makes provision in relation to the revocation and amendment of enforcement orders and failure to comply with such orders.

(13) This section is without prejudice to section 63(3) of the Magistrates' Courts Act 1980 as it applies in relation to contact orders.

11K Enforcement orders: further provision

(1) A court may not make an enforcement order against a person in respect of a failure to comply with a contact order unless it is satisfied that before the failure occurred the person had been given (in accordance with rules of court) a copy of, or otherwise informed of the terms of–

(a)   in the case of a failure to comply with a contact order that was varied before the failure occurred, a notice under section 11I relating to the order varying the contact order or, where more than one such order has been made, the last order preceding the failure in question;

(b)   in any other case, a notice under section 11I relating to the contact order.

(2) A court may not make an enforcement order against a person in respect of any failure to comply with a contact order occurring before the person attained the age of 18.

(3) A court may not make an enforcement order against a person in respect of a failure to comply with a contact order that is an excepted order (within the meaning given by section 11B(4)).

(4) A court may not make an enforcement order against a person unless the person is habitually resident in England and Wales; and an enforcement order ceases to have effect if the person subject to the order ceases to be habitually resident in England and Wales.

11L Enforcement orders: making

(1) Before making an enforcement order as regards a person in breach of a contact order, the court must be satisfied that–

(a)   making the enforcement order proposed is necessary to secure the person's compliance with the contact order or any contact order that has effect in its place;
(b)   the likely effect on the person of the enforcement order proposed to be made is proportionate to the seriousness of the breach of the contact order.

(2) Before making an enforcement order, the court must satisfy itself that provision for the person to work under an unpaid work requirement imposed by an enforcement order can be made in the local justice area in which the person in breach resides or will reside.

(3) Before making an enforcement order as regards a person in breach of a contact order, the court must obtain and consider information about the person and the likely effect of the enforcement order on him.

(4) Information about the likely effect of the enforcement order may, in particular, include information as to–

(a)   any conflict with the person's religious beliefs;
(b)   any interference with the times (if any) at which he normally works or attends an educational establishment.

(5) A court that proposes to make an enforcement order may ask an officer of the Service or a Welsh family proceedings officer to provide the court with information as to the matters in subsections (2) and (3).

(6) It shall be the duty of the officer of the Service or Welsh family proceedings officer to comply with any request under this section.

(7) In making an enforcement order in relation to a contact order, a court must take into account the welfare of the child who is the subject of the contact order.

11M Enforcement orders: monitoring

(1) On making an enforcement order in relation to a person, the court is to ask an officer of the Service or a Welsh family proceedings officer–

(a) to monitor, or arrange for the monitoring of, the person's compliance with the unpaid work requirement imposed by the order;

(b) to report to the court if a report under paragraph 8 of Schedule A1 is made in relation to the person;

(c) to report to the court on such other matters relating to the person's compliance as may be specified in the request;

(d) to report to the court if the person is, or becomes, unsuitable to perform work under the requirement.

(2) It shall be the duty of the officer of the Service or Welsh family proceedings officer to comply with any request under this section.

11N Enforcement orders: warning notices

Where the court makes an enforcement order, it is to attach to the order a notice warning of the consequences of failing to comply with the order.

11O Compensation for financial loss

(1) This section applies if a contact order with respect to a child has been made.

(2) If the court is satisfied that–

(a) an individual has failed to comply with the contact order, and

(b) a person falling within subsection (6) has suffered financial loss by reason of the breach,

it may make an order requiring the individual in breach to pay the person compensation in respect of his financial loss.

(3) But the court may not make an order under subsection (2) if it is satisfied that the individual in breach had a reasonable excuse for failing to comply with the contact order.

(4) The burden of proof as to the matter mentioned in subsection (3) lies on the individual claiming to have had a reasonable excuse.

(5) An order under subsection (2) may be made only on an application by the person who claims to have suffered financial loss.

(6) A person falls within this subsection if he is–

(a) the person who is, for the purposes of the contact order, the person with whom the child concerned lives or is to live;

(b) the person whose contact with the child concerned is provided for in the contact order;

(c) an individual subject to a condition under section 11(7)(b) or a contact activity condition imposed by the contact order; or

(d) the child concerned.

(7) Where the person proposing to apply for an order under subsection (2) is the child concerned, the child must obtain the leave of the court before making such an application.

(8) The court may grant leave to the child concerned only if it is satisfied that he has sufficient understanding to make the proposed application.

(9) The amount of compensation is to be determined by the court, but may not exceed the amount of the applicant's financial loss.

(10) In determining the amount of compensation payable by the individual in breach, the court must take into account the individual's financial circumstances.

(11) An amount ordered to be paid as compensation may be recovered by the applicant as a civil debt due to him.

(12) Subsection (2) has effect subject to the restrictions in section 11P.

(13) Proceedings in which any question of making an order under subsection (2) arises are to be regarded for the purposes of section 11(1) and (2) as proceedings in which a question arises with respect to a section 8 order.

(14) In exercising its powers under this section, a court is to take into account the welfare of the child concerned.

11P Orders under section 11O(2): further provision

(1) A court may not make an order under section 11O(2) requiring an individual to pay compensation in respect of a failure by him to comply with a contact order unless it is satisfied that before the failure occurred the individual had been given (in accordance with rules of court) a copy of, or otherwise informed of the terms of–

(a)   in the case of a failure to comply with a contact order that was varied before the failure occurred, a notice under section 11I relating to the order varying the contact order or, where more than one such order has been made, the last order preceding the failure in question;

(b)   in any other case, a notice under section 11I relating to the contact order.

(2) A court may not make an order under section 11O(2) requiring an individual to pay compensation in respect of a failure by him to comply with a contact order where the failure occurred before the individual attained the age of 18.

(3) A court may not make an order under section 11O(2) requiring an individual to pay compensation in respect of a failure by him to comply with a contact order that is an excepted order (within the meaning given by section 11B(4)).][44]

Prospective amendment—Children and Adoption Act 2006, ss 1–5.

12 *Residence orders and parental responsibility*[45]

(1) Where the court makes a residence order in favour of the father of a child it shall, if the father would not otherwise have parental responsibility for the child, also make an order under section 4 giving him that responsibility.

(2) Where the court makes a residence order in favour of any person who is not the parent or guardian of the child concerned that person shall have parental responsibility for the child while the residence order remains in force.

(3) Where a person has parental responsibility for a child as a result of subsection (2), he shall not have the right–

(a)   ...[46]
(b)   to agree, or refuse to agree, to the making of an adoption order, or an order under [section 84 of the Adoption and Children Act 2002][47], with respect to the child; or
(c)   to appoint a guardian for the child.

(4) Where subsection (1) requires the court to make an order under section 4 in respect of the father of a child, the court shall not bring that order to an end at any time while the residence order concerned remains in force.

[(5) The power of a court to make a residence order in favour of any person who is not the parent or guardian of the child concerned includes power to direct, at the request of that person, that the order continue in force until the child reaches the age of eighteen (unless the order is brought to an end earlier); and any power to vary a residence order is exercisable accordingly.

(6) Where a residence order includes such a direction, an application to vary or discharge the order may only be made, if apart from this subsection the leave of the court is not required, with such leave.][48]

Amendments—Adoption and Children Act 2002, ss 114(1), 139(1), (3), Sch 3, paras 54, 57(a), (b), Sch 5.

---

44   Prospective amendment: Sections 11A-11P prospectively inserted: Children and Adoption Act 2006, ss 1–5, with effect from a date to be appointed (s 17(2)).
45   Provision details: Commencement: 14 October 1991 (SI 1991/828).
46   Amendment: Paragraph repealed: Adoption and Children Act 2002, s 139(1), (3), Sch 3, paras 54, 57(a), Sch 5, with effect from 30 December 2005 (SI 2005/2213).
47   Amendment: Words substituted: Adoption and Children Act 2002, s 139(1), Sch 3, paras 54, 57(b), with effect from 30 December 2005 (SI 2005/2213).
48   Amendment: Subsections inserted: Adoption and Children Act 2002, s 114(1), with effect from 30 December 2005 (SI 2005/2213).

13 *Change of child's name or removal from jurisdiction*[49]

(1) Where a residence order is in force with respect to a child, no person may–

(a)   cause the child to be known by a new surname; or
(b)   remove him from the United Kingdom;

  without either the written consent of every person who has parental responsibility for the child or the leave of the court.

(2) Subsection (1)(b) does not prevent the removal of a child, for a period of less than one month, by the person in whose favour the residence order is made.

(3) In making a residence order with respect to a child the court may grant the leave required by subsection (1)(b), either generally or for specified purposes.

[14B Special guardianship orders: making

(1) Before making a special guardianship order, the court must consider whether, if the order were made –

(a)   a contact order should also be made with respect to the child, ...[50]
(b)   any section 8 order in force with respect to the child should be varied or discharged,
[(c)   where a contact order made with respect to the child is not discharged, any enforcement order relating to that contact order should be revoked, and
(d)   where a contact activity direction has been made as regards contact with the child and is in force, that contact activity direction should be discharged.][51]

(2) On making a special guardianship order, the court may also –

(a)   give leave for the child to be known by a new surname;
(b)   grant the leave required by section 14C(3)(b), either generally or for specified purposes.][52]
       Amendments—Inserted by Adoption and Children Act 2002, s 115(1); amended by Children and Adoption Act 2006, s 15, Sch 2, paras 7, 8(a), (b), Sch 3.

Family assistance orders

16 *Family assistance orders*[53]

(1) Where, in any family proceedings, the court has power to make an order under this Part with respect to any child, it may (whether or not it makes such an order) make an order requiring–

---

49   Provision details: Commencement: 14 October 1991 (SI 1991/828).
50   Amendment: Words repealed; Children and Adoption Act 2006, s 15, Sch 2, paras 7, 8(a), Sch 3.
51   Amendment: Paragraphs inserted; Children and Adoption Act 2006, s 15, Sch 2, paras 7, 8 (b).
52   Amendment: Section inserted; Adoption and Children Act 2002, s 115 (1)
53   Provision details: Commencement: 14 October 1991 (SI 1991/828).

(a)   [an officer of the Service][54] [or a Welsh family proceedings officer][55] to be made available; or

(b)   a local authority to make an officer of the authority available,

to advise, assist and (where appropriate) befriend any person named in the order.

(2) The persons who may be named in an order under this section ('a family assistance order') are–

(a)   any parent[, guardian or special guardian][56] of the child;

(b)   any person with whom the child is living or in whose favour a contact order is in force with respect to the child;

(c)   the child himself.

(3) No court may make a family assistance order unless–

[(a)   it is satisfied that the circumstances of the case are exceptional; and][57]

(b)   it has obtained the consent of every person to be named in the order other than the child.

(4) A family assistance order may direct–

(a)   the person named in the order; or

(b)   such of the persons named in the order as may be specified in the order,

to take such steps as may be so specified with a view to enabling the officer concerned to be kept informed of the address of any person named in the order and to be allowed to visit any such person.

[(4A) If the court makes a family assistance order with respect to a child and the order is to be in force at the same time as a contact order made with respect to the child, the family assistance order may direct the officer concerned to give advice and assistance as regards establishing, improving and maintaining contact to such of the persons named in the order as may be specified in the order.][58]

(5) Unless it specifies a shorter period, a family assistance order shall have effect for a period of [six months][59] beginning with the day on which it is made.

[(6) Where–

---

54   Amendment: Words substituted: Criminal Justice and Court Services Act 2000, s 74, Sch 7, paras 87, 89(a), with effect from 1 April 2001 (SI 2001/919).

55   Amendment: Words inserted: Children Act 2004, s 40, Sch 3, paras 5, 7, with effect from 1 April 2005 (SI 2005/700).

56   Amendment: Words substituted: Adoption and Children Act 2002, s 139(1), Sch 3, paras 54, 58, with effect from 30 December 2005 (SI 2005/2213).

57   Prospective amendment: Paragraph prospectively repealed: Children and Adoption Act 2006, ss 6(1), (2),15, Sch 3, with effect from a date to be appointed (s 17(2)).

58   Prospective amendment: Sub-section prospectively inserted: Children and Adoption Act 2006, s 6(1), (3), with effect from a date to be appointed (s 17(2)).

59   Prospective amendment: Words prospectively substituted: Children and Adoption Act 2006, s 6(1), (4), with effect from a date to be appointed (s 17(2)). New text = "twelve months".

(a)   a family assistance order is in force with respect to a child; and
(b)   a section 8 order is also in force with respect to the child,

the officer concerned may refer to the court the question whether the section 8 order should be varied or discharged.][60]

(7) A family assistance order shall not be made so as to require a local authority to make an officer of theirs available unless–

(a)   the authority agree; or
(b)   the child concerned lives or will live within their area.

(8), (9) ...[61]

Amendments—Criminal Justice and Court Services Act 2000, s 74, Sch 7, paras 87, 89, Sch 8; Adoption and Children Act 2002, s 139(1), Sch 3, paras 54, 58; Children Act 2004, s 40, Sch 3, paras 5, 7.
Prospective amendment—Children and Adoption Act 2006, s 6.

[16A Risk assessments

(1) This section applies to the following functions of officers of the Service or Welsh family proceedings officers–

(a)   any function in connection with family proceedings in which the court has power to make an order under this Part with respect to a child or in which a question with respect to such an order arises;
(b)   any function in connection with an order made by the court in such proceedings.

(2) If, in carrying out any function to which this section applies, an officer of the Service or a Welsh family proceedings officer is given cause to suspect that the child concerned is at risk of harm, he must–

(a)   make a risk assessment in relation to the child, and
(b)   provide the risk assessment to the court.

(3) A risk assessment, in relation to a child who is at risk of suffering harm of a particular sort, is an assessment of the risk of that harm being suffered by the child.][62]

Prospective amendment—Children and Adoption Act 2006, s 7.

---

60   Prospective amendment: Sub-section prospectively substituted: Children and Adoption Act 2006, s 6(1), (5), with effect from a date to be appointed (s 17(2)). New text = "(6) If the court makes a family assistance order with respect to a child and the order is to be in force at the same time as a section 8 order made with respect to the child, the family assistance order may direct the officer concerned to report to the court on such matters relating to the section 8 order as the court may require (including the question whether the section 8 order ought to be varied or discharged)."

61   Amendment: Subsections repealed: Criminal Justice and Court Services Act 2000, ss 74, 75, Sch 7, paras 87, 89(b), Sch 8, with effect from 1 April 2001 (SI 2001/919).

62   Prospective amendment: Section prospectively inserted: Children and Adoption Act 2006, s 7, with effect from a date to be appointed (s 17(2)).

PART IV

CARE AND SUPERVISION

General

31 Care and supervision orders[63]

(1) On the application of any local authority or authorised person, the court may make an order–

(a)   placing the child with respect to whom the application is made in the care of a designated local authority; or

(b)   putting him under the supervision of a designated local authority ...[64].

(2) A court may only make a care order or supervision order if it is satisfied–

(a)   that the child concerned is suffering, or is likely to suffer, significant harm; and

(b)   that the harm, or likelihood of harm, is attributable to–
   (i)   the care given to the child, or likely to be given to him if the order were not made, not being what it would be reasonable to expect a parent to give to him; or
   (ii)   the child's being beyond parental control.

(3) No care order or supervision order may be made with respect to a child who has reached the age of seventeen (or sixteen, in the case of a child who is married).

[(3A) No care order may be made with respect to a child until the court has considered a section 31A plan.][65]

(4) An application under this section may be made on its own or in any other family proceedings.

(5) The court may–

(a)   on an application for a care order, make a supervision order;

(b)   on an application for a supervision order, make a care order.

(6) Where an authorised person proposes to make an application under this section he shall–

(a)   if it is reasonably practicable to do so; and

(b)   before making the application,

---

63   Provision details: Commencement: 14 October 1991 (SI 1991/828).

64   Amendment: Words repealed: Criminal Justice and Court Services Act 2000, ss 74, 75, Sch 7, paras 87, 90, Sch 8, with effect from 1 April 2001 (SI 2001/919).

65   Amendment: Subsection inserted: Adoption and Children Act 2002, s 121(1), with effect from 30 December 2005 (SI 2005/2213).

consult the local authority appearing to him to be the authority in whose area the child concerned is ordinarily resident.

(7) An application made by an authorised person shall not be entertained by the court if, at the time when it is made, the child concerned is–

(a)   the subject of an earlier application for a care order, or supervision order, which has not been disposed of; or

(b)   subject to–

(i) a care order or supervision order;

(ii) an order under [section 63(1) of the Powers of Criminal Courts (Sentencing) Act 2000][66]; or

(iii) *(applies to Scotland only)*

(8) The local authority designated in a care order must be–

(a)   the authority within whose area the child is ordinarily resident; or

(b)   where the child does not reside in the area of a local authority, the authority within whose area any circumstances arose in consequence of which the order is being made.

(9) In this section–

'authorised person' means–

(a)   the National Society for the Prevention of Cruelty to Children and any of its officers; and

(b)   any person authorised by order of the Secretary of State to bring proceedings under this section and any officer of a body which is so authorised;

'harm' means ill-treatment or the impairment of health or development [including, for example, impairment suffered from seeing or hearing the ill-treatment of another][67];

'development' means physical, intellectual, emotional, social or behavioural development;

'health' means physical or mental health; and

'ill-treatment' includes sexual abuse and forms of ill-treatment which are not physical.

(10) Where the question of whether harm suffered by a child is significant turns on the child's health or development, his health or development shall be compared with that which could reasonably be expected of a similar child.

(11) In this Act–

---

66   Amendment: Words substituted: Powers of Criminal Courts (Sentencing) Act 2000, s 165, Sch 9, para 127, with effect from 25 August 2000.

67   Amendment: Words inserted by Adoption and Children Act 2002, s 120, with effect from 31 January 2005 (SI 2004/3203).

'a care order' means (subject to section 105(1)) an order under subsection (1)(a) and (except where express provision to the contrary is made) includes an interim care order made under section 38; and

'a supervision order' means an order under subsection (1)(b) and (except where express provision to the contrary is made) includes an interim supervision order made under section 38.

Amendments—Criminal Justice and Court Services Act 2000, ss 74, 75, Sch 7, paras 87, 90, Sch 8; Powers of Criminal Courts (Sentencing) Act 2000, s 165, Sch 9, para 127; Adoption and Children Act 2002, ss 120, 121(1).

[31A Care orders: care plans

[(1) Where an application is made on which a care order might be made with respect to a child, the appropriate local authority must, within such time as the court may direct, prepare a plan ('a care plan') for the future care of the child.

(2) While the application is pending, the authority must keep any care plan prepared by them under review and, if they are of the opinion some change is required, revise the plan, or make a new plan, accordingly.

(3) A care plan must give any prescribed information and do so in the prescribed manner.

(4) For the purposes of this section, the appropriate local authority, in relation to a child in respect of whom a care order might be made, is the local authority proposed to be designated in the order.

(5) In section 31(3A) and this section, references to a care order do not include an interim care order.

(6) A plan prepared, or treated as prepared, under this section is referred to in this Act as a 'section 31A plan'.][68]

Amendments—Adoption and Children Act 2002, s 121(2).

Powers of court

37 Powers of court in certain family proceedings[69]

(1) Where, in any family proceedings in which a question arises with respect to the welfare of any child, it appears to the court that it may be appropriate for a

---

68   Amendment: Section inserted: Adoption and Children Act 2002, s 121(2), with effect, for certain purposes, from 7 December 2004 (SI 2004/3203), for remaining purposes, from 30 December 2005 (SI 2005/2213).

69   Provision details: Commencement: 14 October 1991 (SI 1991/828).

care or supervision order to be made with respect to him, the court may direct the appropriate authority to undertake an investigation of the child's circumstances.

(2) Where the court gives a direction under this section the local authority concerned shall, when undertaking the investigation, consider whether they should–

(a) apply for a care order or for a supervision order with respect to the child;

(b) provide services or assistance for the child or his family; or

(c) take any other action with respect to the child.

(3) Where a local authority undertake an investigation under this section, and decide not to apply for a care order or supervision order with respect to the child concerned, they shall inform the court of–

(a) their reasons for so deciding;

(b) any service or assistance which they have provided, or intend to provide, for the child and his family; and

(c) any other action which they have taken, or propose to take, with respect to the child.

(4) The information shall be given to the court before the end of the period of eight weeks beginning with the date of the direction, unless the court otherwise directs.

(5) The local authority named in a direction under subsection (1) must be–

(a) the authority in whose area the child is ordinarily resident; or

(b) where the child [is not ordinarily resident][70] in the area of a local authority, the authority within whose area any circumstances arose in consequence of which the direction is being given.

(6) If, on the conclusion of any investigation or review under this section, the authority decide not to apply for a care order or supervision order with respect to the child–

(a) they shall consider whether it would be appropriate to review the case at a later date; and

(b) if they decide that it would be, they shall determine the date on which that review is to begin.

Amendments—Courts and Legal Services Act 1990, s 116, Sch 16, para 16.

---

70 Amendment: Words substituted: Courts and Legal Services Act 1990, s 116, Sch 16, para 16, with effect from 14 October 1991 (SI 1991/1883).

[Representation of child][71]

41 Representation of child and of his interests in certain proceedings[72]

(1) For the purpose of any specified proceedings, the court shall appoint [an officer of the Service][73] [or a Welsh family proceedings officer][74] for the child concerned unless satisfied that it is not necessary to do so in order to safeguard his interests.

(2) The [officer of the Service][75] [or a Welsh family proceedings officer][76] shall–

(a)   be appointed in accordance with rules of court; and
(b)   be under a duty to safeguard the interests of the child in the manner prescribed by such rules.

(3) Where–

(a)   the child concerned is not represented by a solicitor; and
(b)   any of the conditions mentioned in subsection (4) is satisfied,

the court may appoint a solicitor to represent him.

(4) The conditions are that–

(a)   no [officer of the Service][77] [or a Welsh family proceedings officer][78] has been appointed for the child;
(b)   the child has sufficient understanding to instruct a solicitor and wishes to do so;
(c)   it appears to the court that it would be in the child's best interests for him to be represented by a solicitor.

(5) Any solicitor appointed under or by virtue of this section shall be appointed, and shall represent the child, in accordance with rules of court.

(6) In this section 'specified proceedings' means any proceedings–

(a)   on an application for a care order or supervision order;
(b)   in which the court has given a direction under section 37(1) and has made, or is considering whether to make, an interim care order;

71   Amendment: Heading substituted: Criminal Justice and Court Services Act 2000, s 74, Sch 7, paras 87, 91(e), with effect from 1 April 2001 (SI 2001/919).
72   Provision details: Commencement: 14 October 1991 (SI 1991/828).
73   Amendment: Words substituted: Criminal Justice and Court Services Act 2000, s 74, Sch 7, paras 87, 91(a), with effect from 1 April 2001 (SI 2001/919).
74   Amendment: Words inserted: Children Act 2004, s 40, Sch 3, paras 5, 9(1), (2), with effect from 1 April 2005 (SI 2005/700).
75   Amendment: Words substituted: Criminal Justice and Court Services Act 2000, s 74, Sch 7, paras 87, 91(b), with effect from 1 April 2001 (SI 2001/919).
76   Amendment: Words inserted: Children Act 2004, s 40, Sch 3, paras 5, 9(1), (3), with effect from 1 April 2005 (SI 2005/700).
77   Amendment: Words substituted: Criminal Justice and Court Services Act 2000, s 74, Sch 7, paras 87, 91(b), with effect from 1 April 2001 (SI 2001/919).
78   Amendment: Words inserted: Children Act 2004, s 40, Sch 3, paras 5, 9(1), (3), with effect from 1 April 2005 (SI 2005/700).

(c)   on an application for the discharge of a care order or the variation or
       discharge of a supervision order;
(d)   on an application under section 39(4);
(e)   in which the court is considering whether to make a residence order with
       respect to a child who is the subject of a care order;
(f)   with respect to contact between a child who is the subject of a care order
       and any other person;
(g)   under Part V;
(h)   on an appeal against–
       (i) the making of, or refusal to make, a care order, supervision order or
           any order under section 34;
       (ii) the making of, or refusal to make, a residence order with respect to a
            child who is the subject of a care order; or
       (iii) the variation or discharge, or refusal of an application to vary or
             discharge, an order of a kind mentioned in sub-paragraph (i) or (ii);
       (iv) the refusal of an application under section 39(4);
       (v) the making of, or refusal to make, an order under Part V; or
[(hh) on an application for the making or revocation of a placement order
       (within the meaning of section 21 of the Adoption and Children
       Act 2002);][79]
(i)   which are specified for the time being, for the purposes of this section, by
       rules of court.

[(6A) The proceedings which may be specified under subsection (6)(i) include
(for example) proceedings for the making, varying or discharging of a section 8
order.][80]

(7)–(9) ...[81]

(10) Rules of court may make provision as to–

(a)   the assistance which any [officer of the Service][82] [or a Welsh family
       proceedings officer][83] may be required by the court to give to it;
(b)   the consideration to be given by any [officer of the Service][84] [or a Welsh
       family proceedings officer][85], where an order of a specified kind has been
       made in the proceedings in question, as to whether to apply for the
       variation or discharge of the order;

---

79   Amendment: Paragraph inserted: Adoption and Children Act 2002, s 122(1)(a), with effect
     from 30 December 2005 (SI 2005/2213).
80   Amendment: Subsection inserted by Adoption and Children Act 2002, s 122(1)(b), with effect
     from 7 December 2004 (SI 2004/3203).
81   Amendment: Subsections repealed: Criminal Justice and Court Services Act 2000, ss 74, 75,
     Sch 7, paras 87, 91(d), Sch 8, with effect from 1 April 2001 (SI 2001/919).
82   Amendment: Words substituted: Criminal Justice and Court Services Act 2000, s 74, Sch 7,
     paras 87, 91(b), with effect from 1 April 2001 (SI 2001/919).
83   Amendment: Words inserted: Children Act 2004, s 40, Sch 3, paras 5, 9(1), (4)(a), with effect
     from 1 April 2005 (SI 2005/700).
84   Amendment: Words substituted: Criminal Justice and Court Services Act 2000, s 74, Sch 7,
     paras 87, 91(b), with effect from 1 April 2001 (SI 2001/919).
85   Amendment: Words inserted: Children Act 2004, s 40, Sch 3, paras 5, 9(1), (4)(a), with effect
     from 1 April 2005 (SI 2005/700).

(c)   the participation of [officers of the Service][86] [or a Welsh family proceedings officer][87] in reviews, of a kind specified in the rules, which are conducted by the court.

(11) Regardless of any enactment or rule of law which would otherwise prevent it from doing so, the court may take account of–

(a)   any statement contained in a report made by [an officer of the Service][88] [or a Welsh family proceedings officer][89] who is appointed under this section for the purpose of the proceedings in question; and

(b)   any evidence given in respect of the matters referred to in the report,

  in so far as the statement or evidence is, in the opinion of the court, relevant to the question which the court is considering.

(12) ...[90]

> **Amendments**—Criminal Justice and Court Services Act 2000, ss 74, 75, Sch 7, paras 87, 91, Sch 8; Adoption and Children Act 2002, s 122(1)(a); Children Act 2004, s 40, Sch 3, paras 5, 9(1), (2).

Effect and duration of orders etc

91 Effect and duration of orders etc[91]

(1) The making of a residence order with respect to a child who is the subject of a care order discharges the care order.

(2) The making of a care order with respect to a child who is the subject of any section 8 order discharges that order.

[(2A) Where a contact activity direction has been made as regards contact with a child, the making of a care order with respect to the child discharges the direction.[92]

(3) The making of a care order with respect to a child who is the subject of a supervision order discharges that other order.

---

86   Amendment: Words substituted: Criminal Justice and Court Services Act 2000, s 74, Sch 7, paras 87, 91(c), with effect from 1 April 2001 (SI 2001/919).

87   Amendment: Words inserted: Children Act 2004, s 40, Sch 3, paras 5, 9(1), (4)(b), with effect from 1 April 2005 (SI 2005/700).

88   Amendment: Words substituted: Criminal Justice and Court Services Act 2000, s 74, Sch 7, paras 87, 91(a), with effect from 1 April 2001 (SI 2001/919).

89   Amendment: Words inserted: Children Act 2004, s 40, Sch 3, paras 5, 9(1), (5), with effect from 1 April 2005 (SI 2005/700).

90   Amendment: Subsection repealed: Criminal Justice and Court Services Act 2000, ss 74, 75, Sch 7, paras 87, 91(d), Sch 8, with effect from 1 April 2001 (SI 2001/919).

91   Provision details: Commencement: 14 October 1991 (SI 1991/828).

92   Prospective amendment: Subsection prospectively inserted: Children and Adoption Act 2006, s 15, Sch 2, paras 7, 9, with effect from a date to be appointed (s 17(2)).

(4) The making of a care order with respect to a child who is a ward of court brings that wardship to an end.

(5) The making of a care order with respect to a child who is the subject of a school attendance order made under [section 437 of the Education Act 1996]⁹³ discharges the school attendance order.

[(5A) The making of a special guardianship order with respect to a child who is the subject of –

(a)   a care order; or
(b)   an order under section 34, discharges that order.]⁹⁴

(6) Where an emergency protection order is made with respect to a child who is in care, the care order shall have effect subject to the emergency protection order.

(7) Any order made under section 4(1), [4A(1)]⁹⁵ or 5(1) shall continue in force until the child reaches the age of eighteen, unless it is brought to an end earlier.

(8) Any–

(a)   agreement under section 4 [or 4A]⁹⁶; or
(b)   appointment under section 5(3) or (4),

shall continue in force until the child reaches the age of eighteen, unless it is brought to an end earlier.

(9) An order under Schedule 1 has effect as specified in that Schedule.

(10) A section 8 order shall, if it would otherwise still be in force, cease to have effect when the child reaches the age of sixteen, unless it is to have effect beyond that age by virtue of section 9(6) [or 12(5)]⁹⁷.

(11) Where a section 8 order has effect with respect to a child who has reached the age of sixteen, it shall, if it would otherwise still be in force, cease to have effect when he reaches the age of eighteen.

(12) Any care order, other than an interim care order, shall continue in force until the child reaches the age of eighteen, unless it is brought to an end earlier.

(13) Any order made under any other provision of this Act in relation to a child shall, if it would otherwise still be in force, cease to have effect when he reaches the age of eighteen.

---

93   Amendment: Words substituted: Education Act 1996, s 582(1), Sch 37, Pt I, para 90, with effect from 1 November 1996 (s 583(2)).
94   Amendment: Subsection inserted: Adoption and Children Act 2002, s 139(1), Sch 3, paras 54, 68(a), with effect from 30 December 2005 (SI 2005/2213).
95   Amendment: Reference inserted: Adoption and Children Act 2002, s 139(1), Sch 3, paras 54, 68(b), with effect from 30 December 2005 (SI 2005/2213).
96   Amendment: Words inserted by Adoption and Children Act 2002, s 139(1), Sch 3, paras 54, 68(c), with effect from 30 December 2005 (SI 2005/2213).
97   Amendment: Words inserted: Adoption and Children Act 2002, s 114(3), with effect from 30 December 2005 (SI 2005/2213).

(14) On disposing of any application for an order under this Act, the court may (whether or not it makes any other order in response to the application) order that no application for an order under this Act of any specified kind may be made with respect to the child concerned by any person named in the order without leave of the court.

(15) Where an application ('the previous application') has been made for–

(a)   the discharge of a care order;
(b)   the discharge of a supervision order;
(c)   the discharge of an education supervision order;
(d)   the substitution of a supervision order for a care order; or
(e)   a child assessment order,

no further application of a kind mentioned in paragraphs (a) to (e) may be made with respect to the child concerned, without leave of the court, unless the period between the disposal of the previous application and the making of the further application exceeds six months.

(16) Subsection (15) does not apply to applications made in relation to interim orders.

(17) Where–

(a)   a person has made an application for an order under section 34;
(b)   the application has been refused; and
(c)   a period of less than six months has elapsed since the refusal,

that person may not make a further application for such an order with respect to the same child, unless he has obtained the leave of the court.

Amendments—Education Act 1996, s 582(1), Sch 37, Pt I, para 90; Adoption and Children Act 2002, ss 114(3), 139(1), Sch 3, paras 54, 68.
Prospective amendment—Children and Adoption Act 2006, s 15, Sch 2, paras 7, 9.

Jurisdiction and procedure etc

97 *Privacy for children involved in certain proceedings*[98]

(1) [Rules made under section 144 of the Magistrates' Courts Act 1980][99] may make provision for a magistrates' court to sit in private in proceedings in which any powers under this Act [or the Adoption and Children Act 2002][100] may be exercised by the court with respect to any child.

---

98   Provision details: Commencement: 14 October 1991 (SI 1991/828).
99   Prospective amendment: Words prospectively substituted: Courts Act 2003, s 109(1), Sch 8, para 337(1), (2), as from a date to be appointed. New text = "Family Procedure Rules".
100   Amendment: Words inserted: Adoption and Children Act 2002, s 101(3), with effect from 30 December 2005 (SI 2005/2213).

(2) No person shall publish [to the public at large or any section of the public][101] any material which is intended, or likely, to identify–

(a)　any child as being involved in any proceedings before [the High Court, a county court or][102] a magistrates' court in which any power under this Act [or the Adoption and Children Act 2002][103] may be exercised by the court with respect to that or any other child; or

(b)　an address or school as being that of a child involved in any such proceedings.

(3) In any proceedings for an offence under this section it shall be a defence for the accused to prove that he did not know, and had no reason to suspect, that the published material was intended, or likely, to identify the child.

(4) The court or the [Lord Chancellor][104] may, if satisfied that the welfare of the child requires it [and, in the case of the Lord Chancellor, if the Lord Chief Justice agrees][105], by order dispense with the requirements of subsection (2) to such extent as may be specified in the order.

(5) For the purposes of this section–

'publish' includes–

(a)　[include in a programme service (within the meaning of the Broadcasting Act 1990);][106] or

(b)　cause to be published; and

'material' includes any picture or representation.

(6) Any person who contravenes this section shall be guilty of an offence and liable, on summary conviction, to a fine not exceeding level 4 on the standard scale.

(7) Subsection (1) is without prejudice to–

[(a)　the generality of the rule making power in section 144 of the Act of 1980; or][107]

(b)　any other power of a magistrates' court to sit in private.

101　Amendment: Words inserted: Children Act 2004, s 62(1), with effect from 12 April 2005 (SI 2005/847).

102　Amendment: Words inserted: Access to Justice Act 1999, s 72(a), with effect from 27 September 1999 (s 108(3)).

103　Amendment: Words inserted: Adoption and Children Act 2002, s 101(3), with effect from 30 December 2005, (SI 2005/2213).

104　Amendment: Words substituted: Transfer of Functions (Magistrates' Courts and Family Law) Order 1992, Art 3, Sch 2, SI 1992/709, with effect from 1 April 1992.

105　Amendment: Words inserted: Constitutional Reform Act 2005, s 15(1), Sch 4, Pt 1, paras 203, 208(1), (2), with effect from 3 April 2006 (SI 2006/1014).

106　Amendment: Words substituted: Broadcasting Act 1990, s 203(1), Sch 20, para 53 with effect from 1 January 1991 (SI 1990/2347).

107　Prospective amendment: Words prospectively repealed: Courts Act 2003, s 109(1), Sch 8, para 337(1), (2), Sch 10, as from a date to be appointed.

(8) [Sections 69 (sittings of magistrates' courts for family proceedings) and 71 (newspaper reports of certain proceedings) of the Act of 1980][108] shall apply in relation to any proceedings [(before a magistrates' court)][109] to which this section applies subject to the provisions of this section.

[(9) The Lord Chief Justice may nominate a judicial office holder (as defined in section 109(4) of the Constitutional Reform Act 2005) to exercise his functions under subsection (4).][110]

> **Amendments**—Broadcasting Act 1990, s 203(1), Sch 20, para 53; Courts and Legal Services Act 1990, s 116, Sch 16, para 24; SI 1992/709; Access to Justice Act 1999, s 72; Adoption and Children Act 2002, s 101(3); Children Act 2004, s 62(1); Constitutional Reform Act 2005, s 15(1), Sch 4, Pt 1, paras 203, 208(1)–(3).
> **Prospective amendments**—Courts Act 2003, s 109(1), Sch 8, para 337(1), (2), Sch 10.

104 Regulations and orders

(1) Any power of the Lord Chancellor[, the Treasury][111] [, the Secretary of State or the National Assembly for Wales][112] under this Act to make an order, regulations, or rules, except an order under section ...[113], 56(4)(a), 57(3), 84 or 97(4) or paragraph 1(1) of Schedule 4, shall be exercisable by statutory instrument.

(2) Any such statutory instrument, except one made under section [4(1B),][114] 17(4), 107 or 108(2), shall be subject to annulment in pursuance of a resolution of either House of Parliament.

[(2A) Subsection (2) does not apply to a statutory instrument made solely by the National Assembly for Wales.][115]

(3) An order under section [4(1B) or][116] 17(4) shall not be made unless a draft of it has been laid before, and approved by a resolution of, each House of Parliament.

(4) Any statutory instrument made under this Act may –

---

108 Amendment: Words substituted: Courts and Legal Services Act 1990, s 116, Sch 16, para 24, with effect from 14 October 1991 (SI 1991/1883).

109 Amendment: Words inserted: Access to Justice Act 1999, s 72(b), with effect from 27 September 1999 (s 108(3)).

110 Amendment: Subsection inserted: Constitutional Reform Act 2005, s 15(1), Sch 4, Pt 1, paras 203, 208(1), (3), with effect from 3 April 2006 (SI 2006/1014).

111 Amendment: Words inserted by; Tax Credits Act 2002, s 47, Sch 3, paras 15, 19.

112 Amendment: Words substituted by; Children and Adoption Act 2006, s 15, Sch 2, paras 7, 10(a).

113 Amendment: Words revoked by; Care Standards Act 2000, s 117(2), Sch 6.

114 Amendment: Words inserted by; Adoption and Children Act 2002, s 111(6)(a).

115 Amendment: Section inserted by; Children and Adoption Act 2006, s 15(1), Sch 2, paras 7, 10, (b).

116 Amendment: Words inserted by; Adoption and Children Act 2002, s 111(6)(b).

(a)   make different provision for different cases;
(b)   provide for exemptions from any of its provisions; and
(c)   contain such incidental, supplemental and transitional provisions as the
      person making it considers expedient.

> **Amendments**: Care Standards Act 2000, s 117(2), Sch 6; Tax Credits
> Act 2002, s 47, Sch3, paras 15, 19; Adoption and Children Act 2002,
> s 111,(6) (a); (b); Children and Adoption Act 2006, s 15, Sch 2, paras 7,
> 10(a), s 15(1), Sch 2, paras 7, 10 (b)

105 Interpretation

(1) In this Act –

"adoption agency" means a body which may be referred to as an adoption
agency by virtue of [section 2 of the Adoption and Children Act 2002][117];
["appropriate children's home" has the meaning given by section 23;][118]
"bank holiday" means a day which is a bank holiday under the Banking and
Financial Dealings Act 1971;
["care home" has the same meaning as in the Care Standards Act 2000;][119]
"care order" has the meaning given by section 31(11) and also includes any
order which by or under any enactment has the effect of, or is deemed to be, a
care order for the purposes of this Act; and any reference to a child who is in
the care of an authority is a reference to a child who is in their care by virtue of
a care order;
"child" means, subject to paragraph 16 of Schedule 1, a person under the age of
eighteen;
"child assessment order" has the meaning given by section 43(2);
...[120]
["child of the family", in relation to parties to a marriage, or to two people who
are civil partners of each other, means –
      (a)   a child of both of them, and
      (b)   any other child, other than a child placed with them as foster parents
            by a local authority or voluntary organisation, who has been treated
            by both of them as a child of their family;][121]
["children's home" has the meaning given by section 23;][122]
"community home" has the meaning given by section 53;
["contact activity condition" has the meaning given by section 11C;][123]
["contact activity direction" has the meaning given by section 11A;][124]
"contact order" has the meaning given by section 8(1);
"day care" [(except in Part XA)][125] has the same meaning as in section 18;

---

117   Amendment: Words substituted: Adoption and Children Act 2002, s 139(1), Sch 3, paras 54,
      70(a).
118   Amendment: Words inserted; Care Standards Act 2000, s 116, Sch 4, para 14(1), (23)(a)(1).
119   Amendment: Words inserted: Care Standards Act 2000, s 116, Sch 4, para 14(1), (23)(a)(ii).
120   Amendment: Words repealed: Care Standards Act 2000, s 117(2), Sch 6.
121   Amendment: Words substituted: Civil Partnership Act 2004, s 75(1), (3).
122   Amendment: Words substituted: Care Standards Act 2004, s 116, Sch 4, para 14(1), (23)(a)(iii).
123   Amendment: Words inserted: Children and Adoption Act 2006, s 15(1), Sch 2, paras 7, 11.
124   Amendment: Words inserted: Children and Adoption Act 2006, s 15(1), Sch 2, paras 7, 11.
125   Amendment: Words inserted: Care Standards Act 2000, s 116, Sch 4, paras 14(1),(23)(a)(iv).

"disabled", in relation to a child, has the same meaning as in section 17(11); ...[126]

"domestic premises" has the meaning given by section 71(12);

["dwelling-house" includes –

    (a) any building or part of a building which is occupied as a dwelling;

    (b) any caravan, house-boat or structure which is occupied as a dwelling;

and any yard, garden, garage or outhouse belonging to it and occupied with it;]

"education supervision order" has the meaning given in section 36;

"emergency protection order" means an order under section 44;

["enforcement order" has the meaning given by section 11J;][127]

"family assistance order" has the meaning given in section 16(2);

"family proceedings" has the meaning given by section 8(3);

"functions" includes powers and duties;

"guardian of a child" means a guardian (other than a guardian of the estate of a child) appointed in accordance with the provisions of section 5;

"harm" has the same meaning as in section 31(9) and the question of whether harm is significant shall be determined in accordance with section 31(10);

["Health Authority" means a Health Authority established under section 8 of the National Health Service Act 1977;][128]

"health service hospital" has the same meaning as in the National Health Service Act 1977;

"hospital" [(except in Schedule 9A)][129] has the same meaning as in the Mental Health Act 1983, except that it does not include a ...[130][hospital at which high security psychiatric services within the meaning of that Act are provided][131];

"ill-treatment" has the same meaning as in section 31(9);

["income-based jobseeker's allowance" has the same meaning as in the Jobseekers Act 1995;][132]

["independent hospital" has the same meaning as in the Care Standards Act 2000;][133]

"independent school" has the same meaning as in [the Education Act 1996][134];

"local authority" means, in relation to England ...[135], the council of a county, a metropolitan district, a London Borough or the Common Council of the City of London[, in relation to Wales, the council of a county or a county borough][136] and, in relation to Scotland, a local authority within the meaning of section 1(2) of the Social Work (Scotland) Act 1968;

---

126 Amendment: Definition repealed: Health Authorities Act 1995, ss (1), Sch 1, para 118(10)(a), Sch 3.

127 Amendment: Words inserted: Children and Adoption Act 2006, s 15(1), Sch 2, paras 7, 11.

128 Amendment: Words substituted: Health Authorities Act 1995, ss 2(1), 5(1), Sch 1, paras 118(10)(b).

129 Amendment: Words inserted: Care Standards Act 2000, s 116, Sch 4, para 14(1),(23)(a)(v).

130 Amendment: Words repealed: SI 2000/90, arts 2(1),3(2), Sch 2, para 5.

131 Amendment: Words substituted: SI 2000/90, arts 2(1),3(2), Sch 2, para 5.

132 Amendment: Words inserted: Jobseekers Act 1995, s 41(4), Sch 2, para 19(4).

133 Amendment: Words inserted: Care Standards Act 2000, s 116, Sch 4, para (14)(1), (23)(a)(vi).

134 Amendment: Words substituted: Education Act 1996, s 582(1), Sch 37,para 91.

135 Amendment: Words repealed: Local Government (Wales) Act 1994, ss 22(4), 66(8), Sch 10, para 13, Sch 18;

136 Amendment: Words inserted: Local Government (Wales) Act 1994, ss 22(4), 66(8), Sch 10, para 13.

"local authority foster parent" has the same meaning as in section 23(3);
"local education authority" has the same meaning as in [the Education
Act 1996][137];
"local housing authority" has the same meaning as in the Housing Act 1985;
...[138]
...[139]
["officer of the Service" has the same meaning as in the Criminal Justice and
Court Services Act 2000;][140]
"parental responsibility" has the meaning given in section 3;
"parental responsibility agreement" has the meaning given in [sections 4(1) and
4A(2)][141];
"prescribed" means prescribed by regulations made under this Act;
["private children's home" means a children's home in respect of which a person
is registered under Part II of the Care Standards Act 2000 which is not a
community home or a voluntary home;][142]
["Primary Care Trust" means a Primary Care Trust established under
section 16A of the National Health Service Act 1977;][143]
"privately fostered child" and "to foster a child privately" have the same
meaning as in section 66;
"prohibited steps order" has the meaning given by section 8(1);
...[144]
...[145]
"registered pupil" has the same meaning as in [the Education Act 1996][146];
"relative", in relation to a child, means a grandparent, brother, sister, uncle or
aunt (whether of the full blood or half blood or [by marriage or civil
partnership)][147] or step-parent;
"residence order" has the meaning given by section 8(1);
...[148]
"responsible person", in relation to a child who is the subject of a supervision
order, has the meaning given in paragraph 1 of Schedule 3;
"school" has the same meaning as in [the Education Act 1996] or, in relation to
Scotland, in the Education (Scotland) Act 1980;
["section 31A plan" has the meaning given by section 31A(6);][149]

---

137 Amendment: Words substituted: Education Act 1996, s 582(1), Sch 37, para 91.
138 Amendment: Definition repealed: Care Standards Act 2000, s 117(2), Sch 6.
139 Amendment: Words repealed: Care Standards Act 2000, s 117(2), Sch 6.
140 Amendment: Words inserted: Criminal Justice and Court Services Act 2000, s 74, Sch 7, Pt II,
       paras 87,95.
141 Amendment: Words substituted: Adoption and Children Act 2002,s 139(1), Sch 3,
       paras 54,70(c).
142 Amendment: Words inserted: Care Standards Act 2000, s 116, Sch 4, para 14(1), (23)(a)(vii).
143 Amendment: Definition inserted: in relation to England and Wales only, (SI 2000/90),
       arts 2(1), 3(1), Sch1, para 24(1), (10).
144 Amendment: Definition repealed: Adoption and Children Act 2002, s 139(1), (3), Sch 3,
       paras 54,70(d), Sch 5.
145 Amendment: Definition repealed: Care Standards Act 2000, s 117(2), Sch 6.
146 Amendment: Words substituted: Education Act 1996, s 582(1), Sch 37, para 91.
147 Amendment: Words substituted: Civil Partnership Act 2004, s 75(1), (4).
148 Amendment: Definition repealed: Care Standards Act 2000, s 117(2), Sch 6.
149 Amendment: Definition inserted: Adoption and Children Act 2002, s 139(1), Sch 3,
       paras 54,70(b).

"service", in relation to any provision made under Part III, includes any facility;

"signed", in relation to any person, includes the making by that person of his mark;

"special educational needs" has the same meaning as in [the Education Act 1996][150];

["special guardian" and "special guardianship order" have the meaning given by section 14A;][151]

["Special Health Authority" means a Special Health Authority established under section 11 of the National Health Service Act 1977;][152]

"specific issue order" has the meaning given by section 8(1);

["Strategic Health Authority" means a Strategic Health Authority established under section 8 of the National Health Service Act 1977;][153]

"supervision order" has the meaning given by section 31(11);

"supervised child" and "supervisor", in relation to a supervision order or an education supervision order, mean respectively the child who is (or is to be) under supervision and the person under whose supervision he is (or is to be) by virtue of the order;

"upbringing", in relation to any child, includes the care of the child but not his maintenance;

"voluntary home" has the meaning given by section 60;

"voluntary organisation" means a body (other than a public or local authority) whose activities are not carried on for profit;

["Welsh family proceedings officer" has the meaning given by section 35 of the Children Act 2004][154].

(2) References in this Act to a child whose father and mother were, or (as the case may be) were not, married to each other at the time of his birth must be read with section 1 of the Family Law Reform Act 1987 (which extends the meaning of such references).

(3) References in this Act to –

(a)   a person with whom a child lives, or is to live, as the result of a residence order; or

(b)   a person in whose favour a residence order is in force,

shall be construed as references to the person named in the order as the person with whom the child is to live.

(4)   References in this Act to a child who is looked after by a local authority have the same meaning as they have (by virtue of section 22) in Part III.

---

150 Amendment: Words substituted: Education Act 1996,s 582(1), Sch 37, para 91.
151 Amendment: Definition Inserted: Adoption and Children Act 2002, s 1391, Sch 3, paras 54,70(e).
152 Amendment: definition Substituted: Health Authorities Act 1995, ss 2(1), 5(1), Sch 1, para 118(10)(c).
153 Amendment: definition inserted: SI 2002/2469, reg 4, Sch 1, Pt 1, para 16(1), (3).
154 Amendment: definition inserted: Children Act 2004, s 40, Sch 3, paras 5,11.

(5) References in this Act to accommodation provided by or on behalf of a local authority are references to accommodation so provided in the exercise of functions [of that or any other local authority which are social services functions within the meaning of][155] the Local Authority Social Services Act 1970.

[(5A) References in this Act to a child minder shall be construed –

(a) ...[156]

(b) in relation to ...[157] Wales, in accordance with section 79A.][158]

[(5B) References in this Act to acting as a child minder and to a child minder shall be construed, in relation to Scotland, in accordance with section 2(17) of the Regulation of Care (Scotland) Act 2001 (asp 8).][159]

(6) In determining the "ordinary residence" of a child for any purpose of this Act, there shall be disregarded any period in which he lives in any place –

(a) which is a school or other institution;

(b) in accordance with the requirements of a supervision order under this Act or an order under [section 63(1) of the Powers of Criminal Courts (Sentencing) Act 2000][160]; or

(c) while he is being provided with accommodation by or on behalf of a local authority.

(7) References in this Act to children who are in need shall be construed in accordance with section 17.

(8) Any notice or other document required under this Act to be served on any person may be served on him by being delivered personally to him, or being sent by post to him in a registered letter or by the recorded delivery service at his proper address.

(9) Any such notice or other document required to be served on a body corporate or a firm shall be duly served if it is served on the secretary or clerk of that body or a partner of that firm.

(10) For the purposes of this section, and of section 7 of the Interpretation Act 1978 in its application to this section, the proper address of a person –

(a) in the case of a secretary or clerk of a body corporate, shall be that of the registered or principal office of that body;

(b) in the case of a partner of a firm, shall be that of the principal office of the firm; and

---

155 Amendment: Words substituted: Local Government Act 2000,s 107, Sch 5, para 22.
156 Amendment: Subparagraph repealed: Regulation of Care (Scotland) Act 2001, s 79, Sch 3, paras. 15(1), (2)(a), in relation to Scotland only.
157 Amendment: Words repealed: Childcare Act 2006, s 103, para17, Sch 3, Pt 2.
158 Amendment: Subsection inserted: Care Standards Act 2000, s 116, Sch 4, para 14(1), (23)(b).
159 Amendment: Subsection inserted: Regulation of Care (Scotland) Act 2001, s 79, Sch 3, paras 15(1), (2)(b).
160 Amendment: Words substituted: Powers of Criminal Courts (Sentencing) Act 2000, s 165 (1), Sch 9, para 129.

(c)   in any other case, shall be the last known address of the person to be served.

Amendments: Local Government (Wales) Act 1994, ss 22(4), 66(8), Sch 10, para 13, Sch 18; Health Authorities Act 1995, ss (1), Sch 1, para 118(10)(a), Sch 3, ss 2(1), 5(1), Sch 1, paras 118(10)(b), (c); Jobseekers Act 1995, s 41(4), Sch 2, para 19(4); Education Act 1996, s 582(1), Sch 37, para 91; SI 2000/90, arts 2(1), 3(2), Sch2, para 5, arts 2(1), 3(1), Sch 1, para 24(1), (10); Criminal Justice and Court Services Act 2000, s 74, Sch 7, Pt II, paras 87, 95; SI 2002/2469, reg 4, Sch 1, Pt 1, para 16(1), (3). Care Standards Act 2000, s 116, Sch 4, para 14(1), (23)(a)(i), (ii), (iii), (iv), (v), (vi), (vii), (23)(b), s 117(2), Sch 6; Local Government Act 2000, s 107, Sch 5, para 22; Powers of Criminal Courts (Sentencing) Act 2000, s 165(1), Sch 9, para 129; Regulation of Care (Scotland) Act 2001, s 79, Sch 3, paras 15(1), (2)(a), (2)(b); Adoption and Children Act 2002, s 139(1), (3),Sch 3, paras 54, 70(a), (b), (c), (d), (e), s 15(1), Sch 2, paras 7, 11; Civil Partnership Act 2004, s 75(1), (3), (4); Children Act 2004, s 40, Sch 3, paras 5, 11; Childcare Act 2006, s 103, para 17, Sch 3, Pt 2; Powers of Criminal Courts (Sentencing) Act 2000, s 165(1), Sch 9, para 129.

SCHEDULE A1 ENFORCEMENT ORDERS]

Part 1 Unpaid Work Requirement]

[General

1

Subject to the modifications in paragraphs 2 and 3, Chapter 4 of Part 12 of the Criminal Justice Act 2003 has effect in relation to an enforcement order as it has effect in relation to a community order (within the meaning of Part 12 of that Act).

References to an offender

2

Subject to paragraph 3, references in Chapter 4 of Part 12 of the Criminal Justice Act 2003 to an offender are to be treated as including references to a person subject to an enforcement order.

Specific modifications

3

(1) The power of the Secretary of State by order under section 197(3) to amend the definition of "responsible officer" and to make consequential

amendments includes power to make any amendments of this Part (including further modifications of Chapter 4 of Part 12 of the Criminal Justice Act 2003) that appear to the Secretary of State to be necessary or expedient in consequence of any amendment made by virtue of section 197(3)(a) or (b).

(2) In section 198 (duties of responsible officer) –

(a)   in subsection (1) –
    (i) at the end of paragraph (a) insert "and", and
    (ii) omit paragraph (c) and the word "and" immediately preceding it, and

(b)   after subsection (1) insert –

"(1A) Subsection (1B) applies where –
(a)   an enforcement order is in force, and
(b)   an officer of the Children and Family Court Advisory and Support Service or a Welsh family proceedings officer (as defined in section 35 of the Children Act 2004) is required under section 11M of the Children Act 1989 to report on matters relating to the order.

(1B) The officer of the Service or the Welsh family proceedings officer may request the responsible officer to report to him on such matters relating to the order as he may require for the purpose of making a report under section 11M(1)(c) or (d); and it shall be the duty of the responsible officer to comply with such a request."

(3) In section 199 (unpaid work requirement) –

(a)   in subsection (2) (minimum and maximum hours of unpaid work) for paragraph (b) substitute –
"(b) not more than 200.",
(b)   omit subsections (3) and (4), and
(c)   in subsection (5) for the words from the beginning to "of them" substitute "Where on the same occasion and in relation to the same person the court makes more than one enforcement order imposing an unpaid work requirement".

(4) In section 200 (obligations of person subject to unpaid work requirement), for subsection (2) substitute –

"(2) Subject to paragraphs 7 and 9 of Schedule A1 to the Children Act 1989, the work required to be performed under an unpaid work requirement imposed by an enforcement order must be performed during a period of twelve months.

(2A) But the period of twelve months is not to run while the enforcement order is suspended under section 11J(9) of the Children Act 1989."

(5) Section 217 (requirement to avoid conflict with religious beliefs, etc) is omitted.

(6) In section 218 (availability of arrangements in local area), subsection (1) (condition for imposition of unpaid work requirement) is omitted.

(7) Section 219 (provision of copies of relevant order) is omitted.

(8) The power of the Secretary of State to make rules under section 222 in relation to persons subject to relevant orders may also be exercised in relation to persons subject to enforcement orders.

(9) The power of the Secretary of State by order under section 223(1) to amend the provision mentioned in section 223(1)(a) includes power to amend this Part so as to make such modifications of Chapter 4 of Part 12 of the Criminal Justice Act 2003 as appear to the Secretary of State to be necessary or expedient in consequence of any amendment of the provision mentioned in section 223(1)(a).]

Part 2 Revocation, Amendment or Breach of Enforcement Order]

[Power to revoke

4

(1) This paragraph applies where a court has made an enforcement order in respect of a person's failure to comply with a contact order and the enforcement order is in force.

(2) The court may revoke the enforcement order if it appears to the court that –

(a)   in all the circumstances no enforcement order should have been made,

(b)   having regard to circumstances which have arisen since the enforcement order was made, it would be appropriate for the enforcement order to be revoked, or

(c)   having regard to the person's satisfactory compliance with the contact order or any contact order that has effect in its place, it would be appropriate for the enforcement order to be revoked.

(3) The enforcement order may be revoked by the court under sub-paragraph (2) of its own motion or on an application by the person subject to the enforcement order.

(4) In deciding whether to revoke the enforcement order under sub-paragraph (2)(b), the court is to take into account –

(a)   the extent to which the person subject to the enforcement order has complied with it, and

(b)   the likelihood that the person will comply with the contact order or any contact order that has effect in its place in the absence of an enforcement order.

(5) In deciding whether to revoke the enforcement order under sub-paragraph (2)(c), the court is to take into account the likelihood that the person will comply with the contact order or any contact order that has effect in its place in the absence of an enforcement order.

Amendment by reason of change of residence

5

(1) This paragraph applies where a court has made an enforcement order in respect of a person's failure to comply with a contact order and the enforcement order is in force.

(2) If the court is satisfied that the person has changed, or proposes to change, his residence from the local justice area specified in the order to another local justice area, the court may amend the order by substituting the other area for the area specified.

(3) The enforcement order may be amended by the court under sub-paragraph (2) of its own motion or on an application by the person subject to the enforcement order.

Amendment of hours specified under unpaid work requirement

6

(1) This paragraph applies where a court has made an enforcement order in respect of a person's failure to comply with a contact order and the enforcement order is in force.

(2) If it appears to the court that, having regard to circumstances that have arisen since the enforcement order was made, it would be appropriate to do so, the court may reduce the number of hours specified in the order (but not below the minimum specified in section 199(2)(a) of the Criminal Justice Act 2003).

(3) In amending the enforcement order under sub-paragraph (2), the court must be satisfied that the effect on the person of the enforcement order as proposed to be amended is no more than is required to secure his compliance with the contact order or any contact order that has effect in its place.

(4) The enforcement order may be amended by the court under sub-paragraph (2) of its own motion or on an application by the person subject to the enforcement order.

Amendment to extend unpaid work requirement

7

(1) This paragraph applies where a court has made an enforcement order in respect of a person's failure to comply with a contact order and the enforcement order is in force.

(2) If it appears to the court that, having regard to circumstances that have arisen since the enforcement order was made, it would be appropriate to do so,

the court may, in relation to the order, extend the period of twelve months specified in section 200(2) of the Criminal Justice Act 2003 (as substituted by paragraph 3).

(3) The period may be extended by the court under sub-paragraph (2) of its own motion or on an application by the person subject to the enforcement order.

Warning and report following breach

8

(1) This paragraph applies where a court has made an enforcement order in respect of a person's failure to comply with a contact order.

(2) If the responsible officer is of the opinion that the person has failed without reasonable excuse to comply with the unpaid work requirement imposed by the enforcement order, the officer must give the person a warning under this paragraph unless –

(a) the person has within the previous twelve months been given a warning under this paragraph in relation to a failure to comply with the unpaid work requirement, or

(b) the responsible officer reports the failure to the appropriate person.

(3) A warning under this paragraph must –

(a) describe the circumstances of the failure,

(b) state that the failure is unacceptable, and

(c) inform the person that, if within the next twelve months he again fails to comply with the unpaid work requirement, the warning and the subsequent failure will be reported to the appropriate person.

(4) The responsible officer must, as soon as practicable after the warning has been given, record that fact.

(5) If –

(a) the responsible officer has given a warning under this paragraph to a person subject to an enforcement order, and

(b) at any time within the twelve months beginning with the date on which the warning was given, the responsible officer is of the opinion that the person has since that date failed without reasonable excuse to comply with the unpaid work requirement imposed by the enforcement order,

the officer must report the failure to the appropriate person.

(6) A report under sub-paragraph (5) must include a report of the warning given to the person subject to the enforcement order.

(7) The appropriate person, in relation to an enforcement order, is the officer of the Service or the Welsh family proceedings officer who is required under section 11M to report on matters relating to the enforcement order.

(8) "Responsible officer", in relation to a person subject to an enforcement order, has the same meaning as in section 197 of the Criminal Justice Act 2003 (as modified by paragraph 2).

Breach of an enforcement order

9

(1) This paragraph applies where a court has made an enforcement order ("the first order") in respect of a person's failure to comply with a contact order.

(2) If the court is satisfied beyond reasonable doubt that the person has failed to comply with the unpaid work requirement imposed by the first order, the court may –

(a)   amend the first order so as to make the requirement more onerous, or
(b)   make an enforcement order ("the second order") in relation to the person and (if the first order is still in force) provide for the second order to have effect either in addition to or in substitution for the first order.

(3) But the court may not exercise its powers under sub-paragraph (2) if it is satisfied that the person had a reasonable excuse for failing to comply with the unpaid work requirement imposed by the first order.

(4) The burden of proof as to the matter mentioned in sub-paragraph (3) lies on the person claiming to have had a reasonable excuse, and the standard of proof is the balance of probabilities.

(5) The court may exercise its powers under sub-paragraph (2) in relation to the first order only on the application of a person who would be able to apply under section 11J for an enforcement order if the failure to comply with the first order were a failure to comply with the contact order to which the first order relates.

(6) Where the person proposing to apply to the court is the child with respect to whom the contact order was made, subsections (6) and (7) of section 11J have effect in relation to the application as they have effect in relation to an application for an enforcement order.

(7) An application to the court to exercise its powers under sub-paragraph (2) may only be made while the first order is in force.

(8) The court may not exercise its powers under sub-paragraph (2) in respect of a failure by the person to comply with the unpaid work requirement imposed by the first order unless it is satisfied that before the failure occurred the person had been given (in accordance with rules of court) a copy of, or otherwise informed of the terms of, a notice under section 11N relating to the first order.

(9) In dealing with the person under sub-paragraph (2)(a), the court may –

(a)   increase the number of hours specified in the first order (but not above the maximum specified in section 199(2)(b) of the Criminal Justice Act 2003, as substituted by paragraph 3);

(b)   in relation to the order, extend the period of twelve months specified in section 200(2) of the Criminal Justice Act 2003 (as substituted by paragraph 3).

(10) In exercising its powers under sub-paragraph (2), the court must be satisfied that, taking into account the extent to which the person has complied with the unpaid work requirement imposed by the first order, the effect on the person of the proposed exercise of those powers –

(a)   is no more than is required to secure his compliance with the contact order or any contact order that has effect in its place, and

(b)   is no more than is proportionate to the seriousness of his failures to comply with the contact order and the first order.

(11) Where the court exercises its powers under sub-paragraph (2) by making an enforcement order in relation to a person who has failed to comply with another enforcement order –

(a)   sections 11K(4), 11L(2) to (7), 11M and 11N have effect as regards the making of the order in relation to the person as they have effect as regards the making of an enforcement order in relation to a person who has failed to comply with a contact order;

(b)   this Part of this Schedule has effect in relation to the order so made as if it were an enforcement order made in respect of the failure for which the other order was made.

(12) Sub-paragraph (2) is without prejudice to section 63(3) of the Magistrates' Courts Act 1980 as it applies in relation to enforcement orders.

Provision relating to amendment of enforcement orders

10

Sections 11L(2) to (7) and 11M have effect in relation to the making of an order under paragraph 6(2), 7(2) or 9(2)(a) amending an enforcement order as they have effect in relation to the making of an enforcement order; and references in sections 11L(2) to (7) and 11M to an enforcement order are to be read accordingly.]

Amendment—Children and Adoption Act 2006, s 4(2), Sch 1.

Appendix 2

CHILDREN AND ADOPTION ACT 2006

PART 1

ORDERS WITH RESPECT TO CHILDREN IN FAMILY PROCEEDINGS

Contact with children

1 Contact activity directions and conditions

After section 11 of the Children Act 1989 (c 41) insert–

'11A CONTACT ACTIVITY DIRECTIONS

(1) This section applies in proceedings in which the court is considering whether to make provision about contact with a child by making–

(a)   a contact order with respect to the child, or
(b)   an order varying or discharging a contact order with respect to the child.

(2) The court may make a contact activity direction in connection with that provision about contact.

(3) A contact activity direction is a direction requiring an individual who is a party to the proceedings to take part in an activity that promotes contact with the child concerned.

(4) The direction is to specify the activity and the person providing the activity.

(5) The activities that may be so required include, in particular–

(a)   programmes, classes and counselling or guidance sessions of a kind that–
    (i) may assist a person as regards establishing, maintaining or improving contact with a child;
    (ii) may, by addressing a person's violent behaviour, enable or facilitate contact with a child;
(b)   sessions in which information or advice is given as regards making or operating arrangements for contact with a child, including making arrangements by means of mediation.

(6) No individual may be required by a contact activity direction–

(a)   to undergo medical or psychiatric examination, assessment or treatment;
(b)   to take part in mediation.

(7) A court may not on the same occasion–

(a)   make a contact activity direction, and
(b)   dispose finally of the proceedings as they relate to contact with the child concerned.

(8) Subsection (2) has effect subject to the restrictions in sections 11B and 11E.

(9) In considering whether to make a contact activity direction, the welfare of the child concerned is to be the court's paramount consideration.

11B CONTACT ACTIVITY DIRECTIONS: FURTHER PROVISION

(1) A court may not make a contact activity direction in any proceedings unless there is a dispute as regards the provision about contact that the court is considering whether to make in the proceedings.

(2) A court may not make a contact activity direction requiring an individual who is a child to take part in an activity unless the individual is a parent of the child in relation to whom the court is considering provision about contact.

(3) A court may not make a contact activity direction in connection with the making, variation or discharge of a contact order, if the contact order is, or would if made be, an excepted order.

(4) A contact order with respect to a child is an excepted order if–

(a)   it is made in proceedings that include proceedings on an application for a relevant adoption order in respect of the child; or
(b)   it makes provision as regards contact between the child and a person who would be a parent or relative of the child but for the child's adoption by an order falling within subsection (5).

(5) An order falls within this subsection if it is–

(a)   a relevant adoption order;
(b)   an adoption order, within the meaning of section 72(1) of the Adoption Act 1976, other than an order made by virtue of section 14 of that Act on the application of a married couple one of whom is the mother or the father of the child;
(c)   a Scottish adoption order, within the meaning of the Adoption and Children Act 2002, other than an order made–
       (i) by virtue of section 14 of the Adoption (Scotland) Act 1978 on the application of a married couple one of whom is the mother or the father of the child, or
       (ii) by virtue of section 15(1)(aa) of that Act; or
(d)   a Northern Irish adoption order, within the meaning of the Adoption and Children Act 2002, other than an order made by virtue of Article 14 of the Adoption (Northern Ireland) Order 1987 on the application of a married couple one of whom is the mother or the father of the child.

(6) A relevant adoption order is an adoption order, within the meaning of section 46(1) of the Adoption and Children Act 2002, other than an order made–

(a)   on an application under section 50 of that Act by a couple (within the meaning of that Act) one of whom is the mother or the father of the person to be adopted, or

(b)   on an application under section 51(2) of that Act.

(7) A court may not make a contact activity direction in relation to an individual unless the individual is habitually resident in England and Wales; and a direction ceases to have effect if the individual subject to the direction ceases to be habitually resident in England and Wales.

11C CONTACT ACTIVITY CONDITIONS

(1) This section applies if in any family proceedings the court makes–

(a)   a contact order with respect to a child, or

(b)   an order varying a contact order with respect to a child.

(2) The contact order may impose, or the contact order may be varied so as to impose, a condition (a 'contact activity condition') requiring an individual falling within subsection (3) to take part in an activity that promotes contact with the child concerned.

(3) An individual falls within this subsection if he is–

(a)   for the purposes of the contact order so made or varied, the person with whom the child concerned lives or is to live;

(b)   the person whose contact with the child concerned is provided for in that order; or

(c)   a person upon whom that order imposes a condition under section 11(7)(b).

(4) The condition is to specify the activity and the person providing the activity.

(5) Subsections (5) and (6) of section 11A have effect as regards the activities that may be required by a contact activity condition as they have effect as regards the activities that may be required by a contact activity direction.

(6) Subsection (2) has effect subject to the restrictions in sections 11D and 11E.

11D CONTACT ACTIVITY CONDITIONS: FURTHER PROVISION

(1) A contact order may not impose a contact activity condition on an individual who is a child unless the individual is a parent of the child concerned.

(2) If a contact order is an excepted order (within the meaning given by section 11B(4)), it may not impose (and it may not be varied so as to impose) a contact activity condition.

(3) A contact order may not impose a contact activity condition on an individual unless the individual is habitually resident in England and Wales; and a condition ceases to have effect if the individual subject to the condition ceases to be habitually resident in England and Wales.

11E Contact activity directions and conditions: making

(1) Before making a contact activity direction (or imposing a contact activity condition by means of a contact order), the court must satisfy itself as to the matters falling within subsections (2) to (4).

(2) The first matter is that the activity proposed to be specified is appropriate in the circumstances of the case.

(3) The second matter is that the person proposed to be specified as the provider of the activity is suitable to provide the activity.

(4) The third matter is that the activity proposed to be specified is provided in a place to which the individual who would be subject to the direction (or the condition) can reasonably be expected to travel.

(5) Before making such a direction (or such an order), the court must obtain and consider information about the individual who would be subject to the direction (or the condition) and the likely effect of the direction (or the condition) on him.

(6) Information about the likely effect of the direction (or the condition) may, in particular, include information as to–

(a) any conflict with the individual's religious beliefs;

(b) any interference with the times (if any) at which he normally works or attends an educational establishment.

(7) The court may ask an officer of the Service or a Welsh family proceedings officer to provide the court with information as to the matters in subsections (2) to (5); and it shall be the duty of the officer of the Service or Welsh family proceedings officer to comply with any such request.

(8) In this section 'specified' means specified in a contact activity direction (or in a contact activity condition).

11F Contact activity directions and conditions:
financial assistance

(1) The Secretary of State may by regulations make provision authorising him to make payments to assist individuals falling within subsection (2) in paying relevant charges or fees.

(2) An individual falls within this subsection if he is required by a contact activity direction or condition to take part in an activity that promotes contact with a child, not being a child ordinarily resident in Wales.

(3) The National Assembly for Wales may by regulations make provision authorising it to make payments to assist individuals falling within subsection (4) in paying relevant charges or fees.

(4) An individual falls within this subsection if he is required by a contact activity direction or condition to take part in an activity that promotes contact with a child who is ordinarily resident in Wales.

(5) A relevant charge or fee, in relation to an activity required by a contact activity direction or condition, is a charge or fee in respect of the activity payable to the person providing the activity.

(6) Regulations under this section may provide that no assistance is available to an individual unless–

(a)   the individual satisfies such conditions as regards his financial resources as may be set out in the regulations;

(b)   the activity in which the individual is required by a contact activity direction or condition to take part is provided to him in England or Wales;

(c)   where the activity in which the individual is required to take part is provided to him in England, it is provided by a person who is for the time being approved by the Secretary of State as a provider of activities required by a contact activity direction or condition;

(d)   where the activity in which the individual is required to take part is provided to him in Wales, it is provided by a person who is for the time being approved by the National Assembly for Wales as a provider of activities required by a contact activity direction or condition.

(7) Regulations under this section may make provision–

(a)   as to the maximum amount of assistance that may be paid to or in respect of an individual as regards an activity in which he is required by a contact activity direction or condition to take part;

(b)   where the amount may vary according to an individual's financial resources, as to the method by which the amount is to be determined;

(c)   authorising payments by way of assistance to be made directly to persons providing activities required by a contact activity direction or condition.

11G CONTACT ACTIVITY DIRECTIONS AND CONDITIONS: MONITORING

(1) This section applies if in any family proceedings the court–

(a)   makes a contact activity direction in relation to an individual, or

(b)   makes a contact order that imposes, or varies a contact order so as to impose, a contact activity condition on an individual.

(2) The court may on making the direction (or imposing the condition by means of a contact order) ask an officer of the Service or a Welsh family proceedings officer–

(a)   to monitor, or arrange for the monitoring of, the individual's compliance with the direction (or the condition);

(b)   to report to the court on any failure by the individual to comply with the direction (or the condition).

(3) It shall be the duty of the officer of the Service or Welsh family proceedings officer to comply with any request under subsection (2).'

2 Monitoring contact

After section 11G of the Children Act 1989 (c 41) (as inserted by section 1) insert–

'11H MONITORING CONTACT

(1) This section applies if in any family proceedings the court makes–

(a)   a contact order with respect to a child in favour of a person, or
(b)   an order varying such a contact order.

(2) The court may ask an officer of the Service or a Welsh family proceedings officer–

(a)   to monitor whether an individual falling within subsection (3) complies with the contact order (or the contact order as varied);
(b)   to report to the court on such matters relating to the individual's compliance as the court may specify in the request.

(3) An individual falls within this subsection if the contact order so made (or the contact order as so varied)–

(a)   requires the individual to allow contact with the child concerned;
(b)   names the individual as having contact with the child concerned; or
(c)   imposes a condition under section 11(7)(b) on the individual.

(4) If the contact order (or the contact order as varied) includes a contact activity condition, a request under subsection (2) is to be treated as relating to the provisions of the order other than the contact activity condition.

(5) The court may make a request under subsection (2)–

(a)   on making the contact order (or the order varying the contact order), or
(b)   at any time during the subsequent course of the proceedings as they relate to contact with the child concerned.

(6) In making a request under subsection (2), the court is to specify the period for which the officer of the Service or Welsh family proceedings officer is to monitor compliance with the order; and the period specified may not exceed twelve months.

(7) It shall be the duty of the officer of the Service or Welsh family proceedings officer to comply with any request under subsection (2).

(8) The court may order any individual falling within subsection (3) to take such steps as may be specified in the order with a view to enabling the officer of the Service or Welsh family proceedings officer to comply with the court's request under subsection (2).

(9) But the court may not make an order under subsection (8) with respect to an individual who is a child unless he is a parent of the child with respect to whom the order falling within subsection (1) was made.

(10) A court may not make a request under subsection (2) in relation to a contact order that is an excepted order (within the meaning given by section 11B(4)).'

3 Contact orders: warning notices

After section 11H of the Children Act 1989 (c 41) (as inserted by section 2) insert–

'11I CONTACT ORDERS: WARNING NOTICES

Where the court makes (or varies) a contact order, it is to attach to the contact order (or the order varying the contact order) a notice warning of the consequences of failing to comply with the contact order.'

4 Enforcement orders

(1) After section 11I of the Children Act 1989 (as inserted by section 3) insert–

'11J ENFORCEMENT ORDERS

(1) This section applies if a contact order with respect to a child has been made.

(2) If the court is satisfied beyond reasonable doubt that a person has failed to comply with the contact order, it may make an order (an 'enforcement order') imposing on the person an unpaid work requirement.

(3) But the court may not make an enforcement order if it is satisfied that the person had a reasonable excuse for failing to comply with the contact order.

(4) The burden of proof as to the matter mentioned in subsection (3) lies on the person claiming to have had a reasonable excuse, and the standard of proof is the balance of probabilities.

(5) The court may make an enforcement order in relation to the contact order only on the application of–

(a) the person who is, for the purposes of the contact order, the person with whom the child concerned lives or is to live;
(b) the person whose contact with the child concerned is provided for in the contact order;
(c) any individual subject to a condition under section 11(7)(b) or a contact activity condition imposed by the contact order; or
(d) the child concerned.

(6) Where the person proposing to apply for an enforcement order in relation to a contact order is the child concerned, the child must obtain the leave of the court before making such an application.

(7) The court may grant leave to the child concerned only if it is satisfied that he has sufficient understanding to make the proposed application.

(8) Subsection (2) has effect subject to the restrictions in sections 11K and 11L.

(9) The court may suspend an enforcement order for such period as it thinks fit.

(10) Nothing in this section prevents a court from making more than one enforcement order in relation to the same person on the same occasion.

(11) Proceedings in which any question of making an enforcement order, or any other question with respect to such an order, arises are to be regarded for the purposes of section 11(1) and (2) as proceedings in which a question arises with respect to a section 8 order.

(12) In Schedule A1–

(a)   Part 1 makes provision as regards an unpaid work requirement;
(b)   Part 2 makes provision in relation to the revocation and amendment of enforcement orders and failure to comply with such orders.

(13) This section is without prejudice to section 63(3) of the Magistrates' Courts Act 1980 as it applies in relation to contact orders.

11K ENFORCEMENT ORDERS: FURTHER PROVISION

(1) A court may not make an enforcement order against a person in respect of a failure to comply with a contact order unless it is satisfied that before the failure occurred the person had been given (in accordance with rules of court) a copy of, or otherwise informed of the terms of–

(a)   in the case of a failure to comply with a contact order that was varied before the failure occurred, a notice under section 11I relating to the order varying the contact order or, where more than one such order has been made, the last order preceding the failure in question;

(b)   in any other case, a notice under section 11I relating to the contact order.

(2) A court may not make an enforcement order against a person in respect of any failure to comply with a contact order occurring before the person attained the age of 18.

(3) A court may not make an enforcement order against a person in respect of a failure to comply with a contact order that is an excepted order (within the meaning given by section 11B(4)).

(4) A court may not make an enforcement order against a person unless the person is habitually resident in England and Wales; and an enforcement order ceases to have effect if the person subject to the order ceases to be habitually resident in England and Wales.

11L ENFORCEMENT ORDERS: MAKING

(1) Before making an enforcement order as regards a person in breach of a contact order, the court must be satisfied that—

(a) making the enforcement order proposed is necessary to secure the person's compliance with the contact order or any contact order that has effect in its place;

(b) the likely effect on the person of the enforcement order proposed to be made is proportionate to the seriousness of the breach of the contact order.

(2) Before making an enforcement order, the court must satisfy itself that provision for the person to work under an unpaid work requirement imposed by an enforcement order can be made in the local justice area in which the person in breach resides or will reside.

(3) Before making an enforcement order as regards a person in breach of a contact order, the court must obtain and consider information about the person and the likely effect of the enforcement order on him.

(4) Information about the likely effect of the enforcement order may, in particular, include information as to—

(a) any conflict with the person's religious beliefs;

(b) any interference with the times (if any) at which he normally works or attends an educational establishment.

(5) A court that proposes to make an enforcement order may ask an officer of the Service or a Welsh family proceedings officer to provide the court with information as to the matters in subsections (2) and (3).

(6) It shall be the duty of the officer of the Service or Welsh family proceedings officer to comply with any request under this section.

(7) In making an enforcement order in relation to a contact order, a court must take into account the welfare of the child who is the subject of the contact order.

11M ENFORCEMENT ORDERS: MONITORING

(1) On making an enforcement order in relation to a person, the court is to ask an officer of the Service or a Welsh family proceedings officer—

(a) to monitor, or arrange for the monitoring of, the person's compliance with the unpaid work requirement imposed by the order;

(b) to report to the court if a report under paragraph 8 of Schedule A1 is made in relation to the person;

(c) to report to the court on such other matters relating to the person's compliance as may be specified in the request;

(d) to report to the court if the person is, or becomes, unsuitable to perform work under the requirement.

(2) It shall be the duty of the officer of the Service or Welsh family proceedings officer to comply with any request under this section.

11N ENFORCEMENT ORDERS: WARNING NOTICES

Where the court makes an enforcement order, it is to attach to the order a notice warning of the consequences of failing to comply with the order.'

(2) Schedule 1 (which contains a Schedule to be inserted before Schedule 1 to the Children Act 1989 (c 41)) has effect.

5 *Compensation for financial loss*

After section 11N of the Children Act 1989 (as inserted by section 4) insert–

'11O COMPENSATION FOR FINANCIAL LOSS

(1) This section applies if a contact order with respect to a child has been made.

(2) If the court is satisfied that–

(a)   an individual has failed to comply with the contact order, and
(b)   a person falling within subsection (6) has suffered financial loss by reason of the breach,

it may make an order requiring the individual in breach to pay the person compensation in respect of his financial loss.

(3) But the court may not make an order under subsection (2) if it is satisfied that the individual in breach had a reasonable excuse for failing to comply with the contact order.

(4) The burden of proof as to the matter mentioned in subsection (3) lies on the individual claiming to have had a reasonable excuse.

(5) An order under subsection (2) may be made only on an application by the person who claims to have suffered financial loss.

(6) A person falls within this subsection if he is–

(a)   the person who is, for the purposes of the contact order, the person with whom the child concerned lives or is to live;
(b)   the person whose contact with the child concerned is provided for in the contact order;
(c)   an individual subject to a condition under section 11(7)(b) or a contact activity condition imposed by the contact order; or
(d)   the child concerned.

(7) Where the person proposing to apply for an order under subsection (2) is the child concerned, the child must obtain the leave of the court before making such an application.

(8) The court may grant leave to the child concerned only if it is satisfied that he has sufficient understanding to make the proposed application.

(9) The amount of compensation is to be determined by the court, but may not exceed the amount of the applicant's financial loss.

(10) In determining the amount of compensation payable by the individual in breach, the court must take into account the individual's financial circumstances.

(11) An amount ordered to be paid as compensation may be recovered by the applicant as a civil debt due to him.

(12) Subsection (2) has effect subject to the restrictions in section 11P.

(13) Proceedings in which any question of making an order under subsection (2) arises are to be regarded for the purposes of section 11(1) and (2) as proceedings in which a question arises with respect to a section 8 order.

(14) In exercising its powers under this section, a court is to take into account the welfare of the child concerned.

11P ORDERS UNDER SECTION 11O(2): FURTHER PROVISION

(1) A court may not make an order under section 11O(2) requiring an individual to pay compensation in respect of a failure by him to comply with a contact order unless it is satisfied that before the failure occurred the individual had been given (in accordance with rules of court) a copy of, or otherwise informed of the terms of–

(a)   in the case of a failure to comply with a contact order that was varied before the failure occurred, a notice under section 11I relating to the order varying the contact order or, where more than one such order has been made, the last order preceding the failure in question;

(b)   in any other case, a notice under section 11I relating to the contact order.

(2) A court may not make an order under section 11O(2) requiring an individual to pay compensation in respect of a failure by him to comply with a contact order where the failure occurred before the individual attained the age of 18.

(3) A court may not make an order under section 11O(2) requiring an individual to pay compensation in respect of a failure by him to comply with a contact order that is an excepted order (within the meaning given by section 11B(4)).'

Family assistance orders

6 *Provision as to family assistance orders*

(1) Section 16 of the Children Act 1989 (c 41) (family assistance orders) is amended as follows.

(2) In subsection (3) (requirements for making an order), omit paragraph (a) (requirement that circumstances of case be exceptional).

(3) After subsection (4) insert–

'(4A) If the court makes a family assistance order with respect to a child and the order is to be in force at the same time as a contact order made with respect to the child, the family assistance order may direct the officer concerned to give advice and assistance as regards establishing, improving and maintaining contact to such of the persons named in the order as may be specified in the order.'

(4) In subsection (5) (maximum duration of order) for 'six months' substitute 'twelve months'.

(5) For subsection (6) substitute–

'(6) If the court makes a family assistance order with respect to a child and the order is to be in force at the same time as a section 8 order made with respect to the child, the family assistance order may direct the officer concerned to report to the court on such matters relating to the section 8 order as the court may require (including the question whether the section 8 order ought to be varied or discharged).'

Risk assessments

7 *Risk assessments*

After section 16 of the Children Act 1989 (c 41) insert–

'16A RISK ASSESSMENTS

(1) This section applies to the following functions of officers of the Service or Welsh family proceedings officers–

(a) any function in connection with family proceedings in which the court has power to make an order under this Part with respect to a child or in which a question with respect to such an order arises;

(b) any function in connection with an order made by the court in such proceedings.

(2) If, in carrying out any function to which this section applies, an officer of the Service or a Welsh family proceedings officer is given cause to suspect that the child concerned is at risk of harm, he must–

(a) make a risk assessment in relation to the child, and

(b) provide the risk assessment to the court.

(3) A risk assessment, in relation to a child who is at risk of suffering harm of a particular sort, is an assessment of the risk of that harm being suffered by the child.'

Transitional provision

8 Transitional provision

(1) This section applies to any contact order under section 8 of the Children Act 1989 made before, and in force on, the relevant date.

(2) For so long as a contact order to which this section applies continues in force on and after the relevant date without being varied, the circumstances in which a notice under section 11I of the Children Act 1989 is to be attached to the contact order include–

(a) where an application for such a notice to be attached to the contact order is made by a person who, as regards the order, falls within any of paragraphs (a) to (d) of section 11J(5) of the Children Act 1989;

(b) where, in any family proceedings, a question arises with respect to the contact order.

(3) Where the person proposing to apply under subsection (2)(a) is the child with respect to whom the contact order was made, subsections (6) and (7) of section 11J have effect in relation to the application under subsection (2)(a) as they have effect in relation to an application under section 11J for an enforcement order.

(4) If a failure to comply with a contact order to which this section applies occurs while the contact order continues in force as described in subsection (2), each of sections 11K(1) and 11P(1) of the Children Act 1989 is to have effect, in relation to the failure, as if for paragraphs (a) and (b) there were substituted 'a notice under section 11I relating to the contact order'.

(5) In this section 'relevant date' means the day on which sections 3 to 5 come into force.

PART 2

ADOPTIONS WITH A FOREIGN ELEMENT

9 Declaration of special restrictions on adoptions from abroad

(1) This section applies if the Secretary of State has reason to believe that, because of practices taking place in a country or territory outside the British Islands (the 'other country') in connection with the adoption of children, it would be contrary to public policy to further the bringing of children into the United Kingdom in the cases mentioned in subsection (2).

(2) The cases are that a British resident–

(a) wishes to bring, or cause another to bring, a child who is not a British resident into the United Kingdom for the purpose of adoption by the British resident, and, in connection with the proposed adoption, there have been, or would have to be, proceedings in the other country or dealings with authorities or agencies there, or

(b) wishes to bring, or cause another to bring, into the United Kingdom a child adopted by the British resident under an adoption effected, within the period of twelve months ending with the date of the bringing in, under the law of the other country.

(3) It is immaterial whether the other country is a Convention country or not.

(4) The Secretary of State may by order declare, in relation to any such country or territory, that special restrictions are to apply for the time being in relation to the bringing in of children in the cases mentioned in subsection (2).

(5) Before making an order containing such a declaration the Secretary of State must consult–

(a) the National Assembly for Wales, and
(b) the Department of Health, Social Services and Public Safety in Northern Ireland.

(6) A country or territory in relation to which such a declaration has effect for the time being is referred to below in this section as a 'restricted country'.

(7) The Secretary of State must publish reasons for making the declaration in relation to each restricted country.

(8) The Secretary of State must publish a list of restricted countries ('the restricted list') and keep the list up to date.

(9) The restricted list and the reasons are to be published in whatever way the Secretary of State thinks appropriate for bringing them to the attention of adoption agencies and members of the public.

(10) In this section–

(a) 'British resident' means a person habitually resident in the British Islands, and the reference to adoption by a British resident includes adoption by a British resident and another person,
(b) 'the Convention' means the Convention on Protection of Children and Co-operation in respect of Intercountry Adoption, concluded at The Hague on 29th May 1993,
(c) 'Convention country' means a country or territory in which the Convention is in force.

10 Review

(1) The Secretary of State must keep under review, in relation to each restricted country, whether it should continue to be a restricted country.

(2) If the Secretary of State determines, in relation to a restricted country, that there is no longer reason to believe what is mentioned in subsection (1) of section 9, he must by order revoke the order containing the declaration made in relation to it under subsection (4) of that section.

(3) Before making a determination under subsection (2), the Secretary of State must consult–

(a) the National Assembly for Wales, and
(b) the Department of Health, Social Services and Public Safety in Northern Ireland.

(4) In this section, 'restricted country' has the same meaning as in section 9.

11 *The special restrictions*

(1) The special restrictions mentioned in section 9(4) are that, except as mentioned in subsection (2) of this section, the appropriate authority is not to take any step which he or it might otherwise have taken in connection with furthering the bringing of a child into the United Kingdom in the cases mentioned in section 9(2) (whether or not that step is provided for by or by virtue of any enactment).

(2) But nothing in subsection (1) prevents the appropriate authority from taking those steps if, in any particular case, the prospective adopters satisfy–

(a) the appropriate authority, or
(b) in relation to Northern Ireland, in a case which is not a Convention case, the Secretary of State,

that the appropriate authority should take those steps despite the special restrictions.

(3) The Secretary of State may make regulations providing for–

(a) the procedure to be followed by the appropriate authority (or, if subsection (2)(b) applies, the Secretary of State) in determining whether or not he or it is satisfied as mentioned in subsection (2),
(b) matters which the appropriate authority (or the Secretary of State) is to take into account when making such a determination (whether or not he or it also takes other matters into account).

(4) In this section–

'the appropriate authority' means, in a Convention case, the Central Authority in relation to England, to Wales or to Northern Ireland (as the case may be), and in any other case–

(a) in relation to England and Wales, the Secretary of State,
(b) in relation to Northern Ireland, the Secretary of State (for the purposes of steps which he takes) or the Department of Health, Social Services and Public Safety in Northern Ireland (for the purposes of steps which it takes),

'Central Authority' is to be construed in accordance with section 2 of the Adoption (Intercountry Aspects) Act 1999 (c 18) ('the 1999 Act') or, in relation to Northern Ireland, section 2 of the Adoption (Intercountry Aspects) Act (Northern Ireland) 2001 (c 11 (NI)) ('the 2001 Act'),

'Convention case' means a case where–

(a)   the child is intended to be adopted under an adoption order which, by virtue of regulations under section 1 of the 1999 Act or section 1 of the 2001 Act (as appropriate), is made as a Convention adoption order, or

(b)   the child is intended to be adopted under an adoption effected under the law of a Convention country outside the British Islands and certified in pursuance of Article 23(1) of the Convention,

and 'the Convention' and 'Convention country' have the meanings given by section 9(10).

12 *Imposition of extra conditions in certain cases*

(1) The Secretary of State may make regulations providing–

(a)   for him to specify in the restricted list, in relation to any restricted country, a step which is not otherwise provided for by or by virtue of any enactment but which, by virtue of the arrangements between the United Kingdom and that country, the appropriate authority normally takes in connection with the bringing in of a child where that country is concerned, and

(b)   that, if such a step has been so specified in relation to a restricted country, one or more conditions specified in the regulations are to be met in respect of a child brought into the United Kingdom in either of the cases mentioned in section 9(2) (reading the reference there to the 'other country' as being to the restricted country in question).

(2) Those conditions are in addition to any provided for by virtue of–

(a)   section 83 of the Adoption and Children Act 2002 (c 38) (restriction on bringing children in), or

(b)   Article 58ZA of the Adoption (Northern Ireland) Order 1987 (SI 1987/2203 (NI 22)) (restriction on bringing children in),

or under or by virtue of any other enactment.

(3) A person who brings, or causes another to bring, a child into the United Kingdom is guilty of an offence if any condition required to be met by virtue of subsection (1)(b) is not met.

(4) Subsection (3) does not apply if the step specified in the restricted list in relation to any country had already been taken before the publication of the restricted list.

(5) A person guilty of an offence under subsection (3) is liable–

(a)   on summary conviction, to imprisonment for a term not exceeding 12 months (in England and Wales) or 6 months (in Northern Ireland), or a fine not exceeding the statutory maximum, or both,

(b)   on conviction on indictment, to imprisonment for a term not exceeding 12 months, or a fine, or both.

(6) In relation to an offence committed before the commencement of section 154(1) of the Criminal Justice Act 2003 (c 44) (general limit on

magistrates' court's power to impose imprisonment), the reference in subsection (5)(a) to 12 months is to be read as a reference to 6 months.

This subsection does not extend to Northern Ireland.

(7) In this section–

(a)   'the appropriate authority' has the meaning given by section 11(4),

(b)   'restricted country' and 'restricted list' have the same meanings as in section 9.

13 Power to charge

After section 91 of the Adoption and Children Act 2002 (c 38) insert–

'91A POWER TO CHARGE

(1) This section applies to adoptions to which–

(a)   section 83 applies, or

(b)   regulations made under section 1 of the Adoption (Intercountry Aspects) Act 1999 apply.

(2) The Secretary of State may charge a fee to adopters for services provided or to be provided by him in relation to adoptions to which this section applies.

(3) The Assembly may charge a fee to adopters for services provided or to be provided by it as the Central Authority in relation to adoptions to which this section applies by virtue of subsection (1)(b).

(4) The Secretary of State and the Assembly may determine the level of fee as he or it sees fit, and may in particular–

(a)   charge a flat fee or charge different fees in different cases or descriptions of case, and

(b)   in any case or description of case, waive a fee.

(5) But the Secretary of State and the Assembly must each secure that, taking one financial year with another, the income from fees under this section does not exceed the total cost to him or, as the case may be, to it of providing the services in relation to which the fees are imposed.

(6) In this section–

references to adoptions and adopters include prospective adoptions and prospective adopters,

'Central Authority' is to be construed in accordance with section 2 of the Adoption (Intercountry Aspects) Act 1999,

'financial year' means a period of twelve months ending with 31st March.'

14 Other amendments relating to adoptions from abroad

(1) In section 83 of the Adoption and Children Act 2002 (restriction on bringing children into the United Kingdom), in subsection (1)(b), for 'six' substitute 'twelve'.

(2) The amendment made by subsection (1) applies only in relation to a child adopted under an external adoption (see section 83(3) of the Adoption and Children Act 2002 (c 38)) effected after subsection (1) comes into force.

(3) In Schedule 8 to the Children Act 1989 (c 41) (privately fostered children), in paragraph 5 (as amended by paragraph 73 of Schedule 3 to the Adoption and Children Act 2002), after sub-paragraph (c) add–

'or while he is a child in respect of whom a local authority have functions by virtue of regulations under section 83(6)(b) of the Adoption and Children Act 2002 (which relates to children brought into the United Kingdom for adoption), or corresponding functions by virtue of regulations under section 1 of the Adoption (Intercountry Aspects) Act 1999 (regulations to give effect to Hague Convention on Protection of Children and Co-operation in respect of Intercountry Adoption).'

PART 3

MISCELLANEOUS AND FINAL

Miscellaneous provisions

15 Minor and consequential amendments and repeals

(1) Schedule 2 (minor and consequential amendments) has effect.

(2) Schedule 3 (repeals) has effect.

Final provisions

16 Regulations and orders

(1) Any power to make regulations conferred by this Act on the Secretary of State is exercisable by statutory instrument.

(2) The power to make and revoke an order under section 9(4) is also exercisable by statutory instrument.

(3) A statutory instrument mentioned in subsection (1) or (2) is to be subject to annulment in pursuance of a resolution of either House of Parliament.

(4) Regulations made under this Act may make different provision for different purposes.

(5) A power to make regulations under this Act (as well as being exercisable in relation to all cases to which it extends) may be exercised in relation to–

(a)   those cases subject to specified exceptions, or
(b)   a particular case or class of case.

17   Short title, commencement and extent

(1) This Act may be cited as the Children and Adoption Act 2006.

(2) Except as provided in subsection (3), the preceding provisions of this Act shall come into force on such day as the Secretary of State may by order made by statutory instrument appoint; and different days may be appointed for different purposes.

(3) Section 13, so far as relating to adoptions and prospective adoptions in relation to which the National Assembly for Wales may charge a fee under section 91A of the Adoption and Children Act 2002 (c 38), shall come into force on such day as the National Assembly for Wales may by order made by statutory instrument appoint; and different days may be appointed for different purposes.

(4) Before making an order under subsection (2) the Secretary of State must consult the National Assembly for Wales.

(5) Before making an order under subsection (2) bringing sections 9 to 12 into force, the Secretary of State must consult the Department of Health, Social Services and Public Safety in Northern Ireland.

(6) Subject to subsections (7) and (8), this Act extends to England and Wales only.

(7) The amendment or repeal of an enactment has the same extent as the enactment to which it relates.

(8) The following provisions of this Act extend also to Northern Ireland–

(a)   sections 9 to 11;
(b)   section 12(1) to (5) and (7);
(c)   section 16;
(d)   this section.

Schedule 1

Enforcement Orders

Section 4

Before Schedule 1 to the Children Act 1989 (c 41) insert–

'Schedule A1

Enforcement Orders

PART 1

UNPAID WORK REQUIREMENT

1 General

Subject to the modifications in paragraphs 2 and 3, Chapter 4 of Part 12 of the Criminal Justice Act 2003 has effect in relation to an enforcement order as it has effect in relation to a community order (within the meaning of Part 12 of that Act).

2 References to an offender

Subject to paragraph 3, references in Chapter 4 of Part 12 of the Criminal Justice Act 2003 to an offender are to be treated as including references to a person subject to an enforcement order.

3 Specific modifications

(1) The power of the Secretary of State by order under section 197(3) to amend the definition of 'responsible officer' and to make consequential amendments includes power to make any amendments of this Part (including further modifications of Chapter 4 of Part 12 of the Criminal Justice Act 2003) that appear to the Secretary of State to be necessary or expedient in consequence of any amendment made by virtue of section 197(3)(a) or (b).

(2) In section 198 (duties of responsible officer)–

(a)   in subsection (1)–
        (i) at the end of paragraph (a) insert 'and', and
        (ii) omit paragraph (c) and the word 'and' immediately preceding it, and
(b)   after subsection (1) insert–

'(1A) Subsection (1B) applies where–

(a)   an enforcement order is in force, and
(b)   an officer of the Children and Family Court Advisory and Support Service or a Welsh family proceedings officer (as defined in section 35 of the Children Act 2004) is required under section 11M of the Children Act 1989 to report on matters relating to the order.

(1B) The officer of the Service or the Welsh family proceedings officer may request the responsible officer to report to him on such matters relating to the order as he may require for the purpose of making a report under section 11M(1)(c) or (d); and it shall be the duty of the responsible officer to comply with such a request.'

(3) In section 199 (unpaid work requirement)–

(a) in subsection (2) (minimum and maximum hours of unpaid work) for paragraph (b) substitute–
'(b) not more than 200.',
(b) omit subsections (3) and (4), and
(c) in subsection (5) for the words from the beginning to 'of them' substitute 'Where on the same occasion and in relation to the same person the court makes more than one enforcement order imposing an unpaid work requirement'.

(4) In section 200 (obligations of person subject to unpaid work requirement), for subsection (2) substitute–

'(2) Subject to paragraphs 7 and 9 of Schedule A1 to the Children Act 1989, the work required to be performed under an unpaid work requirement imposed by an enforcement order must be performed during a period of twelve months.

(2A) But the period of twelve months is not to run while the enforcement order is suspended under section 11J(9) of the Children Act 1989.'

(5) Section 217 (requirement to avoid conflict with religious beliefs, etc) is omitted.

(6) In section 218 (availability of arrangements in local area), subsection (1) (condition for imposition of unpaid work requirement) is omitted.

(7) Section 219 (provision of copies of relevant order) is omitted.

(8) The power of the Secretary of State to make rules under section 222 in relation to persons subject to relevant orders may also be exercised in relation to persons subject to enforcement orders.

(9) The power of the Secretary of State by order under section 223(1) to amend the provision mentioned in section 223(1)(a) includes power to amend this Part so as to make such modifications of Chapter 4 of Part 12 of the Criminal Justice Act 2003 as appear to the Secretary of State to be necessary or expedient in consequence of any amendment of the provision mentioned in section 223(1)(a).

Part 2

Revocation, Amendment or Breach of Enforcement Order

4 Power to revoke

(1) This paragraph applies where a court has made an enforcement order in respect of a person's failure to comply with a contact order and the enforcement order is in force.

(2) The court may revoke the enforcement order if it appears to the court that–

(a) in all the circumstances no enforcement order should have been made,
(b) having regard to circumstances which have arisen since the enforcement order was made, it would be appropriate for the enforcement order to be revoked, or
(c) having regard to the person's satisfactory compliance with the contact order or any contact order that has effect in its place, it would be appropriate for the enforcement order to be revoked.

(3) The enforcement order may be revoked by the court under sub-paragraph (2) of its own motion or on an application by the person subject to the enforcement order.

(4) In deciding whether to revoke the enforcement order under sub-paragraph (2)(b), the court is to take into account–

(a) the extent to which the person subject to the enforcement order has complied with it, and
(b) the likelihood that the person will comply with the contact order or any contact order that has effect in its place in the absence of an enforcement order.

(5) In deciding whether to revoke the enforcement order under sub-paragraph (2)(c), the court is to take into account the likelihood that the person will comply with the contact order or any contact order that has effect in its place in the absence of an enforcement order.

5 Amendment by reason of change of residence

(1) This paragraph applies where a court has made an enforcement order in respect of a person's failure to comply with a contact order and the enforcement order is in force.

(2) If the court is satisfied that the person has changed, or proposes to change, his residence from the local justice area specified in the order to another local justice area, the court may amend the order by substituting the other area for the area specified.

(3) The enforcement order may be amended by the court under sub-paragraph (2) of its own motion or on an application by the person subject to the enforcement order.

6 Amendment of hours specified under unpaid work requirement

(1) This paragraph applies where a court has made an enforcement order in respect of a person's failure to comply with a contact order and the enforcement order is in force.

(2) If it appears to the court that, having regard to circumstances that have arisen since the enforcement order was made, it would be appropriate to do so, the court may reduce the number of hours specified in the order (but not below the minimum specified in section 199(2)(a) of the Criminal Justice Act 2003).

(3) In amending the enforcement order under sub-paragraph (2), the court must be satisfied that the effect on the person of the enforcement order as proposed to be amended is no more than is required to secure his compliance with the contact order or any contact order that has effect in its place.

(4) The enforcement order may be amended by the court under sub-paragraph (2) of its own motion or on an application by the person subject to the enforcement order.

7 Amendment to extend unpaid work requirement

(1) This paragraph applies where a court has made an enforcement order in respect of a person's failure to comply with a contact order and the enforcement order is in force.

(2) If it appears to the court that, having regard to circumstances that have arisen since the enforcement order was made, it would be appropriate to do so, the court may, in relation to the order, extend the period of twelve months specified in section 200(2) of the Criminal Justice Act 2003 (as substituted by paragraph 3).

(3) The period may be extended by the court under sub-paragraph (2) of its own motion or on an application by the person subject to the enforcement order.

8 Warning and report following breach

(1) This paragraph applies where a court has made an enforcement order in respect of a person's failure to comply with a contact order.

(2) If the responsible officer is of the opinion that the person has failed without reasonable excuse to comply with the unpaid work requirement imposed by the enforcement order, the officer must give the person a warning under this paragraph unless–

(a)   the person has within the previous twelve months been given a warning under this paragraph in relation to a failure to comply with the unpaid work requirement, or
(b)   the responsible officer reports the failure to the appropriate person.

(3) A warning under this paragraph must–

(a)   describe the circumstances of the failure,
(b)   state that the failure is unacceptable, and
(c)   inform the person that, if within the next twelve months he again fails to comply with the unpaid work requirement, the warning and the subsequent failure will be reported to the appropriate person.

(4) The responsible officer must, as soon as practicable after the warning has been given, record that fact.

(5) If–

(a)   the responsible officer has given a warning under this paragraph to a person subject to an enforcement order, and

(b)   at any time within the twelve months beginning with the date on which the warning was given, the responsible officer is of the opinion that the person has since that date failed without reasonable excuse to comply with the unpaid work requirement imposed by the enforcement order,

the officer must report the failure to the appropriate person.

(6) A report under sub-paragraph (5) must include a report of the warning given to the person subject to the enforcement order.

(7) The appropriate person, in relation to an enforcement order, is the officer of the Service or the Welsh family proceedings officer who is required under section 11M to report on matters relating to the enforcement order.

(8) 'Responsible officer', in relation to a person subject to an enforcement order, has the same meaning as in section 197 of the Criminal Justice Act 2003 (as modified by paragraph 2).

9 Breach of an enforcement order

(1) This paragraph applies where a court has made an enforcement order ('the first order') in respect of a person's failure to comply with a contact order.

(2) If the court is satisfied beyond reasonable doubt that the person has failed to comply with the unpaid work requirement imposed by the first order, the court may–

(a)   amend the first order so as to make the requirement more onerous, or

(b)   make an enforcement order ('the second order') in relation to the person and (if the first order is still in force) provide for the second order to have effect either in addition to or in substitution for the first order.

(3) But the court may not exercise its powers under sub-paragraph (2) if it is satisfied that the person had a reasonable excuse for failing to comply with the unpaid work requirement imposed by the first order.

(4) The burden of proof as to the matter mentioned in sub-paragraph (3) lies on the person claiming to have had a reasonable excuse, and the standard of proof is the balance of probabilities.

(5) The court may exercise its powers under sub-paragraph (2) in relation to the first order only on the application of a person who would be able to apply under section 11J for an enforcement order if the failure to comply with the first order were a failure to comply with the contact order to which the first order relates.

(6) Where the person proposing to apply to the court is the child with respect to whom the contact order was made, subsections (6) and (7) of section 11J have effect in relation to the application as they have effect in relation to an application for an enforcement order.

(7) An application to the court to exercise its powers under sub-paragraph (2) may only be made while the first order is in force.

(8) The court may not exercise its powers under sub-paragraph (2) in respect of a failure by the person to comply with the unpaid work requirement imposed by the first order unless it is satisfied that before the failure occurred the person had been given (in accordance with rules of court) a copy of, or otherwise informed of the terms of, a notice under section 11N relating to the first order.

(9) In dealing with the person under sub-paragraph (2)(a), the court may–

(a) increase the number of hours specified in the first order (but not above the maximum specified in section 199(2)(b) of the Criminal Justice Act 2003, as substituted by paragraph 3);

(b) in relation to the order, extend the period of twelve months specified in section 200(2) of the Criminal Justice Act 2003 (as substituted by paragraph 3).

(10) In exercising its powers under sub-paragraph (2), the court must be satisfied that, taking into account the extent to which the person has complied with the unpaid work requirement imposed by the first order, the effect on the person of the proposed exercise of those powers–

(a) is no more than is required to secure his compliance with the contact order or any contact order that has effect in its place, and

(b) is no more than is proportionate to the seriousness of his failures to comply with the contact order and the first order.

(11) Where the court exercises its powers under sub-paragraph (2) by making an enforcement order in relation to a person who has failed to comply with another enforcement order–

(a) sections 11K(4), 11L(2) to (7), 11M and 11N have effect as regards the making of the order in relation to the person as they have effect as regards the making of an enforcement order in relation to a person who has failed to comply with a contact order;

(b) this Part of this Schedule has effect in relation to the order so made as if it were an enforcement order made in respect of the failure for which the other order was made.

(12) Sub-paragraph (2) is without prejudice to section 63(3) of the Magistrates' Courts Act 1980 as it applies in relation to enforcement orders.

10 Provision relating to amendment of enforcement orders

Sections 11L(2) to (7) and 11M have effect in relation to the making of an order under paragraph 6(2), 7(2) or 9(2)(a) amending an enforcement order as they have effect in relation to the making of an enforcement order; and references in sections 11L(2) to (7) and 11M to an enforcement order are to be read accordingly.'

Schedule 2

Minor and Consequential Amendments

Section 15

1 Domicile and Matrimonial Proceedings Act 1973 (c 45)

(1) In Schedule 1 to the Domicile and Matrimonial Proceedings Act 1973 (c 45) (staying of matrimonial proceedings: England and Wales), paragraph 11 (effect of staying matrimonial proceedings on court's power to make certain orders) is amended as follows.

(2) After sub-paragraph (4) insert–

'(4A) Sub-paragraph (4B) applies where–

(a)   proceedings are stayed as described in sub-paragraph (1) or (4), and
(b)   at the time when the stay is imposed, a contact order (within the meaning of the Children Act 1989) made in connection with the stayed proceedings is in force.

(4B) While the stay applies to the proceedings, the court may not–

(a)   make an enforcement order (within the meaning of the Children Act 1989) in relation to the contact order, or
(b)   as regards an enforcement order already made in relation to the contact order, exercise its powers under paragraph 9(2) of Schedule A1 to the Children Act 1989 in relation to the enforcement order.'

(3) In sub-paragraph (5) (certain powers of court not affected) at the beginning insert 'Except as provided in sub-paragraph (4B),'.

Family Law Act 1986 (c 55)

2

The Family Law Act 1986 (c 55) is amended as follows.

3

(1) Section 5 (power of court to refuse application or stay proceedings) is amended as follows.

(2) After subsection (2) (stay where more appropriate for matters to be determined in proceedings outside England and Wales) insert–

'(2A) If the proceedings on the application are proceedings in which a contact activity direction has been made under section 11A of the Children Act 1989 (or an enforcement order has been made under section 11J of that Act), the court may when granting a stay under or by virtue of subsection (2) also suspend the contact activity direction (or the enforcement order).'

(3) After subsection (3A) (removal of stay granted under Article 15) insert–

'(3B) If the stay removed under subsection (3) or (3A) is a stay in relation to which the court suspended a contact activity direction made under section 11A of the Children Act 1989 (or an enforcement order made under section 11J of that Act), the court may when removing the stay under subsection (3) or (3A) also bring the suspension to an end.'

4

In section 29 (enforcement), in subsection (1) after 'enforcing the order' insert '(including, where an order with respect to contact is registered in England and Wales, the powers under section 11O of the Children Act 1989)'.

5

In section 30 (staying or sisting of enforcement proceedings), after subsection (1) insert–

'(1A)   No application may be made under subsection (1) for proceedings to be stayed or sisted if the proceedings are proceedings on an application for an order under section 11O(2) of the Children Act 1989.'

6

In section 31 (dismissal of enforcement proceedings), after subsection (1) insert–

'(1A)   No application may be made under subsection (1) for proceedings to be dismissed if the proceedings are proceedings on an application for an order under section 11O(2) of the Children Act 1989.'

Children Act 1989 (c 41)

7

The Children Act 1989 (c 41) is amended as follows.

8

In section 14B (making of special guardianship orders), in subsection (1)–

(a)   omit the 'and' at the end of paragraph (a), and
(b)   after paragraph (b) insert–
'(c)   where a contact order made with respect to the child is not discharged, any enforcement order relating to that contact order should be revoked, and
(d)   where a contact activity direction has been made as regards contact with the child and is in force, that contact activity direction should be discharged.'

9

In section 91 (effect and duration of orders etc) after subsection (2) insert–

'(2A) Where a contact activity direction has been made as regards contact with a child, the making of a care order with respect to the child discharges the direction.'

10

In section 104 (regulations and orders)–

(a)   in subsection (1) for 'or the Secretary of State' substitute ', the Secretary of State or the National Assembly for Wales';
(b)   after subsection (2) insert–

'(2A) Subsection (2) does not apply to a statutory instrument made solely by the National Assembly for Wales.'

11

In section 105 (interpretation), in subsection (1) at the appropriate place insert–

"contact activity condition' has the meaning given by section 11C;';

"contact activity direction' has the meaning given by section 11A;';

"enforcement order' has the meaning given by section 11J;'.

Family Law Act 1996 (c 27)

12

(1) Schedule 3 to the Family Law Act 1996 (c 27) (stay of proceedings: amendments of Schedule 1 to the Domicile and Matrimonial Proceedings Act 1973 (c 45)) is amended as follows.

(2) In paragraph 9 (amendments of paragraph 11 of Schedule 1) after sub-paragraph (6) insert–

'(6A) In sub-paragraph (4A)(a) for 'sub-paragraph (1) or (4)' substitute 'sub-paragraph (1)'.'

Adoption and Children Act 2002 (c 38)

13

The Adoption and Children Act 2002 (c 38) is amended as follows.

14

(1) Section 26 (effect on contact of placing a child for adoption) is amended as follows.

(2) In subsection (1), after 'have effect' insert 'and any contact activity direction relating to contact with the child is discharged'.

(3) In subsection (6), after 'In this section,' insert "contact activity direction' has the meaning given by section 11A of the 1989 Act and'.

Schedule 3

Repeals

Section 15

Short title and chapter	Extent of repeal
Children Act 1989 (c 41)	In section 14B(1), the word 'and' at the end of paragraph (a).
	Section 16(3)(a).

CRIMINAL JUSTICE ACT 2003

PART 12

SENTENCING

Chapter 4

Further Provisions about Orders under Chapters 2 and 3

Introductory

197 Meaning of 'the responsible officer'

(1) For the purposes of this Part, 'the responsible officer', in relation to an offender to whom a relevant order relates, means–

(a) in a case where the order–
    (i) imposes a curfew requirement or an exclusion requirement but no other requirement mentioned in section 177(1) or, as the case requires, section 182(1) or 190(1), and
    (ii) imposes an electronic monitoring requirement,

the person who under section 215(3) is responsible for the electronic monitoring required by the order;

(b)　in a case where the offender is aged 18 or over and the only requirement imposed by the order is an attendance centre requirement, the officer in charge of the attendance centre in question;

(c)　in any other case, the qualifying officer who, as respects the offender, is for the time being responsible for discharging the functions conferred by this Part on the responsible officer.

(2) The following are qualifying officers for the purposes of subsection (1)(c)–

(a)　in a case where the offender is aged under 18 at the time when the relevant order is made, an officer of a local probation board appointed for or assigned to the [local justice area][1] for the time being specified in the order or a member of a youth offending team established by a local authority for the time being specified in the order;

(b)　in any other case, an officer of a local probation board appointed for or assigned to the [local justice area][2] for the time being specified in the order.

(3) The Secretary of State may by order–

(a)　amend subsections (1) and (2), and

(b)　make any other amendments of this Part that appear to him to be necessary or expedient in consequence of any amendment made by virtue of paragraph (a).

(4) An order under subsection (3) may, in particular, provide for the court to determine which of two or more descriptions of 'responsible officer' is to apply in relation to any relevant order.

Amendments—SI 2005/886.

198 Duties of responsible officer

(1) Where a relevant order has effect, it is the duty of the responsible officer–

(a)　to make any arrangements that are necessary in connection with the requirements imposed by the order,

(b)　to promote the offender's compliance with those requirements, and

(c)　where appropriate, to take steps to enforce those requirements.

(2) In this section 'responsible officer' does not include a person falling within section 197(1)(a).

Requirements available in case of all offenders

199 Unpaid work requirement

(1) In this Part 'unpaid work requirement', in relation to a relevant order, means a requirement that the offender must perform unpaid work in accordance with section 200.

1　Amendment: Words substituted: SI 2005/886, art 2, Sch, para 102, with effect from 1 April 2005.

2　Amendment: Words substituted: SI 2005/886, art 2, Sch, para 102, with effect from 1 April 2005.

(2) The number of hours which a person may be required to work under an unpaid work requirement must be specified in the relevant order and must be in the aggregate–

(a)   not less than 40, and

(b)   not more than 300.

(3) A court may not impose an unpaid work requirement in respect of an offender unless after hearing (if the courts thinks necessary) an appropriate officer, the court is satisfied that the offender is a suitable person to perform work under such a requirement.

(4) In subsection (3) 'an appropriate officer' means–

(a)   in the case of an offender aged 18 or over, an officer of a local probation board, and

(b)   in the case of an offender aged under 18, an officer of a local probation board, a social worker of a local authority ... [3]or a member of a youth offending team.

(5) Where the court makes relevant orders in respect of two or more offences of which the offender has been convicted on the same occasion and includes unpaid work requirements in each of them, the court may direct that the hours of work specified in any of those requirements is to be concurrent with or additional to those specified in any other of those orders, but so that the total number of hours which are not concurrent does not exceed the maximum specified in subsection (2)(b).

   Amendments—Children Act 2004, s 64, Sch 5, Pt

200 Obligations of person subject to unpaid work requirement

(1) An offender in respect of whom an unpaid work requirement of a relevant order is in force must perform for the number of hours specified in the order such work at such times as he may be instructed by the responsible officer.

(2) Subject to paragraph 20 of Schedule 8 and paragraph 18 of Schedule 12 (power to extend order), the work required to be performed under an unpaid work requirement of a community order or a suspended sentence order must be performed during a period of twelve months.

(3) Unless revoked, a community order imposing an unpaid work requirement remains in force until the offender has worked under it for the number of hours specified in it.

(4) Where an unpaid work requirement is imposed by a suspended sentence order, the supervision period as defined by section 189(1)(a) continues until the

---

3   Amendment: Words repealed: Children Act 2004, s 64, Sch 5, Pt 4, with effect, in relation to England, from 1 April 2005 (SI 2005/394), in relation to Wales, from 1 April 2006 (SI 2006/885).

offender has worked under the order for the number of hours specified in the order, but does not continue beyond the end of the operational period as defined by section 189(1)(b)(ii).

Provisions applying to relevant orders generally

220 Duty of offender to keep in touch with responsible officer

(1) An offender in respect of whom a community order or a suspended sentence order is in force–

(a)   must keep in touch with the responsible officer in accordance with such instructions as he may from time to time be given by that officer, and

(b)   must notify him of any change of address.

(2) The obligation imposed by subsection (1) is enforceable as if it were a requirement imposed by the order.

Powers of Secretary of State

222 Rules

(1) The Secretary of State may make rules for regulating–

(a)   the supervision of persons who are subject to relevant orders,

(b)   without prejudice to the generality of paragraph (a), the functions of responsible officers in relation to offenders subject to relevant orders,

(c)   the arrangements to be made by local probation boards for persons subject to unpaid work requirements to perform work and the performance of such work,

(d)   the provision and carrying on of attendance centres and community rehabilitation centres,

(e)   the attendance of persons subject to activity requirements or attendance centre requirements at the places at which they are required to attend, including hours of attendance, reckoning days of attendance and the keeping of attendance records,

(f)   electronic monitoring in pursuance of an electronic monitoring requirement, and

(g)   without prejudice to the generality of paragraph (f), the functions of persons made responsible for securing electronic monitoring in pursuance of such a requirement.

(2) Rules under subsection (1)(c) may, in particular, make provision–

(a)   limiting the number of hours of work to be done by a person on any one day,

(b)   as to the reckoning of hours worked and the keeping of work records, and

(c)   for the payment of travelling and other expenses in connection with the performance of work.

223 Power to amend limits

(1) The Secretary of State may by order amend–

(a)   subsection (2) of section 199 (unpaid work requirement), or
(b)   subsection (2) of section 204 (curfew requirement),

by substituting, for the maximum number of hours for the time being specified in that subsection, such other number of hours as may be specified in the order.

(2) The Secretary of State may by order amend any of the provisions mentioned in subsection (3) by substituting, for any period for the time being specified in the provision, such other period as may be specified in the order.

(3) Those provisions are–

(a)   section 204(3) (curfew requirement);
(b)   section 205(2) (exclusion requirement);
(c)   section 209(3) (drug rehabilitation requirement);
(d)   section 212(4) (alcohol treatment requirement).

Appendix 3

HUMAN RIGHTS ACT 1998

(1998 c 42)

INTRODUCTION

1 The Convention Rights

(1) In this Act, 'the Convention rights' means the rights and fundamental freedoms set out in –

(a)   Articles 2 to 12 and 14 of the Convention, and
(b)   Articles 1 to 3 of the First Protocol, and
(c)   [Article 1 of the Thirteenth Protocol]¹,

as read with Articles 16 to 18 of the Convention.

(2) Those Articles are to have effect for the purposes of this Act subject to any designated derogation or reservation (as to which see sections 14 and 15).

(3) The Articles are set out in Schedule 1.

(4) The [Secretary of State]² may by order make such amendments to this Act as he considers appropriate to reflect the effect, in relation to the United Kingdom, of a protocol.

(5) In subsection (4) 'protocol' means a protocol to the Convention –

(a)   which the United Kingdom has ratified; or
(b)   which the United Kingdom has signed with a view to ratification.

(6) No amendment may be made by an order under subsection (4) so as to come into force before the protocol concerned is in force in relation to the United Kingdom.

Amendments: SI 2003/1887; SI 2004/1574.

---

1   Amendment: Words substituted; Human Rights Act 1998 (Amendment) Order 2004, SI 2004/1574, art 2(1), with effect from 22 June 2004, SI 2004/1574, art 1.

2   Amendment: Words substituted by; Secretary of State for Constitutional Affairs Order 2003; SI 2003/1887, art 9, Sch 2, para 10(1), with effect from 19 August 2003: see SI 2003/1887, art 1(2).

2 Interpretation of Convention rights

(1) A court or tribunal determining a question which has arisen under this Act in connection with a Convention right must take into account any –

(a)   judgment, decision, declaration or advisory opinion of the European Court of Human Rights,

(b)   opinion of the Commission given in a report adopted under Article 31 of the Convention,

(c)   decision of the Commission in connection with Article 26 or 27(2) of the Convention, or

(d)   decision of the Committee of Ministers taken under Article 46 of the Convention,

whenever made or given, so far as, in the opinion of the court or tribunal, it is relevant to the proceedings in which that question has arisen.

(2) Evidence of any judgment, decision, declaration or opinion of which account may have to be taken under this section is to be given in proceedings before any court or tribunal in such manner as may be provided by rules.

(3) In this section 'rules' means rules of court or, in the case of proceedings before a tribunal, rules made for the purposes of this section –

(a)   by ...³ [the Lord Chancellor or]⁴ the Secretary of State, in relation to any proceedings outside Scotland;

(b)   by the Secretary of State, in relation to proceedings in Scotland; or

(c)   by a Northern Ireland department, in relation to proceedings before a tribunal in Northern Ireland-
        (i) which deals with transferred matters; and
        (ii) for which no rules made under paragraph (a) are in force.

Amendments: SI 2003/1887; SI 2005/3429.

LEGISLATION

3 Interpretation of legislation

(1) So far as it is possible to do so, primary legislation and subordinate legislation must be read and given effect in a way which is compatible with the Convention rights.

(2) This section –

(a)   applies to primary legislation and subordinate legislation whenever enacted;

---

3   Amendment: Words repealed; Secretary of State for Constitutional Affairs Order 2003; SI 2003/1887, art 9, Sch 2, para 10(2), with effect from 19 August 2003; SI 2003/1887, art 1(2).

4   Amendment: Words inserted; Transfer of Functions (Lord Chancellor and Secretary of State) Order 2005, SI 2005/3429, art 8, Schedule, para 3, with effect from 12 January 2006, SI 2005/3429, art 1(2).

(b)   does not affect the validity, continuing operation or enforcement of any incompatible primary legislation; and

(c)   does not affect the validity, continuing operation or enforcement of any incompatible subordinate legislation if (disregarding any possibility of revocation) primary legislation prevents removal of the incompatibility.

4 Declaration of incompatibility

(1) Subsection (2) applies in any proceedings in which a court determines whether a provision of primary legislation is compatible with a Convention right.

(2) If the court is satisfied that the provision is incompatible with a Convention right, it may make a declaration of that incompatibility.

(3) Subsection (4) applies in any proceedings in which a court determines whether a provision of subordinate legislation, made in the exercise of a power conferred by primary legislation, is compatible with a Convention right.

(4) If the court is satisfied –

(a)   that the provision is incompatible with a Convention right, and

(b)   that (disregarding any possibility of revocation) the primary legislation concerned prevents removal of the incompatibility,

it may make a declaration of that incompatibility.

(5) In this section 'court' means –

[(a)   the House of Lords;][5]
(b)   the Judicial Committee of the Privy Council;
(c)   the Courts-Martial Appeal Court;
(d)   in Scotland, the High Court of Justiciary sitting otherwise than as a trial court or the Court of Session;
(e)   in England and Wales or Northern Ireland, the High Court or the Court of Appeal.
[-][6]

(6) A declaration under this section ('a declaration of incompatibility') –

(a)   does not affect the validity, continuing operation or enforcement of the provision in respect of which it is given; and

(b)   is not binding on the parties to the proceedings in which it is made.

Prospective amendments: Constitutional Reform Act 2005, s 40(4), Sch 9, Pt 1, para 66(1), (2); Mental Capacity Act 2005, s 67(1), Sch 6, para 43.

---

5   Prospective amendment: Words prospectively substituted; by Constitutional Reform Act 2005, s 40(4), Sch 9, Pt 1, para 66(1), (2), with effect from a date to be appointed; Constitutional Reform Act 2005, s 148(1).New text = "(a) the Supreme Court;".

6   Prospective amendment: sub-paragraph inserted by Mental Capacity Act 2005, s 67(1), Sch 6, para 43, with effect from a date to be appointed; Mental Capacity Act 2005, s 68(1).New text = "(f) the Court of Protection, in any matter being dealt with by the President of the Family Division, the Vice-Chancellor or a puisne judge of the High Court.".

5 *Right of Crown to intervene*

(1) Where a court is considering whether to make a declaration of incompatibility, the Crown is entitled to notice in accordance with rules of court.

(2) In any case to which subsection (1) applies –

(a)   a Minister of the Crown, or
(b)   a member of the Scottish Executive,
(c)   a Northern Ireland Minister,
(d)   a Northern Ireland department,

is entitled, on an application made to the court in accordance with rules of court, to be joined as a party to the proceedings.

(3) An application under subsection (2) may be made at any time during the proceedings.

(4) A person who has been made a party to criminal proceedings (other than in Scotland) as the result of an application under subsection (2) may, with leave, appeal to the [House of Lords][7] against any declaration of incompatibility made in the proceedings.

(5) In subsection (4) –

'criminal proceedings' includes all proceedings before the Courts-Martial Appeal Court; and
'leave' means leave granted by the court making the declaration of incompatibility or by the [House of Lords][8].

> **Prospective amendments:** Constitutional Reform Act 2005, s 40(4), Sch 9, Pt 1, para 66(1), (3).

PUBLIC AUTHORITIES

6 *Acts of public authorities*

(1) It is unlawful for a public authority to act in a way which is incompatible with a Convention right.

(2) Subsection (1) does not apply to an act if –

(a)   as the result of one or more provisions of primary legislation, the authority could not have acted differently; or

---

7   Prospective amendment: Words prospectively substituted by Constitutional Reform Act 2005, s 40(4), Sch 9, Pt 1, para 66(1), (3), with effect from a date to be appointed; Constitutional Reform Act 2005, s 148(1).New text = "Supreme Court".
8   Prospective amendment: Words prospectively substituted by Constitutional Reform Act 2005, s 40(4), Sch 9, Pt 1, para 66(1), (3), with effect from a date to be appointed; Constitutional Reform Act 2005, s 148(1).New text = "Supreme Court".

(b)　in the case of one or more provisions of, or made under, primary legislation which cannot be read or given effect in a way which is compatible with the Convention rights, the authority was acting so as to give effect to or enforce those provisions.

(3) In this section, 'public authority' includes –

(a)　a court or tribunal, and
(b)　any person certain of whose functions are functions of a public nature,

but does not include either House of Parliament or a person exercising functions in connection with proceedings in Parliament.

(4) [In subsection (3) 'Parliament' does not include the House of Lords in its judicial capacity.][9]

(5) In relation to a particular act, a person is not a public authority by virtue only of subsection (3)(b) if the nature of the act is private.

(6) 'An act' includes a failure to act but does not include a failure to –

(a)　introduce in, or lay before, Parliament a proposal for legislation; or
(b)　make any primary legislation or remedial order.

Prospective amendments—Constitutional Reform Act 2005, ss 40(4), 146, Sch 9, Pt 1, para 66(1), (4), Sch 18, Pt 5.

7 Proceedings

(1) A person who claims that a public authority has acted (or proposes to act) in a way which is made unlawful by section 6(1) may –

(a)　bring proceedings against the authority under this Act in the appropriate court or tribunal, or
(b)　rely on the Convention right or rights concerned in any legal proceedings,

but only if he is (or would be) a victim of the unlawful act.

(2) In subsection (1)(a) 'appropriate court or tribunal' means such court or tribunal as may be determined in accordance with rules; and proceedings against an authority includes a counterclaim or similar proceeding.

(3) If the proceedings are brought on an application for judicial review, the applicant is to be taken to have a sufficient interest in relation to the unlawful act only if he is, or would be, a victim of that act.

(4) If the proceedings are made by way of a petition for judicial review in Scotland, the applicant shall be taken to have title and interest to sue in relation to the unlawful act only if he is, or would be, a victim of that act.

9　Prospective amendment: Sub-paragraph prospectively repealed by Constitutional Reform Act 2005, ss 40(4), 146, Sch 9, Pt 1, para 66(1), (4), Sch 18, Pt 5, with effect from a date to be appointed; Constitutional Reform Act 2005, s 148(1).

(5) Proceedings under subsection (1)(a) must be brought before the end of –

(a)   the period of one year beginning with the date on which the act complained of took place; or

(b)   such longer period as the court or tribunal considers equitable having regard to all the circumstances,

but that is subject to any rule imposing a stricter time limit in relation to the procedure in question.

(6) In subsection (1)(b) 'legal proceedings' includes –

(a)   proceedings brought by or at the instigation of a public authority; and

(b)   an appeal against the decision of a court or tribunal.

(7) For the purposes of this section, a person is a victim of an unlawful act only if he would be a victim for the purposes of Article 34 of the Convention if proceedings were brought in the European Court of Human Rights in respect of that act.

(8) Nothing in this Act creates a criminal offence.

(9) In this section 'rules' means –

(a)   in relation to proceedings before a court or tribunal outside Scotland, rules made by ...[10] [the Lord Chancellor] [11]the Secretary of State for the purposes of this section or rules of court,

(b)   in relation to proceedings before a court or tribunal in Scotland, rules made by the Secretary of State for those purposes,

(c)   in relation to proceedings before a tribunal in Northern Ireland –

  (i) which deals with transferred matters; and

  (ii) for which no rules made under paragraph (a) are in force,

rules made by a Northern Ireland department for those purposes,

and includes provision made by order under section 1 of the Courts and Legal Services Act 1990.

(10) In making rules regard must be had to section 9.

(11) The Minister who has power to make rules in relation to a particular tribunal may, to the extent he considers it necessary to ensure that the tribunal can provide an appropriate remedy in relation to an act (or proposed act) of a public authority which is (or would be) unlawful as a result of section 6(1), by order add to –

(a)   the relief or remedies which the tribunal may grant; or

(b)   the grounds on which it may grant any of them.

---

10   Amendment: Words repealed; Secretary of State for Constitutional Affairs Order 2003; SI 2003/1887, art 9, Sch 2, para 10(2), with effect from 19 August 2003; SI 2003/1887, art 1(2).

11   Amendment: Words; inserted; Transfer of Functions (Lord Chancellor and Secretary of State) Order 2005, SI 2005/3429, art 8, Schedule, para 3, with effect from 12 January 2006; SI 2005/3429, art 1(2).

(12) An order made under subsection (11) may contain such incidental, supplemental, consequential or transitional provision as the Minister making it considers appropriate.

(13) 'The Minister' includes the Northern Ireland department concerned.

Amendments: SI 2003/1887; SI 2005/3429.

8 *Judicial remedies*

(1) In relation to any act (or proposed act) of a public authority which the court finds is (or would be) unlawful, it may grant such relief or remedy, or make such order, within its jurisdiction as it considers just and appropriate.

(2) But damages may be awarded only by a court which has power to award damages, or to order the payment of compensation, in civil proceedings.

(3) No award of damages is to be made unless, taking account of all the circumstances of the case, including –

(a)   any other relief or remedy granted, or order made, in relation to the act in question (by that or any other court), and

(b)   the consequences of any decision (of that or any other court) in respect of that act,

the court is satisfied that the award is necessary to afford just satisfaction to the person in whose favour it is made.

(4) In determining –

(a)   whether to award damages, or

(b)   the amount of an award,

the court must take into account the principles applied by the European Court of Human Rights in relation to the award of compensation under Article 41 of the Convention.

(5) A public authority against which damages are awarded is to be treated –

(a)   in Scotland, for the purposes of section 3 of the Law Reform (Miscellaneous Provisions) (Scotland) Act 1940 as if the award were made in an action of damages in which the authority has been found liable in respect of loss or damage to the person to whom the award is made;

(b)   for the purposes of the Civil Liability (Contribution) Act 1978 as liable in respect of damage suffered by the person to whom the award is made.

(6) In this section –

'court' includes a tribunal;
'damages' means damages for an unlawful act of a public authority; and
'unlawful' means unlawful under section 6(1).

9 Judicial acts

(1) Proceedings under section 7(1)(a) in respect of a judicial act may be brought only –

(a) by exercising a right of appeal;
(b) on an application (in Scotland a petition) for judicial review; or
(c) in such other forum as may be prescribed by rules.

(2) That does not affect any rule of law which prevents a court from being the subject of judicial review.

(3) In proceedings under this Act in respect of a judicial act done in good faith, damages may not be awarded otherwise than to compensate a person to the extent required by Article 5(5) of the Convention.

(4) An award of damages permitted by subsection (3) is to be made against the Crown; but no award may be made unless the appropriate person, if not a party to the proceedings, is joined.

(5) In this section –

'appropriate person' means the Minister responsible for the court concerned, or a person or government department nominated by him;
'court' includes a tribunal;
'judge' includes a member of a tribunal, a justice of the peace [(or, in Northern Ireland, a lay magistrate)][12]and a clerk or other officer entitled to exercise the jurisdiction of a court;
'judicial act' means a judicial act of a court and includes an act done on the instructions, or on behalf, of a judge;
'rules' has the same meaning as in section 7(9).

   Amendments: Justice (Northern Ireland) Act 2002, s 10(6), Sch 4, para 39.

REMEDIAL ACTION

10 Power to take remedial action

(1) This section applies if –

(a) a provision of legislation has been declared under section 4 to be incompatible with a Convention right and, if an appeal lies –
   (i) all persons who may appeal have stated that they do not intend to do so;
   (ii) the time for bringing an appeal has expired and no appeal has been brought within that time; or
   (iii) an appeal brought within that time has been determined or abandoned; or

---

12   Amendment: Words inserted by Justice (Northern Ireland) Act 2002, s 10(6), Sch 4, para 39, with effect from 1 April 2005; Justice (Northern Ireland) Act 2002 (Commencement No 8) Order 2005, SR 2005/109, art 2, Schedule.

(b)   it appears to a Minister of the Crown or Her Majesty in Council that, having regard to a finding of the European Court of Human Rights made after the coming into force of this section in proceedings against the United Kingdom, a provision of legislation is incompatible with an obligation of the United Kingdom arising from the Convention.

(2) If a Minister of the Crown considers that there are compelling reasons for proceeding under this section, he may by order make such amendments to the legislation as he considers necessary to remove the incompatibility.

(3) If, in the case of subordinate legislation, a Minister of the Crown considers –

(a)   that it is necessary to amend the primary legislation under which the subordinate legislation in question was made, in order to enable the incompatibility to be removed, and
(b)   that there are compelling reasons for proceeding under this section,

he may by order make such amendments to the primary legislation as he considers appropriate.

(4) This section also applies where the provision in question is in subordinate legislation and has been quashed, or declared invalid, by reason of incompatibility with a Convention right and the Minister proposes to proceed under paragraph 2(b) of Schedule 2.

(5) If the legislation is an Order in Council, the power conferred by subsection (2) or (3) is exercisable by Her Majesty in Council.

(6) In this section 'legislation' does not include a Measure of the Church Assembly or of the General Synod of the Church of England.

(7) Schedule 2 makes further provision about remedial orders.

OTHER RIGHTS AND PROCEEDINGS

11 Safeguard for existing human rights

A person's reliance on a Convention right does not restrict –

(a)   any other right or freedom conferred on him by or under any law having effect in any part of the United Kingdom, or
(b)   his right to make any claim or bring any proceedings which he could make or bring apart from sections 7 to 9.

12 Freedom of expression

(1) This section applies if a court is considering whether to grant any relief which, if granted, might affect the exercise of the Convention right to freedom of expression.

(2) If the person against whom the application for relief is made ('the respondent') is neither present nor represented, no such relief is to be granted unless the court is satisfied –

(a)   that the applicant has taken all practicable steps to notify the respondent; or

(b)   that there are compelling reasons why the respondent should not be notified.

(3) No such relief is to be granted so as to restrain publication before trial unless the court is satisfied that the applicant is likely to establish that publication should not be allowed.

(4) The court must have particular regard to the importance of the Convention right to freedom of expression and, where the proceedings relate to material which the respondent claims, or which appears to the court, to be journalistic, literary or artistic material (or to conduct connected with such material), to –

(a)   the extent to which –
    (i) the material has, or is about to, become available to the public; or
    (ii) it is, or would be, in the public interest for the material to be published;

(b)   any relevant privacy code.

(5) In this section –

'court' includes a tribunal; and
'relief' includes any remedy or order (other than in criminal proceedings).

13 Freedom of thought, conscience and religion

(1) If a court's determination of any question arising under this Act might affect the exercise by a religious organisation (itself or its members collectively) of the Convention right to freedom of thought, conscience and religion, it must have particular regard to the importance of that right.

(2) In this section 'court' includes a tribunal.

DEROGATIONS AND RESERVATIONS

14 Derogations

(1) In this Act, 'designated derogation' means –

...[13]

---

[13]   Amendment: Words repealed; Human Rights Act (Amendment) Order 2001; SI 2001/1216, art 2(a), with effect from 1 April 2001; SI 2001/1216, art 1.

any derogation by the United Kingdom from an Article of the Convention, or of any protocol to the Convention, which is designated for the purposes of this Act in an order made by the [Secretary of State][14].

(2) ...[15]

(3) If a designated derogation is amended or replaced it ceases to be a designated derogation.

(4) But subsection (3) does not prevent the [Secretary of State][16] from exercising his power under subsection (1)...[17] to make a fresh designation order in respect of the Article concerned.

(5) The [Secretary of State][18] must by order make such amendments to Schedule 3 as he considers appropriate to reflect –

(a) any designation order; or
(b) the effect of subsection (3).

(6) A designation order may be made in anticipation of the making by the United Kingdom of a proposed derogation.

Amendments: SI 2001/1216; SI 2003/1887.

15 Reservations

(1) In this Act, 'designated reservation' means –

(a) the United Kingdom's reservation to Article 2 of the First Protocol to the Convention; and
(b) any other reservation by the United Kingdom to an Article of the Convention, or of any protocol to the Convention, which is designated for the purposes of this Act in an order made by the [Secretary of State][19].

(2) The text of the reservation referred to in subsection (1)(a) is set out in Part II of Schedule 3.

(3) If a designated reservation is withdrawn wholly or in part it ceases to be a designated reservation.

---

14 Amendment: Words substituted; Secretary of State for Constitutional Affairs Order 2003; SI 2003/1887, art 9, Sch 2, para 10(1), with effect from 19 August 2003; SI 2003/1887, art 1(2).
15 Amendment: Sub-section repealed; Human Rights Act (Amendment) Order 2001; SI 2001/1216, art 2(b), with effect from 1 April 2001; SI 2001/1216, art 1.
16 Amendment: Words substituted; Secretary of State for Constitutional Affairs Order 2003; SI 2003/1887, art 9, Sch 2, para 10(1), with effect from 19 August 2003; SI 2003/1887, art 1(2).
17 Amendment: Reference repealed; Human Rights Act (Amendment) Order 2001; SI 2001/1216, art 2(c), with effect from 1 April 2001; SI 2001/1216, art 1.
18 Amendment: Words substituted; Secretary of State for Constitutional Affairs Order 2003; SI 2003/1887, art 9, Sch 2, para 10(1), with effect from 19 August 2003; SI 2003/1887, art 1(2).
19 Amendment: Words substituted; Secretary of State for Constitutional Affairs Order 2003; SI 2003/1887, art 9, Sch 2, para 10(1), with effect from 19 August 2003; SI 2003/1887, art 1(2).

(4) But subsection (3) does not prevent the [Secretary of State][20] from exercising his power under subsection (1)(b) to make a fresh designation order in respect of the Article concerned.

(5) The [Secretary of State][21] must by order make such amendments to this Act as he considers appropriate to reflect –

(a)   any designation order; or
(b)   the effect of subsection (3).

   Amendments: SI 2003/1887.

16 Period for which designated derogations have effect

(1) If it has not already been withdrawn by the United Kingdom, a designated derogation ceases to have effect for the purposes of this Act –

...[22]

at the end of the period of five years beginning with the date on which the order designating it was made.

(2) At any time before the period –

(a)   fixed by subsection (1)...[23], or
(b)   extended by an order under this subsection,

comes to an end, the [Secretary of State][24] may by order extend it by a further period of five years.

(3) An order under section 14(1)...[25] ceases to have effect at the end of the period for consideration, unless a resolution has been passed by each House approving the order.

(4) Subsection (3) does not affect –

(a)   anything done in reliance on the order; or
(b)   the power to make a fresh order under section 14(1)...[26].

(5) In subsection (3) 'period for consideration' means the period of forty days beginning with the day on which the order was made.

---

20   Amendment: Words substituted; Secretary of State for Constitutional Affairs Order 2003; SI 2003/1887, art 9, Sch 2, para 10(1), with effect from 19 August 2003; SI 2003/1887, art 1(2).
21   Amendment: Words substituted; Secretary of State for Constitutional Affairs Order 2003; SI 2003/1887, art 9, Sch 2, para 10(1), with effect from 19 August 2003; SI 2003/1887, art 1(2).
22   Amendment: Words repealed; Human Rights Act (Amendment) Order 2001; SI 2001/1216, art 3(a), with effect from 1 April 2001; SI 2001/1216, art 1.
23   Amendment: Words repealed; Human Rights Act (Amendment) Order 2001; SI 2001/1216, art 3(b), with effect from 1 April 2001; SI 2001/1216, art 1.
24   Amendment: Words substituted; Secretary of State for Constitutional Affairs Order 2003; SI 2003/1887, art 9, Sch 2, para 10(1), with effect from 19 August 2003; SI 2003/1887, art 1(2).
25   Amendment: reference repealed; Human Rights Act (Amendment) Order 2001; SI 2001/1216, art 3(c), with effect from 1 April 2001; SI 2001/1216, art 1.
26   Amendment: reference repealed; Human Rights Act (Amendment) Order 2001; SI 2001/1216, art 3(d), with effect from 1 April 2001; SI 2001/1216, art 1.

(6) In calculating the period for consideration, no account is to be taken of any time during which –

(a)   Parliament is dissolved or prorogued; or
(b)   both Houses are adjourned for more than four days.

(7) If a designated derogation is withdrawn by the United Kingdom, the [Secretary of State][27] must by order make such amendments to this Act as he considers are required to reflect that withdrawal.

Amendments: SI 2001/1216; SI 2003/1887.

17 Periodic review of designated reservations

(1) The appropriate Minister must review the designated reservation referred to in section 15(1)(a) –

(a)   before the end of the period of five years beginning with the date on which section 1(2) came into force; and
(b)   if that designation is still in force, before the end of the period of five years beginning with the date on which the last report relating to it was laid under subsection (3).

(2) The appropriate Minister must review each of the other designated reservations (if any) –

(a)   before the end of the period of five years beginning with the date on which the order designating the reservation first came into force; and
(b)   if the designation is still in force, before the end of the period of five years beginning with the date on which the last report relating to it was laid under subsection (3).

(3) The Minister conducting a review under this section must prepare a report on the result of the review and lay a copy of it before each House of Parliament.

JUDGES OF THE EUROPEAN COURT OF HUMAN RIGHTS

18 Appointment to European Court of Human Rights

(1) In this section 'judicial office' means the office of –

(a)   Lord Justice of Appeal, Justice of the High Court or Circuit judge, in England and Wales;
(b)   judge of the Court of Session or sheriff, in Scotland;
(c)   Lord Justice of Appeal, judge of the High Court or county court judge, in Northern Ireland.

---

27   Amendment: Words substituted; Secretary of State for Constitutional Affairs Order 2003; SI 2003/1887, art 9, Sch 2, para 10(1), with effect from 19 August 2003, SI 2003/1887, art 1(2).

(2) The holder of a judicial office may become a judge of the European Court of Human Rights ('the Court') without being required to relinquish his office.

(3) But he is not required to perform the duties of his judicial office while he is a judge of the Court.

(4) In respect of any period during which he is a judge of the Court –

(a) a Lord Justice of Appeal or Justice of the High Court is not to count as a judge of the relevant court for the purposes of section 2(1) or 4(1) of the [Supreme Court Act 1981][28] (maximum number of judges) nor as a judge of the [Supreme Court][29] for the purposes of section 12(1) to (6) of that Act (salaries etc);

(b) a judge of the Court of Session is not to count as a judge of that court for the purposes of section 1(1) of the Court of Session Act 1988 (maximum number of judges) or of section 9(1)(c) of the Administration of Justice Act 1973 ('the 1973 Act') (salaries etc);

(c) a Lord Justice of Appeal or a judge of the High Court in Northern Ireland is not to count as a judge of the relevant court for the purposes of section 2(1) or 3(1) of the Judicature (Northern Ireland) Act 1978 (maximum number of judges) nor as a judge of the [Supreme Court][30] of Northern Ireland for the purposes of section 9(1)(d) of the 1973 Act (salaries etc);

(d) a Circuit judge is not to count as such for the purposes of section 18 of the Courts Act 1971 (salaries etc);

(e) a sheriff is not to count as such for the purposes of section 14 of the Sheriff Courts (Scotland) Act 1907 (salaries etc);

(f) a county court judge of Northern Ireland is not to count as such for the purposes of section 106 of the County Courts Act (Northern Ireland) 1959 (salaries etc).

(5) If a sheriff principal is appointed a judge of the Court, section 11(1) of the Sheriff Courts (Scotland) Act 1971 (temporary appointment of sheriff principal) applies, while he holds that appointment, as if his office is vacant.

(6) Schedule 3 makes provision about judicial pensions in relation to the holder of a judicial office who serves as a judge of the Court.

(7) The Lord Chancellor or the Secretary of State may by order make such transitional provision (including, in particular, provision for a temporary increase in the maximum number of judges) as he considers appropriate in relation to any holder of a judicial office who has completed his service as a judge of the Court.

---

28 Prospective amendment: Words prospectively substituted by Constitutional Reform Act 2005, s 59(5), Sch 11, Pt 1, para 1(2), with effect from a date to be appointed; Constitutional Reform Act 2005, s 148(1).New text = "Supreme Court Act 1981".

29 Prospective amendment: Words prospectively substituted by Constitutional Reform Act 2005, s 59(5), Sch 11, Pt 2, para 4(1), (3), with effect from a date to be appointed; Constitutional Reform Act 2005, s 148(1).New text = "Supreme Court Act 1981".

30 Prospective amendment: Words prospectively substituted; Constitutional Reform Act 2005, s 59(5), Sch 11, Pt 3, para 6(1), (3), with effect from a date to be appointed; Constitutional Reform Act 2005, s 148(1).New text = "Supreme Court Act 1981".

[-]³¹

Prospective amendments: Constitutional Reform Act 2005, ss 15(1), 59(5), Sch 4, Pt 1, para 278, Sch 11, Pts 1–3, paras 1(2), 4(1), (3), 6(1), (3)

PARLIAMENTARY PROCEDURE

19 Statements of compatibility

(1) A Minister of the Crown in charge of a Bill in either House of Parliament must, before Second Reading of the Bill –

(a) make a statement to the effect that in his view the provisions of the Bill are compatible with the Convention rights ('a statement of compatibility'); or

(b) make a statement to the effect that although he is unable to make a statement of compatibility the government nevertheless wishes the House to proceed with the Bill.

(2) The statement must be in writing and be published in such manner as the Minister making it considers appropriate.

SUPPLEMENTAL

20 Orders etc under this Act

(1) Any power of a Minister of the Crown to make an order under this Act is exercisable by statutory instrument.

(2) The power of ...³² [the Lord Chancellor or]³³ the Secretary of State to make rules (other than rules of court) under section 2(3) or 7(9) is exercisable by statutory instrument.

(3) Any statutory instrument made under section 14, 15 or 16(7) must be laid before Parliament.

(4) No order may be made by ...³⁴ [the Lord Chancellor or]³⁵ the Secretary of State under section 1(4), 7(11) or 16(2) unless a draft of the order has been laid before, and approved by, each House of Parliament.

---

31 Prospective amendment: Sub-sections (7A)–(7D) prospectively inserted by Constitutional Reform Act 2005, s 15(1), Sch 4, Pt 1, para 278, with effect from a date to be appointed; Constitutional Reform Act 2005, s 148(1).

32 Amendment: Words repealed; Secretary of State for Constitutional Affairs Order 2003; SI 2003/1887, art 9, Sch 2, para 10(2); with effect from 19 August 2003; SI 2003/1887, art 1(2).

33 Amendment: Words inserted; Transfer of Functions (Lord Chancellor and Secretary of State) Order 2005, SI 2005/3429, art 8, Schedule, para 3; with effect from 12 January 2006; SI 2005/3429, art 1(2).

34 Amendment: Words repealed; Secretary of State for Constitutional Affairs Order 2003; SI 2003/1887, art 9, Sch 2, para 10(2); with effect from 19 August 2003; SI 2003/1887, art 1(2).

(5) Any statutory instrument made under section 18(7) or Schedule 4, or to which subsection (2) applies, shall be subject to annulment in pursuance of a resolution of either House of Parliament.

(6) The power of a Northern Ireland department to make –

(a)   rules under section 2(3)(c) or 7(9)(c), or
(b)   an order under section 7(11),

is exercisable by statutory rule for the purposes of the Statutory Rules (Northern Ireland) Order 1979.

(7) Any rules made under section 2(3)(c) or 7(9)(c) shall be subject to negative resolution; and section 41(6) of the Interpretation Act Northern Ireland) 1954 (meaning of 'subject to negative resolution') shall apply as if the power to make the rules were conferred by an Act of the Northern Ireland Assembly.

(8) No order may be made by a Northern Ireland department under section 7(11) unless a draft of the order has been laid before, and approved by, the Northern Ireland Assembly.

Amendments: SI 2003/1887, SI 2005/3429.

21 Interpretation, etc

(1) In this Act –

'amend' includes repeal and apply (with or without modifications);
'the appropriate Minister' means the Minister of the Crown having charge of the appropriate authorised government department (within the meaning of the Crown Proceedings Act 1947);
'the Commission' means the European Commission of Human Rights;
'the Convention' means the Convention for the Protection of Human Rights and Fundamental Freedoms, agreed by the Council of Europe at Rome on 4th November 1950 as it has effect for the time being in relation to the United Kingdom;
'declaration of incompatibility' means a declaration under section 4;
'Minister of the Crown' has the same meaning as in the Ministers of the Crown Act 1975;
'Northern Ireland Minister' includes the First Minister and the deputy First Minister in Northern Ireland;
'primary legislation' means any –
    (a)   public general Act;
    (b)   local and personal Act;
    (c)   private Act;
    (d)   Measure of the Church Assembly;
    (e)   Measure of the General Synod of the Church of England;
    (f)   Order in Council –

---

35   Amendment: Words inserted; Transfer of Functions (Lord Chancellor and Secretary of State) Order 2005, SI 2005/3429, art 8, Schedule, para 3; with effect from 12 January 2006; SI 2005/3429, art 1(2).

(i) made in exercise of Her Majesty's Royal Prerogative;

(ii) made under section 38(1)(a) of the Northern Ireland Constitution Act 1973 or the corresponding provision of the Northern Ireland Act 1998; or

(iii) amending an Act of a kind mentioned in paragraph (a), (b) or (c);

and includes an order or other instrument made under primary legislation (otherwise than by the National Assembly for Wales, a member of the Scottish Executive, a Northern Ireland Minister or a Northern Ireland department) to the extent to which it operates to bring one or more provisions of that legislation into force or amends any primary legislation;

'the First Protocol' means the protocol to the Convention agreed at Paris on 20th March 1952;

...[36]

'the Eleventh Protocol' means the protocol to the Convention (restructuring the control machinery established by the Convention) agreed at Strasbourg on 11th May 1994;

['the Thirteenth Protocol' means the protocol to the Convention (concerning the abolition of the death penalty in all circumstances) agreed at Vilnius on 3rd May 2002;][37]

'remedial order' means an order under section 10;

'subordinate legislation' means any –

(a) Order in Council other than one –

(i) made in exercise of Her Majesty's Royal Prerogative;

(ii) made under section 38(1)(a) of the Northern Ireland Constitution Act 1973 or the corresponding provision of the Northern Ireland Act 1998; or

(iii) amending an Act of a kind mentioned in the definition of primary legislation;

(b) Act of the Scottish Parliament;

(c) Act of the Parliament of Northern Ireland;

(d) Measure of the Assembly established under section 1 of the Northern Ireland Assembly Act 1973;

(e) Act of the Northern Ireland Assembly;

(f) order, rules, regulations, scheme, warrant, byelaw or other instrument made under primary legislation (except to the extent to which it operates to bring one or more provisions of that legislation into force or amends any primary legislation);

(g) order, rules, regulations, scheme, warrant, byelaw or other instrument made under legislation mentioned in paragraph (b), (c), (d) or (e) or made under an Order in Council applying only to Northern Ireland;

(h) order, rules, regulations, scheme, warrant, byelaw or other

36 Amendment: Definition 'the Sixth Protocol' repealed; Human Rights Act 1998 (Amendment) Order 2004, SI 2004/1574, art 2(2); with effect from 22 June 2004; SI 2004/1574, art 1.

37 Amendment: definition inserted; Human Rights Act 1998 (Amendment) Order 2004, SI 2004/1574, art 2(2); with effect from 22 June 2004; SI 2004/1574, art 1.

instrument made by a member of the Scottish Executive, a Northern Ireland Minister or a Northern Ireland department in exercise of prerogative or

other executive functions of Her Majesty which are exercisable by such a person on behalf of Her Majesty;

'transferred matters' has the same meaning as in the Northern Ireland Act 1998; and

'tribunal' means any tribunal in which legal proceedings may be brought.

(2) The references in paragraphs (b) and (c) of section 2(1) to Articles are to Articles of the Convention as they had effect immediately before the coming into force of the Eleventh Protocol.

(3) The reference in paragraph (d) of section 2(1) to Article 46 includes a reference to Articles 32 and 54 of the Convention as they had effect immediately before the coming into force of the Eleventh Protocol.

(4) The references in section 2(1) to a report or decision of the Commission or a decision of the Committee of Ministers include references to a report or decision made as provided by paragraphs 3, 4 and 6 of Article 5 of the Eleventh Protocol (transitional provisions).

(5) Any liability under the Army Act 1955, the Air Force Act 1955 or the Naval Discipline Act 1957 to suffer death for an offence is replaced by a liability to imprisonment for life or any less punishment authorised by those Acts; and those Acts shall accordingly have effect with the necessary modifications.

Amendments: SI 2004/1574.

22 Short title, commencement, application and extent

(1) This Act may be cited as the Human Rights Act 1998.

(2) Sections 18, 20 and 21(5) and this section come into force on the passing of this Act.

(3) The other provisions of this Act come into force on such day as the Secretary of State may by order appoint; and different days may be appointed for different purposes.

(4) Paragraph (b) of subsection (1) of section 7 applies to proceedings brought by or at the instigation of a public authority whenever the act in question took place; but otherwise that subsection does not apply to an act committed before the coming into force of that section.

(5) This Act binds the Crown.

(6) This Act extends to Northern Ireland.

(7) Section 21(5), so far as it relates to any provision contained in the Army Act 1955, the Air Force Act 1955 or the Naval Discipline Act 1957, extends to any place to which that provision extends.

SCHEDULES

SCHEDULE 1

THE ARTICLES

PART I

THE CONVENTION

Rights and freedoms

Article 2

Right to life

1 Everyone's right to life shall be protected by law. No one shall be deprived of his life intentionally save in the execution of a sentence of a court following his conviction of a crime for which this penalty is provided by law.

2 Deprivation of life shall not be regarded as inflicted in contravention of this Article when it results from the use of force which is no more than absolutely necessary –

(a) in defence of any person from unlawful violence;
(b) in order to effect a lawful arrest or to prevent the escape of a person lawfully detained;
(c) in action lawfully taken for the purpose of quelling a riot or insurrection.

Article 3

Prohibition of torture

No one shall be subjected to torture or to inhuman or degrading treatment or punishment.

Article 4

Prohibition of slavery and forced labour

1 No one shall be held in slavery or servitude.

2 No one shall be required to perform forced or compulsory labour.

3 For the purpose of this Article the term 'forced or compulsory labour' shall not include –

(a)   any work required to be done in the ordinary course of detention imposed according to the provisions of Article 5 of this Convention or during conditional release from such detention;

(b)   any service of a military character or, in case of conscientious objectors in countries where they are recognised, service exacted instead of compulsory military service;

(c)   any service exacted in case of an emergency or calamity threatening the life or well-being of the community;

(d)   any work or service which forms part of normal civic obligations.

Article 5

Right to liberty and security

1 Everyone has the right to liberty and security of person. No one shall be deprived of his liberty save in the following cases and in accordance with a procedure prescribed by law –

(a)   the lawful detention of a person after conviction by a competent court;

(b)   the lawful arrest or detention of a person for non-compliance with the lawful order of a court or in order to secure the fulfilment of any obligation prescribed by law;

(c)   the lawful arrest or detention of a person effected for the purpose of bringing him before the competent legal authority on reasonable suspicion of having committed an offence or when it is reasonably considered necessary to prevent his committing an offence or fleeing after having done so;

(d)   the detention of a minor by lawful order for the purpose of educational supervision or his lawful detention for the purpose of bringing him before the competent legal authority;

(e)   the lawful detention of persons for the prevention of the spreading of infectious diseases, of persons of unsound mind, alcoholics or drug addicts or vagrants;

(f)   the lawful arrest or detention of a person to prevent his effecting an unauthorised entry into the country or of a person against whom action is being taken with a view to deportation or extradition.

2 Everyone who is arrested shall be informed promptly, in a language which he understands, of the reasons for his arrest and of any charge against him.

3 Everyone arrested or detained in accordance with the provisions of paragraph 1(c) of this Article shall be brought promptly before a judge or other officer authorised by law to exercise judicial power and shall be entitled to trial within a reasonable time or to release pending trial. Release may be conditioned by guarantees to appear for trial.

4 Everyone who is deprived of his liberty by arrest or detention shall be entitled to take proceedings by which the lawfulness of his detention shall be decided speedily by a court and his release ordered if the detention is not lawful.

5 Everyone who has been the victim of arrest or detention in contravention of the provisions of this Article shall have an enforceable right to compensation.

Article 6

Right to a fair trial

1 In the determination of his civil rights and obligations or of any criminal charge against him, everyone is entitled to a fair and public hearing within a reasonable time by an independent and impartial tribunal established by law. Judgment shall be pronounced publicly but the press and public may be excluded from all or part of the trial in the interest of morals, public order or national security in a democratic society, where the interests of juveniles or the protection of the private life of the parties so require, or to the extent strictly necessary in the opinion of the court in special circumstances where publicity would prejudice the interests of justice.

2 Everyone charged with a criminal offence shall be presumed innocent until proved guilty according to law.

3 Everyone charged with a criminal offence has the following minimum rights –

(a)   to be informed promptly, in a language which he understands and in detail, of the nature and cause of the accusation against him;
(b)   to have adequate time and facilities for the preparation of his defence;
(c)   to defend himself in person or through legal assistance of his own choosing or, if he has not sufficient means to pay for legal assistance, to be given it free when the interests of justice so require;
(d)   to examine or have examined witnesses against him and to obtain the attendance and examination of witnesses on his behalf under the same conditions as witnesses against him;
(e)   to have the free assistance of an interpreter if he cannot understand or speak the language used in court.

Article 7

No punishment without law

1 No one shall be held guilty of any criminal offence on account of any act or omission which did not constitute a criminal offence under national or international law at the time when it was committed. Nor shall a heavier penalty be imposed than the one that was applicable at the time the criminal offence was committed.

2 This Article shall not prejudice the trial and punishment of any person for any act or omission which, at the time when it was committed, was criminal according to the general principles of law recognised by civilised nations.

Article 8

Right to respect for private and family life

1 Everyone has the right to respect for his private and family life, his home and his correspondence.

2 There shall be no interference by a public authority with the exercise of this right except such as is in accordance with the law and is necessary in a democratic society in the interests of national security, public safety or the economic well-being of the country, for the prevention of disorder or crime, for the protection of health or morals, or for the protection of the rights and freedoms of others.

Article 9

Freedom of thought, conscience and religion

1 Everyone has the right to freedom of thought, conscience and religion; this right includes freedom to change his religion or belief and freedom, either alone or in community with others and in public or private, to manifest his religion or belief, in worship, teaching, practice and observance.

2 Freedom to manifest one's religion or beliefs shall be subject only to such limitations as are prescribed by law and are necessary in a democratic society in the interests of public safety, for the protection of public order, health or morals, or for the protection of the rights and freedoms of others.

Article 10

Freedom of expression

1 Everyone has the right to freedom of expression. This right shall include freedom to hold opinions and to receive and impart information and ideas without interference by public authority and regardless of frontiers. This Article shall not prevent States from requiring the licensing of broadcasting, television or cinema enterprises.

2 The exercise of these freedoms, since it carries with it duties and responsibilities, may be subject to such formalities, conditions, restrictions or penalties as are prescribed by law and are necessary in a democratic society, in the interests of national security, territorial integrity or public safety, for the prevention of disorder or crime, for the protection of health or morals, for the protection of the reputation or rights of others, for preventing the disclosure of information received in confidence, or for maintaining the authority and impartiality of the judiciary.

Article 11

Freedom of assembly and association

1 Everyone has the right to freedom of peaceful assembly and to freedom of association with others, including the right to form and to join trade unions for the protection of his interests.

2 No restrictions shall be placed on the exercise of these rights other than such as are prescribed by law and are necessary in a democratic society in the interests of national security or public safety, for the prevention of disorder or crime, for the protection of health or morals or for the protection of the rights and freedoms of others. This Article shall not prevent the imposition of lawful restrictions on the exercise of these rights by members of the armed forces, of the police or of the administration of the State.

Article 12

Right to marry

Men and women of marriageable age have the right to marry and to found a family, according to the national laws governing the exercise of this right.

Article 14

Prohibition of discrimination

The enjoyment of the rights and freedoms set forth in this Convention shall be secured without discrimination on any ground such as sex, race, colour, language, religion, political or other opinion, national or social origin, association with a national minority, property, birth or other status.

Article 16

Restrictions on political activity of aliens

Nothing in Articles 10, 11 and 14 shall be regarded as preventing the High Contracting Parties from imposing restrictions on the political activity of aliens.

Article 17

Prohibition of abuse of rights

Nothing in this Convention may be interpreted as implying for any State, group or person any right to engage in any activity or perform any act aimed at the destruction of any of the rights and freedoms set forth herein or at their limitation to a greater extent than is provided for in the Convention.

Article 18

Limitation on use of restrictions on rights

The restrictions permitted under this Convention to the said rights and freedoms shall not be applied for any purpose other than those for which they have been prescribed.

PART II

THE FIRST PROTOCOL

Article 1

Protection of property

Every natural or legal person is entitled to the peaceful enjoyment of his possessions. No one shall be deprived of his possessions except in the public interest and subject to the conditions provided for by law and by the general principles of international law.

The preceding provisions shall not, however, in any way impair the right of a State to enforce such laws as it deems necessary to control the use of property in accordance with the general interest or to secure the payment of taxes or other contributions or penalties.

Article 2

Right to education

No person shall be denied the right to education. In the exercise of any functions which it assumes in relation to education and to teaching, the State shall respect the right of parents to ensure such education and teaching in conformity with their own religious and philosophical convictions.

Article 3

Right to free elections

The High Contracting Parties undertake to hold free elections at reasonable intervals by secret ballot, under conditions which will ensure the free expression of the opinion of the people in the choice of the legislature.

[PART III

ARTICLE 1 OF THE THIRTEENTH PROTOCOL

Article 1

Abolition of the death penalty

The death penalty shall be abolished. No one shall be condemned to such penalty or executed.][38]

Amendments: SI 2004/1574.

SCHEDULE 2

REMEDIAL ORDERS

Orders

1

(1) A remedial order may –

(a) contain such incidental, supplemental, consequential or transitional provision as the person making it considers appropriate;
(b) be made so as to have effect from a date earlier than that on which it is made;
(c) make provision for the delegation of specific functions;
(d) make different provision for different cases.

(2) The power conferred by sub-paragraph (1)(a) includes –

(a) power to amend primary legislation (including primary legislation other than that which contains the incompatible provision); and
(b) power to amend or revoke subordinate legislation (including subordinate legislation other than that which contains the incompatible provision).

---

38   Amendment: Part substituted; Human Rights Act 1998 (Amendment) Order 2004, SI 2004/1574, art 2(3); with effect from 22 June 2004; SI 2004/1574, art 1.

(3) A remedial order may be made so as to have the same extent as the legislation which it affects.

(4) No person is to be guilty of an offence solely as a result of the retrospective effect of a remedial order.

Procedure

2

No remedial order may be made unless –

(a) a draft of the order has been approved by a resolution of each House of Parliament made after the end of the period of 60 days beginning with the day on which the draft was laid; or

(b) it is declared in the order that it appears to the person making it that, because of the urgency of the matter, it is necessary to make the order without a draft being so approved.

Orders laid in draft

3

(1) No draft may be laid under paragraph 2(a) unless –

(a) the person proposing to make the order has laid before Parliament a document which contains a draft of the proposed order and the required information; and

(b) the period of 60 days, beginning with the day on which the document required by this sub-paragraph was laid, has ended.

(2) If representations have been made during that period, the draft laid under paragraph 2(a) must be accompanied by a statement containing –

(a) a summary of the representations; and

(b) if, as a result of the representations, the proposed order has been changed, details of the changes.

Urgent cases

4

(1) If a remedial order ('the original order') is made without being approved in draft, the person making it must lay it before Parliament, accompanied by the required information, after it is made.

(2) If representations have been made during the period of 60 days beginning with the day on which the original order was made, the person making it must (after the end of that period) lay before Parliament a statement containing –

(a) a summary of the representations; and

(b) if, as a result of the representations, he considers it appropriate to make changes to the original order, details of the changes.

(3) If sub-paragraph (2)(b) applies, the person making the statement must –

(a) make a further remedial order replacing the original order; and

(b) lay the replacement order before Parliament.

(4) If, at the end of the period of 120 days beginning with the day on which the original order was made, a resolution has not been passed by each House approving the original or replacement order, the order ceases to have effect (but without that affecting anything previously done under either order or the power to make a fresh remedial order).

Definitions

5

In this Schedule –

'representations' means representations about a remedial order (or proposed remedial order) made to the person making (or proposing to make) it and includes any relevant Parliamentary report or resolution; and
'required information' means –

  (a) an explanation of the incompatibility which the order (or proposed order) seeks to remove, including particulars of the relevant declaration, finding or order; and

  (b) a statement of the reasons for proceeding under section 10 and for making an order in those terms.

Calculating periods

6 In calculating any period for the purposes of this Schedule, no account is to be taken of any time during which –

(a) Parliament is dissolved or prorogued; or

(b) both Houses are adjourned for more than four days.

Appendix 4

UNITED NATIONS CONVENTION ON THE RIGHTS OF THE CHILD 1989

The Convention on the Rights of the Child was adopted and opened for signature, ratification and accession by General Assembly resolution 44/25 of 20 November 1989. It entered into force 2 September 1990, in accordance with Article 49.

PREAMBLE

The States Parties to the present Convention,

Considering that, in accordance with the principles proclaimed in the Charter of the United Nations, recognition of the inherent dignity and of the equal and inalienable rights of all members of the human family is the foundation of freedom, justice and peace in the world,

Bearing in mind that the peoples of the United Nations have, in the Charter, reaffirmed their faith in fundamental human rights and in the dignity and worth of the human person and have determined to promote social progress and better standards of life in larger freedom,

Recognising that the United Nations has, in the Universal Declaration of Human Rights and in the International Covenants on Human Rights, proclaimed and agreed that everyone is entitled to all the rights and freedoms set forth therein, without distinction of any kind, such as race, colour, sex, language, religion, political or other opinion, national or social origin, property, birth or other status,

Recalling that, in the Universal Declaration of Human Rights, the United Nations has proclaimed that childhood is entitled to special care and assistance,

Convinced that the family, as the fundamental group of society and the natural environment for the growth and well-being of all its members and particularly children, should be afforded the necessary protection and assistance so that it can fully assume its responsibilities within the community,

Recognising that the child, for the full and harmonious development of his or her personality, should grow up in a family environment, in an atmosphere of happiness, love and understanding,

Considering that the child should be fully prepared to live an individual life in society and brought up in the spirit of the ideals proclaimed in the Charter of the United Nations and in particular in the spirit of peace, dignity, tolerance, freedom, equality and solidarity,

Bearing in mind that the need to extend particular care to the child has been stated in the Geneva Declaration of the Rights of the Child of 1924 and in the Declaration of the Rights of the Child adopted by the General Assembly on 20 November 1959 and recognized in the Universal Declaration of Human Rights, in the International Covenant on Civil and Political Rights (in particular in Articles 23 and 24), in the International Covenant on Economic, Social and Cultural Rights (in particular in Article 10) and in the statutes and relevant instruments of specialised agencies and international organisations concerned with the welfare of children,

Bearing in mind that, as indicated in the Declaration of the Rights of the Child, 'the child, by reason of his physical and mental immaturity, needs special safeguards and care, including appropriate legal protection, before as well as after birth',

Recalling the provisions of the Declaration on Social and Legal Principles relating to the Protection and Welfare of Children, with Special Reference to Foster Placement and Adoption Nationally and Internationally; the United Nations Standard Minimum Rules for the Administration of Juvenile Justice (The Beijing Rules); and the Declaration on the Protection of Women and Children in Emergency and Armed Conflict,

Recognising that, in all countries in the world, there are children living in exceptionally difficult conditions and that such children need special consideration,

Taking due account of the importance of the traditions and cultural values of each people for the protection and harmonious development of the child,

Recognising the importance of international co-operation for improving the living conditions of children in every country, in particular in the developing countries,

Have agreed as follows:

PART I

Article 1

For the purposes of the present Convention, a child means every human being below the age of eighteen years unless under the law applicable to the child, majority is attained earlier.

Article 2

1 States Parties shall respect and ensure the rights set forth in the present Convention to each child within their jurisdiction without discrimination of

any kind, irrespective of the child's or his or her parent's or legal guardian's race, colour, sex, language, religion, political or other opinion, national, ethnic or social origin, property, disability, birth or other status.

2 States Parties shall take all appropriate measures to ensure that the child is protected against all forms of discrimination or punishment on the basis of the status, activities, expressed opinions, or beliefs of the child's parents, legal guardians, or family members.

Article 3

1 In all actions concerning children, whether undertaken by public or private social welfare institutions, courts of law, administrative authorities or legislative bodies, the best interests of the child shall be a primary consideration.

2 States Parties undertake to ensure the child such protection and care as is necessary for his or her well-being, taking into account the rights and duties of his or her parents, legal guardians, or other individuals legally responsible for him or her, and, to this end, shall take all appropriate legislative and administrative measures.

3 States Parties shall ensure that the institutions, services and facilities responsible for the care or protection of children shall conform with the standards established by competent authorities, particularly in the areas of safety, health, in the number and suitability of their staff, as well as competent supervision.

Article 4

States Parties shall undertake all appropriate legislative, administrative and other measures for the implementation of the rights recognised in the present Convention. With regard to economic, social and cultural rights, States Parties shall undertake such measures to the maximum extent of their available resources and, where needed, within the framework of international co-operation.

Article 5

States Parties shall respect the responsibilities, rights and duties of parents or, where applicable, the members of the extended family or community as provided for by local custom, legal guardians or other persons legally responsible for the child, to provide, in a manner consistent with the evolving capacities of the child, appropriate direction and guidance in the exercise by the child of the rights recognised in the present Convention.

Article 6

1 States Parties recognize that every child has the inherent right to life.

2 States Parties shall ensure to the maximum extent possible the survival and development of the child.

Article 7

1 The child shall be registered immediately after birth and shall have the right from birth to a name, the right to acquire a nationality and. as far as possible, the right to know and be cared for by his or her parents.

2 States Parties shall ensure the implementation of these rights in accordance with their national law and their obligations under the relevant international instruments in this field, in particular where the child would otherwise be stateless.

Article 8

1 States Parties undertake to respect the right of the child to preserve his or her identity, including nationality, name and family relations as recognised by law without unlawful interference.

2 Where a child is illegally deprived of some or all of the elements of his or her identity, States Parties shall provide appropriate assistance and protection, with a view to re-establishing speedily his or her identity.

Article 9

1 States Parties shall ensure that a child shall not be separated from his or her parents against their will, except when competent authorities subject to judicial review determine, in accordance with applicable law and procedures, that such separation is necessary for the best interests of the child. Such determination may be necessary in a particular case such as one involving abuse or neglect of the child by the parents, or one where the parents are living separately and a decision must be made as to the child's place of residence.

2 In any proceedings pursuant to paragraph 1 of the present article, all interested parties shall be given an opportunity to participate in the proceedings and make their views known.

3 States Parties shall respect the right of the child who is separated from one or both parents to maintain personal relations and direct contact with both parents on a regular basis, except if it is contrary to the child's best interests.

4 Where such separation results from any action initiated by a State Party, such as the detention, imprisonment, exile, deportation or death (including death arising from any cause while the person is in the custody of the State) of one or both parents or of the child, that State Party shall, upon request, provide the parents, the child or, if appropriate, another member of the family with the essential information concerning the whereabouts of the absent member(s) of the family unless the provision of the information would be detrimental to the

well-being of the child. States Parties shall further ensure that the submission of such a request shall of itself entail no adverse consequences for the person(s) concerned.

Article 10

1 In accordance with the obligation of States Parties under Article 9, paragraph 1, applications by a child or his or her parents to enter or leave a State Party for the purpose of family reunification shall be dealt with by States Parties in a positive, humane and expeditious manner. States Parties shall further ensure that the submission of such a request shall entail no adverse consequences for the applicants and for the members of their family.

2 A child whose parents reside in different States shall have the right to maintain on a regular basis, save in exceptional circumstances personal relations and direct contacts with both parents. Towards that end and in accordance with the obligation of States Parties under Article 9, paragraph 1, States Parties shall respect the right of the child and his or her parents to leave any country, including their own and to enter their own country. The right to leave any country shall be subject only to such restrictions as are prescribed by law and which are necessary to protect the national security, public order (ordre public), public health or morals or the rights and freedoms of others and are consistent with the other rights recognised in the present Convention.

Article 11

1 States Parties shall take measures to combat the illicit transfer and non-return of children abroad.

2 To this end, States Parties shall promote the conclusion of bilateral or multilateral agreements or accession to existing agreements.

Article 12

1 States Parties shall assure to the child who is capable of forming his or her own views the right to express those views freely in all matters affecting the child, the views of the child being given due weight in accordance with the age and maturity of the child.

2 For this purpose, the child shall in particular be provided the opportunity to be heard in any judicial and administrative proceedings affecting the child, either directly, or through a representative or an appropriate body, in a manner consistent with the procedural rules of national law.

Article 13

1 The child shall have the right to freedom of expression; this right shall include freedom to seek, receive and impart information and ideas of all kinds,

regardless of frontiers, either orally, in writing or in print, in the form of art, or through any other media of the child's choice.

2 The exercise of this right may be subject to certain restrictions, but these shall only be such as are provided by law and are necessary:

(a)　For respect of the rights or reputations of others; or
(b)　For the protection of national security or of public order (ordre public), or of public health or morals.

Article 14

1 States Parties shall respect the right of the child to freedom of thought, conscience and religion.

2 States Parties shall respect the rights and duties of the parents and, when applicable, legal guardians, to provide direction to the child in the exercise of his or her right in a manner consistent with the evolving capacities of the child.

3 Freedom to manifest one's religion or beliefs may be subject only to such limitations as are prescribed by law and are necessary to protect public safety, order, health or morals, or the fundamental rights and freedoms of others.

Article 15

1 States Parties recognise the rights of the child to freedom of association and to freedom of peaceful assembly.

2 No restrictions may be placed on the exercise of these rights other than those imposed in conformity with the law and which are necessary in a democratic society in the interests of national security or public safety, public order (ordre public), the protection of public health or morals or the protection of the rights and freedoms of others.

Article 16

1 No child shall be subjected to arbitrary or unlawful interference with his or her privacy, family, home or correspondence, nor to unlawful attacks on his or her honour and reputation.

2 The child has the right to the protection of the law against such interference or attacks.

Article 17

States Parties recognize the important function performed by the mass media and shall ensure that the child has access to information and material from a diversity of national and international sources, especially those aimed at the promotion of his or her social, spiritual and moral well-being and physical and mental health. To this end, States Parties shall:

(a) Encourage the mass media to disseminate information and material of social and cultural benefit to the child and in accordance with the spirit of Article 29;
(b) Encourage international co-operation in the production, exchange and dissemination of such information and material from a diversity of cultural, national and international sources;
(c) Encourage the production and dissemination of children's books;
(d) Encourage the mass media to have particular regard to the linguistic needs of the child who belongs to a minority group or who is indigenous;
(e) Encourage the development of appropriate guidelines for the protection of the child from information and material injurious to his or her well-being, bearing in mind the provisions of Articles 13 and 18.

Article 18

1 States Parties shall use their best efforts to ensure recognition of the principle that both parents have common responsibilities for the upbringing and development of the child. Parents or, as the case may be, legal guardians, have the primary responsibility for the upbringing and development of the child. The best interests of the child will be their basic concern.

2 For the purpose of guaranteeing and promoting the rights set forth in the present Convention, States Parties shall render appropriate assistance to parents and legal guardians in the performance of their child-rearing responsibilities and shall ensure the development of institutions, facilities and services for the care of children.

3 States Parties shall take all appropriate measures to ensure that children of working parents have the right to benefit from child-care services and facilities for which they are eligible.

Article 19

1 States Parties shall take all appropriate legislative, administrative, social and educational measures to protect the child from all forms of physical or mental violence, injury or abuse, neglect or negligent treatment, maltreatment or exploitation, including sexual abuse, while in the care of parent(s), legal guardian(s) or any other person who has the care of the child.

2 Such protective measures should, as appropriate, include effective procedures for the establishment of social programmes to provide necessary support for the child and for those who have the care of the child, as well as for other forms of prevention and for identification, reporting, referral, investigation, treatment and follow-up of instances of child maltreatment described heretofore, and, as appropriate, for judicial involvement.

Article 20

1 A child temporarily or permanently deprived of his or her family environment, or in whose own best interests cannot be allowed to remain in that environment, shall be entitled to special protection and assistance provided by the State.

2 States Parties shall in accordance with their national laws ensure alternative care for such a child.

3 Such care could include, inter alia, foster placement, kafalah of Islamic law, adoption or if necessary placement in suitable institutions for the care of children. When considering solutions, due regard shall be paid to the desirability of continuity in a child's upbringing and to the child's ethnic, religious, cultural and linguistic background.

Article 21

States Parties that recognize and/or permit the system of adoption shall ensure that the best interests of the child shall be the paramount consideration and they shall:

(a)	Ensure that the adoption of a child is authorised only by competent authorities who determine, in accordance with applicable law and procedures and on the basis of all pertinent and reliable information, that the adoption is permissible in view of the child's status concerning parents, relatives and legal guardians and that, if required, the persons concerned have given their informed consent to the adoption on the basis of such counselling as may be necessary;

(b)	Recognise that inter-country adoption may be considered as an alternative means of child's care, if the child cannot be placed in a foster or an adoptive family or cannot in any suitable manner be cared for in the child's country of origin;

(c)	Ensure that the child concerned by inter-country adoption enjoys safeguards and standards equivalent to those existing in the case of national adoption;

(d)	Take all appropriate measures to ensure that, in inter-country adoption, the placement does not result in improper financial gain for those involved in it;

(e)	Promote, where appropriate, the objectives of the present article by concluding bilateral or multilateral arrangements or agreements and endeavour, within this framework, to ensure that the placement of the child in another country is carried out by competent authorities or organs.

Article 22

1 States Parties shall take appropriate measures to ensure that a child who is seeking refugee status or who is considered a refugee in accordance with applicable international or domestic law and procedures shall, whether unaccompanied or accompanied by his or her parents or by any other person, receive appropriate protection and humanitarian assistance in the enjoyment of applicable rights set forth in the present Convention and in other international human rights or humanitarian instruments to which the said States are Parties.

2 For this purpose, States Parties shall provide, as they consider appropriate, co-operation in any efforts by the United Nations and other competent intergovernmental organizations or non-governmental organisations

co-operating with the United Nations to protect and assist such a child and to trace the parents or other members of the family of any refugee child in order to obtain information necessary for reunification with his or her family. In cases where no parents or other members of the family can be found, the child shall be accorded the same protection as any other child permanently or temporarily deprived of his or her family environment for any reason, as set forth in the present Convention.

Article 23

1 States Parties recognise that a mentally or physically disabled child should enjoy a full and decent life, in conditions which ensure dignity, promote self-reliance and facilitate the child's active participation in the community.

2 States Parties recognise the right of the disabled child to special care and shall encourage and ensure the extension, subject to available resources, to the eligible child and those responsible for his or her care, of assistance for which application is made and which is appropriate to the child's condition and to the circumstances of the parents or others caring for the child.

3 Recognising the special needs of a disabled child, assistance extended in accordance with paragraph 2 of the present article shall be provided free of charge, whenever possible, taking into account the financial resources of the parents or others caring for the child and shall be designed to ensure that the disabled child has effective access to and receives education, training, health care services, rehabilitation services, preparation for employment and recreation opportunities in a manner conducive to the child's achieving the fullest possible social integration and individual development, including his or her cultural and spiritual development

4 States Parties shall promote, in the spirit of international cooperation, the exchange of appropriate information in the field of preventive health care and of medical, psychological and functional treatment of disabled children, including dissemination of and access to information concerning methods of rehabilitation, education and vocational services, with the aim of enabling States Parties to improve their capabilities and skills and to widen their experience in these areas. In this regard, particular account shall be taken of the needs of developing countries.

Article 24

1 States Parties recognise the right of the child to the enjoyment of the highest attainable standard of health and to facilities for the treatment of illness and rehabilitation of health. States Parties shall strive to ensure that no child is deprived of his or her right of access to such health care services.

2 States Parties shall pursue full implementation of this right and, in particular, shall take appropriate measures:

(a)   To diminish infant and child mortality;

(b)   To ensure the provision of necessary medical assistance and health care to all children with emphasis on the development of primary health care;

(c)   To combat disease and malnutrition, including within the framework of primary health care, through, inter alia, the application of readily available technology and through the provision of adequate nutritious foods and clean drinking-water, taking into consideration the dangers and risks of environmental pollution;

(d)   To ensure appropriate pre-natal and post-natal health care for mothers;

(e)   To ensure that all segments of society, in particular parents and children, are informed, have access to education and are supported in the use of basic knowledge of child health and nutrition, the advantages of breastfeeding, hygiene and environmental sanitation and the prevention of accidents;

(f)   To develop preventive health care, guidance for parents and family planning education and services.

3 States Parties shall take all effective and appropriate measures with a view to abolishing traditional practices prejudicial to the health of children.

4 States Parties undertake to promote and encourage international co-operation with a view to achieving progressively the full realisation of the right recognised in the present article. In this regard, particular account shall be taken of the needs of developing countries.

Article 25

States Parties recognize the right of a child who has been placed by the competent authorities for the purposes of care, protection or treatment of his or her physical or mental health, to a periodic review of the treatment provided to the child and all other circumstances relevant to his or her placement.

Article 26

1 States Parties shall recognise for every child the right to benefit from social security, including social insurance and shall take the necessary measures to achieve the full realization of this right in accordance with their national law.

2 The benefits should, where appropriate, be granted, taking into account the resources and the circumstances of the child and persons having responsibility for the maintenance of the child, as well as any other consideration relevant to an application for benefits made by or on behalf of the child.

Article 27

1 States Parties recognise the right of every child to a standard of living adequate for the child's physical, mental, spiritual, moral and social development.

2 The parent(s) or others responsible for the child have the primary responsibility to secure, within their abilities and financial capacities, the conditions of living necessary for the child's development.

3 States Parties, in accordance with national conditions and within their means, shall take appropriate measures to assist parents and others responsible for the child to implement this right and shall in case of need provide material assistance and support programmes, particularly with regard to nutrition, clothing and housing.

4 States Parties shall take all appropriate measures to secure the recovery of maintenance for the child from the parents or other persons having financial responsibility for the child, both within the State Party and from abroad. In particular, where the person having financial responsibility for the child lives in a State different from that of the child, States Parties shall promote the accession to international agreements or the conclusion of such agreements, as well as the making of other appropriate arrangements.

Article 28

1 States Parties recognise the right of the child to education and with a view to achieving this right progressively and on the basis of equal opportunity, they shall, in particular:

(a)   Make primary education compulsory and available free to all;
(b)   Encourage the development of different forms of secondary education, including general and vocational education, make them available and accessible to every child and take appropriate measures such as the introduction of free education and offering financial assistance in case of need;
(c)   Make higher education accessible to all on the basis of capacity by every appropriate means;
(d)   Make educational and vocational information and guidance available and accessible to all children;
(e)   Take measures to encourage regular attendance at schools and the reduction of drop-out rates.

2 States Parties shall take all appropriate measures to ensure that school discipline is administered in a manner consistent with the child's human dignity and in conformity with the present Convention.

3 States Parties shall promote and encourage international cooperation in matters relating to education, in particular with a view to contributing to the elimination of ignorance and illiteracy throughout the world and facilitating access to scientific and technical knowledge and modern teaching methods. In this regard, particular account shall be taken of the needs of developing countries.

Article 29

1 States Parties agree that the education of the child shall be directed to:

(a)   The development of the child's personality, talents and mental and physical abilities to their fullest potential;

(b)   The development of respect for human rights and fundamental freedoms, and for the principles enshrined in the Charter of the United Nations;

(c)   The development of respect for the child's parents, his or her own cultural identity, language and values, for the national values of the country in which the child is living, the country from which he or she may originate, and for civilizations different from his or her own;

(d)   The preparation of the child for responsible life in a free society, in the spirit of understanding, peace, tolerance, equality of sexes, and friendship among all peoples, ethnic, national and religious groups and persons of indigenous origin;

(e)   The development of respect for the natural environment.

2 No part of the present article or Article 28 shall be construed so as to interfere with the liberty of individuals and bodies to establish and direct educational institutions, subject always to the observance of the principle set forth in paragraph 1 of the present article and to the requirements that the education given in such institutions shall conform to such minimum standards as may be laid down by the State.

Article 30

In those States in which ethnic, religious or linguistic minorities or persons of indigenous origin exist, a child belonging to such a minority or who is indigenous shall not be denied the right, in community with other members of his or her group, to enjoy his or her own culture, to profess and practise his or her own religion, or to use his or her own language.

Article 31

1 States Parties recognize the right of the child to rest and leisure, to engage in play and recreational activities appropriate to the age of the child and to participate freely in cultural life and the arts.

2 States Parties shall respect and promote the right of the child to participate fully in cultural and artistic life and shall encourage the provision of appropriate and equal opportunities for cultural, artistic, recreational and leisure activity.

Article 32

1 States Parties recognize the right of the child to be protected from economic exploitation and from performing any work that is likely to be hazardous or to interfere with the child's education, or to be harmful to the child's health or physical, mental, spiritual, moral or social development.

2 States Parties shall take legislative, administrative, social and educational measures to ensure the implementation of the present article. To this end and having regard to the relevant provisions of other international instruments, States Parties shall in particular:

(a)   Provide for a minimum age or minimum ages for admission to employment;
(b)   Provide for appropriate regulation of the hours and conditions of employment;
(c)   Provide for appropriate penalties or other sanctions to ensure the effective enforcement of the present article.

Article 33

States Parties shall take all appropriate measures, including legislative, administrative, social and educational measures, to protect children from the illicit use of narcotic drugs and psychotropic substances as defined in the relevant international treaties and to prevent the use of children in the illicit production and trafficking of such substances.

Article 34

States Parties undertake to protect the child from all forms of sexual exploitation and sexual abuse. For these purposes, States Parties shall in particular take all appropriate national, bilateral and multilateral measures to prevent:

(a)   The inducement or coercion of a child to engage in any unlawful sexual activity;
(b)   The exploitative use of children in prostitution or other unlawful sexual practices;
(c)   The exploitative use of children in pornographic performances and materials.

Article 35

States Parties shall take all appropriate national, bilateral and multilateral measures to prevent the abduction of, the sale of or traffic in children for any purpose or in any form.

Article 36

States Parties shall protect the child against all other forms of exploitation prejudicial to any aspects of the child's welfare.

Article 37

States Parties shall ensure that:

(a)   No child shall be subjected to torture or other cruel, inhuman or degrading treatment or punishment. Neither capital punishment nor life imprisonment without possibility of release shall be imposed for offences committed by persons below 18 years of age;

(b)   No child shall be deprived of his or her liberty unlawfully or arbitrarily. The arrest, detention or imprisonment of a child shall be in conformity with the law and shall be used only as a measure of last resort and for the shortest appropriate period of time;

(c)   Every child deprived of liberty shall be treated with humanity and respect for the inherent dignity of the human person and in a manner which takes into account the needs of persons of his or her age. In particular, every child deprived of liberty shall be separated from adults unless it is considered in the child's best interest not to do so and shall have the right to maintain contact with his or her family through correspondence and visits, save in exceptional circumstances;

(d)   Every child deprived of his or her liberty shall have the right to prompt access to legal and other appropriate assistance, as well as the right to challenge the legality of the deprivation of his or her liberty before a court or other competent, independent and impartial authority and to a prompt decision on any such action.

Article 38

1 States Parties undertake to respect and to ensure respect for rules of international humanitarian law applicable to them in armed conflicts which are relevant to the child.

2 States Parties shall take all feasible measures to ensure that persons who have not attained the age of fifteen years do not take a direct part in hostilities.

3 States Parties shall refrain from recruiting any person who has not attained the age of fifteen years into their armed forces. In recruiting among those persons who have attained the age of fifteen years but who have not attained the age of eighteen years, States Parties shall endeavour to give priority to those who are oldest.

4 In accordance with their obligations under international humanitarian law to protect the civilian population in armed conflicts, States Parties shall take all feasible measures to ensure protection and care of children who are affected by an armed conflict.

Article 39

States Parties shall take all appropriate measures to promote physical and psychological recovery and social reintegration of a child victim of: any form of neglect, exploitation, or abuse; torture or any other form of cruel, inhuman or degrading treatment or punishment; or armed conflicts. Such recovery and reintegration shall take place in an environment which fosters the health, self-respect and dignity of the child.

Article 40

1 States Parties recognize the right of every child alleged as, accused of, or recognized as having infringed the penal law to be treated in a manner consistent with the promotion of the child's sense of dignity and worth, which reinforces the child's respect for the human rights and fundamental freedoms of others and which takes into account the child's age and the desirability of promoting the child's reintegration and the child's assuming a constructive role in society.

2 To this end and having regard to the relevant provisions of international instruments, States Parties shall, in particular, ensure that:

(a)   No child shall be alleged as, be accused of, or recognized as having infringed the penal law by reason of acts or omissions that were not prohibited by national or international law at the time they were committed;

(b)   Every child alleged as or accused of having infringed the penal law has at least the following guarantees:

    (i)To be presumed innocent until proven guilty according to law;

    (ii)To be informed promptly and directly of the charges against him or her, and, if appropriate, through his or her parents or legal guardians and to have legal or other appropriate assistance in the preparation and presentation of his or her defence;

    (iii)To have the matter determined without delay by a competent, independent and impartial authority or judicial body in a fair hearing according to law, in the presence of legal or other appropriate assistance and, unless it is considered not to be in the best interest of the child, in particular, taking into account his or her age or situation, his or her parents or legal guardians;

    (iv)Not to be compelled to give testimony or to confess guilt; to examine or have examined adverse witnesses and to obtain the participation and examination of witnesses on his or her behalf under conditions of equality;

    (v)If considered to have infringed the penal law, to have this decision and any measures imposed in consequence thereof reviewed by a higher competent, independent and impartial authority or judicial body according to law;

    (vi)To have the free assistance of an interpreter if the child cannot understand or speak the language used;

    (vii)To have his or her privacy fully respected at all stages of the proceedings.

3 States Parties shall seek to promote the establishment of laws, procedures, authorities and institutions specifically applicable to children alleged as, accused of, or recognised as having infringed the penal law, and, in particular:

(a)   The establishment of a minimum age below which children shall be presumed not to have the capacity to infringe the penal law;

(b)   Whenever appropriate and desirable, measures for dealing with such children without resorting to judicial proceedings, providing that human rights and legal safeguards are fully respected.

4 A variety of dispositions, such as care, guidance and supervision orders; counselling; probation; foster care; education and vocational training programmes and other alternatives to institutional care shall be available to ensure that children are dealt with in a manner appropriate to their well-being and proportionate both to their circumstances and the offence.

Article 41

Nothing in the present Convention shall affect any provisions which are more conducive to the realisation of the rights of the child and which may be contained in:

(a)   The law of a State party; or
(b)   International law in force for that State.

PART II

Article 42

States Parties undertake to make the principles and provisions of the Convention widely known, by appropriate and active means, to adults and children alike.

Article 43

1 For the purpose of examining the progress made by States Parties in achieving the realization of the obligations undertaken in the present Convention, there shall be established a Committee on the Rights of the Child, which shall carry out the functions hereinafter provided.

2 The Committee shall consist of ten experts of high moral standing and recognized competence in the field covered by this Convention. The members of the Committee shall be elected by States Parties from among their nationals and shall serve in their personal capacity, consideration being given to equitable geographical distribution, as well as to the principal legal systems.

3–12 *Not reproduced*

Article 44

1 States Parties undertake to submit to the Committee, through the Secretary-General of the United Nations, reports on the measures they have adopted which give effect to the rights recognised herein and on the progress made on the enjoyment of those rights:

(a)   Within two years of the entry into force of the Convention for the State Party concerned;
(b)   Thereafter every five years.

2 Reports made under the present article shall indicate factors and difficulties, if any, affecting the degree of fulfilment of the obligations under the present Convention. Reports shall also contain sufficient information to provide the Committee with a comprehensive understanding of the implementation of the Convention in the country concerned.

3 A State Party which has submitted a comprehensive initial report to the Committee need not, in its subsequent reports submitted in accordance with paragraph 1(b) of the present article, repeat basic information previously provided.

4 The Committee may request from States Parties further information relevant to the implementation of the Convention.

5 The Committee shall submit to the General Assembly, through the Economic and Social Council, every two years, reports on its activities.

6 States Parties shall make their reports widely available to the public in their own countries.

Appendix 5

PRESIDENT'S GUIDANCE

9 NOVEMBER 2004

THE PRIVATE LAW PROGRAMME

INTRODUCTION

On the 21 July 2004 I announced the implementation of a new **Framework for Private Law** cases. This gave advanced warning to the Designated Family Judges of the principles and key elements of the **Private Law Programme** to enable the judiciary, managers from the Her Majesty's Courts Service (HMCS),[1] and the Children and Family Court Advisory and Support Service (CAFCASS) to begin their discussions about local schemes.

The full text of the guidance, which was published on the 9 November 2004, follows this Introduction. It is intended that the Programme will be a gradual process involving a National roll out of best practice together with the development of local schemes, having in mind good local initiatives already in place, based upon these principles and key elements. The detail has been discussed and agreed by a judicial working party in consultation with representatives of HMCS and CAFCASS.

The guidance provides assistance to the judiciary, HMCS and CAFCASS managers to help develop local schemes and includes examples of information sheets and other documents for court users and certain basic minimum considerations that will be necessary to make the Programme effective.

It is expected that careful consideration will be given to schemes that already exist at Family Proceedings Court level so that they can be incorporated into or enlarged upon in the development of family dispute resolution mechanisms. It is hoped that in due course the Programme will be formally extended to all Family Proceedings Courts.

---

1   On the 1 April 2005 Her Majesty's Courts Service will become the new executive agency, which will incorporate the Court Service, and be responsible for running all courts below the House of Lords – comprising of the Court of Appeal, High Court, Crown Court, County Courts and Magistrates' Family Proceedings Courts.

It is my intention that in each of the Care Centres there will now be a process of consultation between the judiciary, HMCS, CAFCASS and interest groups represented on local Family Court Business Committees and Forums. Having regard to that consultation, local schemes will be implemented by Designated Family Judges as soon as it is practicable to do so in each region.

Elizabeth Butler-Sloss

President

GUIDANCE: THE PRIVATE LAW PROGRAMME

The court process exists in the wider context of parental separation and relationship breakdown. The **court's aim** is to assist parents to safeguard their children's welfare. It is hoped that many families will have received out of court assistance and early intervention from professionals before or upon making an application to the court e.g. by referral to a Family Resolutions Pilot Project and/or information, advice and assistance from specialist legal advisors and others (eg through the Family Advice and Information Service: FAInS). The court to which an application is made will always investigate whether the family has had the benefit of these or similar services and whether any available form of alternative dispute resolution can be utilised.

PRINCIPLES

Where an application is made to the court under Part II of the Children Act 1989, the welfare of the child will be safeguarded by the application of the overriding objective of the family justice system in 3 respects:

1   Dispute resolution at a First Hearing
2   Effective court control including monitoring outcomes against aims
3   Flexible facilitation and referrals (matching resources to families)

The overriding objective is as follows:

> "... to enable the court to deal with every (children) case
>
> (a) justly, expeditiously, fairly and with the minimum of delay;
> (b) in ways which ensure, so far as is practicable, that
>   a. the parties are on an equal footing;
>   b. the welfare of the children involved is safeguarded; and
>   c. distress to all parties is minimised;
> (c) so far as is practicable, in ways which are proportionate
>   a. to the gravity and complexity of the issues; and
>   b. to the nature and extent of the intervention proposed in the private
>   and family life of the children and adults involved"

1 FIRST HEARING DISPUTE RESOLUTION

In every case there shall be an early **First Hearing** dispute resolution appointment:

- That identifies **immediate safety issues**
- That exercises **effective court control** so as to **identify the aim** of the proceedings, the timescale within which the aim can be achieved, the issues between the parties, the opportunities for the resolution of those issues by appropriate referrals for support and assistance and any subsequent steps that may be permitted or required
- That, wherever possible, a **CAFCASS** practitioner shall be available to the court and to the family whose purpose and priority is to **facilitate early dispute resolution** rather than the provision of a formal report
- That, save in exceptional circumstances (e.g. safety) or where immediate agreement is possible so that the principle of **early dispute resolution** can be **facilitated**: directs that **the family** shall be **referred for support and assistance** to:
  - A Family Resolutions Pilot Project (where available)
  - Locally available resolution services (e.g. ADR, including mediation and conciliation, and/or other service, support, facilitation, treatment and therapy options) that are to be listed and publicised by the Family Justice Council/Family Court Business Committee for each Care Centre

(eg provided by CAFCASS, service partnerships – Councils with Social Services Responsibilities and the NHS and/or by voluntary service providers – NACCC (National Association of Child Contact Centres) resources and outreach voluntary workers)

2 EFFECTIVE COURT CONTROL

The overriding objective shall be furthered by **continuous** and **active case management** of every case which shall include:

- **Judicial Availability**: the identification of gatekeeper district judges to undertake early First Hearing dispute resolution appointments
- **Judicial Continuity**: the allocation to the case of private law family judiciary and the identification of dedicated court and CAFCASS practitioners
- **Continuous case management** by the allocated judiciary and identified court officers which shall include a listing scheme in each hearing centre that describes local listing arrangements to ensure judicial availability, continuity and access to the court for review and/or enforcement
- The **avoidance of unnecessary delay** by the early identification of issues and timetabling of the case from the outset
- Maximising Family Court Resources: guidance for the flexible **transfer of cases** between every level of family court so as to make best use of court facilities, judges and FPCs, having regard to availability, urgency and in some cases, complexity
- Identifying **and** achieving **the aim** of each hearing
- **Monitoring** and **reviewing** the **outcome** (if needs be at short notice)
- **Enforcing** the court's orders (if needs be at short notice)
- **Controlling** the use and **cost** of resources

3 FLEXIBLE FACILITATION AND REFERRAL

Best interests decisions and agreements shall be **facilitated** by:

– The use of **Parenting Plans** to assist parents to agree routine childcare questions
– The use of a **CAFCASS practitioner** who where possible shall be continuously involved **to facilitate** and/or supervise the orders made by the court and the arrangements that are necessary to make orders and agreements work
– The flexible use of **rehabilitative, training, therapy, treatment** and **enforcement** powers
– Directions that require parties, referral agencies and, where appropriate, the CAFCASS practitioner to report the **progress** or **outcome** of any step so that the court might respond by **urgent review** to safeguard the welfare of the child

4 PROCESS

Information: The DFJ responsible for each family hearing centre shall liaise with HMCS and CAFCASS and local service providers and shall set out in judicial, listing, parent and child information sheets the procedures, arrangements and facilities that are available to the court and families in the local area.

The **First Hearing** dispute resolution appointment:

– Shall be listed within a target window from the issue of the application of 4 to 6 working weeks;
– Shall be attended by the parents and in court centres where the local scheme provides for it and where resources exist may be attended by any child aged 9 or over

In court centres where resources exist to provide 'in-court conciliation':

– the First Hearing dispute resolution appointment shall be listed so that a duty CAFCASS practitioner is available to the parties and to the court to facilitate agreements, the identification of issues and any appropriate referrals for assistance;
– where the local scheme provides for it, the detailed content of the conciliation discussions may remain confidential;
– the court may adjourn a First Hearing dispute resolution appointment for further in-court conciliation or a report upon the availability or success of any proposal.

In court centres where a duty CAFCASS practitioner is not available:

– the court will identify the issues between the parties and use its best endeavours to facilitate agreements and referrals for assistance;
– in appropriate cases where advice is necessary, the court may adjourn the First Hearing dispute resolution appointment for a CAFCASS practitioner to provide oral or short written advice to the parties and the court limited to the facilitation of matters that are agreed and referrals for further assistance.

In all cases at the conclusion of the First Hearing dispute resolution appointment and generally at the end of any subsequent hearing that may be required the court shall identify on the face of the order:

- the issues that are determined, agreed or disagreed;
- the aim of the order, agreement, referral or hearing that is set out in the order;
- any other basis for the order or directions that are made or the agreement that is recorded;
- in respect of issues that are not agreed and that need to be determined so as to safeguard the welfare of the child:
  - the level of court (and where appropriate the allocated judge(s)) before whom all future non-conciliation hearings and applications are to be heard;
  - the timetable and the sequence of the steps that are required to lead to an early hearing;
  - the filing and service of evidence limited to such of the issues as the court may identify;
  - whether a CAFCASS practitioner's report is necessary and if so, the issues to which the report is to be directed;
  - in respect of all orders, agreements and referrals directions for
    - the facilitation of the same (in particular by a CAFCASS practitioner);
    - the monitoring of the outcome, including by urgent reserved re-listing before the same court **within 10 working days** of a request by CAFCASS;
    - Enforcement.

Model Scheme for In-Court Dispute Resolution

The following is a model based on the principles and key elements of the Programme.

Establishing the Scheme

1 The Designated Family Judge (DFJ) consults with the local Forum, the Family Court Business Committees, the local Family Justice Council (when in place) and the relevant judiciary and Family Proceedings Courts (FPCs) and agrees the structure of the local scheme with Area HMCS and CAFCASS managers

Structure of the Scheme

2 In agreeing the structure of a scheme, regard should be had to the matters set out at Annex A

3 Where a scheme already exists it should be reviewed to ensure that it contains all of the key elements set out in the President's Guidance, having regard to the suggestions contained in this model

4 Provision should be made in every scheme for local review not later than 12 months hence

Information about the Scheme

5 Information sheets for Court Managers and Listing Officers, the parties and children setting out the venues, facilities, arrangements and alternative resources (eg local Alternative Dispute Resolution schemes and support services) should be agreed and published by the DFJ

Examples are at:

Annex B – Information Sheet for Parties
Annex C – Information about leaflets for children
Annex D – Information Sheet for Court Managers and Listing Officers

Practical Arrangements

Before the First Hearing Dispute Resolution Appointment (the FHDRA)

6 Private Law applications are issued on the day of receipt

7 Copy the application is sent or e-mailed to CAFCASS on the day of issue

8 Information sheets about the FHDRA, the role of the CAFCASS practitioner and the court are sent to the parties with the Notice of Hearing. An example is at Annex B. Information about leaflets for children is at Annex C, and there is an approved amended county court Notice of Hearing at Annex E

9 All applications are listed for an FHDRA in a window of 4 to 6 weeks of issue

10 A copy of the acknowledgement form is sent or e-mailed to CAFCASS on day of receipt

11 Prior to the application being listed for the appointment, CAFCASS will undertake their own paper risk assessment in particular as to safety issues

12 CAFCASS may advise the court that a particular case has risk or safety issues that would best be explored before the judge or magistrates/legal advisor at the FHDRA rather than in discussions between the parties and the CAFCASS practitioner

13 Cases that are very urgent or that involve safety issues or issues that are complex may need to be listed or determined separately and should be referred to a resident judge or magistrates/legal advisor for guidance

At Court

14 Subject to any direction to the contrary, in particular as to safety issues, the appointment is listed before a judge or magistrates/legal advisor with a CAFCASS practitioner available to facilitate early dispute resolution in accordance with the local scheme

15 Both parents are expected to attend with their representatives (if they have them). The parties' child or children should only attend where a local scheme provides for it and where the participation can occur in an appropriate child friendly environment

16 Further risk assessment may be undertaken by the CAFCASS practitioner with the child (if appropriate) and each party separately prior to any joint meeting between the practitioner and the parties (it is not expected that any joint meeting between the CAFCASS practitioner and the parties will involve a child unless the CAFCASS practitioner advises that it is in the child's interests and both parties agree)

17 An agreement is reached between the parties

Before the Judge

18 Where an agreement is reached, the terms of the agreement are considered by the judge or magistrates/legal advisor to decide whether the terms are appropriate and whether an order is necessary

19 Where full agreement is not reached the judge or magistrates/legal advisor give directions and a timetable for the case to come back to court dealing in particular with the aim of the next hearing, the issues that need to be determined, the evidence that should be filed for those purposes, and any interim provisions. The timetable will always include the listing of the next, or the full hearing, which should be as soon as is possible consistent with the interests of the child

20 The matters that are ordinarily dealt with by the judiciary are set out at Annex F. It is recommended that the parties and the court consider drafting orders having regard to the content of Annex F to provide a better record for subsequent use

21 Requests for CAFCASS reports should not be made unless a report is necessary. Where a report is necessary, the key issues, to which the report is to be directed, should be identified as should the question of whether the issues can be dealt with in a short report so as to minimise the time taken in preparing the report and to allow CAFCASS to maximise its resources to facilitate agreements and orders

After the First Hearing Dispute Resolution Appointment

22 The court order should indicate if a particular agreement or order is to be facilitated or monitored and whether particular arrangements for enforcement

are provided for e.g. that the first handover for a visiting contact did in fact take place, who is to inform CAFCASS, whether, in what circumstance, and how, CAFCASS is to inform the court (e.g. by e-mail) and whether, how and when the matter is to be listed in the event of non-compliance

23 Where CAFCASS, a party or other agency is asked to inform the court of the success or otherwise of an arrangement, the agreement of that person or agency may need to be sought and the method of informing the court should be specified in the order

24 The local scheme will include the listing and notification arrangements that have been agreed between the DFJ, the judiciary, the FPCs, HMCS and CAFCASS so that a party or CAFCASS is able to bring the matter back to court for enforcement within 10 days where an agreement has not been complied with or is not working effectively

25 Listing of individual cases is a judicial function. When listing a matter for an FHDRA or any subsequent hearing listing officers will follow any listing direction contained in an order in an individual case, the President's guidance and the provisions of the local scheme

26 All applications for the variation of orders or for enforcement other than in accordance with the terms of an order in an individual case or the local scheme are to be made by separate application. Such applications should be referred to a resident judge or magistrates/legal advisor for a decision as to whether the application should be treated as an urgent enforcement hearing or a separate free standing hearing

27 Hearings are allocated to the judge who dealt with the matter previously so as to maintain judicial continuity

28 Arrangements are in place between the Court Managers and the judiciary to release the judge or magistrates for urgent enforcement hearings even if they are sitting at another court

29 A list of useful organisations and links is at Annex G

ANNEX A

Structure of the Scheme

Key Features to be specified in the Scheme

Venues and facilities:

Where do the optimum facilities exist having regard to

 - the available judiciary
 - CAFCASS practitioners
 - Safety requirements
 - the need for interview and/or children's rooms

–   already existing facilities and schemes: Family Hearing Centres may be asked to share a venue (including the Family Proceedings Court) to concentrate resources

Judges:

The availability of the specialist judiciary

–   The identity of the ticketed District Judges, Magistrates and Circuit Judges and their sitting patterns
–   The possibility of listing before District Judges (Magistrates' Courts) and Recorders (and their identity and sittings availability)
–   The existence and availability of similar schemes based in the Family Proceedings Courts

Parenting Plans:

The use of Parenting Plans – families are to be encouraged to consider and make use of the Parenting Plan materials (which are currently in the process of being revised, with the new version to be published in April 2005)

CAFCASS:

The identity and availability of CAFCASS practitioners

Scheme Principles:

Whether the appointment is to be a matter of record or be confidential (i.e. is it privileged, in which case unless adjourned for further discussion or referral with a report back to the same judge or magistrate, the matter would then be listed before a different judge/magistrate for any contested hearing)

What arrangements can be made for the involvement of children? If they are to attend court or elsewhere, is there an appropriate child friendly environment and what are the specific arrangements that are to be made in each case?

Listing:

The local listing scheme

–   to give effect to the timetable for the FHDRA and enforcement applications
–   whether on a dedicated day or days of the week
–   frequency of lists
–   number of judges and magistrates
–   number of CAFCASS practitioners
–   expected number of hearings in each list and expected estimated length of hearing
–   provision for extended discussion after the list is heard (e.g. during an afternoon when mornings
–   only are listed – in like manner to Financial Dispute Resolution appointments – and to allow mention before the end of the court day)
–   provision for adjournment for discussion or to try-out an interim

agreement but to be re-listed before the same judge or magistrate on another day (and, for example, with the same CAFCASS practitioner being available)
–   how to obtain a date for the next hearing

ANNEX B

Information Sheet for Parties

First Hearing Dispute Resolution Appointment

Purpose

The First Hearing Dispute Resolution Appointment is a preliminary meeting at court to help families resolve disputes about arrangements for children and see if a workable solution can be found without further court proceedings.

Before the date of your appointment

When an application is first made to the court a copy of the application form and the respondent's details and response (the other party's acknowledgement form) are sent to the Children and Family Court Advisory and Support Service (CAFCASS). Both these forms give CAFCASS the basic information they need about you and your family. This can include issues about risk to you, or your child(ren). It is very important that you complete these forms carefully.

If any special risks are identified then CAFCASS will advise the court about these. Sometimes this will mean that the First Hearing Dispute Resolution Appointment is not the appropriate form of meeting in which case a judge will decide what form of hearing should take place.

What happens at court

Both parties will be expected to attend the appointment. A CAFCASS Family Court Advisor will be there to help you reach an agreement that will be in your child or children's best interests, without needing to have a full "court hearing".

Before the Judge

Where an agreement is reached, the judge will consider the terms of the agreement and whether a court order is needed to make this work better.

Sometimes the judge will be asked to allow more time so the First Hearing Dispute Resolution Appointment can take longer. Usually this will be on the same day but on occasions may include another appointment on another day.

Sometimes it is not possible to reach a full agreement. In these cases the judge will decide what happens next. This includes making decisions about:

–   If there should be another court hearing

– A date for your case to come back to court
– The purpose of the next hearing
– What evidence will be needed – this can include written statements/and or a report prepared by CAFCASS about the current arrangements

Please contact the court should you have any queries about your appointment

ANNEX C

Information about leaflets for children

There are three leaflets on the DCA website aimed at children whose parents are separating. They are aimed at three age groups: 5–8, 8–13, and 13+.

You can find them on our web site at:

http://www.dca.gov.uk/family/divleaf.htm

The leaflets are as follows:

– Children between 5 and 8 – Me and My Family
– Children between 8 -13 – My Family's Changing
– Children 13+ – My family's Splitting Up

There are also leaflets available for children and teenagers from CAFCASS. They can be found on the following link:

http://www.cafcass.gov.uk/English/Children/childrenIntro.htm

or by contacting:

CAFCASS Headquarters
8th Floor
Wyndham House
189 Marsh Wall
London
E14 9SH
Tel: 020 7510 7000
Fax: 020 7510 7001

ANNEX D

Information Sheet for Court Managers and Listing Officers

How to manage In-Court Dispute Resolution Appointments:

Particular attention should be given to the **Practical Arrangements** in the **Model for In-Court Dispute Resolution** and the **Listing** criteria in **ANNEX A**.

It is essential that:

Discussions take place with the Designated Family Judge and the local CAFCASS managers on the implementation of the Programme

Staff are aware of what is expected of them in respect of:

–   Issuing and listing of private law applications, in particular
    –   An early **First Hearing Dispute Resolution Appointment (FHDRA)** in all cases to be listed before the District Judge or magistrates/legal advisor in a window of between 4 and 6 weeks of an application being issued
    –   Whenever practicable there is access to the allocated judge or magistrates/legal advisor for an **urgent review hearing** and where necessary enforcement of private law orders within 10 working days where an agreement has not been complied with or is not working effectively
    –   All applications for the variation of orders or for enforcement **other than in accordance with the terms of an order** are to be made in form C1 with the appropriate fee
    –   Such applications should be referred to a resident judge or magistrates/legal advisor for a decision as to whether the application should be treated as an urgent enforcement hearing or a separate free standing hearing
    –   Listing is a judicial function. When listing a matter for an FHDRA or any subsequent hearing, listing officers must follow any specific direction made in an individual case, the President's Guidance and the provisions of the local scheme
–   Sending copies of the applications and acknowledgements to CAFCASS
–   Informing the parties of what can be expected of them when they attend the FHDRA and the role of CAFCASS
–   The Notice of Hearing. This may be sent to the parties with a standard paragraph added to inform them that an FHDRA has been made to attempt to resolve the issues within the application, and to explain the conciliation system that runs at the court.[2]
–   Informing parties of the local arrangements (if any) for the involvement of children attending court

---

2   A standard paragraph can be inserted into the county court Notice of Hearing (C6) by using the edit function after committing the C6 on FamilyMan. An example of the standard paragraph is shown in bold in Annex E.

Any current schemes are reviewed to reflect the principles and key elements of the Programme as set out in this guidance

It may be useful to:

Arrange regular meetings with the judiciary, CAFCASS practitioners and court staff to discuss listing arrangements, continuity, accommodation issues, case progression, focus of reports, and the volume of reports requested

ANNEX E

Notice of Proceedings

In the {Court Name}

Case Number: {Case/Parent Number}

Notice of Proceedings

{Hearing/Directions Appointment}

{Applicant Name(s)} {has/have} applied to the court for an order.

The application concerns the following {child/children}: {Children's names}

About the {Hearing/Directions Appointment}

You should attend when the court hears the application at {Court Name}, {Court Address} on {Date of Hearing} at {Time of Hearing (if set)} with a hearing time estimate of {Hearing Time Estimate}

The District Judge has directed that this matter be referred to an appointment at which a Children & Family Court Advisory and Support Service (CAFCASS) practitioner will be available to discuss this matter with the parties and the judge. The object is to see if the matter can be resolved by agreement without the need for further court proceedings. The court can approve any agreement on the same day, if so required. If agreement cannot be reached then the court will normally give further directions as to how the matter should proceed.

What to do next

There is a copy of the application with this Notice. You have been named as a party in the application. Read the application now and the notes overleaf.

When you go to court please take this Notice with you and show it to a court official.

ANNEX F

Recommended Record of Hearing

The Parties

On Notice / Without Notice

The application(s)

Representation and Attendance

The Recitals

The Agreements in principle and as to detail that have been reached and that can be facilitated despite the need for a further hearing on other matters e.g. interim provisions

The method of facilitation and monitoring of agreed matters (if any)

The basis for the order / directions that are made or the agreement that is recorded (e.g. "On the basis that mother says ... and father says ...)

The key ISSUES that remain to be determined, including the issues of fact and any issues relating to safety

The AIM of the hearing that is being timetabled (e.g. to determine the principle / quantum of staying / visiting contact)

Orders and Directions

Any referral to a Family Resolutions Pilot or local ADR schemes

The level of court (and if appropriate the allocated judge) before whom all further hearings are to be conducted

Whether a CAFCASS report or evidence is necessary and, if so, limited to which issues and in what form

The case management timetable including directions as to the filing and service of evidence (and specifying the issues upon which the evidence is permitted)

In the rare cases where independent experts are permitted by the court, the consideration and allocation of the cost of the same

The date of the next hearing / the full hearing

Provisions for Facilitation, Monitoring and Enforcement (including variation and discharge)

Penal Notice and Guidance

Schedules e.g. of evidence / documents considered

ANNEX G

Useful Organisations and Links

CAFCASS Headquarters
8th Floor
Wyndham House
189 Marsh Wall
London
E14 9SH
Tel: 020 7510 7000
Fax: 020 7510 7001
Email: webenquiries@cafcass.gov.uk
www.cafcass.gov.uk

National Association of Child Contact Centres
Minerva House
Spaniel Row
Nottingham
NG1 6EP
Tel: 0870 770 3269

National Family Mediation
9 Tavistock Place
London
WC1H 9SN
Tel 020 7383 5993

Official Solicitors Department
Parent Patient Divisional Manager
Tel: 0207 911 7132
www.offsol.demon.co.uk

Principal Registry of the Family Division
First Avenue House
42–49 High Holborn
London
WC1V 6NP
Tel: 020 7947 6000

Resolution – first for family law
(formerly the Solicitors Family Law Association)
PO Box 302
Orpington
Kent
BR6 8QX
Tel: 01689 850227

The Family Law Bar Association
289 – 293 High Holborn
London

WC1V 7HZ
Tel: 020 7242 1289
Fax: 020 7831 7144
DX 240 LDE
www.FLBA.co.uk

The Association of Lawyers for Children
PO Box 283
East Molesey
KT8 OWH
Tel No: 020 8224 7071
www.ALC.org.uk
CLS Direct
www.clsdirect.org.uk
Tel: 0845 345 4 345

Children and Family Services Division
Legal Services Commission
85 Gray's Inn Road
London
WC1X 8TX
Tel: 020 7759 0315
Fax: 020 7759 0505
E-mail: family@legal services.gov.uk
****

Appendix 6

THE CASC GUIDELINES

GUIDELINES FOR GOOD PRACTICE ON PARENTAL CONTACT IN CASES WHERE THERE IS DOMESTIC VIOLENCE
PREPARED BY THE CHILDREN ACT SUB-COMMITTEE OF THE LORD CHANCELLOR'S ADVISORY BOARD ON FAMILY LAW

April 2002

Extracted from Section 5 of the Report on the Question of Parental Contact in cases where there is Domestic Violence.

Courts to give early consideration to allegations of domestic violence

1.1 In every case in which domestic violence is put forward as a reason for refusing or limiting contact the court should at the earliest opportunity consider the allegations made (and any answer to them) and decide whether the nature and effect of the violence alleged by the complainant (or admitted by the respondent) is such as to make it likely that the order of the court for contact will be affected if the allegations are proved.

Steps to be taken where the court forms the view that its order is likely to be affected if allegations of domestic violence are proved

1.2 Where the allegations are disputed and the court forms the view that the nature and affect of the violence alleged is such as to make it likely that the order of the court will be affected if the allegations are proved the court should:
   (a) consider what evidence will be required to enable the court to make findings of fact in relation to the allegations;
   (b) ensure that appropriate directions under s 11 Children Act 1989 are given at an early stage in the application to enable the matters in issue to be heard as speedily as possible; including consideration of whether or not it would be appropriate for there to be an initial hearing for the purpose of enabling findings of fact to be made;
   (c) consider whether an order for indirect contact pending the final

hearing is in the interests of the child; and in particular that the safety of the child and the residential parent can be secured before, during and after any such contact;

(d) direct a report from a children and family reporter on the question of contact unless satisfied that it is not necessary to do so in order to safeguard the child's interests;

(e) subject to the seriousness of the allegations made and the difficulty of the case consider whether or not the children in question need to be separately represented in the proceedings; and, if the case is proceeding in the Family Proceedings Court whether or not it should be transferred to the County Court; if in the County Court whether or not it should be transferred to the High Court for hearing.

Directions to the Children and Family Reporter in cases involving domestic violence

1.3

(a) Where the court orders a welfare report under s 7 Children Act 1989 in a disputed application for contact in which it considers domestic violence to be a relevant issue, the order of the court should contain specific directions to the children and family reporter to address the issue of domestic violence; to make an assessment of the harm which the children have suffered or which they are at risk of suffering if contact is ordered; to assess whether the safety of the child and the residential parent can be secured before, during and after contact; and to make particular efforts to ascertain the wishes and feelings of the children concerned in the light of the allegations of violence made.

(b) Where the court has made findings of fact prior to the children and family reporter conducting his or her investigation, the court should ensure that either a note of the court. s judgment or of the findings of fact made by the court is made available to the children and family reporter as soon after the findings have been made as is practicable.

(c) Where in a case involving allegations of domestic violence the whereabouts of the child and the residential parent are known to the court but not known to the parent seeking contact; and where the court takes the view that it is in the best interests of the child or children concerned for that position to be maintained for the time being, the court should give directions designed to ensure that any welfare report on the circumstances of the residential parent and the child does not reveal their whereabouts, whether directly or indirectly.

Interim Contact pending a full hearing

1.4 In deciding any question of interim contact pending a full hearing the court should:

(a) specifically take into account the matters set out in s 1(3) Children Act 1989 ('the welfare check-list');

(b) give particular consideration to the likely risk of harm to the child, whether physical and/or emotional, if contact is either granted or refused;

(c) consider, if it decides such contact is in the interests of the child, what directions are required about how it is to be carried into effect; and, in particular, whether it should be supervised, and if so, by whom; and generally, in so far as it can, ensure that any risk of harm to the child is minimised and the safety of the child and residential parent before during and after any such contact is secured;

(d) consider whether it should exercise its powers under s 42(2)(b) Family Law 1996 to make a non-molestation order;

(e) consider whether the parent seeking contact should seek advice and/or treatment as a precondition to contact being ordered or as a means of assisting the court in ascertaining the likely risk of harm to the child from that person at the final hearing.

Matters to be considered at the final hearing

1.5 At the final hearing of a contact application in which there are disputed allegations of domestic violence:

(a) the court should, wherever practicable, make findings of fact as to the nature and degree of the violence which is established on the balance of probabilities and its effect on the child and the parent with whom the child is living;

(b) in deciding the issue of contact the court should, in the light of the findings of fact which it has made, apply the individual items in the welfare checklist with reference to those findings; in particular, where relevant findings of domestic violence have been made, the court should in every case consider the harm which the child has suffered as a consequence of that violence and the harm which the child is at risk of suffering if an order for contact is made and only make an order for contact it can be satisfied that the safety of the residential parent and the child can be secured before during and after contact.

Matters to be considered where findings of domestic violence are made

1.6 In each case where a finding of domestic violence is made, the court should consider the conduct of both parents towards each other and towards the children; in particular, the court should consider:

(a) the effect of the domestic violence which has been established on the child and on the parent with whom the child is living;

(b) whether or not the motivation of the parent seeking contact is a desire to promote the best interests of the child or as a means of continuing a process of violence against or intimidation or harassment of the other parent;

(c) the likely behaviour of the parent seeking contact during contact and its effect on the child or children concerned;

(d) the capacity of the parent seeking contact to appreciate the effect of past and future violence on the other parent and the children concerned;

(e)   the attitude of the parent seeking contact to past violent conduct by
that parent; and in particular whether that parent has the capacity to
change and/or to behave appropriately.

Matters to be considered where contact is ordered in a case where findings of domestic violence have been made

1.7   Where the court has made findings of domestic violence but, having
applied the welfare checklist, nonetheless considers that direct contact is
in the best interests of the child or children concerned, the court should
consider (in addition to the matters set out in paragraphs 5 and 6 above)
what directions are required to enable the order to be carried into effect
under s 11(7) Children Act 1989 and in particular should consider:

(a)   whether or not contact should be supervised, and if so, by whom;

(b)   what conditions (for example by way of seeking advice or treatment)
should be complied with by the party in whose favour the order for
contact has been made;

(c)   whether the court should exercise its powers under s 42(2)(b) Family
Law Act 1996 to make a non-molestation order;

(d)   whether such contact should be for a specified period or should
contain provisions which are to have effect for a specified period;

(e)   setting a date for the order to be reviewed and giving directions to
ensure that the court at the review has full information about the
operation of the order.

Information about local facilities

1.8   The court should also take steps to inform itself (alternatively direct the
children and family reporter or the parties to inform it) of the facilities
available locally to the court to assist parents who have been violent to
their partners and/or their children, and, where appropriate, should
impose as a condition of future contact that violent parents avail
themselves of those facilities.

Reasons

1.9   In its judgment or reasons the court should always explain how its
findings on the issue of domestic violence have influenced its decision on
the issue of contact; and in particular where the court has found domestic
violence proved but nonetheless makes an order for contact, the court
should always explain, whether by way of reference to the welfare
check-list or otherwise why it takes the view that contact is in the best
interests of the child.

Note

1.10 Although not part of our formal guidelines, we think that all courts
hearing applications where domestic violence is alleged should review
their facilities at court and should do their best to ensure that there are

separate waiting areas for the parties in such cases and that information about the services of Victim Support and other supporting agencies is readily available.

Appendix 7

THE HMICA RECOMMENDATIONS

A schedule of the recommendations made by HMICA (HM Inspectorate of Court Administration) in its report *Domestic Violence, Safety and Family Proceedings*, published on 11 October 2005, reproduced with the responses and action plans of CAFCASS and HMCS italicised under each recommendation.

(1) That, in order to improve its service to children and families, CAFCASS should with other agencies, stakeholders and service users devise and disseminate a comprehensive information pack about family proceedings with particular reference to issues relevant to the needs of children and their families in domestic violence cases.

Overall CAFCASS response – in cases where domestic violence is an issue, CAFCASS will work with the HM Courts Service to provide specific information leaflets for children and young people, and for adults.

Overall improvement target – CAFCASS will improve the information provided to children, young people and their families in cases where domestic violence is an issue (target date September 2006).

(2) That, in order to improve its service to children and families, CAFCASS should:
  – ensure that all cases, including conciliation at court, are subject to risk assessment and liaison with other agencies;
  – devise best practice guidance and procedures for preparing reports in domestic violence cases;
  – ensure safety planning is undertaken for all cases.

Overall CAFCASS response – CAFCASS will:
  ● *issue and implement the Domestic Violence Policy and Toolkit to ensure a consistent standard of response;*
  ● *where a safeguarding concern is indicated, conduct relevant checks with other agencies;*
  ● *provide information to the Local Authority where there is a safeguarding concern;*
  ● *embed the CAFCASS Domestic Violence Policy and Toolkit into practice, via the provision of training, quality assurance and review.*

Overall improvement target – the successful implementation of the CAFCASS Domestic Violence Policy and Toolkit (target date June 2006).

(3) That, in order to improve services to children and families, CAFCASS should:
  – implement a strategy to ensure improved practice in domestic abuse cases;

– devise national standards and competencies for work in domestic violence cases;

– ensure compliance with the new domestic violence policy and toolkit;

– create domestic violence champions throughout CAFCASS;

– ensure that the focus on safeguarding is integrated into the casework process and takes priority when considering contact and agreement-seeking in domestic violence cases.

Overall CAFCASS response:

● *CAFCASS will implement a strategy to improve practice – this includes implementation of the recently agreed policy and toolkit, which sets standards, foundation training, communication plan, identified domestic violence 'champions' in each region, requirement for standards of risk assessment to be complied with and demonstrated in appraisal and supervision, and a system to monitor adherence to the policy;*

● *standards for practice have been agreed and staff competencies in risk assessment will form part of the review of the Quality Assurance Framework;*

● *an audit of the system will be carried out in 2006/07;*

● *CAFCASS will work with partner agencies to ensure that the family justice system appropriately addresses safeguarding issues.*

Overall improvement target – demonstrable improvement in the safeguarding provided for children and vulnerable adults through compliance with the Domestic Violence policy and use of the toolkit (target date 30 September 2006).

(4) That, in order to safeguard children and adults, CAFCASS should agree and implement a clear multi-agency protocol regarding information exchange and inter-agency liaison in domestic violence cases.

Overall CAFCASS response – CAFCASS will:

● *promote the inter-agency review of information sharing protocols via ACPC/LSCB[1] agendas;*

● *agree and implement an information sharing protocol with the police.*

Overall improvement target – CAFCASS will improve the standard of the safeguarding service provided to children and families, through working effectively within an inter-agency framework (target date March 2006).

(5) That, in order to improve services to children and families, CAFCASS should provide training:

– in assessment and risk assessment skills;

– on communication skills for direct work with children in domestic violence cases;

– in domestic violence for all staff and, where possible, do so on an inter-agency basis.

---

1 ACPCs (Area Child Protection Committees) are official bodies which bring together a range of statutory and other organisations who share the responsibility for keeping children safe from harm. They are in due course to be replaced with LSCBs (Local Safeguarding Children Boards).

Overall CAFCASS response – CAFCASS will:
- *develop a comprehensive Knowledge, Learning & Development strategy;*
- *ensure that all training properly reflects the domestic violence policy and toolkit;*
- *provide a regional 'launch' event of the policy in each region, for subsequent cascade to local teams.*

Overall improvement target – to provide training to support the domestic violence policy and toolkit, in order to improve the services to children and families (target date September 2006).

(6) That, in order to improve its care of family court users, HMCS should ensure that the information sent to family court users before they attend court includes details of the facilities that may be available for vulnerable parties such as survivors of domestic violence.

Overall HMCS response – HMCS will:
- *publicise the availability of facilities (through information leaflets and a list, such as the one that exists for video conferencing facilities, at each court) to stakeholders (eg children's lawyers) and advise them on how to inform relevant clients;*
- *carry out a sample survey with local solicitors (via Resolution) and/or court user groups to cross-check if they have seen the 'special facilities' poster and if they have ever asked and had access to 'special facilities';*
- *implement a system for early identification of cases where special facilities might be needed, prompting a 'trigger' system on application whereby all courts (county and FPCs) will automatically notify the vulnerable or intimidated party (applicant or respondent) or their legal representatives of special facilities available locally.*

Overall improvement target – all court users (legal representatives and parties in person) to know what 'special facilities' are available at the court that they are attending and how to access them or seek an alternative venue (target date June 2006).

(7) That, in order to improve its care of family court users, HMCS should develop and implement domestic violence policies that address the availability and use of facilities for vulnerable or intimidated parties in family law cases.

Overall HMCS response – HMCS will:
- *develop HMCS national strategy and standards on treatment to be applied in all courts where a case involves domestic violence, building on the established systems for the treatment of victims in the criminal courts and the outcomes to the consultation on the Victim Code of Practice, and linked to the development of specialist family centres – the strategy to include, among other things a 'prompt' to transfer cases so that they may be heard at courthouses across the estate that have special facilities for vulnerable and/or intimidated parties;*
- *promote video conferencing facilities now available in the Care Centres and Magistrates Courts to re-enforce the message that these facilities may be offered, as a matter of course, in any family case application where domestic violence is alleged, as long as local facilities allow;*
- *follow up on the 'special measures' mapping exercise and write again to*

all county courts to ask if they are displaying the 'special facilities' poster and distribute posters for display in FPCs.

Overall improvement target – all family courts to apply a consistent approach to informing and providing special facilities (target date 31 March 2007).

(8) That, in order to improve its care of family court users, HMCS should take steps to ensure an appropriate balance is maintained between safety and service delivery through the use of robust risk assessment procedures.

Overall HMCS response:
- *HMCS Estates Directorate will review current departmental health and safety policies and risk assessments and consider appropriate training for court staff in light of that review;*
- *HMCS will consult with court staff, ushers, security/reception staff, judiciary, court user groups and HMCS Estate as well as DV survivors (and representative bodies – WAFE, Refuge, etc) – locally and nationally – to assist in identifying areas of vulnerability in court buildings;*
- *HMCS will develop instructions to be issued to courts to try to avoid parties leaving chambers unescorted or at the same time;*
- *HMCS will establish the extent to which court located interview room(s) have panic button facilities or staff have personal attack alarms;*
- *HMCS will liaise with senior judiciary and/or court user groups on how vulnerable court users might be directed to 'safe seating';*
- *HMCS will consider adopting existing and/or developing new videos, CD-Rom, website virtual resources for the family court scenario and target user groups where there is a demand.*

Overall improvement target – a national risk assessment procedure to be operated across the court estate (target date 31 March 2006).

(9) That, in order to improve its care of family court users, HMCS should:
- identify the management information required to establish the number of cases that involve domestic violence and the demand for support from survivors;
- identify how such information will be used to improve service delivery;
- collect and use the information systematically to improve service delivery.

Overall HMCS response – HMCS will:
- *continue to collect data from the new gateway forms to establish the number of section 8 cases that involve any form of domestic abuse;*
- *evaluate that information together with qualitative research planned;*
- *consider the use of court user surveys and other methods of engaging with survivor groups to improve service;*
- *pilot an Integrated Domestic Violence Court.*

Overall improvement target – to have effective monitoring systems in place to capture accurate information on DV related cases in the family courts (target date March 2007).

(10) That, in order to improve its care of family court users, HMCS should develop organisational links with national and local community groups to

improve its understanding of the particular difficulties faced by survivors of domestic violence from ethnic minority backgrounds in accessing the family justice system.

Overall HMCS response – HMCS will:

- *establish, via the DV Advisory Group or the mapping exercise a named contact at each county court/court user group to facilitate the exchange of information to and from the DVAG;*
- *establish best practice among Chartermark courts;*
- *back up awareness with article(s) in 'Hearsay' and/or 'In Court' and re-circulate Terms of Reference;*
- *highlight this issue in FJC conferences on DV.*

Overall improvement target – to disseminate best practice guidance on the development of community links (target date March 2006).

(11) That, in order to improve its care of family court users, HMCS should provide appropriate training to assist staff in gaining a greater understanding of domestic violence and its impact on survivors.

Overall HMCS response – HMCS will:

- *carry out a Training Needs Analysis for events such as those directed to Crown Courts (eg 'Dealing with Vulnerable Witnesses & Victims') and other events for security and court staff;*
- *carry out a mapping exercise to establish other examples of where judges, staff and other agencies have designed and carried out joint training events and/or published guidance;*
- *highlight successes and best practices from the evaluation of Specialist DV Courts for incorporation into listing officers' training to provide examples of ways to prioritise DV cases;*
- *investigate the feasibility of adapting the existing criminal court training on 'Vulnerable and Intimidated Witnesses' to suit the family courts;*
- *investigate the processes for passing the best practice examples of staff training material to the Judicial Studies Board for information;*
- *engage court staff (including HM Courts Service Estate) in the delivery of awareness training.*

Overall improvement target – all existing [family] court staff to undergo DV awareness [and safety] training and all new [family court] staff to undergo such training within one year of joining (target date March 2007 for existing staff and a rolling programme for new staff).

Appendix 8

COMPENDIUM OF USEFUL ORGANISATIONS, ADDRESSES AND WEBSITES

In this Appendix, we set out the details of a number of organisations of varying types which provide services, advice and support to children, parents and relatives over a number of different parenting issues, as well as in the specific context of the family justice system. It is not easy to group them in anything other than broad categories, which inevitably to some degree overlap.

CHILDREN'S ORGANISATIONS AND PRESSURE GROUPS

Barnardo's
Multiple regional offices
Website: www.barnardos.org.uk

Barnardo's is a children's charity with a very wide-ranging portfolio: it provides services to more than 120,000 children and their families country-wide, ranging from practical assistance, educational programmes, play-schemes, to direct advice, advocacy and assistance to victims of domestic violence and children leaving care.

ChildLine
Freephone: 0800 1111
Website: www.childline.org.uk

Childline's best known function is the provision of a national 24-hour confidential helpline for children and young people. In addition, however, Childline offers a network of outreach schemes which carry out a large amount of work in schools. Other activities include seminars and conferences, and liaison with policy-makers. At the time of writing, Childline is on the point of joining forces with the NSPCC.

Children Law UK
Unit 15, The Aberdeen Centre
24 Highbury Grove
London N5 2EA
Tel: 020 7704 9919
Fax: 020 7354 1025

Website: www.childrenlawuk.org

A small but influential charity the aim of which is to bring together professionals and policy-makers working in the legal field with the aim of ensuring that children and their families achieve the best outcomes in proceedings. The charity is an important consultee in matters of reform and provides a programme of seminars, lectures and publications in the area of children's law.

Children's Legal Centre
Children's Legal Centre
University of Essex
Wivenhoe Park
Colchester
Essex CO4 3SQ
Tel: 01206 872466
Website: www.childrenslegalcentre.com

The Children's Legal Centre undertakes the full range of legal work relating to the promotion and protection of children's rights. The child lawyers who form its staff have extensive experience in the representation of children.

Children's Rights Alliance
94 White Lion Street
London N1 9PF
Tel: 020 7278 8222
Fax: 020 7278 9552
Website: www.crae.org.uk

The Alliance seeks full compliance with the United Nations Convention on the Rights of the Child through lobbying, supporting children's advocacy and encouraging others to follow their lead.

The Children's Society
The Children's Society
Edward Rudolf House
Margery Street
London WC1X 0JL
Tel: 0845 300 1128 (local rate)
Email: supporteraction@childrenssociety.org.uk
Website: www.the-childrens-society.org.uk

This is a charity the purpose of which is to promote the child's voice and protect vulnerable children. Volunteers run schemes country-wide, including advocacy services for children as well as practical support and assistance for their parents.

Connexions
Website: www.connexions-direct.com

The Connexions service is set up by the Government to offer a range of services for young people from 13–19 years of age. Each person has access to a personal advisor. These advisors are from a range of relevant backgrounds and are qualified to help with a wide range of problems.

Get Connected
Tel: 0808 808 4994
Website: www.getconnected.org.uk
Email: help@getconnected.org.uk

Get Connected is a free, national helpline for young people, who can contact by telephone or email. People wishing to contact get connected are advised to do so 'whatever the problem', and its advisors act as a portal to other specialist services.

The Hideout
Website: www.thehideout.org.uk

The Hideout is a domestic violence website produced by Women's Aid specifically to give advice and information to children.

National Association of Child Contact Centres
Minerva House
Spaniel Row
Nottingham NG1 6EP
Tel: 0845 4500 280
Website: www.naccc.org.uk
Email: contact@naccc.org.uk

Where there is no viable alternative venue, contact between children and parents or other family members must take place in a contact centre. The National Association of Child Contact Centres provides a network of these nationwide. Its mission statement indicates that the paramount aims of the organisation are equality, the safety of the child, respect for individuals and confidentiality.

NCH
NCH Central Office
85 Highbury Park
London N5 1 UD
Tel: 020 7704 7000
Website: www.nchafc.org.uk

NCH is one of the United Kingdom's leading children's charities whose aim is 'helping children to achieve their full potential'. The charity conducts work in a variety of fields including social work research, child protection, adoption and fostering. For children and families needing help on coping with the effects of divorce, NCH has set up a separate website: **www.itsnotyourfault.org.uk**

The 'It's not your fault' website contains advice for children, parents and teenagers. For children, the website aims to give clear explanations of the problems of relationship breakdown, as well as tips for coping with the situation. Similar tips and guidelines are provided for parents.

NCH also offers a family mediation service and directions to this are given in the information for parents on the 'It's not your fault' website.

National Society for the Prevention of Cruelty to Children (NSPCC)
Weston House
42 Curtain Road
London EC2A 3NH
Tel: 0808 800 5000 (24 hour helpline)
Website: www.nspcc.org.uk
Email: help@nspcc.org.uk

The NSPCC has a wide range of objectives, covering as it does the entire field of policy relating to child protection. Its publications include advice to both parents and children on matters that may arise out of family breakdown. At the time of writing, the NSPCC and Childline are on the point of joining forces. The NSPCC operates in England, Wales and Northern Ireland.

National Youth Advocacy Service (NYAS)
99–105 Argyle Street
Birkenhead
Wirral CH41 6AD
Tel: 0151 649 8700
Young persons' advice helpline: 0800 616101
Website: www.nyas.net
Email: help@nyas.net

NYAS represents children and young people up to the age of 25 and works towards promoting and protecting children's rights. Its mission statement is: 'to enable children and young people to have a voice by providing independent and confidential advice, information and advocacy services'.

NYAS is staffed by solicitors and advocates who take instructions from the young people with a problem, and nothing is done without the young person knowing of the action that is to be taken. NYAS is fully committed to the full implementation of Article 12 of the United Nations Convention on the Rights of the Child, which provides that young people should be consulted in all matters that affect them.

NYAS House, located at the above address, is described as an ideal environment for supervised contact for those in the Merseyside area. In addition, NYAS Sign-posting in Birmingham is a preventative service helping people find community-based solutions to family problems.

NYAS is supported by the Community Legal Service (CLS) and has been awarded the CLS Charter Mark.

National Youth Agency
Eastgate House
19–23 Humberstone Road
Leicester LE5 3GJ
Tel: 0116 242 7350
Website: www.nya.org.uk and www.youthinformation.com

Email: nya@nya.org.uk and youthinformation@nya.org.uk

This primarily online resource describes itself as the 'information toolkit' for young people. It provides a range of resources on all youth issues. The section of the website dealing with divorce and separation, located in the 'Family and personal' web-pages, provides an excellent explanation of the court process, what young people can do and how they can best deal with their family separating. This resource is particularly useful in assisting a young person to understand the types and consequences of orders a court can make if a dispute comes to court.

PARENTING ORGANISATIONS AND PRESSURE GROUPS

Action for Prisoners' Families
Unit 21 Carlson Court
116 Putney Bridge Road
London SW15 2NQ
Tel: 020 8812 3600
Website: www.prisonersfamilies.org.uk
Email: info@actionpf.org.uk

The aims of this organisation are to promote the interests of families of prisoners, both in respect of their treatment in society and their family life. In respect of contact, it can offer advice and information on how contact between a prisoner and children or other family members can be managed.

Association for Shared Parenting (ASP)
PO Box 2000
Dudley
West Midlands
Tel: 01789 751157
Website: www.sharedparenting.f9.co.uk
Email: spring.cott@btopenworld.com

This organisation, which is a registered charity in the West Midlands, states its objectives as follows:

> 'The Association for Shared Parenting (ASP) exists to promote the rights of children to the nurture of both parents after separation or divorce and to encourage and support parents in the fulfilment of that right.'

Its specific mission is to provide advice on issues of contact, residence and parental responsibility, and it states that its strength lies in the face-to-face support it is able to offer. The association also plays an active role as a respondent to consultation exercises by the Government and by CAFCASS.

Structurally, ASP comprises autonomous local branches all subscribing to the aims of the association. At the time of writing, there are monthly drop-in centres in Leicester and Birmingham, although telephone advice is available to all.

Both Parents Forever
39 Cloonmore Avenue
Orpington
Kent BR6 9LE
Tel: 01689 854343

Both Parents Forever provides advice and assistance to parents and
grandparents on divorce, separation or in relation to care proceedings.

British Association for Adoption and Fostering (BAAF)
Saffron House
6–10 Kirby Street
London EC1N 8TS
Tel: 020 421 2600
Website: www.baaf.org.uk
Email: mail@baaf.org.uk

The British Association for Adoption and Fostering is the leading charity in the
UK specialising in these services. The website contains a range of useful
resources for prospective adopters or foster carers.

Equal Parenting Council
Website: www.equalparenting.org

This is the UK 'chapter' of an American organisation, the Children's Rights
Council. Its mission statement is as follows:

> 'Equal Parenting Council believes that the law should treat both parents
> equally. This is what we mean by "equal parenting". We are calling upon
> the Government to introduce a legal presumption whereby all separated
> parents will have the right to parenting time with their children unless it can
> be shown (on the basis of credible evidence) that there is some genuine risk
> to a child's safety.'

The website provides links to others advocating shared parenting as well as
supportive forums and resources.

Families Need Fathers
134 Curtain Road
London EC2A 3AR
Tel: 020 7613 5060
Helpline: 08707 607496 (weekdays, 6pm–10pm)
Website: www.fnf.org.uk
Email: fnf@fnf.org.uk

Families Need Fathers is a registered charity in the United Kingdom. It
provides help and support to fathers concerning contact and shared parenting.
The charity's core beliefs are that shared parenting should be encouraged, that
litigation is not the preferred route to resolving disputes, that the family courts
should be backed up by a fully funded mediation service, that both parents'
contributions are unique and valuable, and that children have the right to both
a loving relationship with each parent and to protection from the effects of
parental separation.

Families Need Fathers has local branches across the country, and alongside help and advice provides case studies, responds to consultation papers, collates research and lobbies Parliament and other organisations within the family justice system. Women may become members and there is an online member's forum to run alongside the telephone helpline.

www.family2000.org.uk

A web-based resource, hosted and designed by a family psychotherapist, for all parents, step-parents and grandparents in some way involved in divorce and separation of children from one or other parent. The site contains many useful links and articles.

Family Rights Group
The Print House
18 Ashwin Street
London E8 3DL
Advice line: 0800 731 1696
Website: www.frg.org.uk
Email: office@frg.org.uk

The group is a charity established to provide advice and support for families whose children are involved with social services. The group works to improve services provided to and participation of those families, and advocates for the welfare of children involved with social services from a family-based perspective.

Family Welfare Association
501–505 Kingsland Road
London E8 4AU
Tel: 020 7254 6251
Website: www.fwa.org.uk
Email: fwa.headoffice@fwa.org.uk

The Family Welfare Association aims to help Britain's poorest families or families most in need. It can provide social work support or grants, as well as advice to disadvantaged people.

Fathers Direct
Herald House
Lamb's Passage
Bunhill Row
London EC1Y 8TQ
Tel: 08456 341328
Website: www.fathersdirect.com
Email: mail@fathersdirect.com

The primary purpose of this organisation is to raise awareness of the changing role of both mother and father in the family, working towards a society where both mother and father can earn and undertake childcare without any perception of gender inequality. It undertakes its own research as well as responding to other research, and ultimately aims to provide a national resource for all fathers to draw upon. There is no advice helpline provided by this organisation and it recommends that those seeking such advice should contact Families Need Fathers.

Gingerbread
1st Floor, 7 Sovereign Close
Sovereign Court
London E1W 3HW
Tel: 020 74889300
Advice helpline: Freefone 0800 1484318 (weekdays, 10am–4pm)
Website: www.gingerbread.org.uk

Gingerbread is a national charity providing advice, information and activities for lone parent families. The charity's information helpline can provide advice on all issues, including child maintenance, associated with divorce and separation, as well as providing other types of information targeted to the specific family. Alongside this service, the charity emphasises its services for the children of lone-parent families through attempting to counteract the effects of poverty and enabling the children of lone-parent families to come together.

Gingerbread offers an online members' community by way of an additional help and advice service. On the ground, the charity organises itself through local groups, set up by lone parent volunteers.

Grandparents Association
Moot House
The Stow
Harlow
Essex CM20 3AG
Tel: 01279 444964
Website: www.grandparents-association.org.uk
Email: info@grandparents-association.org.uk

The Grandparents Association was set up in the mid 1980s specifically to tackle the problems facing grandparents wishing to have continued rights of access/contact with their grandchildren. The aims of the association are to provide advice to grandparents on issues relating to contact, to assist those grandparents who have been granted residence by court order, or those grandparents who are seeking a residence order, and to assist those grandparents who are worried about a child being looked after by a local authority.

Match (Mothers Apart from Their Children)
C/O Bm Problems
London WC1N 3XX
Website: www.matchmothers.org
Email: enquiries@matchmothers.org

This organisation is aimed at mothers living apart from their children, and mothers who have little or no contact with their children. It offers support to mothers worldwide. It does not aim to influence judges' decisions, nor does it claim to facilitate or assist with reunification, rather its stated objectives are to make mothers apart from their children feel better about themselves, and to be 'a friend who understands completely'. The organisation is made up of local groups and there is a quarterly newsletter from the central office and a national annual meeting.

Muslim Women's Helpline
Helpline: 0208 9048193/908 6715
Website: www.mwhl.org

The Muslim Women's Helpline aims to provide any Muslim girl or woman in a crisis with a free, confidential listening service and referral to Islamic consultants, plus practical help and information where required.

One Parent Families
255 Kentish Town Road
London NW5 2LX
Tel: 020 7428 5400
Fax: 020 7482 4851
Website: www.oneparentfamilies.org.uk
Tel: Freefone 0800 018 5026

This is a national charity offering help and support to lone parents, with an emphasis on achieving equality for one-parent families in society. To this end, it aims to counter the financial and practical difficulties facing lone parents. Of particular interest is the Lone Parenting Handbook, available on the charity's website, the online help desk, and the advice and information helpline. The website also contains details on how to donate or provide other help. Members can also access a web-based search engine for practical resources in their area.

National Family and Parenting Institute
430 Highgate Studios
53–79 Highgate Road
London NW5 1TL
Tel: 020 7424 3460
Website: www.nfpi.org
Email: info@npfi.org

This charity's website sums up its aims and objectives as follows:

> 'The National Family and Parenting Institute (NFPI) is an independent charity working to support parents in bringing up their children, to promote the wellbeing of families and to make society more family friendly.'

The organisation endeavours to support families by commissioning research, bringing organisations together, working with policymakers and running public campaigns. A wide range of publications are available, some of which are aimed specifically at addressing families' particular needs, such as those where a parent is disabled or those influenced by a particular cultural background.

Parentline Plus
Tel: 020 7284 5500(for general information)
Advice helpline: 0808 800 2222

Website: www.parentlineplus.org.uk

This organisation describes its services as: 'shaped by parents, for parents'. It offers help and support to parents, grandparents, foster carers and others who perform parental duties, on all issues connected with parenting, including the effects of divorce and separation. The services it offers include an email helpline to run alongside its telephone support, both of which are confidential, and various publications dealing with different aspects of parenting.

Refuge
24-hour helpline: 0808 2000 247
Website: www.refuge.org.uk
Email: info@refuge.org.uk

Refuge is a charity committed to a world where domestic violence towards women and children is neither tolerated nor ignored and where women and children can live in safety. The charity works closely with governmental and other policy making bodies to ensure legislation and guidelines provide better services, provision and advocacy for women and children experiencing domestic violence. Refuge provides advice and assistance to women and children victims of domestic violence, as well as safe-houses country wide where victims can live safely in a supportive environment.

Respect
Respect
1st Floor Downstream Building
1 London Bridge
London SE1 9BG
Tel: 020 7022 1801
Fax: 020 7022 1806
Helpline: 0845 122 8609
Website: www.respect.uk.net
Email: info@respect.uk.net

Respect is the UK membership association for domestic violence perpetrator programmes and associated support services. Its key focus is on increasing the safety of those experiencing domestic violence through promoting effective interventions with perpetrators. Respect lobbies government and other statutory agencies across the UK – nationally and locally – to influence public policy in relation to domestic violence perpetrator work. It also develops accredited programmes of work for perpetrators of domestic violence, publishes newsletters to members and offers advice through its helpline.

Shared Parenting Information Group
Website: www.spig.clara.net
Email: nospam@spig.clara.net

The group's mission statement is: 'To promote responsible shared parenting after separation and divorce. To make available information, research and resources to all concerned.' The website provides a large number of articles, search engines, and links to other organisations of relevance to its mission statement.

Women's Aid (WAFE)
Women's Aid Federation of England
Head Office
PO Box 391
Bristol BS99 7WS
Tel (general enquiries only): 0117 944 44 11
Fax: 0117 924 1703
Helpline: 0800 2000 247
Website: www.womensaid.org.uk
Email: helpline@womensaid.org.uk

Women's Aid is the national domestic violence charity that co-ordinates and supports an England-wide network of over 500 local services, who work to end violence against women and children and support over 200,000 women and children each year. Keeping the voices of survivors at the heart of its work, Women's Aid campaigns for better legal protection and services, providing a strategic 'expert view' to government on laws, policy and practice affecting abused women and children. Women's Aid runs public awareness and education campaigns, bringing together national and local action, and developing new training and resources. Women's Aid provides a package of vital, 24-hour lifeline help and information services through its publications, websites for women and children and the Freephone 24-hour National Domestic Violence Helpline, run in partnership with Refuge.

GOVERNMENTAL, LEGAL, ADVISORY AND OTHER PROFESSIONAL BODIES

The Association of Lawyers for Children (ALC)
ALC
PO Box 283
East Molesey KT8 0WH
Tel: 020 8224 7071K
Website: www.alc.org.uk

ALC describes itself as:

> 'a pressure group which lobbies in favour of establishing properly funded legal mechanisms to enable all children and young people to have access to justice and lobbies against the diminution of such mechanisms; a provider of high quality legal training focusing on the needs of lawyers concerned with cases relating to the welfare of children; a forum for the exchange of information and views in relation to the development of the law in relation to children and young people, and a reference point for members of the profession, Governmental organisations and pressure groups interested in the practice of child law and the development and practice in relation to cases involving children.'

ALC organises conferences, seminars and produces newsletters directed towards these aims. It is a frequent consultee in relation to changes in practice and procedure in the law relating to children.

CAFCASS
8th Floor
South Quay Plaza 3
189 Marsh Wall
London E14 9SH
Tel: 020 7510 7000
Website: www.cafcass.gov.uk
Email: webenquiries@cafcass.gov.uk

CAFCASS is the Children and Family Court Advisory and Support Service. It looks after the interests of children involved in family proceedings. It works with children and their families, and then advises the courts on what it considers to be in the children's best interests. CAFCASS only works in the family courts and will therefore be regularly involved in contact and residence cases, as well as proceedings taken by local authorities.

The CAFCASS website aims to give appropriate advice to children, teenagers and parents, and splits its website accordingly. The basic aim of the advice, however, is the same, in that it seeks to explain contact, residence, care and adoption proceedings and the role of CAFCASS within them.

The Collaborative Family Law Group
PO Box 302
Orpington
Kent
BR8 QX
Tel: 01689 820272
Website: www.collablaw.org.uk

A part of Resolution, the Group provides advice and assistance to those interested, professionally or personally, in the collaborative law approach. The website also provides a nationwide database of practitioner members.

Department for Constitutional Affairs
Selborne House
54 Victoria Street
London
SW1E 6QW
Tel: 020 7210 8500
Website: www.dca.gov.uk

Although not the starting-point one might normally expect, this website provides many valuable resources to assist in dealing with the problems arising out of residence and contact disputes in all their different guises. It is, however, not the easiest website to navigate as it embraces so many different fields of information. The relevant sections for parents and children are the pages devoted to family matters and children, and a summary of each is provided below.

The 'Family matters' section of the site's pages on legal policy provides a range of utilities for parents and children in the process of family separation. Of particular interest are the parenting plan, which suggests arrangements considered workable in many cases, and the wide range of leaflets for children of all ages, and parents, to assist families in understanding and coping with family breakdown. Additionally, a link to a mediation guide entitled 'Sorting things out together' is provided.

Of particular interest on the department's web-page devoted to matters concerning children (which is once again found in the 'Family Matters' section) are the links provided to the adoption contact register, Resolution, and useful tools for finding a local solicitor online.

Divorce Aid
Bramble Close
The Beeches
Uppingham
Rutland
LE15 9PH
Website: www.divorceaid.co.uk

This organisation provides advice on all aspects of the divorce process as well as life after divorce. There are separate websites for children, parents and teenagers. Divorce Aid is a professional organisation and expert advice is available from counsellors and solicitors. Divorce Aid is also an advocate of collaborative law.

The Family Justice Council
Family Justice Council
E201 East Block
Royal Courts of Justice
Strand
London WC2A 2LL
Tel: 020 7947 7333/7974/7950
Fax: 020 7947 7875
Website: www.familyjusticecouncil.org.uk

The Council's primary role is to promote an inter-disciplinary approach to the needs of family justice, and, through consultation and research, to monitor the effectiveness of the system and advise on reforms necessary for continuous improvement. There are a number of regional Councils, which meet regularly to discuss and review local policy in the family justice system. The Council co-ordinates and organises professional events such as seminars and lectures for all those involved professionally in the family justice system.

The Family Law Bar Association
289–293 High Holborn
London WC1V 7HZ
Tel: 020 7242 1289
Fax: 020 7831 7144
DX 240 LDE
Email: charris@barcouncil.org.uk
Website: www.flba.co.uk

The Family Law Bar Association is the specialist Bar association for family law barristers. It organises professional conferences and seminars, publishes professionally essential materials, and is a consultee in matters relating to law and procedure in the family law field.

Family Mediation Helpline
Tel: 0845 60 26 627
Website: www.familymediationhelpline.co.uk

The Family Mediation helpline is staffed by specially trained operators who provide:

- general information on family mediation;
- advice on whether your case may be suitable for mediation;
- information about eligibility for public funding; and
- contact details for mediation services in your local area.

The Family Mediators Association
Grove House
Grove Road
Redland
Bristol BS6 6UN
Tel: 0117 946 7062
Helpline: 0808 200 0033
Website: www.fmassoc.co.uk

The Family Mediators Association trains and supports family mediators who work with couples to look at their options relating to their children, their property and financial matters.

NAGALRO
NAGALRO
PO Box 264
Esher
Surrey KT10 0WA
Tel: 01372 818504
Fax: 01372 818505
Email: nagalro@globalnet.co.uk
Website: www.nagalro.com

NAGALRO is the professional association for Children's Guardians and Children and Family Reporters and Independent Social Workers. The website contains sections for parents and children in order to explain and define the role of Guardians in court proceedings. In addition, the website contains a very comprehensive list of links to other useful organisations and resources.

National Family Mediation
Alexander House
Telephone Avenue
Bristol BS1 4BS
Tel: 01392 271610
Website: www.nfm.u-net.com

This charity has, at the time of writing, 60 mediation centres across England and Wales, the vast majority of which have a contract with the Legal Services Commission and are in receipt of funding from CAFCASS. All mediators are trained in accordance with the standards of the UK College of Family Mediators. The website makes it very easy to find a local mediation service by using an interactive map.

www.ondivorce.co.uk
Email: mail@ondivorce.co.uk

This is a web-based information site and community which provides 'friendly community support' for divorcing adults. It contains forums for shared advice, links to other resources and advice and support regarding the impact of divorce upon children.

Relate
Herbert Gray College
Little Church Street
Rugby
Warwickshire CV21 3AP
Tel: 01788 573241
Lo-call: 0845 456 1310
Website: www.relate.org.uk

This organisation was formerly known as Marriage Guidance. It offers help and advice to adults on all aspects of relationships and family life, including the difficulties surrounding separation and the issues that arise as a consequence. There are over 600 local branches of Relate across England, Wales and Northern Ireland, and help is available face-to-face, over the telephone and online.

Resolution (formerly the Solicitors Family Law Association)
PO Box 302
Orpington
Kent BR6 8QX
Tel: 01689 820272
Website: www.resolution.org.uk
Email: info@resolution.org.uk

This is the solicitors' official professional association for family law accredited specialist solicitors. The association can provide information about local family law solicitors, and various fact sheets are also available on all aspects of family law. The association's website contains all these fact sheets as well as a facility to find a solicitor online.

The United Kingdom College of Family Mediators
Alexander House
Telephone Avenue
Bristol BS1 4BS
Tel: 0117 904 7223
Fax: 0117 904 3331
Website: www.ukcfm.co.uk

Email admin@ukcfm.co.uk

The UK College of Family Mediators, established in 1996, sets standards for family mediation and maintains a register of family mediator members who meet those standards; it works to promote best practice in family mediation and to protect the public.

The College keeps a register of family mediators who are College members; it also helps members of the public seeking a mediator to contact its members. The College assesses newly trained mediators and approves the assessment procedures of other family mediation organisations. The College approves foundation and post-qualifying training provided for family mediators. It also organises conferences for family mediators, produces documents and guidelines to support family mediators in their practice; it publishes a newsletter for members, and (jointly with Mediation UK) the journal *Mediation in Practice*. The College also represents the interests of family mediator members nationally.

INDEX